FOLLOWING THE

Master

FOLLOWING THE

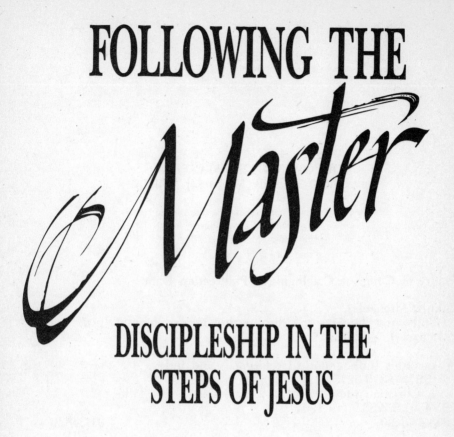

Master

DISCIPLESHIP IN THE
STEPS OF JESUS

MICHAEL J. WILKINS

ZondervanPublishingHouse
Grand Rapids, Michigan

A Division of HarperCollinsPublishers

FOLLOWING THE MASTER
Copyright © 1992 by Michael J. Wilkins

Requests for information should be addressed to:
Zondervan Publishing House
Grand Rapids, Michigan 49530

Library of Congress Cataloging-in-Publication Data

Wilkins, Michael J.
　　Following the Master : discipleship in the steps of Jesus /
Michael J. Wilkins.
　　　　p.　　　cm.
　　Includes bibliograhpical references and index.
　　ISBN 0-310-52151-3
　　1. Christian life–1960-　　　2. Apostles.　　　I. Title.
BV4501.2.W532　　　1991
248.4–dc20　　　　　　　　　　　　　　　　　　　　　91-34820
　　　　　　　　　　　　　　　　　　　　　　　　　　　CIP

Edited by Leonard G. Goss and Laura Weller
Cover design by Vicki Heetderks

Printed in the United States of America

96 97 98 99 00 01 02 / DH / 11 10 9 8 7 6 5 4 3

To my wife Lynne
and our daughters Michelle and Wendy,
fellow followers of the Master

Contents

Abbreviations

AB	Anchor Bible
ABRL	Anchor Bible Reference Library
AThR	*Anglican Theological Review*
BAGD	Walter Bauer, W. F. Arndt, F. W. Gingrich, and F. W. Danker (eds.), *A Greek-English Lexicon of the New Testament and other Early Christian Literature*
BDB	F. Brown, S. R. Driver, and C. A. Briggs, *Hebrew and English Lexicon of the Old Testament*
BHT	Beiträge zur historischen Theologie
BJRL	*Bulletin of the John Rylands University Library of Manchester*
BS	*Bibliotheca Sacra*
BT	*The Bible Translator*
BThB	*Biblical Theology Bulletin*
BZNW	Beihefte zur *Zeitschrift für die neutestamentliche Wissenschaft*
CBQ	*Catholic Biblical Quarterly*
ConBots	Coniectanea biblica, Old Testament Series
EBC	Expositor's Bible Commentary
EstBib	*Estudios biblicos*
ET	*Evangelische Theologie*
EvQ	*Evangelical Quarterly*
GNS	Good News Studies
GOThR	*Greek Orthodox Theological Review*
HTKNT	Herders theologischer Kommentar zum Neuen Testament
HTR	*Harvard Theological Review*
ICC	International Critical Commentary
IDB	G.A. Buttrick (ed.), *Interpreter's Dictionary of the Bible*
IRT	Issues in Religion and Theology
ISBE	The International Standard bible Encyclopedia
JAC	Jahrbuch für Antike und Christentum
JBL	*Journal of Biblical Literature*
JETS	*Journal of the Evangelical Theological Society*
JNSL	*Journal of Northwest Semitic Languages*
JQR	*Jewish Quarterly Review*

JSNT   *Journal for the Study of the New Testament*
JR   *Journal of Religion*
JTS   *Journal of Theological Studies*
LCL   Loeb Classical Library
LexThQ   *Lexington Theological Quarterly*
LumVit   *Lumen Vitae*
NCB   New Century Bible
NICNT   New International Commentary on the New Testament
NICOT   New International Commentary on the Old Testament
NIDNTT   C. Brown (ed.), *The New International Dictionary of New Testament Theology*
NIGTC   The New International Greek Testament Commentary
NovTSup   Novum Testamentum, Supplements
NTA   *New Testament Abstracts*
NTS   *New Testament Studies*
RevQ   Revue de Qumrân
RSR   *Recherches de science reliqieuse*
SANT   Studien zum Alten und Neuen Testament
SBL   Society of Biblical Literature
SBLSP   Society of Biblical Literature Seminar Papers
SBLSBS   Society of Biblical Literature Sources for Biblical Study
SBLSS   Society of Biblical Literature Semeia Studies
SBS   Stuttgarter Bibelstudien
SBT   *Studies in Biblical Theology*
SNTMS   Society for New Testament Studies Monograph Series
TB   Babylonian Talmud
TDNT   G. Kittel and G. Friedrich (eds.), *Theological Dictionary of the New Testament*
TDOT   G. J. Botterweck and H. Ringgren (eds.), *Theological Dictionary of the Old Testament*
THAT   E. Jenni and C. Westermann (eds.), *Theologisches Handwörterbuch zum Alten Testament*
ThE   *Theological Educator*
ThZ   *Theologische Zeitschrift*
TNTC   Tyndale New Testament Commentary
TWOT   R. Laird Harris, Gleason L. Archer, Jr., and Bruce K. Waltke, (eds.), *Theological Wordbook of the Old Testament*
UBS   United Bible Society
WBC   *Wycliffe Bible Commentary*
WMANT   Wissenschaftliche Monographien zum Alten und Neuen Testament
WTJ   *Westminster Theological Journal*

WUNT   Wissenschaftliche Untersuchungen zum Neuen Testament

ZAW   *Zeitschrift für die alttestamentliche Wissenschaft*

ZNW   *Zeitschrift für die neutestamentliche Wissenschaft*

ZPEB   Merrill C. Tenney, et. al. (eds.), *The Zondervan Pictorial Encyclopedia of the Bible*

Preface

When I began to follow Jesus Christ as my Savior and God over twenty years ago, I entered onto a path that has led naturally to the writing of this book. Jesus Christ has been my closest companion during these years. He has also been the subject of my academic study and the focus of my teaching and pastoral ministries. What I have tried to do in this book is share the fruit of my academic, professional, and personal walk with Jesus. Hence, this is a book on discipleship.

But I have not travelled alone. Many people have assisted me and helped me clarify my understanding of the biblical data and the practical implications. I have discussed these issues at length in a variety of classes, training seminars, retreats and conferences. Each has impacted me. In particular, my undergraduate students at Biola University and my graduate students at Talbot School of Theology have stimulated my thinking through research papers, classroom interaction, and individual discussion. Thank-you all for a lively fifteen years! Special appreciation is given to those students in the fall semester, 1990, who carried out research projects on specialized topics for the advanced seminars on biblical discipleship. Thanks also to those students in New Testament Literature, Fall, 1991, who helped compile the indexes. Special thanks to Gary Stratton for his contributions to the interaction questions for each chapter.

To the congregations at Carlsbad (California) Evangelical Free Church, Cayucos Community Evangelical Free Church, and San Clemente Presbyterian Church, thank you for the opportunity of addressing the issues of discipleship on a practical level. You have all influenced my life in major ways.

I would also like to thank the administration of Talbot School of Theology, Biola University, for a sabbatical leave in the spring semester of 1990, during which time the major part of this book took shape. Special thanks go to the dean, W. Bingham Hunter, whose leadership and friendship have been a vital encouragement. Appreciation is also extended to the Faculty Research Committee of Biola University for a research grant that enabled me to take most of the summer of 1990 to continue developing this book.

I am grateful to Fellowship of Faith ministries, Toronto, Canada, for their permission to excerpt from their pamphlet *The Story of Zia Nodrat,*part of their account of a remarkable servant of God. May his story be used to stimulate the faith of many.

Finally, I would like to thank my wife Lynne and our daughters Michelle and Wendy, to whom this book is dedicated. You are my source of greatest earthly joy and peace. With you I find the most fulfillment in living out the wonderful adventure of life. And from you I have learned the most about what it truly means to follow the Master.

PART I

FIRST STEPS
OF THE JOURNEY

1

A Preview
of the Journey

Getting focused:

1. What images come into your mind when you think of the words *disciple* and *discipleship*?
2. Why would someone want to be a disciple of Jesus?
3. How is a study of Jesus and his disciples relevant to modern readers?

THE JOURNEY

Life is a journey. It is a journey that produces exciting adventures, perilous expeditions, monotonous treks, and painful passages. While everyone embarks on the journey without knowing positively what lies ahead, the wonderfully profound truth of the Christian life is that we do not journey alone. Jesus calls us to follow him on the journey as our Guide, Protector, and Example.

In the first century A.D. Jesus of Nazareth called people to follow him. Although our vision is often clouded—not only by time, but also by our own perspectives—that biblical scene remains as one of the most enchanting, challenging, and even poignant portraits for the contemporary church.

Several years ago I was standing by the shoreline at the beach near our home watching one of our daughters and several neighborhood kids out in the water surfing. A young man, whom I knew only casually, walked up and began a conversation with me. He was a professional surfer and a fairly new Christian. As we talked he began to confide to me how difficult it was living as a Christian on the international professional surfing circuit. He expressed to me that he needed help.

He said, "I hear that you help people become better Christians." I loved his innocent way of expressing himself!

"Well, yes. I sure try to help them, Chris," I said.

"I've read about Jesus' disciples," Chris explained. "They seem like a radical group, and I'd like to live like that out there in the professional surfing world. I really don't know very much about all of this, but would you help me to be like those disciples?"

Although Chris did not know very much about the Bible, he knew that when the disciples followed Jesus they were never the same and they made a difference in the world in which they lived. Chris's world was the world of professional surfing; he wanted to live differently and to make a difference in that world. That meant following Jesus as a disciple.

For many of us, Jesus' world seems very far from our own. Technological sophistication, altered worldview, philosophical reasoning, scientific understanding, and psychological analysis have combined to make Jesus' world seem foreign or archaic to modern people. But, paradoxically, Jesus and his disciples continue to fascinate modern people. The vision of Jesus calling and equipping disciples to go and make a difference in their world offers as much hope and meaning to modern men and women as it did to the people of the first century. Jesus still beckons as the Master who offers guidance through the realities of common human experience.

The biblical teaching of discipleship offers the bridge from Jesus' world to our own. In this book we will journey through the biblical picture to explore in depth the meaning of following the Master. We will begin the adventure with the people of Israel in the Old Testament as they walk in covenant relationship with the Lord God. We will also look at the portrait of discipleship found in the world of the Greek philosophers and teachers and then explore the fascinating world of Judaism. After that we will explore the form of discipleship Jesus developed. We will enter into the Gospels' lucid picture of the Master and his disciples walking under Palestinian skies. Then our journey will take us into the expanding world of the early apostolic church, recorded in Acts and the Epistles, as it follows a risen and ascended Jesus, making disciples of all nations. From there we will move ahead and observe the postapostolic church of the late first century as it begins the walk with Jesus down the road of history, a road leading to martyrdom for many. Finally, we will arrive at the dawning of the twenty-first century to ask what it means for us to follow the Master into the third millennium of the common era.

WHY STUDY THE JOURNEY?

Because the last twenty years have witnessed a remarkable, renewed interest in discipleship, our biblical journey is vital. Scholarly studies of biblical teaching and the world of the first century have produced an almost overwhelming mountain of material. Most of it is inaccessible—and often incomprehensible!—to the people of the church. This book draws upon more than fifteen years of study of such material.[1] To be frank, much scholarly work fruitlessly debates issues irrelevant to the church. But, on the other hand, scholarly investigations of narrowly focused biblical and historical conceptions of discipleship can be incredibly enlightening. They can make Jesus' world much more real and practical to us. Our study will benefit from this scholarly work without getting off on insignificant or potentially dangerous side paths.

A flood of practical discipleship books, programs, and applications has swept over the church in the past twenty years. They have come from men and women who have been quite fruitful in various kinds of ministries, both within and outside of established churches. Most of these ministries developed in the practical, day-to-day process of helping people grow as disciples of Jesus. I began my own walk with Jesus during the time when many of them were developing their understanding of discipleship. I have learned much from each of them. In addition to drawing upon scholarly studies of discipleship, our present study profits from the wealth of material to be found within these practical ministries.

However, some practical handbooks are based upon incomplete, sometimes even faulty, understanding of biblical teaching. The goal here is to provide a resource tool from which practical ministries can benefit. While this book is based upon years of scholarly study of biblical discipleship, it also draws upon my nearly twenty years of ministry experience as youth worker, pastor, and Christian educator.[2] The goal here is to furnish students, pastors, layworkers, and

---

[1]E.g., Michael J. Wilkins, *The Concept of Disciple in Matthew's Gospel: As Reflected in the Use of the Term* Μαθητής, Supplements to *Novum Testamentum*, vol. 59 (Leiden: E. J. Brill, 1988); Michael J. Wilkins, "The Use of ΜΑΘΗΤΗΣ ('Disciple') in the New Testament" (unpublished M.Div. thesis, Talbot Theological Seminary, 1977).

[2]"Making disciples" has been the central goal of my ministry as a youth worker, associate pastor, senior pastor, and professor. I have spoken to numerous conferences on the biblical teaching of discipleship and have written practical discipleship guidelines for lay publications; e.g., Michael J. Wilkins, "Radical Discipleship," *Sundoulos*, alumni publication of Talbot School of Theology, Fall 1988; "Contentment: Balancing the Perfect and the Imperfect," *Connections*, alumni publication of Biola University, Winter 1988; "Surfers and Other Disciples," *Discipleship Journal*, vol. 11, 2, no. 62 (March/April 1991): 8–14.

educators with a readable and thorough examination of the biblical teaching so that they can be even more effective in making disciples Jesus' way.

The subtitle of this book, *Discipleship in the Steps of Jesus*, hints at another important issue. This book is an exercise in developing a biblical theology of discipleship. We will describe the biblical data before attempting to reconcile it with any specific theological system. We will follow the biblical portrait of discipleship as it unfolds in its historical and literary environment, from the Old Testament to the New Testament. Once we clearly see the biblical portrait, we can attempt to see the implications for our theological system (e.g., whether Arminian or Calvinistic). For example, Jesus' teaching on "counting the cost of discipleship" has crucial implications for theological debates. If we hope to understand this teaching as Jesus originally intended it, we must try to comprehend it first within its historical and literary context before we see its implications for our particular system. Too often we allow our theological perspective to interpret the passage before we hear it as God originally intended it. Hopefully this study will profit anyone from any theological position.

The study of ancient discipleship is a rewarding task today because various academic disciplines have been harnessed by biblical scholars to help remove the shroud that time has placed over first-century discipleship practices. Historical, sociological, and philological methods now help us understand more clearly what it meant to be a disciple in ancient times. We will combine recent philological methods with traditional word study approaches to understand the most common words for "disciples" found in the New Testament. Social scientific methods aid us in understanding the sociocultural environment within which master-disciple relationships existed. Historical analysis helps us arrive at an objective understanding of the events of history that lead to Jesus calling his disciples. Used together in conjunction with the biblical record, these various disciplines assist us in pulling back the shroud of time that obscures the ancient world of disciples.

Since this is a biblical theological study, understanding the biblical data must precede practical application. Many of us have developed various discipleship "programs" that have served the church well. Are our programs based upon a comprehensive understanding of the biblical teaching? Biblical study must always precede application, but we ought also emphasize that application must always follow biblical study. Since I teach in an academic setting, I know the very real danger to myself and to my students of not applying the material we have studied. We become intellectually gluttonous and spiritually sterile. Therefore, once we examine the biblical teachings we will explore ways of applying them to our own particular settings, whether in a church, a parachurch organization, our homes, or relationships in the world.

FOR WHOM IS THIS WRITTEN?

This book is designed as a general introduction to the biblical teaching, theology, and history of the concept of discipleship. It is designed as a resource tool for those who are involved in making disciples. The body of the text interacts with the biblical data. That interaction is our primary concern. However, the footnotes carry on a discussion and interaction with scholarly treatments of the topic. The advanced student or scholar will want to consult those notes. The "Implications" section of each chapter addresses some of the practical issues from which the reader can develop methods for applying the material of the chapter. These implications are merely suggestive, not exhaustive.

This book is written for serious Bible students and church workers who want to understand more clearly the biblical teaching of discipleship. This means pastors, seminary students, biblical studies students, and persons in the church or in parachurch organizations who want a more in-depth understanding of what Jesus intended by calling, training, and commissioning disciples to go into the world. This study has profound implications for all those who are involved in developing disciples today. The intent is to put within reach of those who are serious about biblical discipleship a tool that draws upon the wealth of scholarly research and sifts the myriad of popular discipleship handbooks. This book is not intended primarily for scholars, although I trust that it can be used profitably by them. It is not intended as popular, light reading, although I trust that it could be accessible to anyone who wants to study biblical teaching on discipleship.

This study attempts to inform readers by treating the biblical, extrabiblical, and secondary literature. But it also attempts to involve readers by using real-life analogies, experiences, and implications. Much of my own life is involved here; this is not merely an academic exercise.

WALKING IN THE WORLD

As we study and apply the biblical teaching of discipleship, the conviction will grow upon us that Jesus is with us. We do not study a dead religious leader whose memory we revere. Rather, we study a risen Lord whose presence is near. Our study will become simply a "means to the end" of helping us walk more effectively with Jesus in the world.

Sometimes our discipleship programs thwart true discipleship. What I mean by this is that we can become so involved with our programs that we isolate ourselves from real life. Jesus called his disciples to him so that he could teach them how to walk with him in the real world. That is true discipleship. As the early church gathered week by week for study, prayer, fellowship, and worship they were equipped to walk more effectively with their risen Lord and to go out more boldly with him into the world to make disciples of all the nations. While we journey through this study, our goal must be to learn how Jesus' first disciples were trained to walk with him so that we can apply that training to our own lives as we walk with Jesus in the real world.

Scripture paints a lucid picture of the Master and his disciples walking under Palestinian skies. Once Jesus has ascended back to his heavenly father, the scene changes to those disciples going out to make disciples of all the nations. From those portraits, Jesus still issues a call to the modern church to follow him. Do we hear his summons clearly? Is our vision of the Master properly focused? Many voices call for our attention; sometimes those voices muffle Jesus' call. Many authority figures want to set the direction for our lives; sometimes we see them more clearly than we see Jesus.

My young surfer friend, Chris, knew that he needed help following Jesus out into the world of professional surfing. He knew that what he read of the disciples' lives was not what he was experiencing, so he wanted help getting there. That is the kind of open door none of us can walk by if we are really interested in helping people around us grow as Christians! Are you prepared to help the "Chris" who comes into your life asking for help? Whether it is the neighbor next door, the person with whom we share an office, or the child the Lord has given us to raise, these all are precious people who have come into our lives from the Lord. As we learn to follow Jesus more closely, we will in turn be a source of guidance for those whom the Lord sends our way.

With this study I offer two prayers: First, I pray that we see Jesus clearly and that his Word, not this book, becomes the authoritative voice that we follow. As we hear his voice more and more clearly, we will be able to follow him more closely and to offer help to those around us who are seeking support. Second, I pray that you, the reader, and I will develop a sense of camaraderie as we make this journey. Together we follow the Master.

Following up:

1. In what ways will becoming a more dynamic disciple of Jesus affect our daily lives?
2. How does the discipleship commitment you have made to Jesus compare to the radical commitments made by the first disciples?
3. Is there any place in this world where Jesus would not walk? Why or why not?
4. How would you have responded to Chris (the surfer) if he had asked you to help him to be like the first disciples?
5. What would you do with him to help him accomplish his goal of radical discipleship?

2

Jesus and Disciples Today

Getting focused:

1. What is a good definition of a disciple of Jesus?
2. Do you agree with the statement, "All disciples are believers, but not all believers are disciples"? Why or why not?
3. Are you a disciple of Jesus? Who is a disciple of Jesus today? Is discipleship optional?

Being a disciple of Jesus is a phenomenon that is simple to appreciate yet incredibly complex fully to comprehend.

Witness this scene. A young sailor is sitting on the floor of a Christian coffee house next to a couch on which is seated a somewhat older man. The young sailor is visibly agitated, wringing his hands, looking desperate. Then he raises his voice and cries out, pleading with the other man, "When will I finally be a disciple of Jesus? What else do I have to do? I want to be one so badly, but I just don't know what else to do!"

That scene haunts me to this day. I was a fairly new believer and had been asked to give my testimony of conversion at a Christian servicemen's center; that sailor was the first person I encountered when entering the center. Here was a young man who had the sincerest desires, yet his conception of discipleship was such that it caused him severe personal turmoil.

The young sailor was captivated by the same complex phenomenon that has captivated the Christian world in the last quarter century. Discipleship appears simple to understand at first glance, yet the more we examine what Jesus was doing with his disciples, the more complex the issues become. John Vincent, writing over thirty years ago, foresaw the essence of the young sailor's dilemma.

24

Commenting on Jesus' teaching about discipleship, "Anyone who loves his father or mother more than me is not worthy of me. . . . Anyone who does not take up his cross and follow me is not worthy of me. Whoever finds his life will lose it, and whoever loses his life for my sake will find it" (Mt 10:37–39, paraphrase), Vincent wrote:

> These words—the *discipleship words* of the Synoptic Gospels—and others like them, have always been either a *fascination* or an *embarrassment* to the Church. For the hermit or the monastic, for the prophet and even for the mystic, they have exercised an irresistible attraction. For some of the greatest names in Christian biography—Benedict, Francis of Assisi, Jacob Boehme, William Law, Soren Kierkegaard, Dietrich Bonhoeffer—here lay the key to the mystery of Christian existence. But for the Church in general, they have always constituted a problem. If the words are to be taken literally, then there can be but few who can be disciples. If they are to be taken symbolically or spiritually, then they plainly mean something different for us than they meant for those who were first called.[1]

For many people in the church, as for the young sailor, Vincent's vexation over the discipleship words of Jesus expresses the dilemma clearly. To illustrate this dilemma, when I teach or speak on discipleship in classes or churches or conferences, I regularly ask this question: "How many of you can say, in the humble confidence of your heart, that you are convinced that you are a true disciple of Jesus Christ? Please raise your hand." People are visibly confused as they attempt to answer the question. Most do not put their hand up at all, some do so hesitantly, some put it up then take it down, others put it up half-way.

Then I ask another question: "How many of you can say, in the humble confidence of your heart, that you are convinced that you are a true Christian? Please raise your hand." Immediately most hands shoot up—no hesitation, no doubt!

In the last twenty-plus years, a virtual flood of discipleship studies has swept over the church, yet people may be more confused now than ever. The reason? No consensus reigns in understanding what Jesus was doing and in what we should be doing in making disciples. What is a disciple of Jesus? What should we be like as disciples? Who are to be the objects of discipleship?

DISCIPLESHIP MODELS

Different answers are given to those questions today. As we look at the various responses, we can see several models of discipleship that

[1]John James Vincent, "Discipleship and Synoptic Studies," *Theologische Zeitschrift* 16 (1960): 456.

result from those who have studied the biblical data. While some diversity is to be found within each model, distinct characteristics mark each one. We have isolated five models here. Each view of discipleship has both strengths and weaknesses. Which of the following discipleship models represents your own understanding of what it means to be a disciple of Jesus?

Disciples Are Learners

Some suggest that a disciple is a learner who follows a great teacher. They suggest that the term *disciple* refers to one who puts himself/herself under the teaching authority of a great teacher but that it has no reference to whether or not the person is a Christian.[2] For example, Charles Ryrie suggests the following general definition of a "disciple." "A follower of a teacher and his teachings, involving, in Bible times, traveling with that teacher wherever he went."[3] Kenneth Wuest says, "The word merely refers to one who puts himself under the teaching of someone else and learns from him. . . . In the case of the word 'disciple' the context must rule as to whether the particular disciple mentioned is saved or unsaved, not the word itself."[4] Livingston Blauvelt takes it one step further by saying that

> the Greek word "disciple" ($\mu\alpha\theta\eta\tau\acute{\eta}\varsigma$ [*mathētēs*]) comes from the verb "to learn" ($\mu\alpha\nu\theta\acute{\alpha}\nu\omega$ [*manthanō*]). Many people, both saved and unsaved, were learning of Jesus. So He exhorted those who would follow Him to count the cost (Luke 9:23; 14:25–35). That the terms "disciple" and "Christian" are not synonymous is clear from John's Gospel. "From this time many of his disciples turned back and no longer followed him" (John 6:66). Then there was Judas, an unsaved disciple.[5]

This view is instructive because it emphasizes the early linguistic relationship between the noun *disciple* and the verb *learn*. Further, this model emphasizes that a variety of different kinds of followers were called disciples. In the Gospels we find that a disciple may be a believer in Jesus Christ or may be a follower of someone else, such as John the Baptist (Jn 1:35) or the Pharisees (Mt 22:15–16).[6] This

---

[2]E.g., Charles C. Ryrie, *So Great Salvation: What It Means to Believe in Jesus Christ* (Wheaton, Ill.: Victor Books, 1989), 155; Livingston Blauvelt, Jr., "Does the Bible Teach Lordship Salvation?" *BS* 143 (1986): 41; Kenneth S. Wuest, *Studies in the Vocabulary of the Greek New Testament*, vol. 3, *Wuest's Word Studies* (Grand Rapids: Eerdmans, 1966), 25.
[3]Ryrie, *So Great Salvation*, 155.
[4]Wuest, *Studies*, 3:25.
[5]Blauvelt, "Does the Bible. . . ?" 41.
[6]A variation on this view suggests that discipleship was appropriate to Jesus' day, while people could follow him around physically, but that today, since Jesus

model also indicates the historical development of the "disciples" of Jesus within his earthly ministry. At an early point in Jesus' ministry, people became "disciples" of Jesus even though it was revealed later that they were not believers.

This model has two basic difficulties. First, the Greek term for "disciple" (*mathētēs*) is used in Scripture in a manner different than simply to designate a "learner." For example, the followers of John the Baptist are more like adherents to the prophet and the movement surrounding him than students of a teacher. The second difficulty appears when we note the normal use of the term *disciple* in the book of Acts. In Acts the term is generally used without any qualifiers simply to designate "Christians." For example, Acts 11:26 says, "The disciples were called Christians first at Antioch." The disciples appear to be more than simply learners.

Disciples Are Committed Believers

Several others suggest that a disciple is a committed Christian, a believer who has made a commitment to follow Jesus and obey his radical demands of discipleship.[7] Juan Carlos Ortiz answers one of our original questions by saying, "What is a disciple? A disciple is one who follows Jesus Christ. But because we are Christians does not necessarily mean we are his disciples, even though we are members of his kingdom. Following Christ means acknowledging Him as Lord; it means serving Him as a slave."[8] Dwight Pentecost similarly asserts that "there is a vast difference between being saved and being a disciple. Not all men who are saved are disciples although all who

has ascended to heaven and believers can no longer follow him physically, it is inappropriate for us to speak of ourselves as disciples. See, for example, Donald R. Rickards, "Discipleship: A Biblical Doctrine?" *Voice* 55 (1976): 5–18; Fred L. Fisher, *Jesus and His Teachings* (Nashville: Broadman, 1972). This view will be considered directly in later chapters.

[7]E.g., Allan Coppedge, *The Biblical Principles of Discipleship* (Grand Rapids: Zondervan, 1989), 40–42; Leroy Eims, *The Lost Art of Disciple Making* (Grand Rapids/Colorado Springs: Zondervan/NavPress, 1978), 61ff., 83ff., 181–88; Walter A. Henrichsen, *Disciples Are Made—Not Born* (Wheaton, Ill.: Victor, 1974), 18, 40; Zane C. Hodges, *The Gospel Under Siege: A Study on Faith and Works* (Dallas: Redención Viva, 1981), 36–45; *Absolutely Free: A Biblical Reply to Lordship Salvation* (Grand Rapids/Dallas: Zondervan/Redención Viva, 1989), 67–68, 87; Gary W. Kuhne, *The Dynamics of Discipleship Training: Being and Producing Spiritual Leaders* (Grand Rapids: Zondervan, 1978), 15; Juan Carlos Ortiz, *Disciple* (Carol Stream, Ill.: Creation House, 1975), 9; J. Dwight Pentecost, *Design for Discipleship* (Grand Rapids: Zondervan, 1971), 14; Paul W. Powell, *The Complete Disciple* (Wheaton, Ill.: Victor, 1982), 11–12; J. Oswald Sanders, *Spiritual Maturity* (Chicago: Moody, 1962), 108–9.

[8]Ortiz, *Disciple*, 9.

are disciples are saved. In discussing the question of discipleship, we are not dealing with a man's salvation. We are dealing with a man's relationship to Jesus Christ as his teacher, his Master, and his Lord.[9] Walter Henrichsen points to the average Christian in the church who has not become fully committed to Jesus' discipleship teachings and says, "See that man? He is a believer who has refused to pay the price of becoming a disciple. In making that decision, he has relegated himself to a life of mediocrity. Given a chance to be first, he has chosen to be last. To use the words of the Lord Jesus, he is savorless salt. Whatever you do, don't become like him."[10]

This discipleship model emphasizes Jesus' radical challenge to count the cost of discipleship. It points to the small group of disciples who followed Jesus and emphasizes that when they left all to follow Jesus they became models of a higher spiritual calling. It compares Jesus' disciples with the crowds around him and concludes that the difference lay in responding to Jesus' call to commitment. The beginning point of discipleship, therefore, was commitment. This model suggests that there are two levels within the church today—disciples and ordinary believers. A disciple is a more committed Christian than the average Christian. This model of discipleship is quite widespread, being found in several different forms. Some who hold this view make a distinction between active "disciples" (found in some renewal movements and parachurch organizations) and ordinary Christians. Others who hold to this position make a distinction between "Spirit-filled disciples" (found in some churches in the charismatic movement)[11] and other Christians.

This model also encounters difficulties. One difficulty lies in the interpretation of Jesus' discipleship messages and the spiritual nature of the audiences to whom he directs his messages. For example, when Jesus gives a message directed to the "crowds," which calls them to count the cost before they become his "disciples" (Lk 14:25–33), or when he tells the rich young ruler to go give all his riches to the poor before he can enter into eternal life (Mt 19:16–22), what is the spiritual nature of the crowds? of the ruler? Are they already believers or not? What is the meaning of the message? Is it a call to deeper commitment or a call to salvation? An additional difficulty appears when we notice that in its various forms this model relies

[9]Pentecost, *Design for Discipleship*, 14.

[10]Henrichsen, *Disciples Are Made*, 40.

[11]An extreme of this view is discovered in the "Shepherding Movement" founded in North America in the 1970s, which, tellingly, has also been called the "Discipleship Movement."

upon a two-class system of Christians, a problematic concept of
biblical discipleship.[12]

Disciples Are Ministers

Another model of discipleship suggests that a disciple is the
believer who has been called out from among lay believers in order
to enter into ministry. Discipleship means to be with Jesus in order to
learn from him how to serve the crowd, the church.[13] Focusing on the
distinction between the crowds and the disciples in the gospel of
Matthew, Paul Minear maintains that because the crowds represent
followers of Jesus, his disciples "form a much more limited and
specialized group than is usually supposed. They are those chosen
and trained as successors to Jesus in His role as exorcist, healer,
prophet, and teacher."[14] Dennis Sweetland has a similar perspective
when he says: "Everyone is called to participate in the reign of God,
but only some are called to be followers of Jesus. . . . The disciple of
Jesus is called to serve other members of the eschatological community (cf. Mk 1:31) and, through the missionary enterprise, those
outside the community as well."[15]

This model results from observing the close relationship of the
twelve disciples with Jesus in his ministry and in their later ministry
to the early church.[16] It concludes that the radical call to discipleship

[12]Among those biblical scholars who say that a two-class distinction of
Christians cannot be supported from a biblical concept of discipleship are Martin
Hengel (*The Charismatic Leader and His Followers* [New York: Crossroad,
1981], 62–63) and Kvalbein ("'Go Therefore,'" 51).

[13]E.g., H.-J. Degenhardt, *Lukas—Evangelist der Armen. Besitz und Besitzver-
zicht nach den lukanischen Schriften: Eine traditions- und redaktionsgeschicht-
liche Untersuchung* (Stuttgart: Katholisches Bibelwerk, 1965); Karl Hermann
Schelkle, *Discipleship and Priesthood*, trans. Joseph Disselhorst, rev. ed. (New
York: 1965); Mark Sheridan, "Disciples and Discipleship in Matthew and
Luke,"*BThB* 3 (1973): 235–55; Paul S. Minear, "The Disciples and the Crowds in
the Gospel of Matthew," *AThR* Sup. Series, 3 (March 1974): 28–44; R. Thysman,
Communauté et directives éthiques: la catéchèse de Matthieu, Recherches et
Synthéses: Section d'exégèse, no. 1 (Gembloux: Duculot, 1974); Gerhard Lohfink,
Jesus and Community: The Social Dimension of Christian Faith (Philadelphia:
Fortress, 1984), 31–33; Demetrios Trakatellis, "'Ἀκολούθει μοι/Follow Me' (Mk
2:14): Discipleship and Priesthood," *GOThR* 30 (3, 1985): 271–85; Dennis M.
Sweetland, *Our Journey with Jesus. Discipleship According to Mark*, GNS 22
(Wilmington, Del.: Michael Glazier, 1987).

[14]Minear, "Disciples and Crowds," 31.

[15]Sweetland, *Our Journey*, 17, 35.

[16]This is the implication of Gerd Theissen's study when he distinguishes
"wandering charismatics" (the disciples) from the "sympathizers" in the local
communities. Gerd Theissen, *Sociology of Early Palestinian Christianity*, trans.
John Bowden (Philadelphia: Fortress, 1978), 8–23.

was intended to be a model of how a believer today is called into ministry. This model of discipleship is also quite widespread, found especially in church traditions that emphasize a hierarchical order within their denominational structure and usually emphasize a distinction between the clergy and the laity. This model is also employed quite often by those who point to Jesus' training of his disciples as examples of how Christian leaders should be trained today.[17]

The same difficulties encountered in the second model apply here, but an additional difficulty is encountered because the twelve disciples are often used as the example. A problem arises when a clear distinction is not made between the Twelve as disciples and the Twelve as apostles. Most scholars agree that the terms *disciple* and *apostle* point to significantly different aspects of the Twelve. When do the Twelve function as disciples and when do they function as apostles? That is a crucial distinction for us to make.

Disciples Are Converts; Discipleship Comes Later

Others propose that disciples are converts to Jesus and that discipleship comes later. A disciple is one who has been evangelized, and the later process of growth is called "perfecting" or "discipleship."[18] Donald McGavran says, "Church-growth men use the word 'discipling' to mean the initial step by which people come to Christ and become baptized believers. We go on and say that the second part of church growth is 'perfecting' or growing in grace."[19] Another leader in the church growth movement, Peter Wagner, similarly declares that

a person is not a disciple just because he has been born in a Christian country or in many cases, even if he is a church member. . . . The basic meaning of disciple in the New Testament is equivalent to a true, born-again Christian. . . . Some have confused "making disciples" with "discipleship." Making disciples is the right goal of evangelism and missions according to the Great Commission. Once disciples are made, they then begin the lifetime road of discipleship.[20]

---

[17]E.g., P. T. Chandapilla, *The Master Trainer* (Bombay: Gospel Literature Service, 1974); M. E. Drushal, "Implementing Theory Z in the Church: Managing People as Jesus Did," *Ashland Theological Bulletin* 20 (1988): 47–62; Leroy Eims, *The Lost Art of Disciple Making* (Grand Rapids/Colorado Springs: Zondervan/NavPress, 1978), 61ff., 83ff., 181–88.

[18]E.g., Donald A. McGavran and Win Arn, *How to Grow a Church* (Glendale, Calif.: Gospel Light, 1973); C. Peter Wagner, *Stop the World I Want to Get On* (Glendale, Calif.; Regal, 1974), 79.

[19]McGavran and Arn, *How to Grow a Church*, 80.

[20]Wagner, *Stop the World*, 79–80. Wagner confuses the issue somewhat because of his distinction between disciple and discipleship. Elsewhere he

This discipleship model emphasizes that the meaning of the Great Commission's imperative, "make disciples" of all nations, is to make converts out of non-Christians. It stresses conversion as the beginning point of the Christian life, which means that conversion is the beginning point of becoming a disciple. Further, it recognizes that the term *disciple* is the most common designation for a "believer" in the Gospels and Acts.

The difficulty with this model is that it seems to separate the imperative of the Great Commission, "make disciples," from the following participles, "baptizing" and "teaching." The discrepancy may lie in the use of the English terms *disciple, discipling,* and *discipleship.* Is it possible to be a *disciple* without being on the road of *discipleship?* Is *discipling* different than *discipleship?*

Disciples Are Converts Who Are in the Process of Discipleship

Still others suggest that a disciple is a true believer who enters the life of discipleship at the time of conversion. In this model, as with the prior view, conversion is the beginning point of becoming a disciple, but discipleship is vitally linked to it as the natural result. Discipleship is not a second step in the Christian life but rather is synonymous with the Christian life. At conversion one becomes a disciple of Jesus, and the process of growth as a Christian is called discipleship. For Dietrich Bonhoeffer, to speak of entrance to the Christian life without recognizing that it also means entrance into the life of discipleship, is to cheapen the grace of God. He says:

> Cheap grace is grace without discipleship, grace without the cross, grace without Jesus Christ, living and incarnate. . . . Happy are they who know that discipleship means the life which springs from grace, and that grace simply means discipleship. Happy are they who have become Christians in this sense of the word. For them the word of grace has proved a fount of mercy.[21]

Dallas Willard stresses that discipleship is not an optional, second step in the Christian life, and he declares that to conceive of the Christian life in terms of discipleship is not to imply salvation by works. He says, "We are not speaking of perfection, nor of earning God's gift of life. Our concern is only with the manner of entering into that life. While none can merit salvation, all must act if it is to be

---

seems to make the two synonymous; cf. C. Peter Wagner, "What Is 'Making Disciples'?" *Evangelical Missions Quarterly* 9 (1973): 285–93.

[21]Dietrich Bonhoeffer, *The Cost of Discipleship,* trans. R. H. Fuller, 2d rev. ed. (New York: Macmillan, 1963), 47, 60.

theirs."[22] Similarly, James Montgomery Boice asserts that "discipleship is not a supposed second step in Christianity, as if one first becomes a believer in Jesus and then, if he chooses, a disciple. From the beginning, discipleship is involved in what it means to be a Christian."[23]

This model of discipleship emphasizes that as Jesus called men and women to him, and as he sent his disciples out to make other disciples, he was calling men and women into a saving relationship with himself that would make a difference in the new disciples' lives. Therefore, Jesus' purpose in the Great Commission included both conversion and growth—that is, "making disciples" meant that one became a disciple at the moment of conversion and that growth in discipleship was the natural result of the new disciple's life. As Jesus sent the disciples out to make converts, the demands for discipleship made by Jesus in his teaching were directed, not only to his first followers, but to all true believers.

This model of discipleship is quite widespread, appearing in several different contexts. Some emphasize the personal side of the disciple's committed walk with Jesus,[24] while others accentuate the social ramifications of the disciple's impact upon society.[25] Some concentrate on the growth that must occur within the context of life within the Christian discipleship community as a witness to the world,[26] while others accent leadership training for selective disci-

---

[22]Dallas Willard, *The Spirit of the Disciplines: Understanding How God Changes Lives* (San Francisco: Harper & Row, 1988), 264. This quote is taken from an appendix entitled "Discipleship: For Super-Christians Only?" which first appeared in *Christianity Today*, October 10, 1980.

[23]James Montgomery Boice, *Christ's Call to Discipleship* (Chicago: Moody, 1986), 16.

[24]E.g., Boice (*Christ's Call*), Bonhoeffer (*Cost of Discipleship*), and Willard, *The Spirit of the Disciplines*, as well as Michael Griffiths, *The Example of Jesus*, The Jesus Library, ed. Michael Green (Downers Grove, Ill.: InterVarsity Press, 1985), 43; Hans Kvalbein, " 'Go Therefore and Make Disciples. . .': The Concept of Discipleship in the New Testament," *Themelios* 13 (1988): 48–53; John F. MacArthur, *The Gospel According to Jesus: What Does Jesus Mean When He Says "Follow Me"?* (Grand Rapids: Zondervan, 1988), 196ff.; William MacDonald, *True Discipleship* (Kansas City, Kans.: Walterick, 1975), 3–9.

[25]E.g., Bonhoeffer (*Cost of Discipleship*), as well as Jim Wallis, *Agenda for Biblical People* (New York: Harper & Row, 1976), 23–26; Christopher Sugden, *Radical Discipleship* (Hants, England: Marshall, Morgan, & Scott, 1981), cf. 75; John R. Martin, *Ventures in Discipleship: A Handbook for Groups or Individuals* (Scottdale, Pa.: Herald, 1984), 17; Tom Sine, *Taking Discipleship Seriously: A Radical Biblical Approach* (Valley Forge, Pa.: Judson, 1985); Ched Myers, *Binding the Strong Man: A Political Reading of Mark's Story of Jesus* (Maryknoll, N.Y.: Orbis, 1988), 7–8.

[26]E.g., Alice Fryling, ed., *Disciplemakers' Handbook: Helping People Grow in Christ* (Downers Grove, Ill.; InterVarsity Press, 1989), 18; Allen Hadidian, *Successful Discipling* (Chicago: Moody, 1979), 19ff.; Bill Hull, *The Disciplemak-*

ples,[27] and still others focus on the evangelistic and missionary work that will result from right discipleship emphases.[28] In spite of the diversity, the common denominator of this model is that all true believers are seen as disciples, and the Christian life is the outworking of Jesus' discipleship teachings.

This model of discipleship displays several difficulties. First, this model does not always clarify which of the demands of discipleship given by Jesus were for whom, nor does it specify the purpose for which the demands were given. Jesus' radical discipleship admonitions are often presented as a whole without distinguishing the audience to whom they were presented nor the purpose for which they were given. Are all disciples/believers under the obligations of all of the discipleship teachings? For example, does discipleship today mean that everyone must literally leave everything to follow Jesus, including family and occupation? Must all Christians give all their riches to the poor? What was the purpose of the discipleship challenges given by Christ in his public ministry?

This last question leads to the second difficulty. This model has been accused of confusing conversion and commitment because it does not always clarify what it means to "count the cost" prior to becoming a believer. Must a person perform acts of commitment prior to conversion? If so, how does this square with grace? If not, what does it mean to count the cost?

A third difficulty appears, as with some of the other discipleship models, when this model does not clarify the difference between the Twelve as disciples and the Twelve as apostles. What was uniquely intended for the Twelve as apostles, and what was directed to them as disciples?

Fourth, is there a difference between discipleship as it is found in the Gospels and as it is found in the early church in Acts? Pentecost seemed to mark a major turning point in the lives of the disciples. Did Pentecost make a difference in what it meant to be a disciple? Finally, what of the church today? If—as this model emphasizes—a two-level conception of Christianity is not valid, then what is the

---

ing Pastor: The Key to Building Healthy Christians in Today's Church (Old Tappan, N.J.: Revell, 1988), 52; John R. Martin, *Ventures in Discipleship: A Handbook for Groups or Individuals* (Scottdale, Pa.: Herald, 1984), 17.

[27]E.g., A. B. Bruce, *The Training of the Twelve*, 1871, reprint (Grand Rapids: Kregel, 1971). Bruce calls all believers disciples but notes that some, like the Twelve, are called to leadership roles (cf. 11–12).

[28]E.g., Robert E. Coleman, *The Master Plan of Evangelism*, 2d ed. (Old Tappan, N.J.: Revell, 1964), 52; Richard R. DeRidder, *Discipling the Nations*, 1971, reprint (Grand Rapids: Baker, 1975), 183; Carl Wilson, *With Christ in the School of Disciple Building: A Study of Christ's Method of Building Disciples* (Grand Rapids: Zondervan, 1976), 79ff.

spiritual state of the many people in churches today who apparently are not living their lives in conformity with Jesus' discipleship teachings? Is there a clear understanding of a relationship between salvation and discipleship in the church today? Are the discipleship teachings of Jesus so radical that they are no longer a practical reality for us in the modern world?

OVERCOMING DIFFICULTIES IN DISCIPLESHIP STUDIES

No wonder that poor young sailor I met in the servicemen's center was so troubled! Each of these models is represented by wonderful men and women of God who are serious about heeding Jesus' call to discipleship. If they cannot agree, how could he hope to understand Jesus' call to discipleship! Each model has correctly accented—at least partially—biblical teaching. Why the different models? Why the problems?

These various models have come about as people have attempted to get at the heart of Jesus' conception of discipleship and then have attempted to apply that conception to present-day ministry. The major problems surface when each model attempts to reconcile seemingly contradictory passages, especially when reconciling Jesus' gracious call to discipleship with his stringent demands of discipleship, or when reconciling Jesus' ministry to the crowds with his ministry to the disciples, or when reconciling general discipleship passages with the role of the Twelve, or when reconciling the portrait of disciples in the Gospels with their occurrence in the Acts and the nonoccurrence of the term *disciple* in the Epistles. The strength of each discipleship model lies in its emphasis upon a particular type of discipleship teaching. The weakness of each discipleship model lies in its deemphasis of other types of discipleship teachings. As we prepare to embark upon our journey through the first-century world of discipleship, several observations should be kept in mind.

Enter Jesus' First-Century World
Before Following Him in Ours

Many difficulties can be overcome if we try to understand, first, the dynamics of discipleship as they occurred within the cultural setting of the first century before we try to apply those dynamics to our own lives.

With each new class studying the Gospels I like to perform a fun exercise. I take a few volunteers and ask them to stand on the platform in the large auditorium in which the lecture is held. I inform them that when I was a drill sergeant in the Army one of my responsibilities was to teach the new recruits how to march. "So," I tell them, "I'm going to teach you how to march through the Gospels." As the volunteers line up, I call out, "Forward, march!" They go a few steps and then, after they stop, I ask them to tell me which foot they started out on. Some say right; some say left; others don't remember! Then I tell them how it is that military people always stay in step with each other: they always start out on the same foot, and that is always the *left* foot.

Likewise, when walking through the Gospels we must always start out on the same foot, the left foot. The left foot represents starting with understanding the Gospels first from the standpoint of what was happening in the first century as Jesus walked and taught all around Palestine. What did the discipleship saying of Jesus mean to those who first heard it while Jesus was with them? What was Jesus' intention in his first-century setting? Then, after our left foot is solidly planted, we can go to the right foot, which represents applying the passage to our lives today. Once we understand what the discipleship sayings meant to Jesus' original audience, we will be able to take the essential principles and apply them to our own setting. If we start with the right foot, we run the risk of reading our own set of values and circumstances back into the Gospels. We must allow the original intention to interpret our own application.[29] Several difficulties found in the above discipleship models result from starting with the right foot! We must be as clear as possible in our understanding of what it meant to follow Jesus in the first century if we are to be clear about what it means to follow Jesus in our modern world. We must start with the left foot!

Identify with the Appropriate Audience

Several difficulties in the discipleship models result from a lack of precision concerning the audiences who heard Jesus' teachings. Even as preachers and teachers today try to know their audiences so that they can minister to appropriate needs and circumstances, Jesus gave teaching that was appropriate for the spiritual state of his listeners. He gave teaching and offered invitations that were uniquely suited for the particular audience that surrounded him. For example, in his parabolic discourse Jesus gave parables that had one intention for the crowds (hiding the mysteries of the kingdom) and one intention for the disciples (revealing the mysteries of the

---

[29]On the technical side, this reveals my hermeneutical approach, which flies in the face of much contemporary hermeneutics, especially certain literary-critical approaches that deny the reality of authorial intentionality.

kingdom) (cf. Mt 13:1–2, 10–17; Mk 4:1–12). If we do not precisely specify the audience, we will not identify with the audience and teaching that is appropriate for our spiritual state. Overall, discipleship teaching that is directed to the crowds deals with the act of becoming a disciple (evangelism), whereas teaching directed to the disciples deals with growth in discipleship (Christian growth).

Distinguish Between the Twelve as Disciples and the Twelve as Apostles

Throughout the history of the church a certain tension has been felt when looking at the lives of the Twelve. Special comfort has been drawn from recognizing that they are really not that much different than we are. If Jesus could make something of their lives, then he certainly can do something with ours! Yet, on the other hand, they seem so different than we are. The Twelve were used in the founding of the early church in ways not duplicated. When have we experienced such a ministry?

This points to a special difficulty that was observed when the Twelve were used in the above discipleship models: a clear distinction was not always made between the Twelve as disciples and the Twelve as apostles. Although the Twelve were both disciples and apostles, scholars agree that the terms *disciple* and *apostle* point to significantly different aspects. Indeed, while in the Gospels the Twelve are almost always called disciples, in the book of Acts the Twelve are never called disciples. In Acts they are only called apostles, to emphasize their leadership role in the early church. Therefore our preliminary observation is that as disciples the Twelve give us an example of how Jesus works with all believers, and as apostles the Twelve give us an example of how Jesus works with leaders of the church.

A. B. Bruce, in his classic study, *The Training of the Twelve*, provides clarification when he recognizes three stages in the history of the Twelve's relationship with Jesus. In the first stage they were simply believers in Jesus as the Christ and were his occasional companions (e.g., Jn 2:1, 12, 17, 22; 3:22; 4:1–27, 31, 43–45). In the second stage fellowship with Christ assumed the form of an uninterrupted attendance on his person, involving entire, or at least habitual abandonment of secular occupations (e.g., Mt 4:18–22; 9:9). In the third stage the twelve entered on the last and highest stage of their life's calling when they were chosen by the Master from the mass of his followers and formed into a select band to be trained for the great work of the apostleship.[30] What is important to note is that in every stage, whether they were first-stage believers, second-stage attendants, or third-stage apostles, the Twelve were *disciples*. The word *disciple* expressed the most basic aspect of their life with Jesus: they were *his followers*, not followers of any other master. The second and third stages represent different points in their relationship with the Lord as he trained them for later ministry.

My own experience has certain similarities. As new believers, my wife and I were a part of the fellowship of other believers. When we were asked to lead a high school youth group we were called church workers. When we were led to go to seminary and later entered into the pastorate, I was designated a pastor. At each stage we considered ourselves to be disciples of Jesus, no different than any other disciples in the church. Yet at the same time we were different because of the different leadership roles to which the Lord called us. If we are to learn from the example of the Twelve, we must be careful to observe the role they played at any one particular point in their relationship with their Lord.

Allow the Book of Acts to Help Us Interpret the Meaning of Discipleship Terminology

Several difficulties have already been mentioned which are best resolved when we allow the book of Acts to help us interpret discipleship terminology. By the time of the early church, as recorded in Acts, the term *disciple* was synonymous with the true believer in Jesus. Luke speaks of the multitude of "believers" in Acts 4:32 and the multitude or congregation of "disciples," in Acts 6:2. In Luke's writings, the expressions "those who believe" and "the disciples" signify the same group of people (cf. Ac 6:7; 9:26; 11:26; 14:21–22). Acts clarifies for us that the common word for a believer in the early church was *disciple*. *Disciple* was also the earliest synonym for *Christian* (11:26).

Luke also makes clear the use of the terms *disciple* and *apostle* with reference to the Twelve. Unlike in his gospel, Luke in Acts never calls the Twelve "disciples." Since the Twelve are only called apostles in Acts, Luke stresses the distinctive role that the Twelve played as apostles in the early church. In Acts the Twelve are called apostles to accentuate their leadership role, and the common name for a believer is *disciple*.

The book of Acts also helps us see the transitions that took place in discipleship terminology. In the Gospels *disciple* is the most

---

[30]A. B. Bruce, *Training of the Twelve*, 11–12.

common word used to designate the followers of Jesus, but the word does not occur at all in the Epistles. Instead, other terms, such as *brother/sister, saints, believers*, and *Christians* came to be the prominent terms used to designate followers of Jesus. We will explore the reasons for this transition in terminology in a later chapter. For now we simply need to point to the transition and emphasize that although the term *disciple* does not occur in the epistles, the book of Acts allows us to see that at the same basic historical period as the writing of the Epistles the terminology and concept of discipleship flourished.

DISCIPLES IN HISTORICAL CONTEXT

Today the English terms *disciple, discipleship*, and *discipling* imply different things to different users, depending upon the background of the user and the context of use. This is part of the problem behind the different discipleship models in existence today. We need standardized definitions of these very important terms or else we will not be talking about the same things. As we define them we must keep in mind three categories of usage: (1) How were the terms used in the general context of the first-century world? (2) How were the terms used in the biblical context? and (3) How are the terms used today? Although we will go into more background of these terms in the following chapters, a brief overview of the history of the term *disciple* is necessary before we can offer our definitions.

Behind our English word *disciple* lie the Latin terms *discipulus* (masculine) /*discipula* (feminine) and the Greek words *mathētēs* (masculine) /*mathētria* (feminine). Since these Latin and Greek nouns have a linguistic relationship to verbs for "learn"[31] in their earliest history, they were used to refer to "learners" and "students." Eventually the meaning broadened so that they were used to refer to "adherents" of a great master. The Greek term especially, by the late Hellenistic period during the time when the New Testament was written, was used increasingly to refer to an adherent. The type of adherence was determined by the master, but it ranged from being the companion of a philosopher, to being the follower of a great thinker and master of the past, to being the devotee of a religious figure. Therefore, in most common usage, whether in the Roman or Greek world, a "disciple" was a person who was committed to a significant master.[32] To say that a disciple is a learner is true, but this

---

[31]Latin *discere*; Greek *manthanein*.

[32]For a discussion of the classical and Hellenistic background to these terms see Wilkins, *Concept of Disciple*, 11–42.

overemphasizes one aspect of the term's meaning and misses what the term primarily signified in the New Testament era. For example, the disciples of John the Baptist were not primarily learners since John was not primarily a teacher but a prophet. A disciple was one who made a life commitment to a particular master and his way of life. The type of "disciple" and the corresponding life of "discipleship" was determined by the type of master, but commitment to the master and his ways was central.

Therefore, it is not enough to ask what a disciple is. Rather, we must ask of whom the person is a disciple and at what period of time. A disciple of Jesus during his earthly ministry was one who made a life commitment to him. Among those who made an early commitment were some who gave up following Jesus around when his way proved to be different than what they had expected (cf. Jn 6:60–66). And one, Judas Iscariot, was proven to be a false disciple. But as Jesus increasingly revealed his messianic identity, those who believed in him claimed him as their Savior and God, and those who remained with him were Jesus' true disciples. Possibly the clearest declaration of what this meant was given by Simon Peter right after many of Jesus' early disciples left him (v. 66). Jesus turned to the Twelve and asked, "You do not want to leave too, do you?" Then Peter stepped forward and said, "Lord, to whom shall we go? You have the words of eternal life. We believe and know that you are the Holy One of God" (vv. 67–69). Although even Jesus' closest followers, the Twelve, proved to be less than completely faithful when he went to the cross, the basic word used to designate a true follower of Jesus during his earthly life and the time of the early church was *disciple* (*mathētēs*).

DEFINITIONS

We are now prepared to give basic definitions for some crucial terms. These definitions will be fleshed out as we go through the biblical data, but at this point they should provide some orientation for our journey.

Disciple

In the New Testament the primary word for *disciple* is the Greek term *mathētēs* (*mathētai*, pl.). The definition of a disciple must be given in a general sense as well as in a specific sense with reference to what Jesus intended his disciples to be. This specific sense is seen most clearly toward the end of Jesus' earthly ministry, in the Great Commission, and in the early church.[33]

In the general sense, we may define a disciple as a committed follower of a great master. The general sense of the term has two common applications. (1) It was used nonreferentially to distinguish the disciple from the teacher (Mt 10:24–25; Lk 6:40). (2) It was also used to designate the followers of a great leader or movement. Thus, we find disciples of Moses (Jn 9:28), disciples of the Pharisees (Mt 22:16; Mk 2:18; Lk 5:33), disciples of John the Baptist (Mt 9:14; Mk 2:18; Lk 5:33; Jn 1:35; 3:25), and disciples of Jesus.

In the specific sense, a disciple of Jesus is one who has come to Jesus for eternal life, has claimed Jesus as Savior and God, and has embarked upon the life of following Jesus. *Disciple* is the primary term used in the Gospels to refer to Jesus' followers and is a common referent for those known in the early church as *believers, Christians, brothers/sisters, those of the Way,* or *saints,* although each term focuses upon different aspects of the individual's relationship with Jesus and others of the faith. The term was used most frequently in this specific sense; at least 230 times in the Gospels (e.g., Jn 6:66–71) and 28 times in Acts (e.g., Acts 9:1, 10, 19–20).

An interesting and important observation for us to make is that the plural form *disciples* is normally used. The singular form *disciple* never occurs in Mark, but it is frequent in John, where it always refers to a particular person (e.g., Jn 9:28; 18:15, 16; 19:26–28; 20:2–4, 8; 21:7, 20, 23, 24). The singular occurs in Matthew and Luke only on Jesus' lips, where it is used in teachings about the nature of discipleship (Mt 10:24, 25, 42; Lk 6:40; 14:26, 27, 33). The singular occurs only four times in Acts, where it always refers to a particular person (9:10, 26; 16:1; 21:16). The singular form designates an individual who professes to believe in and follow Jesus.[34] That the plural form is normally used expresses an important point: *individual disciples* are always seen in conjunction with the *community of disciples,* whether as Jesus' intimate companions or as the church.[35]

The English term *disciple* has undergone much the same development as did the Greek and Latin terms. Although *disciple* has roots in the Latin noun *discipulus,* which is related to the verb "to learn"

---

[33]Cf. Johannes P. Louw and Eugene A. Nida, eds., *Greek Lexicon of the New Testament: Based on Semantic Domains,* 2 vols. (New York: United Bible Societies, 1988), 1:470–71.

[34]We should note that Judas is called one of Jesus' disciples (Jn 12:4). Here is an individual who professes to be but is not a true believer. See the discussion of Judas in chap. 8.

[35]The significance of this concept will be discussed in full in later chapters, esp. chap. 13.

(*discere*), present English usage only secondarily associates *disciple* with a person who is a student or learner. The English noun is now associated most often with the words *supporter, follower,* or *adherent.* The word *disciple* in contemporary usage "pertains exclusively to someone devoted to a master or patron. Most strictly, *disciple* suggests a religious situation: the *disciples* of Buddha who codified his teachings. In general usage, the word refers to someone's ardent advocacy of any prominent figure or theory: an early disciple of Freud. . . ."[36] The words *supporter* and *follower* are perhaps the nearest synonyms: "Supporter is the general term for one who allies himself with a cause or shows allegiance to its leader. . . . Follower and disciple are related in that they emphasize devotion to a leader rather than to its doctrine or cause."[37] Hence, in the Christian sense, a disciple of Jesus is one who has come to him for eternal life, has claimed him as Savior and God, and has embarked upon the life of following him.

Discipleship and Discipling

The terms *discipleship* and *discipling,* are English words derived, obviously, from *disciple.* The nearest equivalent to these expressions in the New Testament is the verbal form, *mathēteuō,* "make or become disciples," which occurs only four times (Mt 13:52; 27:57; 28:19; Ac 14:21). In common parlance, *discipleship* and *discipling* today relate to the ongoing life of the disciple. *Discipleship* is the ongoing process of growth as a disciple. *Discipling* implies the responsibility of disciples helping one another to grow as disciples. Therefore, discipleship and discipling can be narrowly understood as a technical discussion of the historical master-disciple relationship, but these terms can also be understood in a broader way as Christian experience—that is, the self-understanding of the early Christian believers as believers: what such a way of life requires, implies, and entails.[38] Thus, when we speak of Christian discipleship and discipling we are speaking of what it means to grow as a Christian in every area of life. Since *disciple* is a common referent for *Christian,* discipleship and discipling imply the process of becoming like Jesus

---

[36]S. I. Hayakawa et al., "Student: Pupil, Scholar, Learner, Disciple, Protége," *Use the Right Word: Modern Guide to Synonyms and Related Words* (Pleasantville, N.Y.: Reader's Digest Association, 1979), 596–97.

[37]Ibid., "Supporter," 607.

[38]Fernando F. Segovia, "Introduction: Call and Discipleship—Toward a Reexamination of the Shape and Character of Christian Existence in the New Testament," in *Discipleship in the New Testament,* ed. Fernando F. Segovia (Philadelphia: Fortress, 1985), 2.

Christ. Discipleship and discipling mean living a fully human life in this world in union with Jesus Christ and growing in conformity to his image.

This definition is much broader than what many conceive of discipleship and discipling. Most conceive of discipleship as a more narrow program or training time. But when Jesus says that "a student is not above his teacher, but everyone who is fully trained will be like his teacher" (Lk 6:40), he enunciates a principle common to all master-disciple relationships: a disciple is involved in a natural process that will bring him or her to be like the master. That principle is central to biblical discipleship: in this life a disciple is always in a discipleship process, the process of becoming like the Master, Jesus. This establishes a link between explicit discipleship sayings in the Gospels and Acts with similar concepts in the rest of the New Testament, such as Paul's statement that the goal of God's calling in the life of the Christian is to be conformed to the image of Christ (cf. Ro 8:28–30). As one author says, "Indeed, full discipleship and full Christlikeness are the same thing."[39] Hence, all who are called to be Jesus' disciples are in the process of becoming more like the Master, Jesus Christ—that is, the process of *discipleship*. Each disciple also has the responsibility to be involved in helping other disciples grow—that is, *discipling*.

IMPLICATIONS

I wish that I could go back and talk to that young sailor in the servicemen's center, but I never saw him again after that night. What would I tell him if I could talk to him right now? I would like to comfort him, to tell him that I understand what he was struggling with, that the issues are complex, indeed as complex as the Christian life itself. But at the same time I would like to encourage him! Jesus wants him to get up and follow him right now as his disciple!

As I have studied and taught and pastored over the years I have seen many other younger and older Christians struggle with the same issues. Most of the difficulties can be attributed to the tension found in many areas of the Christian life, especially in the tension between the "already and the not yet." I want to tell that young sailor that if he is a Christian, he already is a disciple, but during this life he is not yet a complete disciple. He will continue to grow and to develop and to become more fully a disciple of Jesus.

The tendency is to emphasize one over the other. Some of us focus on the "not yet" in a perfectionistic way, and we in ministry often set

---

[39]Pierson Parker, "Disciple," *IDB*, 1:845.

up standards that only a few attain. This creates a heavy burden that can result in defeatism or exclusivism. Or some of us focus on the "already" and become so comfortable with the work of grace God has performed in saving us that we do not heed Jesus' call to press forward and grow as his disciples. Once we have responded to Jesus' invitation to follow him, we have become his disciples; we need to rest with that assurance. At the same time, as we rest with this assurance, we must get up and walk on the path of discipleship down which Jesus leads us in this life. We must balance the already and the not yet of discipleship. Everett Harrison declares:

> The future-oriented emphasis on life in the Synoptics is congruent with the emphasis they give to the theme of discipleship. People are summoned to follow Jesus, which suggests present incompleteness and progress toward a goal. The consummation lies ahead. Parenthetically, in the very nature of the case discipleship involves protest against any doctrine of sinless perfection in the present life: we will continue to be followers.[40]

The implications of this balanced approach to following the Master will impact significantly our choice of words, our theology, and the practical outworking of our lives. Many other implications will be examined in the process of our study, but these are important to raise now.

Semantical

Some implications are simply semantical. I recently gave a guest lecture at the University of Aberdeen on the occurrence of disciple groups in the first century. I was intrigued by the way two professors were almost convinced that we should give up the use of the English term *disciple* because it is so closely tied to certain expectations in the mind of hearers today. The more we talked, the more we agreed that we need to be more accurate in our use of terminology and not read modern usage back into the first-century context. We need to communicate by the use of our words as closely as possible what Jesus intended his followers to understand and what the biblical authors desired for us to know.

Several discipleship ministries have developed wonderful methods of helping Christians grow, but they have created confusion by their choice of words. Some ministries refer to those only with advanced commitment as "disciples." This implies that those with

---

[40]Everett F. Harrison, *The Apostolic Church* (Grand Rapids: Eerdmans, 1985), 142.

less commitment are not disciples. Instead, we should call all believers disciples and those with advanced commitment something like "mature disciples."

Some organizations designate only those who are active in the practice of Christian disciplines as "disciples." This implies that certain activities make a person a disciple. Rather, we should emphasize that Jesus called all believers to activity; those who are faithful we might refer to as something like "faithful disciples." Remember, for a period of time, even some of the Twelve were less than completely faithful yet continued to be called disciples.

Some ministries reserve the terminology "discipleship training" for a method that focuses on only a few people who have advanced in the Christian life. Instead, we might speak of "leadership training." Jesus chose the Twelve out from a "multitude of disciples" in order to train them for their future leadership role as apostles. The rest of the disciples continued to be under his teaching as they grew as disciples (cf. Lk 6:12–17).

Our choice of terminology determines the kind of expectations that we communicate to people. Since all true Christians are disciples, the ministry of the church may be seen in its broadest sense as "discipleship." Various ministries within the church should be seen as specialization, aspects, or stages of discipleship training. If we incorrectly use discipleship terminology, we run the risk of communicating that the uncommitted have the option to remain that way if they so desire, or else we place unrealistic expectations upon the committed ones. Discipleship teaching is applicable to all Christians.

Theological

While our study is intended primarily as an inquiry into the nature of biblical discipleship, it will also have profound theological implications. A case in point is the impact serious discipleship study should have on the "Lordship salvation" debate that has raged in some circles of North American evangelicalism off and on throughout the twentieth century. Although both sides of the controversy have used discipleship passages as support, their discussion of those passages tends—at times—to be more polemical than informed. Polemicism can have a place in debate if it helps clarify the issues, but in this case it tends to fuzz them.

For example, both sides of the debate come to amazingly different conclusions when they point to Jesus' startling discipleship words addressed to the crowds, "If anyone comes to me and does not hate his father and mother, his wife and children, his brothers and sisters—yes, even his own life—he cannot be my disciple" (Lk

14:26). One advocate of "non-Lordship salvation" points to those words and says, ". . . it should be clear that they have nothing to do with the terms on which we receive eternal life."[41] Because those words delineate conditions for entrance to discipleship, this author apparently interprets all "entrance to discipleship" passages in like manner, saying that none of them addresses the issue of entrance to eternal life. In this case, he even includes the Great Commission's imperative to "make disciples of all nations" (Mt 28:19) as only a broad call into a vital experience with God, not as entrance to eternal life.[42] While we can appreciate his struggle with Jesus' difficult words, eliminating the Great Commission as a message on entrance to salvation is a tenuous interpretation which even few other "non-Lordship salvation" advocates would hold.[43]

On the other side, one advocate of "Lordship salvation" points to the same discipleship words of Jesus cited above and says that Jesus uses these words "because He is eager to chase the uncommitted away and to draw true disciples to Himself. He does not want half-hearted people deceived into thinking that they are in the kingdom. Unless He is the number one priority, He has not been given His rightful place."[44] Further, when suggesting that the term *disciple* is a synonym for *Christian*, he says "the call to Christian discipleship explicitly demands just that kind of total dedication. It is full commitment, with nothing knowingly or deliberately held back. No one can come to Christ on any other terms."[45] The expressions "number one priority," "total dedication," "full commitment," and "nothing held back" have very strong overtones that may confuse people in the church. What do these expressions mean to a person who is coming to Christ for salvation? Such statements need to be carefully explained, or else they can be misunderstood to imply a works salvation. While we appreciate this endeavor to take Jesus' words seriously, we must also be clear about what Jesus intended the crowds to understand by his words and be clear in delivering those words to a present-day audience. We must be sure that we have communicated Jesus' invitation appropriately.

[41]Zane C. Hodges, *Absolutely Free: A Biblical Reply to Lordship Salvation* (Grand Rapids/Dallas: Zondervan/Redención Viva, 1989), 68.

[42]Ibid., 160–61.

[43]E.g., Charles C. Ryrie understands the Great Commission's imperative to mean entrance to eternal salvation and to be the missionary task of the church; cf. Charles C. Ryrie, *So Great Salvation: What It Means to Believe in Jesus Christ* (Wheaton, Ill.: Victor, 1989), 103–6; and *The Ryrie Study Bible* (Chicago: Moody, 1978), 1502, n. on Mt 28:19.

[44]John F. MacArthur, *The Gospel According to Jesus: What Does Jesus Mean When He Says "Follow Me"?* (Grand Rapids: Zondervan, 1988), 201.

[45]Ibid., 197.

Both sides of the contemporary "Lordship/non-Lordship salvation" issue have wonderful men and women of God who contend for their position. Both sides are contending for what they perceive to be the essence of the Gospel message. Although our theological discussions are important to modern life and doctrine, we must be careful not to let our theological agendas compel an interpretation of the text. And we must not cloud the meaning of the text with our rhetoric. What did Jesus mean by those startling discipleship words? What would the crowds have understood those words to mean? We will discuss them more fully in later chapters, but we suggest here in preliminary fashion that they are a challenge for people to count the cost of claiming Jesus Christ as their God. But that challenge was delivered to a particular group of people in first-century Palestine whom Jesus assumed understood what he intended for them to understand.

Jesus' words have caused scholars down through the centuries to struggle with his intended meaning. We will continue to struggle with them here. Our study of his discipleship teachings will have profound theological implications, but we need to allow Jesus to inform our theology rather than allowing our theological agendas to determine our interpretation. We need to hear Jesus' radical discipleship teachings as he intended them to be understood and then appropriately apply them to our own setting. We need to walk with the "left foot" first through such sayings before we interpret them from the "right foot"!

Practical

Serious discipleship study has implications that are forcibly practical as well. Since the discipleship life is the life expected of all believers, then the gauntlet is now thrown down by Jesus for all of us to follow him. Yes, some of us are called to specific areas of ministry and service not intended for all disciples, but when we hear the word *disciple*, do the ears of all of us open with expectancy? Far too often we think, "Disciple? Oh, that's for an extremist. I'm just a normal Christian." Far too often we imply when we say that we are "discipling" someone or when we are starting a "discipleship program," that we have in mind the extraserious Christian. Rather, we need to recognize that when Jesus spoke of disciples he had in mind what would be the *normal* Christian, not the abnormal.

A RADICAL YET REALISTIC SUMMONS

What will our churches and ministries be like if we live out the message that the expectations of discipleship found in the Gospels are expectations for all Christians, not just for a few committed ones? Jesus wants a church full of disciples who dare to go out into the world to make a difference and to live life the way it was intended to be lived. Yet, as the old hymn goes, "God never gives a call without the enabling." As he calls us to discipleship he is also right there with us to lead the way. Our young sailor needed to understand that Jesus' call to discipleship was a radical yet realistic summons to follow the Master out into the adventure of life's journey. That is precisely the message that Jesus gives to each of us.

Following up:

1. Which of the five models listed above reflects the definition of biblical discipleship you gave at the beginning of this chapter? Under which model were you raised spiritually?
2. How have the strengths and weaknesses of the model under which you were "discipled" affected your life?
3. Why do you think that there are so many models of discipleship?
4. What would you do to help the sailor out of his dilemma? What advice would you give him?

PART II

JESUS' DISCIPLESHIP ENVIRONMENT

3

The People Called to Follow God: Discipleship in the Old Testament

Getting focused:

1. How can people show that they love God with all their heart, soul, mind, and strength?
2. What did it mean for the Old Testament believers to "follow God"?
3. What is the difference between being a "disciple" in the Old Testament and being a disciple today?
4. Did God "disciple" Israel in the Old Testament? Explain.

"Roots." When I hear that word I invariably have memories of Alex Haley's book and the subsequent movie, which deeply impacted the lives of many people several years ago. The book and the movie depicted the African Americans' quest to remember their historical/cultural heritage. Cruelly uprooted from land, family, and dignity and forced to become slaves of white people in a faraway place, African Americans were separated from many elements that made them a distinctive people. However, through a spirit of oneness brought about by common origins, memories of a former time of freedom, and mutual suffering, they endured. Their "roots" held them firm while they pressed onward toward a time of freedom. I have the deepest respect for such a people of roots.

I have no such roots. I am like many Americans whose ancestry is made up of a hodge-podge of ancestries only barely remembered by my family. My Uncle Leon has tried to help me trace some of our family roots. He is the main person who has provided some kind of insight into our family heritage. He has a wonderful way of bringing the past to life. What an enlightening experience! Strains of Norwegian, English, Scottish, and probably many other nationalities run through our blood! I'm especially proud to point to an American Indian among our distant ancestors who has unknowingly supplied me with many "imaginary roots." My lack of roots has been playfully overcome through stories I made up to entertain my daughters when they were little. I would tell stories of incredible escapades with my imaginary Indian relatives, getting my little girls to scream with delight as I "reminisced" about hunting buffalo with bow and arrow, tracking deer through the forest, and riding the range with Sitting Bull! Unfortunately for my story telling, my daughters are now old enough so that when I start up with a wild tale they immediately get that "knowing" look and say, "Dad's telling his stories again!" I guess I have to wait for future grandchildren now to tell those stories of my imaginary "roots."

But I do have another set of roots—roots of faith. Once I became a Christian I was immediately adopted into a family of faith that has a long and well-documented genealogy. Through church history I can trace back through nearly two thousand years to the family of faith initiated by Jesus. The apostle John tells us: "He came to that which was his own, but his own did not receive him. Yet to all who received him, to those who believed in his name, he gave the right to become children of God—children born not of natural descent, nor of human decision or a husband's will, but born of God" (Jn 1:11–13). Contrasting his earthly family and his family of faith, his disciples, Jesus asked, "Who is my mother, and who are my brothers?" Pointing to his disciples, he said, "Here are my mother and my brothers. For whoever does the will of my Father in heaven is my brother and sister and mother" (Mt 12:48–50). I have the privilege of teaching men and women from all over the world who are my brothers and sisters of faith. Despite the diversity of backgrounds, races, colors, languages, and cultures, we have common roots. We belong to the same family of faith through responding to Jesus' call to follow him.

Jesus' call echoes throughout the Gospels and down through the centuries, the call which initiates discipleship, then and now. Whether it comes from the sandy seaside, beckoning fishermen to follow Jesus to become fishers of men (Mk 1:16–20), or comes from the hilly countryside, challenging the multitudes surrounding him to take up their cross and follow him (Lk 14:25–33), or comes from the dusty town-center in an alien land, inviting a scandalous woman to participate in his good news of salvation (Jn 4:1–42), Jesus' call brings men and women into a right relationship with the living God and into a life of discipleship.

Jesus' call had a long prehistory, however. As radical as it was, Jesus' call in the first century was a reiteration and extension of the call God had proffered to the people of Israel centuries before. When

God directed Abraham "Leave your country, your people and your
father's household and go to the land I will show you" (Ge 12:1), a
calling motif was established among the covenantal people of Israel
which later reverberated in Jesus' challenge: "If anyone would come
after me, he must deny himself and take up his cross and follow me.
For whoever wants to save his life will lose it, but whoever loses his
life for me and for the gospel will save it" (Mk 8:34–35). Likewise,
God called Israel into a special relationship that guaranteed his
presence in every circumstance:

> But now, this is what the LORD says—
>   he who created you, O Jacob,
>   he who formed you, O Israel:
> "Fear not, for I have redeemed you;
>   I have summoned you by name; you are mine.
> When you pass through the waters,
>   I will be with you;
> and when you pass through the rivers,
>   they will not sweep over you.
> When you walk through the fire,
>   you will not be burned;
>   the flames will not set you ablaze.
> For I am the LORD, your God,
>   the Holy One of Israel, your Savior." (Isa 43:1–3a)

That motif resonates through Jesus' call to men and women to be with
him, to confess him as Savior, to enter into a special relationship with
him which guarantees his presence in their activities even when they
go throughout all the world: "Go and make disciples of all nations. . . . And surely I am with you always, to the very end of the
age" (Mt 28:19–20).

The roots of biblical discipleship go deep into the fertile soil of
God's calling. That calling is expressed in the pattern of divine
initiative and human response that constitutes the heart of the
biblical concept of covenant, and is manifested in the recurrent
promise, "I will be your God, and you shall be my people" (e.g., Ex
6:7).[1] That call from the awesome Yahweh of the Old Testament is
reiterated in the tender call of Jesus when he said, "Come to me, all
you who are weary and burdened, and I will give you rest. Take my
yoke upon you and learn from me, for I am gentle and humble in
heart, and you will find rest for your souls. For my yoke is easy and
my burden is light" (Mt 11:28–30). God has called his people to

[1]For an extensive study of Israel and the church as a called community, see
Paul D. Hanson, *The People Called: The Growth of Community in the Bible* (San
Francisco: Harper & Row, 1986).

represent him upon the earth, to be with him in every circumstance of life, to be transformed in their personal character to be like him.

That calling is at the heart of biblical discipleship, both in the Old and New Testaments. Discipleship does not exist in the same form in the Old Testament as it is found elsewhere in the ancient world of the nations surrounding Israel. Israel's special covenantal relationship with God dominates all relationships within the national life. Certain basic similarities may be found with other forms of discipleship in the ancient world, but biblical discipleship in the Old Testament is distinctly different from that found elsewhere. Therefore, analogous discipleship concepts must not be sought primarily in the secular world of master-disciple relationships. Rather, the one master-disciple relationship that is analogous to the Old Testament's is the relationship between Jesus and his disciples. The God of the Old Testament who calls his people to a covenantal relationship is the same God of the New Testament who, in Jesus, calls his people to the new covenantal relationship.

Continuity and discontinuity characterize discipleship between the Old and New Testaments, as is the case with biblical theology generally.[2] This cautions us not to press too far in either direction. We should not press too far in the direction of drawing unwarranted analogous continuity between what we see in the Old Testament and the New Testament, nor too far in the direction of claiming unwarranted discontinuity. To understand the heart of biblical discipleship and the heart of God's purposes for humankind, we must follow the Master's call from the Old into the New.[3]

THE TERMS FOR *DISCIPLE* IN THE OLD TESTAMENT

One striking feature that stands out when going to the Old Testament to study discipleship is the relative absence of disciple terminology. The terms that later normally specified master-disciple relationships in Judaism (i.e., *talmîdh* and *limmûdh*) are virtually absent from the Old Testament. They are found only four times. *Talmîdh* is the Hebrew equivalent of the common Greek term for

---

[2]Cf. Gerhard Hasel, *Old Testament Theology: Basic Issues in the Current Debate*, 3d ed. (Grand Rapids: Eerdmans, 1982), 145–67. For a discussion of specific points of tension, see John S. Feinberg, ed., *Continuity and Discontinuity: Perspectives on the Relationship Between the Old and New Testaments.* Essays in Honor of S. Lewis Johnson, Jr. (Westchester, Ill.: Crossway, 1988).

[3]For this possibility, we heed the positive note sounded generally by Kenneth Barker in his presidential address to the Evangelical Theological Society; Kenneth L. Barker, "False Dichotomies Between the Testaments," *JETS* 25 (1982): 3–16.

disciple, *mathētēs*. Just as *mathētēs* ("learner," "disciple") derived from the verb for "learn" (*manthanō*), so *talmîdh* derived from the Hebrew verb for "learn" (*lāmadh*), meaning "taught one."[4] *Talmîdh* is the equivalent of *mathētēs* in later rabbinical Hebrew, although it normally designates a "beginning scholar" in rabbinical use.[5]

Surprisingly, *talmîdh* is used only once in the Hebrew Old Testament. Within a classification of musicians, the noun indicates a pupil in contrast to a teacher (*mebhîn*), or a novice in contrast to a master: "Young and old alike, teacher as well as student (*talmîdh*), cast lots for their duties" (1Ch 25:8).[6] Some have understood this to mean that a formal school existed in Jerusalem for the training of temple musicians.[7] The existence of a school is a possibility, but the text merely states that the musicians, whether small or great, or whether (chiastically) accomplished or learning, all cast lots for their duties. R. N. Whybray argues that the text ". . . implies no more than the obvious fact that there must have been musical instruction in order to preserve a continuity of skilled musicians; but such instruction may well have been private and comparable to the normal instruction in the hereditary craft of the family given by fathers to their sons."[8] *Talmîdh* in 1 Chronicles 25:8 is best understood in the most basic sense of the term: one engaged in the learning process or an apprentice learning a trade.

The adjective *limmûdh*, "taught," also derived from the verb *lāmadh*, occurs six times, always in the Prophets (Isa 8:16; 50:4 [2x]; 54:13; Jer 2:24; 13:23). *Limmûdh* was rendered as a substantive, "taught one," but it did not become a common term for a "disciple"

---

[4]Ernst Jenni, *"lmd," THAT*, 2, ed. Ernst Jenni and Claus Westermann (München: Chr. Kaiser, 1971), col. 872; Francis Brown, S. R. Driver, and Charles A. Briggs, *A Hebrew and English Lexicon of the Old Testament* (Oxford: Clarendon, 1974), 541 (hereafter BDB). This derivation is also true for the Aramaic term *talmîdha'*; cf. Marcus Jastrow, ed., *A Dictionary of the Targumim, the Talmud Babli and Yerushalmi, and the Midrashic Literature* (New York: Pardes, 1950), 2:1673.

[5]M. Aberbach, "The Relations Between Master and Disciple in the Talmudic Age," *Essays Presented to Chief Rabbi Israel Brodie on the Occasion of His Seventieth Birthday*, ed. H. J. Zimmels, J. Rabbinowitz, and I. Finestein, vol. 1, Jews' College Publications, new ser., no. 3 (London: Soncino, 1967): 1–24.

[6]Options for translating *talmîdh* are given by Jacob M. Myers, *I Chronicles*, AB, 2d ed. (Garden City, N. Y.: Doubleday, 1974), 12:170.

[7]C. F. Keil renders *talmîdh* "scholar" and tends to imply a formal school setting (this is also the rendering of the KJV). Quite possibly this was assumed from later rabbinic usage (cf. C. F. Keil and F. Delitzsch, *The First Book of Chronicles*, trans. Andrew Harper, *Commentary on the Old Testament*, reprint [Grand Rapids: Eerdmans, 1975], 272–73).

[8]R. N. Whybray, *The Intellectual Tradition in the Old Testament*, BZAW 135, ed. Georg Fohrer (Berlin: Walter de Gruyter, 1974), 37.

in later Judaism as did the related noun *talmîdh*. In Jeremiah the adjective has the meaning of "accustomed to" something,[9] while in Isaiah it means "taught" or "instructed" (8:16; 50:4 [2x]; 54:13).[10]

The occurrences of *limmûdh* in Isaiah have the most significance for this study, especially since lexicographers have given the adjective the force of "taught, as disciples," or "disciple, follower" in these passages.[11] Isaiah 8:16 reads, "Bind up the testimony and seal up the law among my disciples." This indicates that a group of disciples were gathered around the prophet Isaiah, listening to the words of God through him. Isaiah 50:4 (NASB) declares:

> The Lord GOD has given Me the tongue of disciples,
> That I may know how to sustain the weary one with a word.
> He awakens Me morning by morning,
> He awakens My ear to listen as a disciple.

This suggests a recognizable category of persons in Israel known as "disciples/taught ones" who were assumed to have facility in speaking and attentive listening. Isaiah 54:13 notes that the sons of Zion will be directly instructed by the Lord: "All your sons will be taught by the LORD, and great will be your children's peace." The context does not indicate the content of the teaching, but the prophetic picture of sons of Zion characterized as "God-taught" is the same as saying that they are God's disciples.[12]

THE CONCEPT OF DISCIPLESHIP IN THE OLD TESTAMENT

While a curious scarcity of Hebrew and Aramaic words for "disciple" leads some to minimize discipleship concepts in the Old Testament,[13] other terms and expressions point to abundant concepts of discipleship. Most clearly, discipleship relationships can be

---

[9]E.g., Jer 2:24: a wild donkey accustomed to the wilderness; Jer 13:23: a person accustomed to doing evil.

[10]Jenni, *"lmd,"* cols. 872, 875; BDB, 541; Walter C. Kaiser, *"lamadh," TWOT,* ed. R. Laird Harris; Gleason L. Archer, Jr.; and Bruce K. Waltke (Chicago: Moody, 1980), 1:480.

[11]BDB, 541; Ludwig Koehler and Walter Baumgartner, eds., *Lexicon in Veteris Testamenti Libros* (Leiden: E. J. Brill, 1951), 1:483. The KJV and RSV render the use in 8:16 "disciples"; the NASB renders the use in 50:4 "disciple" and also gives that translation as an alternate in 54:13.

[12]The RSV and NASB give "disciples" as a possible translation in their respective margins.

[13]E.g., Karl H. Rengstorf, *"μαθητής," TDNT* 4:427, who says, "If the term is missing, so, too, is that which it serves to denote. Apart from the formal relation of teacher and pupil, the OT, unlike the classical Greek world and Hellenism, has no master-disciple relation. Whether among the prophets or the scribes we seek in vain for anything corresponding to it."

observed on three levels: (1) on the national level, in the covenant relationship of Israel and God; (2) on the individual to God level, in the relationships of certain individuals who followed God; and (3) on the human relationship level, in relationships found within the national life.

National Discipleship to God

Karl Rengstorf correctly stresses that the "ideal" of discipleship in the Old Testament is the covenant relationship between Israel and God.[14] Although the call came from God to individuals—Abraham, Isaac, and Jacob—the covenantal relationship was directed toward their offspring (e.g., Ge 13:15). God was creating a national community that would be called his people. In turn his people were to be a source of blessing to all peoples on the earth (12:1–3). That calling was reiterated and confirmed in the exodus from Egypt, where God demonstrated his loving care and grace by providing deliverance from bondage and protective guidance as he went ahead of them during their travels in the wilderness (Ex 13:21–22).

GOD WITH HIS PEOPLE

When giving the law to Israel in the wilderness, God stressed his covenantal intent: "I will walk among you and be your God, and you will be my people" (Lev 26:12). The nation was called to a relationship in which God was with his people. No other person or god was to take a place of preeminence that would usurp God. While God called men and women to leadership roles (e.g., Moses, Joshua, the judges, prophets), they were only intermediate leaders. God alone was to have the place of preeminence.

In fact, no human king ruled over Israel. In their covenantal relationship with God, God was their sovereign. But having an invisible sovereign was difficult for the people of Israel. The people of Israel wanted to be like the surrounding nations who had kings whom they could see and follow; they wanted their own king. God recognized that wanting a human king was equivalent to rejecting him as King (1Sa 8:7). He considered this an evil thing (1Sa 12:17). Later God allowed a human king to rule for him, even establishing Saul and calling David's line, but God intended to be Israel's King himself. The promise of a coming Davidic Messiah is intertwined with the promise that God himself would be with his people (e.g., Eze 37:24–28).

---

[14]Rengstorf, "μαθητής," 427. Cf. also Paul Helm, "Disciple," *Baker Encyclopedia of the Bible*, ed. Walter A. Elwell (Grand Rapids: Baker, 1988), 1:630.

THE PEOPLE FOLLOW GOD

The abstract covenantal relationship with God—"How does the nation display its single-hearted devotion to God?"—finds concrete expression in "following God" and "walking in his ways," explicit discipleship-type terminology.[15] When the nation is fulfilling its commitment to the covenant it is said to be following God (e.g., Dt 4:1–14; 1Sa 12:14) and walking in his ways (Dt 10:12). Moses, in his final charge to the people, asks, "And now, O Israel, what does the LORD your God ask of you but to fear the LORD your God, to walk in all his ways, to love him, to serve the LORD your God with all your heart and with all your soul, and to observe the LORD's commands and decrees that I am giving you today for your own good?" (Dt 10:12–13). When the nation has violated the covenant, it is said to be following the gods of the heathen and walking in their ways (Dt 6:14; Jdg 2:10–13; Isa 65:2). Elijah, on Mount Carmel provides a graphic statement of the choice when he calls to the people of Israel and says, "How long will you waver between two options? If the LORD is God, follow him; but if Baal is God, follow him" (1Ki 18:21).

Deuteronomy 6:4–9, known in the Jewish tradition as the *Shema'*, contains the "fundamental truth of Israel's religion" and "the fundamental duty founded upon it." The fundamental truth declares that in his nature God is One: "Hear, O Israel: The LORD our God, the LORD is one" (v. 4). The fundamental duty declares the response of love that God requires of man: "Love the LORD your God with all your heart and with all your soul and with all your strength" (v. 5).[16] Following God is the concrete expression of what it means to love the Lord God with all of one's heart and soul.

> If a prophet . . . says, "Let us follow other gods" (gods you have not known) "and let us worship them," you must not listen to the words of that prophet or dreamer. The LORD your God is testing you to find out whether you love him with all your heart and with all your soul. It is the LORD your God you must follow, and him you must revere. Keep his commands and obey him; serve him and hold fast to him (Dt 13:1–4).

Following God is understood in a metaphorical sense of walking in the ways of God.[17] Because God is holy, Israel is to be holy (Lev

---

[15]Cf. John James Vincent, *Disciple and Lord: The Historical and Theological Significance of Discipleship in the Synoptic Gospels*, Dissertation zur Erlangung der Doktorwuerde der Theologischen Fakultaet der Universitaet Basel (Sheffield: Sheffield Academic Press, 1976), 18–19.

[16]See Peter C. Craigie, *The Book of Deuteronomy*, NICOT (London/Grand Rapids: Hodder and Stoughton/Eerdmans, 1976), 168.

[17]F. J. Helfmeyer, הלך *hālakh*, *TDOT* 3:388–403; Gerhard Kittel, "ἀκολουθέω," *TDNT* 1:211.

11:44–45). Walking with God points to human life as a journey with God. It is the experience of God's benevolent presence (Ge 24:40; 48:15; cf. Ps 56:13; 116:9), designating a happy human life exclusively in the presence of God.[18]

Individual Discipleship to God

The same themes, God with his people and the people following God, are found not only on the national level, but also on the individual level, where individuals follow God in discipleship. This is seen clearly in Isaiah 54:13, where the ideal relationship is for the sons of Zion to be directly taught of the Lord. While the nation as a whole was in covenant relation with God, the individual was not lost within the nation. Individual relationships with God were understood within the covenantal relationship. This also included the individual called to "follow" God in this metaphorical sense. As the individual followed God, it was an expression of living in covenantal relationship with God. To stop following God indicated consciously breaking the covenant. Isaiah says:

> The way of the righteous is smooth;
> O Upright One, make the path of the righteous level.
> Indeed, while following the way of Thy judgments, O LORD,
> We have waited for Thee eagerly;
> Thy name, even Thy memory, is the desire of our souls.
>
> (Isa 26:7–8 NASB)

The leaders of the people were evaluated by the criteria of whether or not they were following God and walking in his ways. For example, Joshua (Nu 32:12) and Caleb (Nu 32:12; Jos 14:8, 9, 14) were singled out and commended for following God when the rest of the people did not (Nu 32:11–12). The high priest was given a conditional blessing based upon whether or not he walked in God's ways (e.g., Zec 3:7). Kings were good or bad, depending upon whether or not they followed God while leading the people. David is the supreme example of the king whose life was characterized by following God: ". . . my servant David, who kept my commands and followed me with all his heart, doing only what was right in my eyes" (1Ki 14:8). Solomon was exhorted by God to set the proper example for his people by following God or else he would be cut off (9:6–7). Hezekiah (2Ki 18:6) and Josiah (23:3) epitomized what it meant to be godly kings, because they did not turn aside from following God. The covenant is specifically tied to following God, and, as Josiah followed God, the people came after him: "The king stood by the pillar and

---

[18]Helfmeyer, הלך *hālakh,* 403.

renewed the covenant in the presence of the LORD—to follow the LORD and keep his commands, regulations and decrees with all his heart and all his soul, thus confirming the words of the covenant written in this book. Then all the people pledged themselves to the covenant" (2Ki 23:3; cf. Nu 32:11–12).

Individual discipleship in the Old Testament is a personalization of national discipleship. The individual makes a personal commitment to the national covenant, which means to love God with all of one's heart and soul and to follow after God within the parameters of the covenant. One of the most beautiful expressions of this relationship is found in Psalm 25.

> Make me know Thy ways, O LORD;
> Teach me Thy paths.
> Lead me in Thy truth and teach me,
> For Thou art the God of my salvation;
> For Thee I wait all the day.
> . . . .
> Good and upright is the LORD;
> Therefore He instructs sinners in the way.
> He leads the humble in justice,
> And He teaches the humble His way.
> All the paths of the LORD are lovingkindness and truth
> To those who keep His covenant and His testimonies.
> For Thy name's sake, O LORD,
> Pardon my iniquity, for it is great.
> Who is the man who fears the LORD?
> He will instruct him in the way he should choose.
>
> (vv. 4–5, 8–12 NASB)

Human Discipleship Relationships

Discipleship in the Old Testament entailed placing God as the focal point for the nation and the individual to follow. Other forms of discipleship in the ancient world usually involved following a great human master, leader, or teacher (we will explore some of the other forms in the next chapter). Therefore, some scholars have suggested that ancient Israel avoided human discipleship relationships, because relationships between human masters and disciples potentially could usurp the central place of God and make false distinctions between members of the chosen community.[19] While the scarcity of

---

[19]Especially, Rengstorf, "μαθητής," 427–31. Rengstorf's influential article has been followed by many, including Jenni, "lmd," col. 875; Dietrich Müller, "μαθητής," *NIDNTT* 1:485; Andre Feuillet, "Disciple," *Dictionary of Biblical Theology*, ed. Xavier Leon-Dufour, 2d. ed. (New York: Seabury, 1973), 125.

discipleship terminology and the extreme reverence with which Israel held the centrality of God may indeed point in this direction, this is too narrow a view of what "discipleship" means. For example, Philip Sigal states, "Three figures shared the spiritual leadership of ancient Israel: the priest (*kohen*), the prophet (*nabi*), and the sage (*hakam*). All three were responsible for the transmission of torah and, in their respective circles, were teachers and role models for the populace to emulate."[20] Recent study has examined various human relationships within the matrix of national life with Yahweh and concludes that these should be called "discipleship" relationships. In particular, evidence of human master-disciple relationships appear within the structure of Israel's national leadership; within the priestly, prophetic, and scribal groups; and within the wisdom tradition.

Although human masters and their disciples in Israel developed an important relationship, God never lost his central place. In fact, these master-disciple relationships were brought about by God to serve the nation with the result that the nation was enabled to hear God's voice more clearly and to follow him more closely. Therefore, certain similarities occur between human discipleship relationships found in Israel and those found in the surrounding nations, but the form of discipleship found in Israel has a uniqueness that cannot be exactly paralleled.[21] All discipleship relationships are designed to lead Israel and individuals within the nation into a closer walk with the living God.

INDIVIDUAL LEADERS

Several relationships between individuals in the Old Testament could be called "discipleship" relationships. Most prominent among them are the relationships between Moses and Joshua, between Elijah and Elisha, and between Jeremiah and Baruch.[22] In each, we find a person called to serve God and the nation and another person in a subordinate role. Josephus, writing at approximately the same time as the New Testament writers, provides an interesting and important perspective. Josephus looked back on each of these

---

[20]Philip Sigal, *Judaism: The Evolution of a Faith*, rev. and ed. Lillian Sigal (Grand Rapids: Eerdmans, 1988).

[21]I treated this in some depth in an earlier study; Michael J. Wilkins, *The Concept of Disciple in Matthew's Gospel: As Reflected in the Use of the Term Μαθητής, NovTSup* 59 (Leiden: E. J. Brill, 1988), 51–91. For a succinct overview see Pheme Perkins, *Jesus As Teacher, Understanding Jesus Today* (Cambridge: Cambridge Univ. Press, 1990), 1–22.

[22]Martin Hengel, *The Charismatic Leader and His Followers*, trans. J. Greig, 1968 (New York: Crossroad, 1981); Vincent, *Disciple and Lord*, 17–18.

relationships and used the same term to designate the subordinate person as the gospel writers used to designate the disciples of Jesus (*mathētēs*).[23] From Josephus's perspective, the association between each of these pairs is that of a master and disciple.

After evaluating the evidence from the Old Testament, we should agree with Josephus. The association between these individuals is a discipleship relationship. But when we look closely, we should recognize that there are unique characteristics of this Old Testament form of discipleship. First, the relationship was oriented toward service. On the one hand, this means that the subordinate person is the "servant" of the master. Joshua is called the "servant of Moses." "So Moses arose with Joshua his servant (*shārath*), and Moses went up to the mountain of God" (Ex 24:13 NASB). On the other hand, we must also recognize that the master is the servant of God. God admonished Aaron and Miriam by saying, "Why then were you not afraid to speak against my servant [*ebed*] Moses" (Nu 12:8). Later, after Joshua is called to take over the role of leadership from Moses, he is also called the "servant [*ebed*] of the LORD" (cf. Jos 5:14; 24:29), who carries out the task Moses began. Although the subordinate person is designated as a "servant" of the master, this is not menial service as rendered by a slave. Rather, he is an "assistant" who performs a vital and essential function to help the master carry out his leadership role. Ultimately, both are servants of God, serving God by serving the people of Israel.[24]

Second, both master and disciple were chosen by God to carry out his work. The disciple was in training to carry out the master's work once the master passed from the scene. Joshua succeeded Moses in his work of serving God in retaking the Promised Land. God said to Joshua, "No one will be able to stand up against you all the days of your life. As I was with Moses, so I will be with you; I will never leave you nor forsake you" (Jos 1:5). This succession in carrying out the work of God is classically portrayed in the scene after Elijah is taken up to heaven in the whirlwind and chariot. Elisha tore his clothes and "he also took up the mantle of Elijah that fell from him, and returned and stood by the bank of the Jordan. And he took the mantle of Elijah that fell from him, and struck the waters and said, 'Where is the LORD, the God of Elijah?' And when he also had struck the waters, they were divided here and there; and Elisha crossed

---

[23]For Joshua as the disciple (*mathētēs*) of Moses, see Josephus, *Antiq.* 6.84; for Elisha as the disciple (*mathētēs*) of Elijah, see *Antiq.* 8.354; 9.28, 33; for Baruch as the disciple (*mathētēs*) of Jeremiah, see *Antiq.* 10.158, 178. Josephus uses the term only fifteen times, and eight of those describe the above individuals.

[24]Joshua-Moses in Ex 24:13; 33:11; Nu 11:28; Jos 1:1; Elisha-Elijah in 1Ki 19:19–21; 2Ki 2:3; 3:11; Baruch-Jeremiah in Jer 36:26; 43:3.

over" (2Ki 2:13–14 NASB). In the miraculous parting of the waters with Elijah's mantle, God confirms to Elisha that he will be with Elisha even as he has been with Elijah. Both Joshua and Elisha are designated by God to carry out the work of their masters, Moses and Elijah.[25] The discipleship relationship is intended for the purpose of carrying out God's work. The disciple was being trained to carry out the work of the master.[26]

Third, the relationships between these individual masters and disciples were functionally related to crisis periods in Israel's history. God brought these relationships into existence in order to meet the leadership needs within the national life. But the relationship was not perpetuated to other generations. For example, the prophet Jeremiah was called to provide a prophetic voice during the time of Judah's crisis. Baruch assisted him in that role, writing down what Jeremiah dictated (Jer 36:27, 32–33). But Baruch did not perpetuate the prophetic role once Babylon conquered Judah. Once the crisis ended and the leadership need was met, we hear no more of later leaders who carried on their role. The relationship was not intended as an institution within the nation. It was a special relationship for a special time to carry out a special work for God.[27]

Fourth, the human master never took primary place of importance. The master always pointed beyond himself to God so that the disciple was ultimately following, serving, and walking with God. This was recognized by the human master, the disciple, and the people.[28]

> Then Moses summoned Joshua and said to him in the presence of all Israel, "Be strong and courageous, for you must go with this people into the land that the LORD swore to their forefathers to give them, and you must divide it among them as their inheritance. The LORD himself goes before you and will be with you; he will never leave you nor forsake you. Do not be afraid; do not be discouraged (Dt 31:7–8).

Therefore, individual master-disciple relationships within the leadership of the nation enabled the leadership function to be passed from one leader to the next until God had accomplished his purposes through them to meet the need of his people.

---

[25]T. R. Hobbs, *2 Kings, WBC* 13 (Waco: Word, 1985), 19, 27.

[26]Joshua-Moses in Dt 3:28; Jos 1:1ff.; Elisha-Elijah in 1Ki 19:16 cf. 19:19–21; 2Ki 2:13–14; Baruch-Jeremiah in Jer 36:26.

[27]Joshua-Moses in Dt 3:21–22, 28; Elisha-Elijah in 1Ki 19:16 cf. 19:19–21; Baruch-Jeremiah in Jer 36:1–32.

[28]Joshua-Moses in Dt 31:7–8; Elisha-Elijah in 2Ki 3:11–12; Baruch-Jeremiah implied in the prophet office.

THE PROPHETS

We already observed disciples gathered around the prophet Isaiah (Isa 8:16). Other prophets demonstrate master-disciple relationships. Groups of prophets were found around Samuel (1Sa 10:5–10). He appears to have exercised some kind of "mentor" authority over them (19:20–24). The relationship was not a school setting but rather a "fellowship" of prophets who looked to Samuel as an authority. A similar type relationship is found with the "sons of the prophets" and Elisha (cf. 1Ki 20:35; 2Ki 2:3, 5, 7, 15; 4:1, 38; 5:22; 6:1; 9:1). Elisha exercised leadership authority over these prophets, but again it is not in a school setting. The sons of the prophets were not prophets in training but were rather gathered around Elisha for guidance in performing their own prophetic activities. This is not a school setting; it is a master-disciple relationship in mutual commitment to service of God.[29]

THE SCRIBES

The scribes also demonstrate characteristics of master-disciple relationships. Based on the nature of their profession, the scribes would naturally be involved in apprentice-type training in the rudimentary skills of their trade—e.g., reading, writing, and transcribing. Other skills are also associated with the Old Testament scribes, such as political responsibilities as advisers in the royal court (cf. 2Sa 8:16–18; 20:23–25; 1Ki 4:1–6).[30] After the Exile Ezra's responsibilities as scribe centered on teaching the law (Ne 8:1ff.), but such responsibility was also in evidence prior to the Exile (cf. Jer 8:8–9). Much of the training for these various scribal responsibilities appears to have occurred within the family and clan, which would speak of master-disciple training in these skills being from father to son. But as advanced training and specialization was needed, the most likely place for this to occur would have been within the scribal guild. Such a guild might be described as a "fellowship of professionals."[31] This might refer to a school for scribes, possibly located at the court, but evidence for such a school is lacking. Some kind of master-disciple relationship is required to account for the continuity of the scribal arts in Israel. There appears to be a sociological development from scribal families to a fellowship of scribes within

---

[29]Cf. Robert R. Wilson, *Prophecy and Society in Ancient Israel* (Philadelphia: Fortress, 1980), 202; 300–301; E. J. Young, *My Servants the Prophets* (Grand Rapids: Eerdmans, 1955), 92–94; Hengel, *Charismatic Leader*, 17–18.

[30]The Hebrew term for scribe is *sōphēr* (סֹפֵר).

[31]William McKane, *Prophets and Wise Men*, SBT 44 (Naperville, Ill.: Alec R. Allenson, 1965), 22ff.

the nation, to the sophistication of the court, to the Torah-centered activities of Ezra, to later rabbinic thinking.[32] Such a development implies master-disciple relationships.[33]

THE WISE MEN

'Wisdom" as it is found in the Old Testament is understood in a threefold manner: wisdom is a world outlook, a teaching position, and a folk tradition.[34] Understood from this point of view, "wisdom" requires master-disciple relationships for its acquisition and use, but the types of relationship vary in form and function. Master-disciple relationships behind the perpetuation and dissemination of the wisdom tradition would be found in informal father-son relationships, in training of elders for making judicial decisions in the city gate, in the wisdom orientation of advisers in the court, and within certain groups who specialized in wisdom and were involved with the recording of wisdom sayings.[35] Those specializing in wisdom (e.g., elders and court advisers) would help regulate and fine-tune the wisdom that was originally disseminated throughout the cultural milieu by means of family/clan education and contextualization.[36] A wisdom school is often suggested as being behind this nationwide wisdom specialty, and evidence of wisdom emphasis at the royal court gives some weight to this suggestion. But the absence of "school" evidence suggests that the master-disciple relationship was more apt to be found in the family/clan, in elder/leader training, and among "wise men" who were specialists in the wisdom tradition.[37]

In spite of the relative absence of disciple terminology and explicit teaching on discipleship, the nature of the prophetic ministry, the writing prophets, the scribes, and the wisdom tradition speak strongly of the existence of master-disciple relationships in Israel.

[32]Bernhard Lang, *Monotheism and the Prophetic Minority: An Essay in Biblical History and Sociology,* The Social World of Biblical Antiquity Series, no. 1 (Sheffield: Almond, 1983), 128ff.

[33]For a discussion of the scribe within the prophetic, political, and wisdom lines of Israel's history, see David E. Orton, *The Understanding Scribe: Matthew and the Apocalyptic Ideal,* JSNTSup 25 (Sheffield: Sheffield Academic Press, 1989), 39–51.

[34]Cf. James L. Crenshaw, *Old Testament Wisdom: An Introduction* (Atlanta: John Knox, 1981), 17–25.

[35]Cf. Friedemann W. Golka, "Die Israelitische Weitheitsschule oder 'Des Kaisers neue Kleider,' " *VT* 33, 3 (1983), 257ff.

[36]Roland E. Murphy, "Wisdom—Theses and Hypotheses," *Israelite Wisdom: Theological and Literary Essays in Honor of Samuel Terrien,* ed. J. Gammie, W. Brueggemann, W. L. Humphreys, and J. Ward (Missoula, Mont.: Scholars, 1978), 39.

[37]William McKane, *Prophets and Wise Men,* SBT 44 (Naperville, Ill.: Alec R. Allenson, 1965), 40–47.

These types of relationships are quite different from the formal, institutionalized models found especially in Hellenistic relationships and would in no way preempt the place of discipleship to God. Indeed, when these master-disciple relationships are viewed in the manner suggested here, they are recognized to be part of various means of communicating to Israel the revelation of God, and as such, promote a greater depth of discipleship to God within the national life.

IMPLICATIONS OF OLD TESTAMENT EXPECTATIONS

The Old Testament richly portrays the nation and individuals following after God, walking in his ways, and serving him. There are several implications that provide continuity with later New Testament forms of discipleship. We must be extremely careful not to overanachronize the Old Testament teaching, but more complete understanding comes to light from reading the New Testament.

God with His People

First, the Old Testament theme of God with his people finds explicit fulfillment in Jesus with his people. The ideal form of discipleship for Israel was for the nation to be in covenantal relationship with God. That ideal is richly expressed in the prophets as they look ahead to the time when Israel would have the ultimate realization of that relationship. Isaiah tells the nation, "Although the Lord has given you bread of privation and water of oppression, He, your Teacher will no longer hide Himself, but your eyes will behold your Teacher. And your ears will hear a word behind you, 'This is the way, walk in it,' whenever you turn to the right or to the left" (Isa 30:20–21 NASB). When giving the law to Israel in the wilderness God stressed his covenantal intent: "I will walk among you and be your God, and you will be my people" (Lev 26:12). The nation was called to a relationship in which God was with his people.

The promise of a coming Davidic Messiah is intertwined with the promise that God himself would be with his people (e.g., Eze 37:24–28). The significance of Matthew's interpretation of the meaning of Jesus' name, "Immanuel," therefore, cannot be overstated: "'The virgin will be with child and will give birth to a son, and they will call him Immanuel'—which means, 'God with us'" (Mt 1:23). In Jesus, God has come to be with his people to fulfill the deepest meaning of the covenant—God with his people as Master, Lord, and Savior. The centrality of God in the life of his people is also found in the New Testament epistles. The apostle Paul rightly understood the central place that God alone should have. Paul explains that the basis of differentiation between righteousness and wickedness, between light and darkness, between Christ and Belial, between believers and unbelievers, between the temple of God and idols, is that, "as God has said: 'I will live with them and walk among them, and I will be their God, and they will be my people. . . .'"

> "Therefore come out from them
>   and be separate,
>   says the Lord.
>
> Touch no unclean thing,
>   and I will receive you."
> "I will be a Father to you,
>   and you will be my sons and
> daughters,
>   says the Lord Almighty."
>
>   (2Co 6:16–18)

The intimacy of the relationship cannot be overlooked. It is an intimacy that is fulfilled only when God is with his people.

The People Follow God

Second, the relationship established between God and Israel was a divine-human relationship that anticipated the relationship to which Jesus would call his followers.[38] To fulfill the covenantal relationship means simply that God must be God, signifying giving him preeminence in all things. Following God is the concrete expression of what it means to love the Lord God with all of one's heart and soul. Following God is understood in a metaphorical sense of walking in the ways of God.[39] Because God is holy, Israel is to be holy (Lev 11:44–45). Walking with God points to human life as a journey with God. It is the experience of God's benevolent presence (Ge 24:40; 48:15; cf. Ps 56:13; 116:9), designating a happy human life exclusively in the presence of God.[40] When we recognize that these themes are taken up by Jesus to express the heart of discipleship (Mt 5:48; 22:37; Mk 12:29–30; Lk 10:27), we understand that the relationship initiated by God in the Old Testament is a discipleship relationship that was to find its fulfillment in Jesus.

---

[38]For a position close to this, see Howard Clark Kee, *Knowing the Truth: A Sociological Approach to New Testament Interpretation* (Minneapolis: Fortress, 1989), 84–88.

[39]F. J. Helfmeyer, הלך *hālakh*, *TDOT* 3:388–403; Gerhard Kittel, "ἀκολουθέω," *TDNT* 1:211.

[40]Helfmeyer, הלך *hālakh*, *TDOT* 3:403.

The Old Testament metaphorical language of "following God" and "walking with God" points ahead to Jesus. The God of the Old Testament has come to earth in Jesus to be with his people (Mt 1:23) and will be with his people forever (28:20), dwelling in each of his disciples through the Spirit (2Co 6:16), and will come again to be with us (Rev 21:3).

Serving God and His People

Third, the various human discipleship relationships we see in the Old Testament prepare us for the kinds of relationships to which Jesus would call the apostles and the kinds of relationships that would develop within the church. At least three points can be observed here. (1) We can see a form of "mentoring" initiated in the Old Testament which carries over into the New. As God called individuals (e.g., Moses, Elijah) to serve him within the nation, he prepared them personally to carry on his work. In turn, those individuals prepared others (e.g., Joshua, Elisha) to carry on the work that remained. This readies us to see that as Jesus called individuals (e.g., Peter, Paul) to carry out his work within the church, he prepared them personally to carry out his work. In turn, those individuals prepared others (e.g., John, Mark, Timothy) to carry out the work that remained. (2) These mentoring relationships, both in the Old and New Testaments, were "service" oriented. The goal of these mentoring relationships was to prepare individuals to serve God's people, either within the nation or within the church. Individuals were equipped for service through these relationships. When we hear the words "discipleship" and "mentoring" we often think of personal growth or some such thing. Growth is important, but the goal of growth is service. (3) These service-oriented mentoring relationships provided leaders who could point the way to Yahweh. Whether it was as a national leader (e.g., Moses), or as a wise man instructing younger generations (e.g., the wise men of Proverbs), or as a prophetic voice of God (e.g., Jeremiah), these Old Testament leaders were called to help the nation "follow God" and "walk in his ways." The individual relationships of the Old Testament reveal certain similarities to the training of Jesus' twelve disciples for their leadership role in the church. Jesus' disciples were to point the way to Jesus. They were to "make disciples of all nations" (Mt 28:19), disciples who would have only one Master, Jesus.

"But you are not to be called 'Rabbi,' for you have only one Master and you are all brothers. And do not call anyone on earth 'father,' for you have one Father, and he is in heaven. Nor are you to be called 'teacher,' for you have one Teacher, the Christ. The greatest among you will be your servant. For whoever exalts himself will be humbled, and whoever humbles himself will be exalted" (Mt 23:8–12).

The roots of biblical discipleship go deep into the fertile soil of the Old Testament. We who read from the standpoint of the church must recognize our heritage in the ancient people of Israel. We may not have traceable personal roots, but we do have spiritual roots that cause us to stand firm in declaring God's purposes for his people. There are indeed differences from the Old to the New Testaments, as we will see clearly in the following chapters. But the strong disciple of Jesus Christ, like the strong tree, will stand firm as his or her roots go deep into the whole Word of God. The psalmist says:

> Blessed is the man
>   who does not walk in the counsel of the wicked
> or stand in the way of sinners
>   or sit in the seat of mockers.
> But his delight is in the law of the LORD,
>   and on his law he meditates day and night.
> He is like a tree planted by streams of water,
>   which yields its fruit in season
> and whose leaf does not wither.
>   Whatever he does prospers. (Ps 1:1–3)

Following up:

1. How are the qualifications for discipleship in the Old Testament different from those in the New Testament?
2. In what ways was Jesus' call to discipleship a fulfillment of God's Old Testament call to Israel as a nation?
3. What can the Old Testament believers who tried to follow God teach us about following God today?
4. In what ways does your discipleship commitment evidence that you love the Lord your God with all of your heart, soul, mind, and strength?

4

Disciples in the Greco-Roman World

Getting focused:

1. When you hear the word *disciple*, what comes to mind? A student? A zealous follower? A religious devotee?
2. What kinds of disciples, other than Jesus', might have existed in the Greco-Roman world of the first century? What would have been their characteristics?

"I had never before considered the history of discipleship until reading this book. I had not realized how common the master-disciple relationship was, and that it had originated long before Jesus ever came to earth. That explained to me why Jesus' command to 'Follow Me' was not so unusual, though it required radical commitment."

Those words are from one of my undergraduate students, Roslynn, a bright young lady who was raised in very good churches. She included that statement in an analysis of a book on discipleship required for a course I was teaching on the life of Christ. As I have discovered over the years, Roslynn is representative of most people in our churches. Because of her good church background, she was quite well informed about Jesus' disciples. But Jesus' disciples can seem like flat characters, almost like fictional figures in a story, if they are not viewed within their social-historical context. After studying other types of disciples in the first-century world, Roslynn pointed to "the extremes to which other disciples have gone in order that they might be more closely identified with their masters" and then asked, "Can others really tell, by my testimony, that Jesus is my master? Do my actions stand out as being different than those who follow others?"[1]

That is a question for all of us to ask! What difference exists between being a disciple of Jesus and being a disciple of any other master? Jesus said that, since certain characteristics will mark his disciples' lives, "all men will know that you are my disciples." What marks us out as distinct from other types of disciples? What differences were readily apparent between those who followed Jesus and those who followed other masters during the first century?

The world Jesus encountered when he entered human history displayed a variety of religious, philosophical, and political leaders. Each of these leaders had followers who were committed to their cause, teaching, and beliefs. While several different terms designated these followers, *disciple* (in its various language forms) was one of the most common. It also became the most commonly used term to designate the followers of Jesus. His ministry of calling and training disciples was similar to other masters of the first century, yet it was distinctive. Our purpose in this chapter is to explore the world of discipleship that existed when Jesus arrived on the scene of history so that we can understand more clearly his unique calling upon the lives of his own disciples.

The study of ancient discipleship is a rewarding task today because various academic disciplines have been harnessed by biblical scholars which help remove the shroud that time has placed over first-century discipleship practices. Historical, sociological, and philological studies can now help us understand more clearly what it meant to be a disciple in ancient times. We will combine recent philological methods with traditional word study approaches in order to understand the most common words for "disciples" found in the New Testament. Social scientific methods help us understand the sociocultural environment within which master-disciple relationships existed. Historical analysis helps us arrive at an objective understanding of the events of history that lead to Jesus calling his disciples. Used together in conjunction with the biblical record, these various disciplines help us to understand the world of the disciples. In this chapter we will enter the intriguing Greco-Roman world. In the next chapter we will explore the fascinating world of Judaism.

THE GRECO-ROMAN WORLD

Greece is the birthplace of Western civilization. Many of our modern institutions and ways of thinking—democracy, mathematics,

---

[1]Thank you for giving me permission to quote from your paper, Roslynn!

literature, education, philosophy, even the Olympics—were born in ancient Greece. The Greeks also influenced their own world. When Alexander the Great conducted his military conquest of the Mediterranean world, he also conducted another form of conquest—a cultural conquest. He initiated a program in his empire called "Hellenism," in which Greek culture and language became the dominate factors in Near Eastern and Western life. Although his empire was conquered by the Romans, and Rome became the dominant military/political power during Jesus' time on earth, Hellenism continued to dominate much of the sociolcultural ways of the Mediterranean world.

It was the Greek world that gave birth to the term *mathētēs* (pl. *mathētai*), the primary word the evangelists used to designate the followers of Jesus in the New Testament. The historical development of the use of the term *mathētēs* is important for understanding its meaning during the New Testament era.

MATHĒTĒS IN ANCIENT GREECE

The word *mathētēs* appears for the first time in the writings of Herodotus in the fifth century before Jesus. Herodotus used the word casually, indicating that it had a history in the oral language of Greece prior to its appearance in writing. After Herodotus, *mathētēs* appeared frequently in Greek literature. Depending upon its context, the term had a field of meaning in classical Greek literature that ranged from learner, to disciple, to pupil.

Learner/Apprentice

Very early in its history the noun *mathētēs* was commonly used to indicate a person who was a learner or apprentice. We find an early relationship between the noun *mathētēs* and the verb "to learn" (*manthanein*). The learner might be engaged in a course of instruction in dancing and wrestling,[2] music,[3] astronomy,[4] writing,[5] hunting,[6] or medicine.[7] The learner was acquiring knowledge or a skill from a person who was an expert in the area of study. The emphasis in these learning situations is not so much upon the person teaching as upon the skill or knowledge acquired by the learner.

---

[2]Plato, *Laws* 796.A.8.
[3]Xenophon, *Memorabilia* 1.2.27.3; Plato, *Laches* 180.D; Plato, *Meno* 90.E.6.
[4]Plato, *Epistles* 360.C.4.
[5]Plato, *Euthydemus* 276.A.7.
[6]Xenophon, *On Hunting* 1.2.2.
[7]Plato, *Republic* 599.C.4.

Pupil/Academician

The idea of a "learner" easily transitioned to the idea of a "pupil." Here was a person not only involved in learning but who had become committed to a prominent teacher or teaching within an academic setting. The subject under study might be a course in etymology,[8] metaphysics,[9] drama,[10] or religion,[11] but the significant feature is that the student had become committed to a great teacher or master. For example, Isocrates uses *mathētēs* to designate several different types of master-disciple relationships, including those who were studying philosophy-religion with Pythagoras,[12] those who were companions in dialogue with Socrates,[13] and even his own students of oratory.[14] In each case, education alone is not in view. Commitment to the master-teacher and his ways was the primary focus.

An important development occurred when the Sophists adopted *mathētēs* as the word to designate their students. The relationship between the Sophists and their students was primarily academic. The Sophists were a philosophical-educational movement of the fifth and fourth centuries B.C. who are famous for being the first teachers in recorded history to require fees from their students. Their teaching centered on skepticism about law, morality, and knowledge, and in practice they concentrated on how to win arguments regardless of truth.[15] The Sophists were ardently opposed by some of the most influential thinkers of the day, including Aristophanes and Socrates. Because these men opposed the Sophists, they directed specific criticism toward the students of the Sophists. In a satirical comedy, Aristophanes parodied the Sophists' students by characterizing them as literally imitating the mannerisms and rhetoric of their teachers. When Socrates attacked the philosophical foundation of the Sophists' teaching and practices, he included intense criticism of the teacher-student relationships they developed. Because of these attacks upon the Sophists, the word *mathētēs,* when used in Sophistic contexts,

---

[8]Plato, *Cratylus* 428.B.4.

[9]Aristotle, *Metaphysics* 5.986b.22.

[10]Aristophanes, *Frogs* (964).

[11]Isocrates, *Busiris* 28.6.

[12]Isocrates, *Busiris* 29.3, 7.

[13]Isocrates, *Busiris* 5.11.

[14]Isocrates, *Antidosis* 5.5; 30.7; 31.3; 41.5; 42.4; 87.2; 92.3; 98.5; 183.2,5; 185.3; 205.4; 220.3; 222.2,7; 235.7; 243.8.

[15]Socrates was vehemently opposed to Sophistic philosophy and practices, and his attacks upon them are well documented in the writings of Plato. His attacks and the parodies of the Sophists found in the comedies of Aristophanes are still reflected in the modern word *sophistry.*

aroused thoughts of an "academician" or "pupil" in the minds of the hearers.[16]

Since Socrates (and those of the Socratic line; e.g., Plato, Xenophon, and Aristotle) was opposed to the Sophists on philosophical and pedagogical grounds, he avoided calling his followers *mathētai* because he did not want his followers to be confused with the *mathētai* of the Sophists. The Sophists were much more focused upon formal education, while Socrates believed in dialogue and mutual growth with his followers in discovering truth. This has led some to the conclusion that Socrates rejected the term outright.[17] However, Socrates used the term freely to refer to "learners" (Plato, *Republic* 618.C.2), "disciples" (Plato, *Symposium* 197.B.1), and "pupils" (Plato, *Cratylus* 428.B.4) when there was no danger of misunderstanding.[18] Socrates rejected the Sophists' philosophy and manner of training their students, not the term itself.

Disciple/Adherent

From its very earliest use, *mathētēs* was not simply a learner or a pupil in an academic setting. In fact, Herodotus, in whose writings the noun occurs for the first time in written Greek, uses the term to indicate a person who made a significant, personal, life commitment. Anacharsis, a member of the nomadic Scythians raiders from the north, while traveling through Greece observing the practices and wisdom of the various city-states, became "a *mathētēs* of the ways of Hellas."[19] Anacharsis was so enchanted by the customs of Greece that he became personally committed to living them out. His commitment became so intense that when he returned to his homeland he performed some of the Greek ritual practices, including a ritual sacrifice to the Cyzicenes' Mother of Gods. His attachment to foreign ways incited his countrymen to the degree that he was killed by his own brother and banished from memory among the Scythians, "because he left his country for Hellas and followed the customs of

---

[16]For an analysis of the complex use of the term in the writings of Plato, which contain Socrates' attacks, see the chapter on the classical and Hellenistic background to μαθητής in Michael J. Wilkins, *The Concept of Disciple in Matthew's Gospel: As Reflected in the Use of the Term* Μαθητής, NovTSup 59 (Leiden: E. J. Brill, 1988), 15–22.

[17]Rengstorf, "μαθητής," 418. Cf. the similar statements in his article on μανθάνω (Rengstorf, "μανθάνω," *TDNT* 4:394–99) and his article on διδάσκαλος (Rengstorf, "διδάσκω, διδάσκαλος," *TDNT* 2:150).

[18]See Wilkins, *Concept of Disciple*, 15–22.

[19]Herodotus, *Books 3 and 4*, trans. A. D. Godley, vol. 2, *Loeb Classical Library* (hereafter *LCL*) (Cambridge: Harvard Univ. Press, 1921), 277.

strangers."[20] Anacharsis made a life commitment to the ways of Greece, which made him a "disciple" or "adherent" of the Greek way of life.

Socrates speaks similarly of disciples/adherents of the Spartan culture: "All these were enthusiasts, lovers and disciples (*mathētai*) of the Spartan culture; and you can recognize that character in their wisdom by the short, memorable sayings that fell from each of them."[21] In another place, he speaks of certain men who were called disciples (*mathētai*) of Marathon because they were representative of the city's cultural distinctives.[22] Becoming a disciple of a particular culture meant that one's lifestyle now reflected that culture.[23]

Varied Relationships

By now we can see that relationships between the *mathētēs* and the master varied considerably. The relationship between Pythagoras and his followers was intellectually oriented around mathematics and philosophy, yet, since his followers soon equated him with the god Apollo, the relationship became much more religiously oriented. Socrates wanted a relationship that was characterized by shared community, so he used words such as *friend (hetairos)*, *knowledgeable one (gnōrimos)*, and *follower (akolouthos)* to describe those around him. Isocrates' relationship with his followers was primarily oriented toward study of oratory and achieving the highest ethical good.

The type of relationship is not to be found within the inherent meaning of the term *mathētēs* but within the dynamic created by the master and the kind of commitment to him. This is one of the most important developments in the history of the term, a development important to keep in mind when we get to the New Testament environment.

MATHĒTĒS IN HELLENISM OF THE NEW TESTAMENT ERA

During the Hellenistic period,[24] the time when the New Testament was written, the trend toward a variety of relationships associated

---

[20]Herodotus 4.76–77. All translations from Greek literature are taken from the *Loeb Classical Library* unless otherwise stated.

[21]Plato, *Protagoras* 343.A.6.

[22]Plato, *Menexenus* 240.E.5.

[23]For a similar usage see Isocrates, *Panegyricus* 50.5–8 and *Antidosis* 296.8.

[24]This section is referred to as the Hellenistic period for convenience only. Technically the Hellenistic period extends from the death of Alexander in 323 B.C.

with the term *mathētēs* continued. While learners and pupils in an academic setting could still be designated *mathētai*, disciples or adherents of various kinds of great masters became the more common usage. Correspondingly, as the learning emphasis decreased, the focus shifted increasingly to the relationship between the master and the disciple. The type of relationship was determined by the master, ranging from being the companion of a great thinker and master of the past like Socrates (Dio Chrysostom, *On Homer and Socrates* 1.2), to being the follower of a philosopher like Pythagoras (Diodorus *Bibliotheca Historica* 12.20.1.3), to being the devotee of a religious master like Epicurus (Plutarch, *Pleasant Life* 1100.A.6). Prominently in view was a person who had become a committed follower, a "disciple," of a great master or religious figure.

Disciples of a Great Master

The relationship between a great thinker or leader and his follower involved a commitment that affected the follower's entire life. The follower was truly a "disciple" of the leader and was known primarily for the character of the relationship shared with the master. For example, Euripides is honored because he is the disciple of Anaxagoras, a natural philosopher,[25] and Zaleucus, who was known for his noble birth as a Locrian of Italy, was admired because he was a disciple of the philosopher Pythagoras.[26] Hesiod was able to compose and chant his poems because "he held converse with the Muses and had become a *disciple* of those very beings."[27] Hesiod was a disciple and imitator of the Muses; he was an adherent of their art. Plutarch, writing very near to the time when the New Testament was written, indicates a broad range of masters, each of whom had disciples—e.g., Zeno;[28] Theophrastus;[29] Xenocrates;[30] Socrates, Plato, and Alexan-

---

to the Battle of Actium in 31 B.C. The period from 31 B.C. to A.D. 313 is technically known as the "Roman" period (cf. F. A. Wright, *A History of Later Greek Literature: From the Death of Alexander in 323 B.C. to the Death of Justinian in 565 A.D.* [London: Routledge and Kegan Paul, 1932], 3–6). Since this section is only background to the use in the New Testament, a more precise delineation of use in the separate "Hellenistic" and "Roman" periods is unnecessary.

[25]Diodorus of Sicily, *Bibliotheca Historica* 1.7.7.3; 1.38.4.4.

[26]Ibid., 12.20.1.3.

[27]Dio Chrysostom, *On Envy* 60, 61.1.4.

[28]Plutarch, *Agis and Cleomenes* 23.3.2; *How a Man May Become Aware of His Progress in Virtue* 78.E.2; *On Moral Virtue* 443.A.8; *On Stoic Self-Contradictions* 1034.F.1.

[29]Plutarch, *How a Man* 78.E.2; *On Praising Oneself Inoffensively* 545.F.6.

[30]Plutarch, *Sayings of Kings and Commanders* 192.A.9.

der;[31] Isocrates;[32] and Epicurus.[33] In common usage, a *mathētēs* was a committed follower of a significant master.

Disciples of a Great Religious Leader

By the time of the New Testament, religious adherents, especially those within the mystery religions, were commonly called *mathētai,* "disciples." Dio Chrysostom, another near contemporary to the New Testament authors,[34] speaks of "disciples of the gods," and "disciples of religious leaders." For example, he refers to mortal kings as disciples of Zeus because they are "Zeus-nurtured" and "like Zeus in counsel." Dio writes, "In fact, it stands to reason that practically all the kings among Greeks or barbarians who have proved themselves not unworthy of this title [king] have been disciples and emulators of this god."[35] Elsewhere Dio says that since Homer calls King Minos "an associate of Zeus," this would virtually be calling him his *disciple.*[36] Plutarch also refers to "disciples of the gods"[37] and says that Epicurus, who had attained godlike stature, was revered by his *disciples.*[38]

Learning is minimized in these contexts. Instead, religious commitment and imitation of the religious figure's life and character characterize the relationship.

Imitation of Conduct

Imitation of the conduct of a human master became a significant feature of a disciple of a great master, either secular and religious, during the Hellenistic period. On the secular side, Linus, admired for his skill in poetry and singing, had several disciples who were always characterized by the traits of their master.[39] The disciple was so committed to the master that he or she wanted to imitate the master's conduct. On the religious side, a long history of "imitation" came to be associated with religious disciples. Plato had advocated imitation

---

[31]Plutarch, *On the Fortune or the Virtue of Alexander* 328.B.10.

[32]Plutarch, *Lives of the Ten Orators* 837.B.7.

[33]Plutarch, *That Epicurus Actually Makes a Pleasant Life Impossible* 1100.A.6; *Reply to Colotes in Defence of the Other Philosophers* 1108.E.6.

[34]Also known as Dion of Prusa in Bithynia, Dio Chrysostom lived approximately A.D. 40–120.

[35]Dio Chrysostom, *Kingship* 1.38.6.

[36]Ibid., 4.40.3.

[37]Plutarch, *That a Philosopher Ought to Converse Especially With Men in Power* 776.E.11.

[38]Plutarch, *That Epicurus Actually Makes a Pleasant Life Impossible* 1100.A.6; *Reply to Colotes in Defence of the Other Philosophers* 1108.E.6.

[39]Diodorus of Sicily, *Bibliotheca Historica* 3.67.2.2; 3.67.4.1.

of God in a philosophical sense, because the present world was the visible, imperfect copy of the invisible archetype in the higher world of Ideas.[40] The mystery religions focused upon cultic and magical imitation of God.[41] With this influence the concept of imitation became a characteristic associated with religious disciples.[42] Sometimes the disciple literally mimicked physical characteristics of the master, but mostly the disciple was so committed to his master's ability to carry out his or her teaching into life that the disciple tried to emulate the overall lifestyle of the master. Therefore, the master-disciple relationship moved away from "learning" to be characterized more readily by imitation of conduct.

IMPLICATIONS

The historical development of the term *mathētēs* is important for comprehending the way in which people would have understood its meaning at the time of the writing of the New Testament. A *mathētēs* was a committed follower of a great master, although the type of master ranged from philosopher to great thinker-master of the past to religious figures.[43] The commitment assumed the development of a sustained relationship between the follower and the master, and the relationship extended to imitation of the conduct of the master. This is the notion of the word understood by a Greek audience at the time of the writing of the New Testament.

This broad range of disciples was important to recognize once Christianity moved into the Hellenistic world and the world of the Diaspora. As the apostles went into Greek-speaking regions, they encountered people who already had some kind of conception of the meaning of "disciple." "Disciples" were individuals who were committed to a master who provided a philosophy/teaching and pattern of life that they could follow. Therefore, when the apostles went about fulfilling Jesus' Great Commission to "make disciples" among the nations (cf. Mt 28:18–20; Acts 14:21), they were able to build upon a prevailing master-disciple concept. Yet they needed to be careful to proclaim exactly what it meant to be a disciple of Jesus in distinction from being a disciple of another type of master.

When we use the English term *disciple* to render the Greek term

---

[40]Karl F. Morrison, *The Mimetic Tradition of Reform in the West* (Princeton, N.J.: Princeton, 1982), 3–31.

[41]Hans Dieter Betz, *Nachfolge und Nachahmung Jesu Christi im Neuen Testament*, BHT 37 (Tübingen: Mohr/Siebeck, 1967), 48–84.

[42]See, e.g., Dio Chrysostom, *On Homer* 11.7.

[43]See Wilkins, *Concept of Disciple*, 32–42. See also Martin Hengel, *The Charismatic Leader and His Followers* (New York: Crossroad, 1981), 25–31.

mathētēs of the New Testament, we also need to be careful to define it. As we go about "making disciples" of all the nations, we will also find people who have varied understandings of what it means to be a "disciple." *Webster's New World Dictionary* defines a "disciple" as "a pupil or follower of any teacher or school of religion, learning, art, etc." There are a variety of types of disciples out there. What did Jesus intend his disciples to be like? We must be clear about this so that as we obey the Great Commission we are in line with Jesus' expectations and goals.

On our journey through the ancient world of disciples, we will spend a great deal of time walking with the Master through the biblical revelation of discipleship. But before we do so, we must make one more side trip in the next chapter. On this side trip we will enter the world of Judaism, the very social/religious world into which Jesus was born. It is a fascinating world. Combined with our journey through the world of Greco-Roman disciples, the journey through the world of Judaism's disciples will prepare us to understand Jesus' form of discipleship much more clearly.

Following up:

1. What differences exist between being a disciple of Jesus rather than being a disciple of any other master? What differences were readily apparent between those who followed Jesus and those who followed other masters during the first century?
2. Ask yourself the same questions that Roslynn asked herself: "Can others really tell, by your testimony, that Jesus is your master? Do your actions stand out as being different than those who follow others?"

5

Disciples in the
World of Judaism

Getting focused:

1. What kinds of disciples, other than Jesus', might have existed in
   the world of Judaism in the first century? What would have been
   their characteristics?
2. The Gospels speak of the disciples of John the Baptist, the
   disciples of the Pharisees, and the disciples of Jesus. How were
   they alike? How were they different?
3. What unique characteristics ought to distinguish Jesus' disciples
   from the disciples of all other masters?

Family activities, surfing, and working around the house comprise
some of the most enjoyable moments of my life. They point to one
distinct side of my character. However, there is another side to me.
As a professor, I love to read, research, write, and teach. The one side
(family, surfing, home) is what I call living in the "real" world. The
other side (reading, researching, writing, teaching) is more of the
"ivory tower" world. Sometimes those two sides do not seem to fit
together, but I enjoy the diversity of life that they bring!

At a recent national meeting of other professors of biblical studies,
I had a long talk over lunch with a Jewish professor who was
intrigued by my involvement in the "real" world of surfing. He could
not quite fathom spending time at the beach with a group of surfers.
He had a stereotype of surfers that he had inherited from television
commercials. The stereotype pictures surfers as a bit dim-witted, laid
back, loose-living, and always saying "dude"! That portrait tends to
be true among some of the beach-bum type of surfers, but among
truly dedicated surfers it is an unwarranted categorization. I don't
think I know even one person who says "dude"!

However, as we talked about the stereotype of surfers, it brought up another equally fascinating discussion of stereotypes: the stereotype he had of Christians. He is a world reknowned scholar, especially focusing his research on the interplay of Judaism and Christianity in the first century. He was intrigued by the early Christians who left Judaism to become the foundation of the early church. His explanation for the departure centered on sociological/psychological reasons. In so doing, he was creating a stereotype of the early disciples of Jesus. He readily acknowledged the stereotype, and then asked me to explain my own conversion to Christianity, which resulted in a remarkably lengthy, animated, and profound conversation.

My Jewish professor friend is an extremely bright, honest, and observant person, yet he had a stereotype of Jesus and his followers. The young lady I mentioned in the preceding chapter also had a stereotype of Jesus' disciples. What is the true picture of Jesus' disciples? What caused them to follow Jesus? What is it that made them so unique in history? To answer those questions, we must view Jesus' disciples in the light of the other kinds of disciples found within Judaism. When Jesus began his earthly ministry he found a variety of types of disciples. Because of that variety, we must take a very careful look into the fascinating world of first-century Judaism.

DISCIPLESHIP IN THE WORLD OF JUDAISM

Discipleship in Judaism reflects the remarkably complex character of Judaism as a whole at the turn of the Christian era. Since renewed study of Jewish culture, history, and literature by both Jewish and Christian scholars in the last century has brought to light the diversity of social groups that comprised Judaism, many now speak of the *Judaisms* of the first century. For example, Jacob Neusner says, "A Judaism comprises a world view and a way of life that together come to expression in the social world of a group of Jews. 'Judaisms' . . . therefore constitute several such ways of life and world views addressed to groups of Jews."[1] Exactly that diversity characterizes the various forms of discipleship found within Judaism.[2]

---

[1]Jacob Neusner, William S. Green, Ernest Frerichs, eds., *Judaisms and Their Messiahs at the Turn of the Christian Era* (Cambridge: Cambridge Univ. Press, 1987), ix. Cf. also Richard A. Horsley, *Sociology and the Jesus Movement* (New York: Crossroad, 1989), 72.

[2]Therefore, the use of the singular *Judaism* implies the Jewish people as a whole, with all of its diversity as found in the first century. The Judaisms of Judaism were united in two characteristics: (1) the address "Israel" and (2) the common holy writing of the Old Testament, written Torah, even as the diverse

Several different types of individuals were called "disciples," using primarily the Greek word *mathētēs* and the Hebrew word *talmîdh*, but other words and concepts designated discipleship relationships as well. These disciples were individuals who were committed to a recognized leader or teacher or movement, and the relationships ran the spectrum from philosophical (in Philo, *Sacrifices* 7.4; 64.10; 79.10) to technical (rabbinical scribes; *Aboth* 1.1; *Shabbat* 31a) to sectarian (Pharisees in Josephus, *Antiq.* 13.289; 15.3, 370) to revolutionary (zealotlike nationalists in Midrash *Shir Hashirim Zuta*).

We find evidence of discipleship relationships in the writings from Philo, the Qumran community, the Gospels, Josephus, and the rabbinical literature. Each of these relationships reflects the religious/cultural influence surrounding the writer(s).[3] Philo's conception of discipleship reflects diaspora Judaism with Greek influence upon Jews who were scattered throughout the Mediterranean world. The conception of discipleship found within the Qumran writings reflects an ascetic community that had withdrawn from the rest of Judaism and saw itself as the true Israel. The gospel writers indicate types of discipleship within Judaism that are viewed from both the Jewish social perspective as well as from the perspective of discipleship to Jesus. The conception of discipleship in Josephus reflects a person with a Palestinian Jewish background who has gone over to become a part of the Roman establishment and who now tries to write an apologetic for traditional Jewish ways to his Roman audience. The conception of discipleship found in the rabbinical literature reflects relationships established in the wake of the fall of Jerusalem and the development of rabbinical Judaism.

Jewish conceptions of discipleship in the first century help us to appreciate the diversity of ways in which the Jewish people sought to follow the God of the Old Testament. Our focus will be upon five representative groups that reflect biblical and extrabiblical conceptions of discipleship within Judaism of the first century. They also help us to understand better the commonalities and distinctives of Jesus' form of discipleship within Judaism.

Disciples of Israel's Religious Heritage

The Old Testament portrait of the people of Israel following God carried over into Judaism of the first century and acquired explicit

---

Christianities of Christianity are united in the Cross and Resurrection (cf. Neusner's comments in the preface to *Judaisms and Their Messiahs*, ix–xi).

[3]Cf. Max Wilcox, "Jesus in the Light of His Jewish Environment," *Aufstieg und Niedergang der Römischen Welt*, 2:25, 1, ed. H. Temporini and W. Haase (Berlin: Walter de Gruyter, 1982), 159–85.

disciple terminology to describe it. Philo of Alexandria, a diaspora Jew who was strongly influenced by both the Old Testament and Greek philosophy,[4] spoke often of various kinds of master-disciple relationships. But his favorite was the person who was a direct disciple of God, one who was guided directly by God and who could in turn guide others. In his allegorical discussion of Rebecca and the servant, Philo presents Rebecca as the personification of the virtuous teacher and presents the servant as her disciple (cf. *Posterity* 132.2; 147.1). As his commentary unfolds, Philo begins to refer to Rebecca as a disciple of God. By this Philo shows that the perfect teacher is also a disciple of God. An inherent characteristic of the disciple is true humility, the lack of self-conceit. This implies the ability to learn from God himself without recourse to external instruction (Moses is described this way as well; cf. *Sacrifices* 8–9).[5]

The apostle John, writing in his gospel, recorded an incident in which being a "disciple of Moses" indicated commitment to God and his revelation. The "Jews"[6] who questioned the parents of the man born blind (Jn 9:18ff.) attempted to scorn the man by saying that, although the blind man was a disciple of Jesus, they were disciples of Moses (Jn 9:28). Their claim was to a direct line with the revelation of God to Moses through Torah (cf. v. 29). While this is similar to some Greek forms of "discipleship" (e.g., "disciples of Socrates," who lived long after his death) and later specialized rabbinic use,[7] in this context there is no specialized meaning of discipleship. Rather, the emphasis is on following a type of teaching: i.e., following a person known to receive a revelation of God (Moses), or one who claims it (Jesus). Here discipleship is a personal commitment to a type of teaching as represented in a person who is known to speak for God. Any true Jew would have called himself a "disciple of Moses" in this sense, regardless of any secondary sectarian commitments (i.e., to John, the Pharisees, Sadducees, Essenes, Qumran, etc.). Therefore,

---

[4]Cf. Samuel Sandmel, *Philo of Alexandria: An Introduction* (Oxford: Oxford Univ. Press, 1979) and Peder Borgen, "Philo of Alexander," *Jewish Writings of the Second Temple Period*, ed. M. E. Stone, *Compendia Rerum Iudaicarum ad Novum Testamentum*, 2 (Assen/Philadelphia: Van Gorcum/Fortress, 1984), 233–82.

[5]Cf. Michael J. Wilkins, *The Concept of Disciple in Matthew's Gospel: As Reflected in the Use of the Term* Μαθητής, *NovTSup* 59 (Leiden: E. J. Brill, 1988), 100–104.

[6]The consensus in Johannine studies is that "the Jews" stands for the religious leaders of Judaism; see C. K. Barrett, *The Gospel According to St. John*, 2d ed. (Philadelphia: Westminster, 1978), 171–72; Leon Morris, *The Gospel According to John*, *NICNT* (Grand Rapids: Eerdmans, 1971), 130–32.

[7]See Karl H. Rengstorf, "μαθητής," *TDNT* 4:437, for examples. The rabbinic use became specialized because it signified a rabbinic-type study of the Law of Moses and the oral tradition concerning it.

as a development from the Old Testament portrait of discipleship to God, the ideal of Judaism was that every Israelite was a disciple to Moses and to Torah.[8]

Disciples of a Religious Institution

The various subgroups that existed within Judaism in the first century each had their own followers. Several of them could be described by master-disciple terminology. The Pharisees, whether they were called a philosophical school, a religious sect, or a political interest group,[9] are one such group. Josephus and two of the gospel writers (Mt 22:15–16; Mk 2:18) mention "disciples (*mathētai*) of the Pharisees." Josephus alludes to John Hyrcanus, one of the rulers of the Maccabean line, as a disciple of the Pharisees (*Antiq.* 13.289),[10] indicating that Hyrcanus was an adherent of the Pharisaic organization or a follower of the organization's way of thinking. While Hyrcanus is not actually a member of the Pharisees, he is their disciple, since, like the crowds, he is influenced by their teaching. Josephus speaks of another disciple of the Pharisees in *Antiquities* 15.3. Here the Pharisee Pollion and his disciple Samaias are described as working together in a scheme on behalf of Herod. In *Antiquities* 15.370, other followers are attached to them both. This reflects the school setting of the Pharisees but also shows two individuals, one senior to the other, who are linked together in a project. The former usage by Josephus emphasizes that disciples of the Pharisees could be a part of a larger group of people who were

[8]Emil Schürer, *The History of the Jewish People in the Age of Jesus Christ (175 B.C.–A.D. 135)*, A New English Version, rev. and ed. Geza Vermes, Fergus Millar, and Matthew Black, 3 vols., rev. ed. (Edinburgh: T. & T. Clark, 1979), 1:332.

[9]A great deal of debate surrounds this terminology, generated mostly by sociological investigations of Judaism and the major subgroups of Israel mentioned in Josephus, Philo, and the New Testament. The Pharisees were called a philosophical school by Josephus (*Antiq.* 13.9). They are commonly called a religious sect by many scholars (e.g., Alan F. Segal, *Rebecca's Children: Judaism and Christianity in the Roman World* [Cambridge: Harvard Univ. Press, 1986], 52). Recent sociological approaches contrast them to sectarian movements such as the Samaritans and call the Pharisees a political interest group within the retainer class of Judaism: e.g., Anthony J. Saldarini, *Pharisees, Scribes and Sadducees in Palestinian Society: A Sociological Approach* (Wilmington, Del.: Michael Glazier, 1988), ch. 12; Horsley, *Sociology and the Jesus Movement*, 73; L. Michael White, "Shifting Sectarian Boundaries in Early Christianity," *BJRL* 70 (3, 1988): 11–13. A balanced approach to the issue is found in the community approach of Paul D. Hanson, *The People Called: The Growth of Community in the Bible* (San Francisco: Harper & Row, 1986), 349–57.

[10]The parallel passage in TB *Qiddushim* 66a does not use the term *talmîdh*, and neither does the book of Maccabees.

influenced by Pharisaic ideals and practice, while the latter indicates that individual disciples could attach themselves to individual Pharisees in order to study with them and to become involved in their projects.

The disciples of the Pharisees appear also in the Gospels. Mark tells us that the disciples of the Pharisees (along with the disciples of John the Baptist) were concerned about fasting (Mk 2:18). Matthew tells us that the disciples of the Pharisees were involved in a dispute about another important Pharisaic issue: paying taxes to Caesar (Mt 22:16–17).[11] These passages accentuate key ingredients of Pharisaism. The Pharisees were committed to an intense study of the Scriptures and uniquely the oral tradition, but they were also fully committed to living out the Law and the traditions. Donald Hagner suggests that "Pharisaism was at heart, though tragically miscarried, a movement for righteousness. It was this concern for righteousness that drove the Pharisees to their legalism with such a passion."[12] All through the Gospels the Pharisees are concerned with fidelity to the Scripture, the traditions, and the unblemished practice of both. Therefore it would be expected that their disciples were students of the Law and tradition and were practitioners of legalistic adherence to both.

An interesting contrast is found in Mark 2:16, where the scribes (*grammateis*) of the Pharisees are mentioned. The scribes were the official interpreters of the Law within the Pharisaic party.[13] Each group had their scribes or official interpreters. A disciple, by contrast, was a person outside of the official party and was most likely in training to become an official member. If a person was a disciple of the Pharisees, then that one was an adherent of the teachings of the Pharisees, was in training to become a part of that group, and possibly even belonged to one of the academic institutions. The disciples of the Pharisees, therefore, would have centered their activities on traditional interpretations that would lead to a more complete understanding and personal application of Torah.

The Pharisaic system is quite likely the forerunner of the later rabbinic master-disciple relationships that evolved into a formal educational system for training rabbis.[14] The rabbinical portrait indicates an institutionalized form of discipleship where the student centered his studies on learning and practicing Torah. His studies

---

[11]See TB *Pesahim* 112b and *Babba Kamma* 113a–b and 114a. See David Hill, *The Gospel of Matthew, NCB* (London: Marshall, Morgan & Scott, 1972), 304.

[12]Donald A. Hagner, "Pharisees," *ZPEB* 4:752.

[13]Schürer, *History*, 1:329.

[14]Cf. Segal, *Rebecca's Children*, 52–54.

especially centered on oral Torah because he had to spend much time hearing it from his master in order to become proficient in its use. Therefore, the rabbinic *talmîdh* is primarily a student of oral Torah. *Aboth* 1:1 attributes a saying to the Great Synagogue which became a standard of Israel: "Be patient in [the administration of] justice, rear many disciples [*talmîdhîm*], and make a fence round the Torah." Many youths would eagerly gather around the more popular rabbis to study. Josephus mentions that there were so many "young men" gathering in Herod's day that they were like an army (*Wars* 1, 33.2), and Gamaliel II (A.D. 100–130) is said to have had a thousand *talmîdhîm* at one time (*Sotah* 49b). In the rabbinic literature disciples (*talmîdhîm*) characteristically directed their study toward mastering the complex and extensive oral Torah.[15] Since all of Israel had the Pentateuch and the rest of Scripture regularly read to them in the synagogue, the common people had an extensive knowledge of religious observances. Thus, what separated rabbis and their disciples from the rest of the people was knowledge of the oral Torah.[16]

Disciples of a Prophet

Judging from the reports of Josephus, several prophetic-type figures appeared among the people around the time of Jesus.[17] Some of these prophets proclaimed God's impending judgment and gathered followers around them to wait for the judgment. Others sought to lead their followers into revolutionary activity.[18] The New Testament gives singular attention to the prophetic activity of John the Baptist's ministry of preparing the way for Messiah. The interesting feature is that John had his own disciples who apparently assisted him in his ministry.

John the Baptist appeared out of the wilderness of Judea somewhere shortly after A.D. 25, a lone, hermitlike prophet preaching repentance for sins in the light of the soon-coming kingdom of God. His message of repentance was known to be intended for all of Israel, and people from all parts of Israel came to be baptized by him.[19] In

---

[15]Schürer, *History*, 1:332–33.

[16]Jacob Neusner, *Invitation to the Talmud: A Teaching Book* (New York: Harper, 1973), 13.

[17]E.g., Josephus, *Wars* 2.259; *Antiq.* 20.97–98.

[18]This twofold breakdown of prophetic types is emphasized by Richard A. Horsley and John S. Hanson, *Bandits, Prophets, and Messiahs: Popular Movements in the Time of Jesus* (Minneapolis: Winston, 1985), chap. 4.

[19]Jn 1:9–34, esp. v. 31; cf. also Mt 3:1–12 (esp. vv. 1–5); Mk 1:2–8; Lk 3:3ff. See also Josephus, *Antiq.* 18:117, who notes that John commended the Jews as a whole to exercise virtue.

addition to the crowds who came to hear him preach, a group of regular followers, his disciples, accompanied John.

Very little is known about how John gathered his disciples around him.[20] His disciples first appeared in the Gospels at the baptism of Jesus (Jn 1:35–37), and some became the first disciples of Jesus. John's disciples next appeared in a controversy with a Jew about purification, most likely having to do with John's (and Jesus') practice of baptism (3:22–26). At the reception of Matthew Levi, the disciples of John came with the disciples of the Pharisees and asked why Jesus' disciples were not fasting ("and praying" in Luke) as they were (Mt 9:14; Mk 2:18; Lk 5:33). While he was in prison, John sent his disciples to ask about Jesus' messianic identity (Mt 11:2–3; Lk 7:18–19). Later John's own disciples buried his body (Mt 14:12; Mk 6:29). After John's death they continued with the prayer he had taught them (Lk 11:1), and many continued for years as his disciples, scattered to such distant places as Alexandria (cf. Ac 18:24–25)[21] and Ephesus (19:1–3).

The circle of disciples around John did not include all those who came for baptism but initially may have been a group who assisted him in baptizing the crowds, similar to the way Jesus' disciples assisted him (Jn 4:1–2). There is no mention of John expounding Scripture to his disciples[22] but only of teaching his disciples a special prayer (Lk 5:33; 11:1) and of them having their own fasting practices (Mt 9:14; Mk 2:18). His disciples centered their lives on the practice of piety as had John.[23] The prophetic and eschatological form of his activity was the purest expression of ancient Judaism, especially in distinction from the Pharisaic and scribal activity.[24] Since John was preparing the way for Jesus and the messianic age, Günther Bornkamm is correct in stressing that the disciples of John represent the closest analogy to the disciples of Jesus, even though they are not exactly parallel.[25]

The evidence indicates that the disciples of John continued as a movement within Judaism after his death. Although John did not

---

[20]Cf. Poul Nepper-Christensen, "Die Taufe im Matthäusevangelium," *NTS* 31 (1985): 189–207.

[21]Rengstorf notes that "this account shows that the preaching of the Baptist had spread to the Egyptian *diaspora*" (Rengstorf, "μαθητής," 456, n. 271). Josephus (*Antiq.* 18:118–19) notes the great influence Josephus had over the crowds.

[22]Although his disciples did call him rabbi at least once (Jn 3:26) and John teaches the multitudes in Lk 3:10ff.

[23]Martin Hengel, *The Charismatic Leader and His Followers* (New York: Crossroad, 1981), 35–37.

[24]Hengel, *Charismatic Leader*, 37.

[25]Günther Bornkamm, *Jesus of Nazareth* (London: Hodder & Stoughton, 1960), 145.

consider himself anything other than the forerunner of the Messiah,[26] near his death he appeared to have some personal confusion about Jesus' role. This confusion quite likely passed on to certain disciples who continued his ministry as a movement.[27] John's disciples were a unique sort within Judaism. They were fully committed to John as a person but primarily as John led the way to repentance and Messiah. Their activities did not center on intellectual and scribal pursuits but on righteousness and piety toward God. These activities appear to be dichotomized in their thinking,[28] something not envisioned in rabbinic Judaism. Even their disputations with the Jews (Jn 3:25) and Jesus' disciples (Mt 9:14) concerned pietistic practices, not interpretation of Scripture or tradition. They were adherents of a movement, not members of a religious institution.[29]

Disciples of the Remnant of Israel

On the northwestern shore of the Dead Sea, in a desolate desert area, lies Khirbet Qumran, the ancient site of a community of Jews who left civilization behind in order to purify themselves through study, ascetic practices, prayer, and communal life in anticipation of the arrival of Messiah.

The Qumran community produced a significant body of literature, popularly called the Dead Sea Scrolls, most of which has been closely scrutinized. Although neither Hebrew nor Aramaic terms for *disciple* are found in the Qumran literature,[30] the organization of this community demonstrates concepts of discipleship. The community at

---

[26]Cf. Hengel, *Charismatic Leader,* 36.

[27]Rengstorf, "μαθητής," 456–57. Rengstorf rightly points out that even though the relation of John to Jesus might not always have been clear in the minds of his followers, men like Apollos and the disciples at Ephesus were easily able to turn to Jesus because John's way of preparation for the soon-coming Messiah remained central in the movement.

[28]See the interesting comment to this effect by Josephus, *Antiq.* 18:117.

[29]Dietrich Müller, "μαθητής," *NIDNTT* 1:488.

[30]The concordances to the available literature list no occurrences of either *talmîdh* or *sh^ewalya'*; cf. Karl Georg Kuhn, ed., *Konkordanz zu den Qumrantexten* (Göttingen: Vandenhoeck & Ruprecht, 1960); Karl Georg Kuhn, "Nachträge zur Konkordanz zu den Qumrantexten," *RevQ* 4 (1963–1964), 163–234; Jean Carmignac, "Concordance hébräique de le 'Règle de la Guerre,' " *RevQ* 1 (1958): 7–49; Hubert Lignée, "Concordance de '1 Q Genesis Apocryphon,' " *RevQ* 1 (1958), 163–86; A. M. Habermann, *Megilloth Midbar Yehudah: The Scrolls From the Judean Desert* (Tel Aviv: Machbaroth Lesifruth, 1957). Related terms are found in 1QH 2, 17, where *talmidu* is a verbal construction meaning "you have taught," and in 4QpNah 2, 8, where *talmud* means "teaching," (the origin of "Talmud").

Qumran saw itself as the righteous remnant of Israel.[31] The Teacher of Righteousness was the founder/organizer of the community (CD 1:10–11), and it developed into a cloistered, communal, brotherhood in the desert.

Specific guidelines were developed for admission to the community (1QS 6:13–23), involving the following: (1) After examination by an official, (2) the initiate entered into agreement with the "Covenant," after which followed (3) an examination by the "Many." (4) Investigation of the person's spirit and work was conducted by the community for a year, with an examination of his understanding of Torah at the end of that year. (5) After that examination, the initiate yielded his possessions, turning them over to the common use and control of the group. (6) Then came a second trial year with an examination for final admission following the second year. A second group of "physical" qualifications existed for entrance into the "Assembly" (1QSa 1:19–21; 2:3–9). An order of precedence or rank within the community was also specified (CD 14:3–6) which governed the life of the community. Spiritual qualifications were the basic criteria for advancement up the hierarchical order, and advancement was a desirable objective (cf. 1QS 2:22–23; 6:3–4).[32]

This was a community gathered out from the rest of Judaism for a communal life of strict dedication to the study of Torah and obedience to God. The community believed that God had sent the Teacher of Righteousness to guide the community's study and discovery of the true meaning of Torah (cf. 1QS 1:1–2; 8:10–16). The lack of any technical terminology for *disciple* indicates that all were part of one brotherhood. The various classifications were functionally and spiritually oriented to help each individual carry out a life of obedience to God as prescribed in Torah. For example, Culpepper suggests that there was a school at Qumran within the community.[33] This school interpreted Scripture and tradition according to the precepts of its revered Teacher of Righteousness and wrote down its

---

[31]The extensive discussion as to the identity of this community, especially as it relates to the Essenes, does not significantly affect this study. Those favoring an identification of the Essenes and the people of Qumran are in the majority; cf. the discussion and bibliographies in Schürer, ed. Vermes, *History*, 2:575–90. For a discussion of the minority position, which sees the Essenes and Qumran community as separate movements, cf. William S. LaSor, *The Dead Sea Scrolls and the New Testament* (Grand Rapids: Eerdmans, 1972), 131–41.

[32]Othmar Schilling, "Amt und Nachfolge im Alten Testament und in Qumran," *Volk Gottes: zum Kirchenverständnis der Katholischen, Evangelischen, und Anglikanischen Theologie. Festgabe für Josef Höfer*, ed. Remigius Bäumer and Heimo Dolch (Freiberg: Herder, 1967), 211–12.

[33]R. Alan Culpepper, *The Johannine School: An Evaluation of the Johannine-School Hypothesis Based on an Investigation of the Nature of Ancient Schools*, SBL Dissertation Series, no. 26 (Missoula: Scholars, 1975), 156–70.

interpretation in order to guide the life of the community.[34] If there was such a school, the members were not set aside in the literature as the true "disciples" in distinction from the rest of the brotherhood.

Discipleship for Qumran was not a scribal or academic or philosophical pursuit but rather was expressed in imitation and community conviction (CD 4:19).[35] The shared communal lifestyle and commitment to the interpretations of the revered Teacher made the community one brotherhood and made them distinct within Israel. Indeed, as the remnant of Israel the Qumran community saw itself as the true people of God; all in the brotherhood were the true disciples of God. In this sense they saw themselves, not as a movement within Israel, but as *the* Israel.[36]

The absence of the common words for *disciple* is problematic, but, as in the Old Testament, the concept of discipleship is revealed in other terms and activities. Perhaps it is best to see that discipleship for Qumran was understood as communal isolation for practical devotion to God and Torah as interpreted by the Teacher of Righteousness. Therefore, Qumran appears similar to the Old Testament organization. Primary discipleship was given to God, but they had social structures that could be described as master-disciple relationships. This community appears strongly in line with the Old Testament picture.

Disciples of a Messianic Movement

Josephus tells us that during the time of Jesus several messianic movements flourished in Palestine.[37] While they differed significantly, the common characteristic of each was that a group of followers gathered around their leader and acclaimed him as king.[38] A great deal of social unrest existed in Palestine, prompted in large measure by the military oppression of Rome and the harsh economic conditions of the people. A popular hope among the people was that a military king would arise who would throw off the yoke of Roman oppression and lead them into economic prosperity. Judas, the son of the brigand chief Ezekias; Simon, a former servant of Herod; and

---

[34]Ibid., 170.

[35]Schilling suggests that *"Nachahmung und Gesinnungsgemeinschaft"* is the essence of discipleship for Qumran ("Amt und Nachfolge," 211).

[36]Ephraim Urbach, *The Sages: Their Concepts and Beliefs*, trans. Israel Abrahams, 2d ed. (Jerusalem: Magnes, 1979), 584–85.

[37]E.g., Josephus, *Wars* 2.56, 71–75; *Antiq.* 17.271–72, 278–85.

[38]Cf. Horsley and Hanson, *Bandits, Prophets, and Messiahs*, chap. 3; Neusner, Green, and Frerichs, eds., *Judaisms and Their Messiahs at the Turn of the Christian Era*.

Arthronges, an obscure shepherd, were all leaders of such movements.

John's gospel records two incidents that indicate that some of Jesus' followers mistook him for one of these popular messianic figures. After the feeding of the five thousand, John tells us that Jesus left the crowds because he knew that they intended to take him by force to make him king (6:15). John then tells us that Jesus gave a discourse on eating his flesh and drinking his blood, teaching which was particularly hard for some of his disciples to accept (v. 60). Then John says, "From this time many of his disciples (*mathētai*) turned back and no longer followed him" (v. 66). The expressions "going away to the things left behind" and "no longer walking with him" are Hebraic[39] and mark the return of these disciples to their old lives before they had begun to follow Jesus.[40] The expressions may reflect merely a literal "following around," but John's usage most likely indicates that these disciples were followers of Jesus because he was an exciting new miracle-worker and teacher (cf. 2:23–25).[41] The disciples were people who had made a commitment to Jesus, quite likely because of their expectations of a messianic movement. When they encountered teaching that disturbed them, they left. This is simply a loose attachment to a movement.[42]

The rabbinical literature looks back upon similar kinds of disciples. Although the common picture of "disciples" in the rabbinical literature is of a professional student of Torah, they are not found exclusively in this manner. One intriguing passage speaks of Jesus and his followers. Jesus' followers were called "disciples" (*talmîdhîm*) even though he was not called "*Rabh*" in the context. On the contrary, Jesus was described as practicing sorcery and enticing Israel to apostasy (*Sanhedrin* 43a). Each of Jesus' disciples are ridiculed in the text, in no way elevated as exemplars.

Two other rabbinic sources speak of "disciples" (*talmîdhîm*) who are equipped as soldiers and do battle (Midrash *Shir Hashirim*

---

[39]See Hengel, *Charismatic Leader*, 16–18; Barrett, *John*, 306; Raymond E. Brown, *The Gospel According to John (i–xii): Introduction, Translation, and Notes*, AB 29, 2d ed. (Garden City, N.Y.: Doubleday, 1966), 297.

[40]Morris, *John*, 387, n. 154.

[41]Jn 2:23–25 is determinative for the reaction of people observing Jesus' ministry.

[42]As John's gospel unfolds Jesus makes the definition of discipleship explicit so that anyone following would know what was expected of a true disciple (see Jn 8:31–32; 13:34–35; 15:8). This defining process indicates movement toward a "specialized" use of disciple, as does the movement from the use of "his disciples" to "the disciples" (*hoi mathetai autou* to *hoi mathetai*) (Leon Morris, *Studies in the Fourth Gospel* [Grand Rapids: Eerdmans, 1969], 142). See the later chapters on the Jesus Movement and John.

Zuta).[43] One reads, "In the time of Menahem and Hillel, when a dissension arose between them, Menahem left together with eight hundred disciples [talmîdhîm] who were dressed in golden scale armor." Disciples dressed in armor is not the usual sense of pupils! The other reads, "Eleazar and the disciples [talmîdhîm] arose and killed Elhanan and cut him in pieces. At that time the Romans went and encamped in Jerusalem where they defiled all the women. Eleazar and the disciples [talmîdhîm] arose and brought the soldiers down from the camp." These disciples are the "Idumeans" to whom Josephus refers (Wars 4.5.2), and to whom an old Tannaitic source (Sifre Zuta) refers as Idumean disciples (talmîdhîm).[44] Here we find disciples who were involved in warfare, not in discussions of Torah. Furthermore, they are Idumeans, and in Josephus they are said to be associated with zealots.

There were several different messianic movements during the time of Jesus, each involving a messianic figure and disciples. The common feature of each was hope for military overthrow of Roman rule and ensuing political peace and prosperity.

IMPLICATIONS

At least two significant implications stand out from this study of discipleship within Judaism at the time of Christ. First, the type of discipleship found in Judaism depended upon the kind of master or group to which the disciple belonged. Specific lifestyle changes were associated with each follower, and each change resulted in certain expectations of how a true disciple should conduct himself (e.g., the questions about fasting brought on by the disciples of John and the Pharisees). But the requirements differed for each group (e.g., entrance requirements, instructional methodology and content, advancement).

Second, on the surface Jesus' disciples appeared to be similar to other forms of Jewish disciples. Some of Jesus' own disciples quite likely followed him in a mistaken fashion, expecting Jesus to be like other revolutionary leaders and their disciples (e.g., Jn 6:60–66).

How then did Jesus establish his unique form of discipleship? One of the great New Testament scholars of the twentieth century suggested that Jesus emphasized his form of discipleship in every

---

[43]See in Saul Lieberman, Greek in Jewish Palestine: Studies in the Life and Manners of Jewish Palestine in the II–IV Centuries C.E. (New York: Jewish Theological Seminary of America, 1942), 179–83.

[44]See Lieberman, Greek in Jewish Palestine, 182–83, n. 199, for text and translation.

way, even to the point of calling his disciples by a different Hebrew/Aramaic name from other Jewish disciples. Several years ago T. W. Manson suggested that Jesus chose a specific term, *sh*ᵉ*walya'*, to designate his followers instead of the more common word for disciples, *talmîdh*. Manson suggested that Jesus was indicating by his choice of terms that discipleship was not a theoretical life of scholarship but a practical task of labor in God's vineyard or harvest field. "Jesus was their Master not so much as a teacher of right doctrine, but rather as a master-craftsman whom they were to follow and imitate. Discipleship was not matriculation in a Rabbinical College, but apprenticeship to the work of the Kingdom."[45] Manson's perspective of Jesus' form of discipleship has been followed by many students because he rightfully sees it as distinctive. And we should agree in the main with the above quotation. However, his attempt to make Jesus' form of discipleship distinctive on the basis of a hypothetical difference in the linguistic substratum misses an important element in Jesus' approach to discipleship. Jesus started out by basing his form of discipleship in the common stream of Jewish hope as based upon Old Testament expectations and then slowly clarified his distinctive form of discipleship. Jesus worked contextually from the commonalities to the distinctive. In fact, in the fasting dispute, the very similarity of Jesus' disciples to John the Baptist's and the Pharisees' disciples created the controversy (Mk 2:18).[46]

Discipleship in the ancient world was a common phenomenon. It primarily involved commitment of an individual to a great master or leader. The kind of commitment varied with the type of master. The important feature for us to understand is that when Jesus came and called for men and women to follow him, not all understood him in the same way. Not all understood the apostles in the same way when they went into the furthest reaches of the known world calling for men and women to become disciples of Jesus. Depending upon the background of the audience, some might have heard quite a different thing than what was meant by Jesus or his apostles.

Jesus took a commonly occurring phenomenon, discipleship, and used it as an expression of his kind of relationship with his followers. Yes, Jesus' form of discipleship was misunderstood, even by some of his closest followers. But Jesus patiently taught his disciples what it meant for them to be his kind of disciple, his kind of follower. May

---

[45]T. W. Manson, *The Teaching of Jesus: Studies of Its Form and Content*, 2d ed. (Cambridge: Cambridge Univ. Press, 1935), 239–40.

[46]See my discussion of Manson's proposal in Wilkins, *Concept of Disciple*, 109–11.

we hear him clearly as we now turn to an examination of Jesus' distinctive form of discipleship.

Following up:

1. If Jesus had approached a representative of each of the discipleship groups within Judaism and said, "Follow me and become my disciple," how would each have understood what Jesus was requiring of them?
2. Whose understanding would have been most accurate? Why?
3. When Peter, Andrew, James, and John heard the word *disciple* at the outset of Jesus' ministry, how do you think they would have defined the word?
4. If you could have been a disciple in any of these first-century discipleship groups within Judaism, which one would you choose? Why?

PART III

JESUS' FORM OF DISCIPLESHIP

In the days between his resurrection and ascension, Jesus spent important time with his followers preparing them for the days ahead when they would continue the work of carrying the good news of salvation to all the world. One message continues to stand out as a central focus for the ministry of the church today. That message is known as the Great Commission, in which Jesus told his followers to go "make disciples" of all nations.

Apparently his followers would know what Jesus meant by this commission, yet we have already seen that a variety of disciples existed in the first century. What difference was to be found between Jesus' disciples and other disciples of the first century? What did Jesus expect of his disciples in particular, in distinction from other disciples in Palestine?

Early in the twentieth century the great Jewish scholar C. G. Montefiore declared that the form of discipleship created by Jesus was something clearly unique, not at all patterned after other forms of discipleship found in Palestine at that time: "Discipleship such as Jesus demanded and inspired (a following, not for *study* but for service—to help the Master in his mission, to carry out his instructions and so on) was apparently a *new thing*, at all events, something that *did not fit in,* or was not on all-fours, with usual Rabbinic customs or with customary Rabbinic phenomena."[1] Since that writing many scholars have attempted to classify Jesus' ministry according to other types of social/religious movements of the first century; e.g., wandering charismatics,[2] political revolutionaries,[3] cynic philosophers,[4] Qumran/Essene isolationaries,[5] Jewish rabbis,[6] apocalyptic

---

[1]C. G. Montefiore, *Rabbinic Literature and Gospel Teachings* (1939), 218.

[2]Gerd Theissen, *Sociology of Early Palestinian Christianity*, trans. John Bowden (Philadelphia: Fortress, 1978), esp. 8−16.

[3]S. G. F. Brandon, *Jesus and the Zealots* (Manchester: Manchester Univ. Press, 1967); C. B. Caird, *Jesus and the Jewish Nation* (London: Athlone Press, 1965).

[4]Gerd Theissen, "Itinerant Radicalism: The Tradition of Jesus Sayings from the Perspective of the Sociology of Literature," in *The Bible and Liberation: A Radical Religion Reader* (Berkeley: Community for Religious Research and Education, 1976), 84−93.

[5]For an evaluation of the evidence, see James H. Charlesworth, *Jesus Within Judaism*, ABRL (Garden City, N.Y.: Doubleday, 1988), 54−75; Richard A. Horsley, *Sociology and the Jesus Movement* (New York: Crossroad, 1989), 95, 137.

[6]Rudolph Bultmann, *Jesus and the Word* (New York: Scribner, 1958), 57−61; Hans Dieter Betz, *Nachfolge und Nachahmung Jesu Christi im Neuen Testament, BHT* 37 (Tübingen: J. C. B. Mohr/Siebeck, 1967), 10−27; Anselm Schulz, *Nachfolgen und Nachahmen: Studien über das Verhältnis der neutestamentlichen Jüngerschaft zur urchristlichen Vorbildethik, SANT* 6 (Munich: Kösel, 1962); a more nuanced view of Jesus as a Jewish teacher is advanced by those

scribes,[7] and Israelite prophet figures.[8] While these studies certainly touch on some parallel characteristics, Montefiore's declaration remains: Jesus' call to follow him defies satisfactory categorization.[9]

What is it that made Jesus' particular form of discipleship so unique? In this section we will take an overview of the full picture of the kind of discipleship Jesus initiated. We will see how it began and how it grew within its social-historical context and how Jesus shaped and molded his disciples' understanding of what it meant to be his disciple. Then we will look closely at the group of disciples known as "the Twelve." In the following section we will take a close view of discipleship from the particular perspectives of the individual evangelists, Matthew, Mark, Luke, and John. As in the previous chapters, we will explore the biblical data first and then draw implications for present-day discipleship.

following Birger Gerhardsson, *Memory and Manuscript: Oral Tradition and Written Transmission in Rabbinic Judaism and Early Christianity* (Lund: C. W. K. Gleerup, 1961), such as Rainer Riesner, *Jesus als Lehrer: Eine Untersuchung zum Ursprung der Evangelien-Überlieferung,* WUNT 2:7 (Tübingen: J. C. B. Mohr [Paul Siebeck], 1981); James D. G. Dunn, *Unity and Diversity in the New Testament,* 2d ed. (London: SCM, 1990), 104.

[7]David E. Orton, *The Understanding Scribe: Matthew and the Apocalyptic Ideal, JSNTSup* 25 (Sheffield: Sheffield Academic Press, 1989).

[8]Oscar Cullman, *The Christology of the New Testament* (Philadelphia: Westminster, 1963), 44; David Aune, *Prophecy in Early Christianity and the Ancient Mediterranean World* (Grand Rapids: Eerdmans, 1983); Richard A. Horsley, *Sociology and the Jesus Movement* (New York: Crossroad, 1989), 140–44.

[9]This is also the conclusion of Martin Hengel, *The Charismatic Leader and His Followers* (New York: Crossroad, 1981), 84–88; and Paul D. Hanson, *The People Called: The Growth of Community in the Bible* (San Francisco: Harper & Row, 1986), 430–38.

6

The Jesus Movement

Getting focused:

1. Who were Jesus' first followers? How did they find out about Jesus?
2. When Jesus said, "Follow me"; "If you would be my disciple. . ."; "Believe in me," to whom was he speaking?
3. What did Jesus mean when he said that unless a person hated father and mother, he or she could not become his disciple?

The "Jesus movement" of the late 1960s and early 1970s was an electrifying time. I consider it electrifying because it surged onto the scene in such a surprising manner, it had shocking effects on traditional Christianity, it brought power to a generation of the church, and it was an energized beacon of light in the world testifying to the ability of Jesus Christ to change lives. Arising from the social/political/religious unrest of the 1960s, the Jesus movement offered hope to a generation of idealistic hippies who had become disillusioned with alternative solutions.

I was one of those who turned to Jesus at that time. Raised in a nominally religious environment in California where church was very important but where a personal relationship with Jesus Christ was not emphasized, I left church in my teens to try to find my own way. Right out of high school I got caught up in the Vietnam War and served three years in the army. I spent one of those years with an airborne infantry combat unit in Vietnam, a year that sowed seeds of personal, social, and religious turmoil. Returning from Vietnam in 1969, I entered into the diverse quests of the 60s generation. I explored revolutionary solutions, religious alternatives, social/political agendas, drug-induced revelations, diverse sensory experiences, and philosophical ventures. I found some help but nothing of lasting or monumental import. In fact, I became even more confused and disturbed. Feelings of emptiness, futility, and despair began to dominate my consciousness.

Then I was introduced to the message and teachings of Jesus. Here was a solution that was amazingly unique. It was quite unlike anything I had explored up to that point, and when I heard a personal call to follow Jesus it turned my world upside-down. I knew that if I followed Jesus I was committing my entire life. I was not just entering into a religion; I was not just gaining a new philosophical perspective; I was not just obtaining a new social/ethical ideal. Jesus' call to follow him was a challenge to enter into a relationship with him that would result for me in an entirely different worldview and an entirely different lifestyle.

It was scary stepping out onto that unknown path to follow Jesus, but I felt strangely comforted as I read of Jesus' first disciples. They too were part of a Jesus movement. They too were challenged with a new phenomenon, quite unlike anything they had experienced before they began to follow Jesus. The call to men and women to follow him in the first century resulted in the first Jesus movement. That movement changed the course of history. Later Jesus movements, including the Benedictine in the fifth century, the Franciscan in the twelfth, the Puritan and Methodist in the seventeenth and eighteenth, and the most recent phenomenon of the early 1970s, are simply variations on the first, variations that continue to have significant impact on the course of history.[1] While people within the church will appraise the value of each later movement differently, all will agree that the movement Jesus initiated in the first century was the most significant turning point of history.

The study of the original Jesus movement has been undertaken in several different dimensions in recent years. On the scholarly level, insights have been drawn from sociological and anthropological disciplines that have helped us to see the dynamic of Jesus' life and ministry within the social/cultural context of life in first-century Palestine.[2] These kinds of studies have contributed to a clearer

---

[1]Geoffrey Wainright's discussion of H. Richard Niebuhr's fivefold typology of the relations between Christ and culture leads to this conclusion as well. Cf. Geoffrey Wainright, "Types of Spirituality," *The Study of Spirituality,* ed. Cheslyn Jones, Geoffrey Wainwright, and Edward Yarnold (Oxford: Oxford Univ. Press, 1986), 592–605.

[2]Especially starting with Martin Hengel, *The Charismatic Leader and His Followers* (New York: Crossroad, 1968); John G. Gager, *Kingdom and Community: The Social World of Early Christianity* (Englewood Cliffs, N.J.: Prentice-Hall, 1975); Gerd Theissen, *Sociology of Early Palestinian Christianity,* trans. John Bowden (Philadelphia: Fortress, 1977); Bruce J. Malina, *The New Testa-*

theological understanding of Jesus' person and work and his relationship to his most intimate followers.[3] And these studies, in turn, have contributed to popular writings that have put this perspective of Jesus' life and ministry within the reach of the people of the church.[4]

In this chapter we will focus on the Jesus movement as it relates to the unfolding conception of discipleship within Jesus' earthly ministry. In particular, we will observe how the first followers came to Jesus, how the movement grew and expanded, and how it ebbed and flowed with the tides of popular opinion. We will then observe how Jesus began to assert his own remarkable form of discipleship in the face of opposition and misunderstanding. As Jesus' earthly ministry drew to a climactic close, we will see how Jesus established a permanent definition of discipleship for his followers, which then became the standard in the early church.

As we turn now to walk through the biblical data that describes the first-century movement to follow Jesus, we must once again remember to begin our walk with the "left foot," keenly alert to the social-historical setting of Jesus and those who followed him in the first century. Then we must eagerly shift to the "right foot" so that we can discerningly apply the principles to following Jesus in our own day.

STAGES OF THE JESUS MOVEMENT

Movements inevitably start when a perceived need within a group of people is addressed by a person (or persons) who offers a solution to that need. As the solution is recognized among a wider and wider

ment World: Insights from Cultural Anthropology (Atlanta: John Knox, 1981); and *Christian Origins and Cultural Anthropology: Practical Models for Biblical Interpretation* (Atlanta: John Knox, 1986). Recent advances have been made, among many others, by Richard A. Horsley, *Jesus and the Spiral of Violence* (San Francisco: Harper & Row, 1987); and *Sociology and the Jesus Movement* (New York: Crossroad, 1989), 95, 137; Alan F. Segal, *Rebecca's Children: Judaism and Christianity in the Roman World* (Cambridge: Harvard Univ. Press, 1986); Derek Tidball, *The Social Context of the New Testament: A Sociological Analysis* (Grand Rapids: Zondervan, 1984).

[3]An intriguing blend of sociological and theological analysis is found in a recent work by Ben Witherington III, *The Christology of Jesus* (Minneapolis: Fortress, 1990), esp. chap. 2, "Christology and the Relationships of Jesus," 33–143.

[4]E.g., the popular-level series edited by Howard Clark Kee entitled *Understanding Jesus Today*, with books by Pheme Perkins, *Jesus As Teacher* (Cambridge: Cambridge Univ. Press, 1990); and James D. G. Dunn, *Jesus and Discipleship* (Cambridge: Cambridge Univ. Press, forthcoming). In a recent article, I employed background studies that were designed to inform and stimulate believers in their present lives; Michael J. Wilkins, "Surfers and Other Disciples," *Discipleship Journal*, 62, Vol. 11, No. 2 (March/April 1991): 8–14.

group, the movement grows. But as the movement grows it often begins to include people who have varied needs and expectations of the proper solution to their need. As the movement continues to grow, so does the diversity of followers, until finally the solution has to be clarified by the leader. Then people within the movement either reaffirm their commitment to the leader and solution, or they leave the movement because the leader's solution is not in line with their expectations.

Such is the case surrounding the movement to follow Jesus. We find a variety of types of people who came to Jesus in the beginning, a variety who had different needs and different expectations of how their needs would be met. As the movement grew, Jesus clarified the goals of his ministry. That clarification had significantly different effects upon those who were following him: some agreed with him, others disagreed; some became more committed to Jesus, others abandoned him; some readjusted their thinking, others rebelled against Jesus' way. Finally, at the end of his ministry, only a few followers remained. A unique feature of the Jesus movement was that it "centred and depended wholly and solely on Jesus himself."[5] As Jesus clarified his identity and the purpose of his ministry, the movement itself found its own identity and purpose.[6] People were either with him or against him.

We can discern several important stages in the development of the Jesus movement, each stage reflecting an important light upon what it meant to be a disciple of Jesus in the first century. These stages correspond with the major turning points in Jesus' public ministry.[7]

Stage One: Personal Initiative to Follow Jesus

We can see evidence that the first stage of the Jesus movement was characterized by people who took a personal initiative to follow Jesus. That initiative was motivated by various levels of understanding John the Baptist's and Jesus' message of the Gospel.

---

[5]James D. G. Dunn, *Unity and Diversity in the New Testament*, 2d ed. (London: SCM, 1990), 106.

[6]For an excellent discussion of Jesus' sense of purpose and mission, see Witherington, *Christology of Jesus*, 120–26.

[7]E.g., a biblical historian developed similar "reference points" while unfolding a chronological exposé of Jesus' activities within his public ministry; cf. Paul Barnett, *Behind the Scenes of the New Testament* (Downers Grove: InterVarsity, 1990). Although many scholars today deny the possibility of harmonizing the callings in John and the synoptics (e.g., C. K. Barrett, *The Gospel According to St. John: An Introduction with Commentary and Notes on the Greek Text*, 2d ed. [Philadelphia: Westminster, 1978], 179), as their records stand, the gospel accounts give substantial insight to the early Jesus movement.

The beginning of Jesus' public ministry is commonly understood to have begun with his baptism by John the Baptist. Therefore, we should expect to find here also the beginning of the Jesus movement. Such is indeed the case. John's gospel tells us that the movement began the day after Jesus' baptism. Notice carefully the early progression of the movement in this narrative.

> The next day John was there again with two of his disciples. When he saw Jesus passing by, he said, "Look, the Lamb of God!"
>
> When the two disciples heard him say this, they followed Jesus. Turning around, Jesus saw them following and asked, "What do you want?"
>
> They said, "Rabbi" (which means Teacher), "where are you staying?"
>
> "Come," he replied, "and you will see."
>
> So they went and saw where he was staying, and spent that day with him. It was about the tenth hour.
>
> Andrew, Simon Peter's brother, was one of the two who heard what John had said and who had followed Jesus. The first thing Andrew did was to find his brother Simon and tell him, "We have found the Messiah" (that is, the Christ). And he brought him to Jesus. (Jn 1:35–42)

Some of those in the early days of the movement came to Jesus because they recognized his messianic identity.[8] These first followers originally were disciples of John the Baptist. John had come "preaching a baptism of repentance for the forgiveness of sins" (Mk 1:4) and preparing the way for the coming One: "After me will come one more powerful than I, the thongs of whose sandals I am not worthy to stoop down and untie. I baptize you with water, but he will baptize you with the Holy Spirit" (vv. 7–8). Since the Baptist's ministry prepared the way for Jesus' ministry, the natural transition was for John's disciples to follow Jesus. Therefore, Jesus' first recorded followers were originally disciples of John the Baptist.

These first followers were Andrew and another unnamed disciple.[9] Andrew, convinced that Jesus was the Messiah, brought his brother, Simon Peter, to Jesus. Philip, from the same hometown as Andrew and Peter, was next called by Jesus, and he in turn brought Nathaniel to Jesus (cf. Jn 1:35–49). These first followers all displayed some recognition of Jesus' messianic identity. They were most likely the same "disciples" (2:2) who traveled with Jesus to the wedding celebration at Cana and even stayed with Jesus and his family in Capernaum a few days (v. 12).[10] But we should note that full

---

[8]Note the extended network of people who recognized various aspects of Jesus' messianic identity in Jn 1:35–51.

[9]Many think this was the apostle John.

[10]Cf. the notes on this incident and the chronology in Barrett, *Gospel According to St. John*, 190.

recognition of Jesus' identity was a developing process for these disciples. As Jesus performed his first miracle at Cana, the evangelist records, "This beginning of His signs Jesus did in Cana of Galilee, and manifested His glory, and His disciples believed in Him" (v. 11 NASB). Although they were already following Jesus (1:35ff.) and were already called "his disciples" (2:2, 11), it was not until after Jesus performed the miraculous sign at Cana that they "believed." In this first stage of the Jesus movement, Jesus' disciples followed him in a way similar to other masters, e.g., John the Baptist, but they soon discovered that Jesus' was a much different type of discipleship!

But not all those who came to Jesus in the early days came for the same reasons. People followed Jesus based upon their own personal background and understanding of who Jesus was. Many people who observed Jesus' activities in Jerusalem became "believers" of a sort, but the evangelist notes that it was a deficient sort of belief. "Now while he was in Jerusalem at the Passover Feast, many people saw the miraculous signs he was doing and believed in his name. But Jesus would not entrust himself to them, for he knew all men. He did not need man's testimony about man, for he knew what was in a man" (Jn 2:23–25). The early movement produced some followers of a different kind than what Jesus was looking for.

Some people apparently came to Jesus through a process of curiosity, questioning, and commitment. For example, Nicodemus, part of the Pharisaic establishment in Jerusalem, whose curiosity was stimulated by Jesus' teaching and miraculous signs, came to question Jesus in the earliest part of his ministry in Jerusalem. Nothing is said about Nicodemus' commitment, but he appears uncomprehending and incredulous in spite of his professional knowledge of the Old Testament, which should have prepared him to see Jesus as its fulfillment.[11] We do not know when he became a disciple of Jesus, but we do see that by the time of the crucifixion Nicodemus came forward as one of Jesus' disciples to claim his body. On the other hand, other individuals came forward curious and questioning but turned away. The rich young ruler approached Jesus with questions of how to inherit eternal life, but his riches were more important to him than following Jesus (Lk 18:18–27).

In the early stages of the movement, Jesus' disciples did not seem to be much different from other types of disciples who surrounded other masters in Israel, especially John the Baptist's. The early ministries of Jesus and John the Baptist were not only carried out in close geographical proximity to one another, but they were carried out in much the same manner: people from the surrounding regions

---

[11]Ibid., 203.

came to Jesus and John for baptism and to become their disciples (Jn 3:22–26; 4:1–2).[12] The similarity between John's and Jesus' early ministries provoked comparison from some of John's own disciples and some of the Jews (cf. 3:25–30) and from the Pharisees (4:1–3). The common people expected Jesus' disciples to observe the same discipleship practices (e.g., fasting) as did both John's disciples and the Pharisees' disciples (Mk 2:18). And Jesus' own disciples wanted to have a prayer like John's disciples (Lk 11:1–4).

The first stage of the Jesus movement was characterized by people who took a personal initiative to follow Jesus. That initiative was motivated by various levels of understanding John the Baptist's and Jesus' message. They came for a variety of reasons. Some came to Jesus because they thought he was the Messiah. Others were attracted by his teaching and miraculous signs. Others came to Jesus because he was a prophetic figure like John the Baptist. Some came because their friends or family told them about Jesus. Among those who came to Jesus were some of the disciples who followed Jesus throughout his public ministry (e.g., Andrew and Peter), but we also find many others who came to Jesus during this stage. Among this larger group were some whose expectations of discipleship differed from those of Jesus. In many ways it appears that the first stage was preparatory for Jesus' later distinctive form of discipleship. It was not until the second stage of the movement that Jesus' distinctive form of discipleship began to be established.

Stage Two: Jesus' Call

The second stage of the Jesus movement occurred when Jesus shifted his public ministry to Galilee after the arrest of John the Baptist and began preaching that the kingdom of God was near (Mt 4:12–17; Mk 1:14–16). During this second stage Jesus initiated his unique approach to discipleship. Passing by the sea, he called two sets of brothers to follow him (Mt 4:18–22; M. 1:16–20). Abruptly introduced by both Matthew and Mark, this calling established a pattern that governed entrance to true discipleship.[13] It is important

---

[12]Recent scholars debate not only the theological implications of the relationship between Jesus and John the Baptist but also the sociological implications of discipleship relations between the two. E.g., William B. Badke, "Was Jesus a Disciple of John?" *EvQ* 62 (3, 1990): 195–204; Jerome Murphy-O'Connor, "John the Baptist and Jesus: History and Hypotheses," *NTS* 36 (1990): 359–74; Mark Hollingsworth, "Rabbi Jesus and Rabbi John: Opponents and Brothers," *BibToday* 28 (5, 1990): 284–90.

[13]Rudolf Pesch, *Das Markusevangelium* (Freiburg: Herder, 1976), 1:109; Anselm Schulz, *Nachfolgen und Nachahmen* (München: Kösel, 1962), 98–99;

to note that these first individuals had already become acquainted with Jesus. They were those disciples of John who had left John to become Jesus' first followers (cf. Jn 1:35ff.). The movement gained momentum as the news of Jesus traveled through social relationships in this relatively localized area. Since Jesus focused his ministry in the Galilee region, early disciples were drawn from existing networks of relatives (e.g., brothers: Andrew and Simon Peter; John and James), business partners (e.g., Peter and Andrew were partners in the fishing industry with James and John, Lk 5:10), neighbors and acquaintances (most of the twelve disciples were from Capernaum and Bethsaida).

But Jesus' ministry in Galilee created a stir among far-flung crowds as well, and a great ground swell of people began following him from all over the surrounding regions. Matthew's gospel tells us:

> Jesus went throughout Galilee, teaching in their synagogues, preaching the good news of the kingdom, and healing every disease and sickness among the people. News about him spread all over Syria, and people brought to him all who were ill with various diseases, those suffering severe pain, the demon-possessed, those having seizures, and the paralyzed, and he healed them. Large crowds from Galilee, the Decapolis, Jerusalem, Judea and the region across the Jordan followed him (4:23–25).

As the news of Jesus spread throughout Galilee and the surrounding areas, great crowds of people began following him around. The crowds were astonished when he taught in the synagogue (Mk 1:22, 27) or on the open mountainside (Mt 7:28–29) because he taught as one having authority and not as their scribes. The crowds marveled at his miracles (9:33; 15:31), and Jesus had compassion for them (9:36; 14:14; 15:32). But not all of the people responded. Jesus reproached entire cities for remaining unrepentant (11:20–24), and he declared that great crowds could not understand his parables because they were hard-hearted (13:10–17; Mk 4:10–12).

While the movement around him ebbed and flowed, Jesus' call established the high-tide mark of his form of discipleship. That call must be understood within the broader biblical concept of "calling"[14] because it is a call that demands a decision of life commitment from those who are curious. The call focused people on making a commitment to Jesus, summoning them to place their unreserved

---

Ernest Best, *Following Jesus: Discipleship in the Gospel of Mark*, JSNTSup 4 (Sheffield: Univ. of Sheffield, 1981), 166.

[14]Note the important biblical terms related to calling, such as *kaleō, klēsis, klētos, ekklēsia*: K. L. Schmidt, "kaleō, k.t.l," *TDNT* 3:487–536; L. Coenen, "Call; *kaleō*," "Church, Synagogue; *ekklēsia*," *NIDNTT* 1:271–76; 291–307.

faith in him as the One coming with the proclamation of the kingdom.
The call at this stage meant commitment to Jesus personally. It also
included some sense of joining with Jesus in his announcement that
the kingdom of God had arrived. For some, not all, this meant that
they were to accompany Jesus physically.

When we look at various calls in the Gospels, we see a pattern.
While some variation is found in the different summons and
responses, the expressions used are essentially synonymous. Note the
following "calls":

Philip:
  Call: "Follow me" (*akolouthei moi*) (Jn 1:43);[15]
  Response: No recorded response, but he went and told others (Jn
              1:44–45).

Peter and Andrew, James and John:
  Call: "Come, follow me" (*deute opisō*) (Mk 1:17); "He called
              them" (*ekalesen autous*).
  Response: "They . . . followed him" (*ēkolouthēsan autō*) (Mk
              1:18); "They . . . followed him" (*apēlthon opisō autou*)
              (Mk 1:20).

Matthew Levi:
  Call: "Follow me" (*akolouthei moi*) (Mk 2:14).
  Response: "[He] followed him" (*ēkolouthēsen autō*) (Mk 2:14).

"Another person":[16]
  Call: "Follow me" (*akolouthei moi*) (Lk 9:59/Mt 8:21).
  Response: "Lord, first let me go and bury my father" (Lk 9:59/Mt
              8:22).

The rich young ruler—
  Call: "Come, follow me" (*deuro akolouthei moi*) (Mt 19:21).
  Response: "He went away sad, because he had great wealth" (Mt
              19:22).

The challenge to counting the cost of discipleship:
  Call: "If anyone comes to me and does not hate his father . . .
              he cannot be my disciple" (*ei tis erchetai pros me kai
              ou misei ton patera eautou . . . ou dunatai einai mou
              mathētēs*) (Lk 14:26).

The challenge of the cost of following Jesus:

---

[15]This calling occurred during the first stage of the Jesus movement, an
indication that "calling" was an inherent aspect of Jesus' form of discipleship
from the beginning.

[16]Matthew calls this person "another disciple," probably an indication that he
was one of those in the early enthusiastic movement.

Call: "If anyone wishes to come after Me, let him deny
             himself, and take up his cross, and follow Me" (*ei tis
             thelei opisō mou akolouthein, aparnēsasthō eauton kai
             aratō ton stauron autou kai akoloutheitō moi*) (Mk
             8:34).

The pattern of the calling is clear: (1) while going about the
countryside Jesus "sees" (i.e. selects, chooses) the ones he would
call; (2) he summons them; and (3) at once those who respond
rightly "follow him." That same general pattern is found repeatedly
in the Gospels, and the force of the pattern is obvious:

> It serves to accentuate the great authority with which Jesus calls
> persons to become his disciples and the absolute obedience and
> commitment with which those summoned answer his call. In elucidat-
> ing how one becomes a disciple, this pattern shows that the initiative
> lies exclusively with Jesus. It is by virtue of his authority alone that one
> can embark upon the life of discipleship and sustain it.[17]

JESUS INITIATES THE CALL

We can see, therefore, that a change has occurred in the way one
becomes a disciple of Jesus. Up to this point people had come to
Jesus at will. But now Jesus extends a gracious, enabling call. Those
who hear and respond to his call become disciples or followers,
essentially synonymous terms. This kind of calling was not to be
found among other first-century master-disciple relationships.

A contrast is seen in Matthew 8:19 where, instead of responding to
a call, a scribe takes the initiative to come to Jesus and announce that
he will follow him wherever he goes. This scribe has in mind the
kind of master-disciple relationship in which the would-be disciple
examined various masters and then enlisted himself in following the
most popular or the best-equipped master. Jesus' stern reply checks
this enthusiastic recruit because his form of discipleship is different
from what the scribe anticipated. Jesus had no school or synagogue or
prestigious place of honor among the religious establishment. He had
nowhere to lay his head, and such would be the lot of those who
followed him.[18]

Although discipleship was a voluntary initiative with other types of
master-disciple relationships in the first century, with Jesus the
initiative lay with his choice and call of those who would be his
disciples.[19] In the early stages of the Jesus movement it was difficult

---

[17]Jack Dean Kingsbury, "On Following Jesus: The 'Eager' Scribe and the
'Reluctant' Disciple (Matthew 8.18–22)," *NTS* 34 (1988): 49.
[18]Ibid., 47–52.
[19]Hengel, *Charismatic Leader*, 50ff.

to tell the difference between true and false disciples, but ultimately the true disciple of Jesus was the one who responded with true faith to Jesus' call.

JESUS BREAKS THROUGH RELIGIOUS BARRIERS

The disciples were not called on the basis of their special abilities; they were called on the basis of God's grace alone. Eduard Schweizer notes that the calling of the disciples "takes place in sovereign liberty and can at once assume the character of an act of divine grace."[20] Jesus' summons was an act of grace, calling unworthy sinners to follow him. This is especially evident in the types of people to whom Jesus extended an invitation. Unlike some of the sectarians within Judaism, Jesus broke through the barriers that separated the clean and unclean, the obedient and sinful. He summoned the fisherman as well as the tax collector and zealot. A decisive factor is that Jesus called to himself those who, in the eyes of sectarians, did not seem to enjoy the necessary qualifications for fellowship with him (Mt 9:9–13; Mk 2:13–17). In calling the despised to himself, in sitting down to a meal with publicans, in initiating the restoration of a Samaritan woman, Jesus demonstrated that they had been adopted into fellowship with God.[21]

THE PIVOTAL RESPONSE

Once Jesus extended his call, a response had to be made. That response was the pivotal point of the person's life. From that point, a person was either a disciple of Christ or turned away from him. It was an either-or situation, because Jesus said that "he who is not with me is against me" (Lk 11:23a). The response to Jesus' call involved recognition and belief in Jesus' messianic identity (Jn 2:11; 6:68–69), obedience to his summons (Mk 1:18, 20), and a personal commitment that was undertaken after counting the cost of allegiance to him (Mt 19:23–30; Lk 14:25–33).

Once the response was made it marked the beginning of a new life; it meant losing one's old life (Mk 8:34–37; Lk 9:23–25) and finding new life in the family of God through obeying the will of the Father (Mt 12:46–50).

---

[20]Eduard Schweizer, *Lordship and Discipleship*, SBT 28, rev. ed. (Naperville, Ill.: Allenson, 1960), 20. Cf. also Hans Kvalbein, "'Go Therefore and Make Disciples. . .': The Concept of Discipleship in the New Testament," *Themelios* 13 (1988): 50.

[21]Dietrich Müller, "Disciple/*mathētēs*," *NIDNTT* 1:488; Karl Rengstorf, "mathētēs," *TDNT* 4:444; Schweizer, *Lordship and Discipleship*, 14.

COMING OUT OF THE CROWD

The Gospels reveal to us that Jesus attracted large audiences, "crowds" or "multitudes," for much of his public ministry. But Jesus did not want people to remain spectators; he called for individuals to come out of the crowd to follow him as his disciple. The crowds were a curious, though basically neutral, group who were not attached in a serious way to Jesus. Although they followed Jesus at times in a literal sense (Mt 4:25), they did not exhibit the twin prerequisites of discipleship—cost and commitment.[22] The crowds were the people of Israel of Jesus' day who were the object of his evangelistic ministry. They flocked to him for healing (Mt 15:29–31) and teaching (5:28–29) but could not understand because they were not true believers (13:10ff). At different times they were either positively or negatively oriented toward him. They were amazed at his teaching (7:28; 21:9–10) and shouted "Hosanna!" at his entry into Jerusalem; but at other times they laughed at him (9:23–25), came to arrest him (26:47), were led astray by the chief priests and elders to ask for Barabbas (27:20), and, finally, accepted reponsibility for the blood of Jesus (v. 24).[23]

The objective of Jesus' ministry among the crowd was to make them disciples. As he taught and preached, the sign of faith was when one came out of the crowd and called Jesus "Lord" (Mt 8:18–21; 17:14–15; 19:16–22).[24] Although Jesus issued an open call to the crowd (cf. Lk 14:25ff.), he was not an apocalyptic enthusiast calling the crowd to mass demonstrations.[25] In fact, on the occasion of the feeding of the five thousand, when the crowd rushed him to make him king, Jesus withdrew from them (Jn 6:15). Jesus' intention was to make disciples not simply enthusiasts. As the crowd heard Jesus' message they were called to a personal decision, either for him or against him. When a person made a personal decision to believe on Jesus, that one would come out of the crowd to become a disciple of Jesus. Making disciples from among the crowd was the object of Jesus' ministry in Israel (Mt 9:35–38), and the worldwide commis-

---

[22]Jack Dean Kingsbury, "The Verb AKOLOUTHEIN ('To Follow') as an Index of Matthew's View of His Community," *JBL* 97 (1978): 61.

[23]T. W. Manson, *The Sayings of Jesus*, 1937, reprint (Grand Rapids: Eerdmans, 1979), 19.

[24]Günther Bornkamm, "End-Expectation and Church in Matthew," *Tradition and Interpretation in Matthew*, trans. Percy Scott (Philadelphia: Westminster, 1963), 40–41; Kingsbury, "On Following Jesus," 51.

[25]Hengel stresses so strongly the literal nature of following Jesus that he virtually eliminates the possibility of a figurative sense; Hengel, *Charismatic Leader*, 62–63.

sion he gave before his ascension was to make disciples of the nations (28:19).

COUNTING THE COST/BEARING THE CROSS

Jesus' call regularly included a demand for the listeners to count the cost of discipleship and to take up their cross. That demand took various forms, but in each case it meant the cost of allegiance to Jesus. Although entrance into the way of salvation and discipleship is found through faith alone (Lk 7:50; 8:48; 17:19; cf. Ac 10:43; 13:38–39; 16:31), true faith meant having no allegiances that would hinder following after Jesus and carrying out the life of discipleship that would emanate.[26]

Jesus' call to count the cost of discipleship included seemingly harsh statements. In one, directed to the crowds who wanted to follow him, he said, "If anyone comes to me and does not hate his father and mother, his wife and children, his brothers and sisters—yes, even his own life—he cannot be my disciple" (Lk 14:26). In another statement, directed to would-be followers, one of whom wanted to bury his father and another who wanted to say good-bye to his family, Jesus said, "Let the dead bury their own dead" and "no one who puts his hand to the plow and looks back is fit for service in the kingdom of God" (9:59–62). Jesus knew that all kinds of good things, even family, can keep a person from making a commitment to him.

Yet the same cost of discipleship is not demanded for all. Jesus personalizes the cost of discipleship according to what he knows are the priorities of a person's heart. For example, the above sayings on hating father and mother and leaving family must be balanced with incidents such as the one involving the Gerasene demoniac. The Gerasene man, out of whom were cast a legion of demons, begged to accompany Jesus, yet Jesus redirected his attention, telling him, "Go home to your family and tell them how much the Lord has done for you, and how he has had mercy on you" (Mk 5:18–19; Lk 8:38–39). Here the person is told to go back specifically to his household and friends (*oikon sou tous sous*) to tell them of Jesus. Jesus knew the heart of the person, knew what was best for the proclamation of the Gospel, and did not call this person to the same kind of "cost" to which others were called. His calling was personalized in line with Jesus' knowledge of the priorities of his life and Jesus' intentions for him.[27]

---

[26]See the next chapter and chap. 11, for a more complete discussion.

[27]See Wolfgang Schrage, *The Ethics of the New Testament* (Philadelphia: Fortress, 1988), 49–50.

Jesus called people to exchange the allegiances of this world for following him. Obeying Jesus' call to follow him was to make him the central focus of one's life. Whatever kept a person from following Jesus must be considered, as the apostle Paul would say later, as loss, as rubbish "compared to the surpassing greatness of knowing Christ Jesus my Lord" (Php 3:8).

THE CALL TO DISCIPLESHIP AND THE CALL TO APOSTLESHIP

The harshness of some of the calls is also understood more clearly when we recognize that some of those disciples we see most often in the Gospels have received an additional calling to service. Their original "calling" was to discipleship, which was a call to salvation, while the additional calling was to apostleship, which was a call to service. The call to service required additional "costs" as they followed Jesus around in his public ministry.

The call to discipleship

Jesus directed his call to discipleship to the multitude of people who came to hear him. They were challenged to count the cost and to take up their cross in order to become Jesus' disciples (Lk 14:25–33). When the rich young man came to Jesus asking how he might obtain eternal life, he assured Jesus that he had observed the commandments from his youth. Then "Jesus looked at him and loved him. 'One thing you lack,' he said. 'Go, sell everything you have and give to the poor, and you will have treasure in heaven. Then come, follow me'" (Mk 10:21). This call follows the same pattern that was evident in the other callings, and it explicitly relates to following Jesus in order to obtain eternal life.

The disciples of Jesus, therefore, were all those who responded to Jesus' call to follow him. It was a call to salvation, a call to the kingdom of God, a call to believe on Jesus for eternal life. The term *disciple* designated a believer in Jesus.

The broad assembly of disciples/followers revealed a remarkable diversity, including, among others, a large number of common people (Lk 6:13), a variety of men and women who supported Jesus' ministry and accompanied him from Galilee (Mt 8:21; Mk 15:41; Lk 8:2–3; 23:49, 55; 24:13, 18, 33), tax collectors (Lk 19:1–10, Zacchaeus),[28] scribes (Mt 13:52), and religious leaders (Mt 27:57; Jn 19:38–42, Joseph of Arimathea and Nicodemus).[29] At the end of Jesus' ministry,

---

[28]Matthew tells of a teacher of the law or scribe (*grammateus*) and "another disciple" who desired to follow Jesus (Mt 8:18–22).

[29]Cf. Hengel, *Charismatic Leader*, 81–82, n. 163; Benno Przybylski, *Righteousness in Matthew and His World of Thought*, SNTSMS 41 (Cambridge: Cambridge Univ. Press, 1980), 108–10.

at the triumphal entry into Jerusalem, Luke records that a "crowd of disciples began joyfully to praise God in loud voices for all the miracles they had seen" (Lk 19:37). This larger group was composed of all those who responded to Jesus' call but who were not included in the inner group of Twelve who followed Jesus around.

The call to apostleship

The Gospels are unanimous in witnessing to a core of twelve disciples who were called by Jesus into a special relationship with him. The Twelve displayed the same remarkable diversity that was found among the broader group, including businessmen (Peter, Andrew, James, and John), a tax collector (Matthew), and a zealous revolutionary (Simon [Thaddaeus]).[30] These twelve disciples became so prominent in the ministry of Jesus that, at many points in the Gospel record, to speak of the disciples was to speak of the Twelve.

However, the distinction between the Twelve and the rest of the disciples resided primarily in the fact that the Twelve received an additional call that designated them as "apostles." In the light of Luke's wording, we can see that Jesus chose the Twelve out from among the larger number of disciples and then named them as apostles (cf. Lk 6:13, 17). The Twelve were first called to follow Jesus, by which they became disciples; then they were chosen and named as apostles (cf. Mt 4:18–22; Mk 1:16–20 with Mt 10:1–4 and Mk 2:14). The circumstances of the lives of these Twelve were quite different from the circumstances of the lives of other disciples, because they were called to follow Jesus around and to join him in the missionary outreach to Israel.

At least the inner four disciples—Peter, Andrew, James, and John—had a relationship with Jesus that progressed through the various stages of the Jesus movement. During the first stage, these four had a somewhat lengthy acquaintance with Jesus (cf. Jn 1:35–42). At the beginning of the second stage of the Jesus movement they received their formal call (cf. Mk 1:16–20; Lk 5:1–11). Scholars debate the precise time when these disciples became convinced believers, because we can see a slow growth of faith as they understood more and more clearly who Jesus was. However, the call that the four received in the second stage of the Jesus movement appears to include a call to Jesus' person and also a call to service. "Come, follow me," Jesus said, "and I will make you fishers of men" (Mk 1:17). Then later in the second stage of the Jesus movement these four, along with the rest of the Twelve, received their call to become apostles. Luke tells us, "One of those days Jesus went out to

---

[30]See chap. 13 for a more extended study of Jesus and the Twelve.

a mountainside to pray, and spent the night praying to God. When morning came, he called his disciples to him and chose twelve of them, whom he also designated apostles" (6:12–13). Later these Twelve joined with Jesus in proclaiming the message of the kingdom as they were sent out on a preaching mission in Israel. "When Jesus had called the Twelve together, he gave them power and authority to drive out all demons and to cure diseases, and he sent them out to preach the kingdom of God and to heal the sick" (Lk 9:1–2).

While it is somewhat difficult to put together the exact chronology of the Twelve's spiritual pilgrimage,[31] the clue to the role of the Twelve as we see it in the Gospels is that they are not only Jesus' disciples (believers), but they are also in training to be his apostles (commissioned representatives). The term *apostle* has a significantly different meaning than *disciple*, designating as it does the leaders of the early church in Acts.[32] As "disciples" the Twelve are examples of what Jesus accomplishes in all believers; as "apostles" the Twelve are specified as the leaders within the new movement to come, the church.

The second stage of the Jesus movement is characterized by Jesus' gracious, enabling call to men and women to follow him. Some of those whom he called were already following him, but Jesus now makes clear his form of discipleship. Jesus emphasizes that his disciples must be committed to him personally as the One who has initiated the kingdom answer. Jesus is not just another teacher or prophetic figure. Jesus calls men and women to come to him as their Lord for forgiveness of sins and for entrance to the kingdom. Therefore, the call is couched in terms that cause people to count the cost of what it means to have Jesus as their Messiah. No other allegiances must compete. Jesus alone is God; he alone is their only hope for salvation; he is the only way to eternal life. This kind of call was incredibly unique in the first century, but it began to clarify for the people exactly what kind of persons could be Jesus' followers. In the third stage we see that this created a tension for those who had come to Jesus for reasons other than what Jesus intended for his followers.

---

[31]It is difficult to clarify the exact chronology and character of the calling of the Twelve because first-stage verses occur only in John (Jn 2:1–2, 12, 13, 17, 22; 3:22; 4:1–27, 31, 43–45), and second stage verses occur only in the synoptics (Mt 4:18–22; 9:9; Mk 1:16–20; 2:14; Lk 5:1–11). The synoptics seem to combine the first two stages and use the calling as the crisis point of faith. Luke especially combines coming to faith with attendance upon Jesus' person (cf. Lk 5:8–11).

[32]See chap. 13 for an extended discussion of the distinction between the disciples and apostles.

Stage Three: Jesus Sifts the Followers

The third stage of the Jesus movement came to light at the time of the feeding of the multitude at Passover. Now came the need to sift those who said they were his followers. The Jesus movement had accelerated rapidly. In the early stages of his ministry a great company of disciples attached themselves to Jesus (Lk 6:17; 10:1; Jn 6:60). As Jesus ministered to the multitude of people, a ground swell of followers came after him to become his disciples. But as the Jesus movement continued to expand, the expectations of many of those following were not in line with Jesus' expectations. Jesus' call clarified the purposes for his earthly ministry and his expectations for his followers. But many people continued to misunderstand him (see Jesus' comments about the crowds not understanding his parabolic teaching in Mt 13:10–17; Mk 4:10–12).

The feeding of the five thousand marked a significant point when Jesus' expectations and the people's expectations clashed. John tells us, "After the people saw the miraculous sign that Jesus did, they began to say, 'Surely this is the Prophet who is to come into the world.' Jesus, knowing that they intended to come and make him king by force, withdrew again to a mountain by himself" (6:14–15). This is an intriguing passage because of the complexity of the reactions. The people demonstrate a high regard for Jesus. They regarded Jesus as "the Prophet who [was] to come into the world," (Jn 6:14), most likely declaring a messianic reference to the prophet foretold by Moses (Dt 18:15).[33] But their messianic expectations, fueled by the miraculous feeding, were probably militaristic: Jesus perceived that they wanted to make him king by force. Messianic expectations within first-century Judaism were diverse, but there was a common hope for an overthrow of the Roman government and the establishment of a golden age of peace and prosperity for Israel.[34] But Jesus' purposes included a more thoroughgoing understanding of the kingdom of God. Feeding the people miraculously indicated that earthly needs are important to Jesus, but it was not yet the time to establish the kingdom of God on earth. Rather than falling prey to their misguided aspirations, Jesus withdrew by himself alone.

At this point, the third stage of the Jesus movement, Jesus began to emphasize the true nature of his earthly ministry. By doing so, he sifted out those who were not in line with his expectations. Having

---

[33]Barnabas Lindars, *The Gospel of John*, NCB (London/Grand Rapids: Marshall, Morgan & Scott/Eerdmans, 1972), 244.

[34]See Jacob Neusner, William S. Green, Ernest Frerichs, eds., *Judaisms and Their Messiahs at the Turn of the Christian Era* (Cambridge: Cambridge Univ. Press, 1987).

miraculously supplied the people with bread, he used the feeding as an occasion to teach on the spiritual food which they were to eat and drink, his body and blood (Jn 6:22–59).

The evangelist surprises us by noting the reaction of many of Jesus' disciples to his teaching. "On hearing it, many of his disciples said, 'This is a hard teaching. Who can accept it?'" (Jn 6:60). Not the common people, not the religious leaders, but *Jesus' disciples* had difficulty accepting his teaching! Jesus, however, was ready for this reaction. In fact, the teaching apparently was designed to elicit this very reaction, because it revealed who were true believers and who were not. Jesus pointed to the disciples and said, "There are some of you who do not believe" (v. 64). Jesus knew from the beginning which of his disciples did not believe, just as he also knew who would betray him (v. 64). Among the disciples were those who were not believers. On the surface they appeared like Jesus' other disciples, but their expectations of what they wanted from Jesus were different from Jesus' purposes. Jesus wanted people who would believe on him as the Son of God for eternal life (20:30–31).

We can see, therefore, that the early company of disciples was mixed. As Jesus pointed out his expectations "many of his disciples turned back and no longer followed him" (Jn 6:66). Apparently these disciples were following Jesus because he was an exciting new miracle worker and teacher (cf. Jn 2:23–25). When Jesus' teaching did not conform to their expectations, they left him. These individuals had attached themselves as "disciples" to the Jesus movement, but they were not truly in line with Jesus' goals.

Through this incident Jesus established a definition of what it meant to be his disciple. Once the disciples left, Jesus turned to the Twelve and asked, "You do not want to leave too, do you?" Simon Peter stepped forward and made a statement that is a hallmark of true discipleship to Jesus: "Lord, to whom shall we go? You have the words of eternal life. We believe and know that you are the Holy One of God" (Jn 6:67–69). Peter functioned as a spokesperson for the definition of true discipleship. Jesus' true followers, his true disciples, are people who make a faith commitment to him (although some continue to do so falsely, like Judas; vv. 70–71).

At this stage of the Jesus movement the contrast between true and false discipleship was starkly drawn, and faith in Jesus clearly shifted to faith in him for eternal life. Those disciples who left did not rightly understand Jesus' messianic ministry and did not truly believe on him. They were following Jesus with earthly expectations. Peter spoke for the other disciples by stating that true discipleship means basing one's hope of eternal life on Jesus as the Holy One of God.

Discipleship for Peter and the other disciples was a matter of eternal life. Leon Morris comments on those disciples who left:

> The events of this chapter had made it all too clear that following Him meant something different from anything they had anticipated. Nothing is said to give us a clear idea of their views, but the probability is that they were interested in a messianic kingdom in line with the general expectation. Instead they are invited to believe, to receive Christ, to eat His flesh and drink His blood, to enter into that eternal life that He proclaimed. It was too much for them. They rejected these words of life. They went back.[35]

This third stage of the Jesus movement resulted in a sifting of Jesus' disciples. Now the people and the disciples themselves understood more clearly what Jesus' purposes were for coming to earth. Through h's teaching Jesus effectively sifted out from among his disciples those who did not truly believe. Those who remained had to align themselves with Jesus' purposes by reaffirming true belief. Hence, in the fourth stage of the Jesus movement we find a much more limited group of disciples.

Stage Four: The Limited Group of Followers

The fourth stage of the Jesus movement came during the final weeks of Jesus' earthly ministry. Now we find that the number of those around him became fewer and fewer as Jesus traveled from Galilee to Jerusalem for his encounter with the cross. This decrease in number corresponds with the increasing clarification he gave to his earthly ministry. Jesus had not come to overthrow the Roman Empire and he had not come to establish an earthly kingdom. He had come to proclaim the good news of spiritual salvation; he had come for the purpose of going to the cross. Although during the latter part of Jesus' ministry his popularity increased when he performed miraculous signs (e.g., the raising of Lazarus, Jn 11:1–45) or when he was perceived as a national deliverer (e.g., the triumphal entry in to Jerusalem, 12:9–19), the overall popularity of the Jesus movement was decreasing. This is seen tragically during the last days of his life. Luke tells us that a large number of the disciples had been at the Triumphal Entry (Lk 19:37), but in less than a week the crowds of people were persuaded by the religious leaders to ask for Barabbas's release and Jesus' death (Mt 27:15–26), and Jesus was abandoned by all of his disciples until at the cross only John the apostle and the

---

[35]Leon Morris, *The Gospel According to John*, NICNT (Grand Rapids: Eerdmans, 1971), 387.

women who had followed Jesus from Galilee were present. This was the time of the Jesus movement when a correct understanding of Jesus' intended ministry was absolutely crucial. The faith of his followers was now tested.

This was especially true for two disciples, Nicodemus and Joseph of Arimathea, who came forward at this critical moment to claim the body of their crucified Master. We noted that in the earliest stage of the Jesus movement Nicodemus had come to Jesus by night, curious and questioning Jesus' activities. We can now see that the discipleship process had been slow but steady for Nicodemus. Nicodemus seemed uncomprehending and incredulous at Jesus' statements to him at the first encounter. But later, when Jesus made another trip to Jerusalem, Nicodemus appeared on the scene to defend Jesus before his fellow Pharisees. The evangelist introduces him in the narrative as "Nicodemus, who had gone to Jesus earlier and who was one of their own number" (Jn 7:50). Although Nicodemus did not make an open profession of faith, he infuriated his fellow Pharisees by demanding a fair trial for Jesus (vv. 50–52). One commentator notes, "However little understanding he showed during that nocturnal dialogue, his encounter with Jesus did not fail to make an impression on him."[36] Apparently he had not yet become committed, but he had been marked by Jesus.[37] When Nicodemus became a committed disciple we do not know for sure, but the next time he appears in the biblical narrative he puts his faith on the line. At the crucifixion, he and Joseph of Arimathea claim Jesus' body (19:38–42). Joseph is called a "secret disciple" of Jesus, and the way that the evangelist introduces Nicodemus, "the impression is forced upon us that Nicodemus too in a similar way to Joseph of Arimathea, is pictured as a man for whom Jesus' death leads to a breakthrough of a more decisive attitude of his faith."[38] Leon Morris comments strikingly on this incident. "It is not without its interest that, whereas the disciples who had openly followed Jesus ran away at the end, the effect of Jesus on these two secret disciples was exactly the opposite. Now, when they had nothing at all to gain by affirming their connection with Jesus, they came right out into the open."[39] Nicodemus's initial encounter with Jesus was stimulated by curiosity. We do not know when he became a disciple of Jesus, but watching Jesus' ministry

---

[36]Rudolf Schnackenburg, *The Gospel According to St. John*, 3 vols., *HTKNT* 4 (New York: Crossroad, 1990), 2:160.

[37]Morris, *Gospel According to John*, 433.

[38]Schnackenburg, *Gospel According to St. John*, 3:297.

[39]Morris, *Gospel According to John*, 826.

unfold produced a faith that declared itself openly at the necessary time.

At this stage of the Jesus movement, the number of Jesus' disciples had been severely reduced. Only a few remained with him until the end. However, after the Resurrection, faith was renewed when Jesus appeared to the Twelve (now only eleven), the women, and over five hundred others (cf. 1Co 15:5–6). But the reduction in number of those who could be called Jesus' disciples sets the stage for Jesus' declaration of the Great Commission. Now there could be no mistaking what it means to be his disciple. He had issued his radical summons, he had sifted out those who were merely curious or those who did not have his kingdom perspective, he had taught his disciples what it means to be his true followers, so now he could boldly declare that the disciples must dedicate themselves to "make disciples" of all nations. A disciple is a person who comes out of the crowd of unbelievers (the nations) to claim Jesus as Savior and Master and to lead the way down the discipleship road.

Stage Five: The Early Church

The fifth stage in the Jesus movement came with the birth of the church at Pentecost. Jesus had promised the disciples that whereas the Holy Spirit had been *with them (par' humin)* during Jesus' earthly ministry, the Spirit would later be *in them (en humin)*. The significance of this work of the Spirit for the Jesus movement was dramatically revealed at Pentecost, when thousands of new believers joined the movement in the first few days (cf. Ac 2:37–42; 4:1–4). The empowering of the Spirit marked a completely new stage in the Jesus movement. From the time the church came into existence, the movement expanded to the rest of Judea and Samaria (Ac 8), Gentiles were brought into the church (Ac 10), and persecution could not wipe it out (e.g., Ac 4, 5, 7, 8, 12).

The word *disciple,* which was subject to some confusion during Jesus' earthly ministry because of the existence of other types of disciples and because of the inherent implication that a disciple follows the master around, was used freely during this stage of the Jesus movement to designate a believer in Jesus. Now all believers were in his presence continually because of the indwelling Spirit. The multitude of "believers" (Ac 4:32) is a synonymous expression for the multitude of "disciples" (*mathētai*) (Ac 6:2), and the expressions "those who believe" and "the disciples" signify the same group of people (cf. Ac 6:7; 9:26; 11:26; 14:21–22). Although followers of other masters still continued to be called "disciples" (cf. Ac 19:1ff.), Jesus' followers most commonly referred to themselves as "Jesus' disciples." Only later were his disciples called "Christians" (cf. Ac 11:26).

The growth of the church is a direct fulfillment of the Great Commission. The disciples went to the surrounding nations to make disciples of unbelievers, and then they baptized and taught the new converts to obey Jesus' teachings. The Commission found remarkable verbal fulfillment as Paul and Barnabas ministered in Gentile cities in Asia Minor. Luke records, "And after they had preached the gospel to that city and had made many disciples, they returned to Lystra and to Iconium and to Antioch, strengthening the souls of the disciples, encouraging them to continue in the faith, and saying, 'Through many tribulations we must enter the kingdom of God' " (Ac 14:21–22 NASB). All that Jesus had taught the original disciples was now to be taught to new believers so that new converts could be obedient disciples following the ever-present Jesus (cf. Mt 28:18–20). The Jesus movement of the first century continued as disciples made other disciples and then helped them to grow in faith until the time when they would enter into the glorified kingdom of God. Of such is what all true Jesus movements are made.

IMPLICATIONS

Taking a close look at the original Jesus movement brings to light several important implications for those of us who live in the wake of its passing. Those implications will guide us as we look at the general topic of discipleship as well help us as we look at later Jesus movements.

First, we can now see that various discipleship models in existence today result from focusing on one or two particular stages of the Jesus movement. For example, those who emphasize disciples simply as learners seem to focus on the first and third stages, when a variety of people simply attached themselves to Jesus but later left him. Those who emphasize discipleship as a radical form of commitment focus on the second stage of the movement, when individuals left everything to follow Jesus around. Those who see discipleship as ministry also focus on the second stage but in particular see the call to the Twelve as determinative. Those who say that all Christians are disciples focus primarily on the fifth stage.

We should recognize, therefore, that all of the models of discipleship we discussed in chapter 2 are partially correct. A more comprehensive and accurate understanding of discipleship will be found by seeing the historical progression of the Jesus movement and the various stages through which the disciples went. The stage of the movement with which we can most readily identify today is the stage of the early church. But we can, and should, also learn from each stage, especially from the way in which Jesus clarified his form of discipleship. The Great Commission, which concludes Jesus' earthly ministry, is intended for the church, and in it we find the culmination of his purposes in calling and training disciples.

Second, our evangelistic practices need to allow for historical and individual preparation and stages of faith. By viewing the four Gospels together, we gain insights into the progression of time and faith that occurred in the relationship between Jesus and his followers. We have difficulty understanding clearly the chronology of the Jesus movement because of the difference of the synoptic and Johannine narrative accounts. This is especially evident in that neither Matthew, Mark, nor Luke show the historical preparation behind the call of the disciples. They simply start out with it (Mt 4:18–22; Mk 1:16–20; Lk 5:1–11), either because they assume their readers had knowledge of this background or because they wanted to accentuate Jesus' authoritative call and the disciples' immediate response. By leaving this out, their picture of Jesus' call and the disciples' response can be misunderstood by present-day readers. John's gospel informs us that the four—Peter, Andrew, James, and John—were quite likely disciples of John the Baptist first, heard of Jesus through the Baptist, saw miraculous signs and "believed," and quite likely joined Jesus in making and baptizing people, all before their calling and response as recorded in the Synoptic Gospels.

Third, this perspective of the Jesus movement should alert us to the fact that not all of those who respond are true believers. Even as Jesus had many disciples who had followed him around for some time, including one of the Twelve, who were not true believers, so we should expect to find people among us who claim to be believers but are not. This became a significant problem for "Jesus movements" later in church history when pagans flooded into the church, sometimes seemingly more politically motivated than spiritually.[40] We will examine this more fully in our discussion of discipleship in John's gospel (chap. 12), but we should emphasize here that Jesus indicates that external claims to be a disciple/believer are accompanied by a change of life that works from the inside-out.

This leads to the fourth implication. Both in his earthly ministry in Palestine and in his ascended ministry after Pentecost, Jesus emphasized that the Holy Spirit is the key to discipleship. The Spirit is the One who convicts unbelievers, regenerates new believers, and causes growth. We must allow for the work of the Spirit in all that we

---

[40]Max Warren, *I Believe in the Great Commission* (Grand Rapids: Eerdmans, 1976), 84–87.

do while making disciples. Although various programs and methods can be helpful, discipleship practices must rely on the work of the Spirit from beginning to end. And we cannot program the Spirit.

My wife and I met during our days in the Jesus movement of the early 1970s. It was a wonderful time as God moved among former so-called "hippies." There was genuine excitement and a refreshing naivete in our new-found faith. We rejoiced in seeing people set free from drugs and hopelessness. Our worship experiences were moving expressions of joy and thankfulness and wonder for our new relationship with Jesus Christ. Bumper stickers covered our old Volkswagen van, and we eagerly lifted a "one-way" finger to passing Jesus people. We sang and laughed as we traveled around and eagerly witnessed to anyone who would listen.

But there was a tragic side as well. For many it was just another high. Of the fifty-plus of our really close friends in the movement, my wife and I know of only a handful who are walking with Jesus today. Not long ago we ran across a particularly close friend from those days. He had been one of the leaders. He did not look much different now, but he did not seem quite as friendly. As we talked, I asked (using our old jargon), "How's your head with the Lord?" He looked at me quizzically and then slowly responded, "You mean Jesus? We don't talk any more. That was a long time ago. That was a different time."

Movements are exciting times. Jesus can produce new life, genuine change, entirely different perspectives, redirected dreams, enthusiastic throngs of people. But the commitment should not be to the movement so much as to Jesus. Our own expectations and agendas have a way of blurring his purposes. The proof of any movement is to be found in the reality of the disciples that follow the Master.

Following up:

1. Are you a disciple of Jesus? How do you know?
2. What is the cost you have had to count and cross you have had to bear by following Jesus?
3. How does your own calling compare to the calling of the Twelve?
4. If you were put in charge of training counselors for a Billy Graham crusade, how would you train the counselors to help those who come forward to "count the cost" before making a decision to follow Christ?
5. What is the minimum commitment someone needs to make to Jesus in order to be truly one of his disciples?

7

Becoming Like Jesus

Getting focused:

1. What are the characteristics of a disciple of Jesus? How do Jesus' disciples differ from other types of disciples found in the first century?
2. What did Jesus' form of discipleship mean in the first century? What does it mean today?
3. Was personal discipleship more or less important than the community of disciples around Jesus? Why?

This is a great year! This year as I write I celebrate my twentieth anniversary, twice! Twice? That's right. This year is the anniversary of the two most important events of my adult life. Twenty years ago this New Year's Eve my life was forever turned around when I asked Jesus Christ to be my Savior and Lord. I had struggled with the decision for months. I went to Bible studies, I talked with people, I read books and struggled with biblical teachings. Finally, I knew that the struggle was over. I was convinced in my mind and heart that Jesus was God, that he had come to this earth to show people, including me, the way to know him in a personal way. So, at a college conference to which I was invited, I quietly became a disciple of Jesus Christ.

The second most important event of my adult life occurred twenty years ago this coming December. That was the day I married a wonderful young lady from Pismo Beach, California. Her name was Lynne, and we started going out just one week after I became a Christian. In spite of the many wonderful men and women of God that I have known since then, Lynne has had more influence on my life than any other living person.

Twenty remarkable years have flown by. Twenty years that have marked the transformation of a desperately sinful and confused young man. Today I thank God every day for the adventure of being a disciple of Jesus Christ. I still have a long way to go in my growth (just ask my wife!), but these twenty years have made a wonderful difference in my life as a disciple. Let me explain part of what has happened.

I begin a class I teach, entitled "A Biblical Theology of Discipleship," with the following question: "Has anyone ever 'discipled' you?" Surprisingly, the most common answer I encounter is no. As I follow up on the question with other questions, I discover that what most people mean is that they have never been in a formal relationship with a more mature Christian who guides them step by step in a process of growth as a disciple of Jesus Christ. I then move the questioning in a slightly different direction by asking, "Are you right now involved in discipling anyone else?" Again, the most common response is no. Why? One reason predominates: "Since I have never been discipled, I don't know what to do or how to do it."

Fair enough. I can understand what these students mean, because in the twenty years in which I have been a Christian, I have never been on the receiving end of that formal type of discipleship relationship. At first it used to bother me. I longed for that type of relationship. But given the circumstances I was in, it was virtually impossible. You will remember from the last chapter that I became a Christian during the Jesus movement of the late 1960s/early 1970s. There were no people within our particular group who were really mature enough as believers to carry out a formal discipleship relationship. We were pretty much on our own.

But that is where the two anniversaries this year are so significant. Once I realized that I was not going to be in a formal discipleship relationship, I committed myself to two things. First, I committed myself to learning how to walk with Jesus in an intimate way every moment of every day. Second, I committed myself to grow in an unqualified way in my relationship with my wife. As I now realize, these two commitments have been the most important "discipling" relationships of my life. Since those early days, I have had formal Christian training, I have been to intensive training seminars, I have had many study/fellowship relationships, but I still look to those two commitments as the most important discipling ingredients in my life.

In many ways this is what I try to instill in my students. Discipleship is not simply a program. Discipleship is becoming like Jesus as we walk with him in the real world. And the real world begins in my home, in my closest relationships, in the moment-to-moment circumstances of life. When the Lord brought Lynne into my life in those early days, we were two very young, immature Christians. But we committed our relationship to the Lord and we began to grow together. As we grew in the Word together, she was the human instrument Jesus used to help me to open up, to point to my weaknesses, to provide encouragement and support as he slowly transformed me into his image.

Have I been discipled? Not in the way that many speak of a formal relationship. But I certainly have been in the sense that I have had a companion in real life who has helped me to become like Jesus. And it is that orientation that focuses discipleship relationships that I develop with other people. I have helped direct many people through formal discipleship relationships, but I realize that such relationships are often one dimensional. They tend to focus only on the development of the spiritual life, especially through some kind of directed study. I certainly enjoy this kind of relationship, but increasingly I am aware that discipleship in the way that Jesus directed it is much more multidimensional. Jesus impacted the whole person in every area of life. When I am helping someone to grow as a disciple, I must also help that person develop in every area of life.

This is exactly the place where I believe we need to take a close look at what Jesus was doing with his disciples and what the early church was doing after his ascension. During Jesus' earthly ministry his disciples were to "follow" him, an allegiance to his person that is regarded as *the* decisive act.[1] Later rabbinic disciples would follow a master around, often physically imitating the master's teaching of Torah, because "imitating the master is imitating Moses' imitation of God."[2] The goal of Jewish disciples was someday to become masters, or rabbis, themselves, and to have their own disciples who would follow them.[3] But Jesus' disciples were to remain disciples of their Master and Teacher, Jesus, and to follow him only (cf. Mt 23:1–12). Even though it is probable that Jesus' disciples memorized much of his teaching and passed it on as the tradition of the church, the disciples were committed to his person; they were not simply committed to his teaching as in the rabbinic form of discipleship.[4]

Discipleship was not simply a program through which Jesus ran the disciples. Discipleship was life. That life began in relationship with the Master and moved into all areas of life. Discipleship was not

[1]Eduard Schweizer, *Lordship and Discipleship*, SBT 28, rev. ed. (Naperville, Ill.: Allenson, 1960), 20.

[2]Jacob Neusner, *Invitation to the Talmud: A Teaching Book* (New York: Harper & Row, 1973), 70.

[3]Dietrich Müller, "Disciple/*mathētēs*," *NIDNTT* 1:488.

[4]Gerald F. Hawthorne, "Disciple," *ZPEB* (Grand Rapids: Zondervan, 1975), 2:130.

just development of the religious or spiritual dimension, discipleship was directed toward the whole person. In this chapter we will look at Jesus with his disciples. We will see the kind of relationship he developed with them and the kinds of goals that he established for them. We start by looking at the various kinds of relationships Jesus developed with those who were called his disciples.

THE DISCIPLES AROUND JESUS

The Gospels reveal to us several ways in which people "followed Jesus." Sometimes the word is used simply in a spatial sense, as, for example, people "followed" Jesus from one point to another (Lk 22:54), or even as Jesus "followed" the ruler to his house so that he could heal his daughter (Mt 9:19). But there is another sense in which following means "discipleship." That is the metaphorical sense of the word—accompanying Jesus as his disciple. "Following Jesus" is a technical expression for going after him as his disciple. The disciple is the one who has counted the cost, has made a commitment of faith, and has then "followed" Jesus.[5] However, we should recognize that variation occurs in the metaphorical sense. Some disciples physically followed Jesus around as disciples in his earthly ministry (e.g., the Twelve), while other disciples followed Jesus as his disciples only in a figurative sense (e.g., Joseph of Arimathea, Jn 19:38). Following Jesus meant togetherness with him and service to him while traveling on the Way, but that following was manifested in either a physical or figurative sense, depending upon the ministry to which Jesus called his followers.

The Twelve

The four Gospels witness unanimously to a core of twelve disciples who were called by Jesus into a special relationship with him. Jesus chose twelve out from among a much larger number of disciples. These Twelve became his constant companions. They joined with him in the proclamation of the kingdom message and were in training to become the apostles of the future church (cf. Lk 6:13, 17). These twelve disciples were so prominent in Jesus' ministry that at many points in the gospel record the word *disciple* is synonymous with the

___
[5]Jack Kingsbury suggests that the presence or absence of two factors—cost and commitment—is the key to understanding whether "following Jesus" should be taken literally or metaphorically in Matthew's gospel (Jack Dean Kingsbury, "The Verb AKOLOUTHEIN ('To Follow') as an Index of Matthew's View of His Community," *JBL* 97 [1978]: 58). I would extend those two criteria to the usage in the other gospels and Acts as well.

Twelve. Indeed, the majority of modern scholarship accepts the thesis that the Evangelists tend to identify the terms *disciple* and *the Twelve* with one another.[6] But the Evangelists were not implying that the term *disciple* should be limited to the Twelve.[7] Rather, they focused on the Twelve as an example of how Jesus deals with all believers and of how Jesus trained those who were to be leaders of the movement after his ascension.

It is well-known that the Twelve were called to leave all and to follow Jesus around. That included leaving their families, professions, and property. Often this is misunderstood as a necessary sacrifice for anyone who desired to be a disciple of Jesus. Rather, we should recognize that following Jesus around physically was part of the special role of the Twelve as coworkers with Jesus. Leaving all to follow Jesus was a necessary sacrifice in order to join with him in the proclamation of the kingdom of God (cf. Mt 10:1–15) and as a training time for their future role in the church (cf. Mt 19:23–30).[8]

However, among the broader group of disciples outside of the Twelve we also find others who were called to such a following around (cf. Lk 9:59–62; 23:49, 55; Jn 6:66), including seventy whom Jesus sent out on a mission and an important group of women who physically followed Jesus during portions of his earthly ministry.

The Seventy

Jesus also appointed seventy (-two)[9] others whom he sent out ahead of himself on a missionary tour (Lk 10:1–20). Luke is the only evangelist to mention this mission, which is often said to foreshadow

---

[6]Robert Meye, *Jesus and the Twelve: Discipleship and Revelation in Mark's Gospel* (Grand Rapids: Eerdmans, 1968), 98–140, 228–30; Ulrich Luz, "Die Jünger im Matthäusevangelium," ZNW 62 (1971): 142–43. That this is not a consensus is observed in Martin Hengel, *The Charismatic Leader and His Followers,* trans. James Greig (New York: Crossroad, 1981), 81–82, n. 163.

[7]Contra Georg Strecker, *Der Weg der Gerechtigkeit: Untersuchung zur Theologie des Matthäus,* 3d ed., reprint (Göttingen: Vandenhoeck & Ruprecht, 1971), 191–92; W. F. Albright and C. S. Mann, *Matthew,* AB 26 (Garden City, N.Y.: Doubleday, 1971), lxxvii; R. Pesch, "Levi-Mätthaus (Mc 2:14/Mt 9:9; 10:3). Ein Beitrag zur Lösung eines alten Problems," ZNW 59 (1968): 40–56.

[8]See the discussion of this very point as the consequences that stem from seeing Jesus as God's *shaliach* and the Twelve as his *shalihim,* in Ben Witherington III, *The Christology of Jesus* (Minneapolis: Fortress, 1990), 137–40.

[9]The manuscript evidence for "seventy" or "seventy-two" is evenly divided. Either reading is understood by most scholars to be a symbolic reference to the Gentiles (cf. the number of Gentile nations in Ge 10) and the future universal mission. Cf. the discussion by Metzger and Aland in Bruce M. Metzger, ed., *A Textual Commentary on the Greek New Testament: A Companion Volume to the UBS Greek NT,* 3d ed. (Philadelphia: UBS, 1971), 150–51.

the Gentile mission. Some important points arise with Luke's record of this mission of the Seventy. We can see here that individuals other than the Twelve are involved in the missionary enterprise. We will see later that the missionary activity of the church in Acts is not restricted to the Twelve. Whether the Seventy illustrate a mission to the seventy Gentile nations (Gen 10), or are representative of the elders of ancient Israel (Ex 24:1; Num 11:25), or suggest a supplanting of the ruling Sanhedrin, they indicate that Jesus had many disciples besides the Twelve whom he trained and used in his earthly ministry.[10] These seventy missionaries, like the Twelve, were closely associated with the same mission Jesus undertook. They had the same authority bestowed upon them that Jesus gave to the Twelve (Lk 10:19; cf. 9:1), and they preached the same message (Lk 10:9; cf. 9:2). Dennis Sweetland has written, "The Seventy, like the Twelve sent out earlier by Jesus, work miracles, preach the word of God, and demand a decision from the members of their audience. Those who hear the authoritative words of these missionaries and/or witness their powerful deeds must either accept or reject them and their message of salvation."[11] Hence, the Seventy went out as Jesus' messengers, exercising the same authority, proclaiming the same message, working the same miraculous works. But when the Seventy returned, rejoicing at their authoritative power over demonic spirits, Jesus declared to them what was truly important. "Do not rejoice that the spirits submit to you, but rejoice that your names are written in heaven" (Lk 10:20). The salvation Jesus proclaimed is the most important motivation for mission.[12]

The Women Who Followed Jesus

A prominent place is given in the Gospels and Acts to various women who were disciples of Jesus. Luke tells of a group of women who accompanied Jesus and the Twelve on a particular preaching tour through Galilee.

After this, Jesus traveled about from one town and village to another, proclaiming the good news of the kingdom of God. The Twelve were with him, and also some women who had been cured of evil spirits and diseases: Mary (called Magdalene) from whom seven demons had come out; Joanna the wife of Cuza, the manager of Herod's household;

---

[10]Cf. E. Earle Ellis, *The Gospel of Luke, NCB*, rev. ed. (London/Grand Rapids: Marshall, Morgan & Scott/Eerdmans, 1974), 156–57.

[11]Cf. Dennis M. Sweetland, *Our Journey with Jesus. Discipleship According to Luke-Acts*, Good News Studies 23 (Wilmington, Del.: Michael Glazier, 1990), 39.

[12]Cf. I. Howard Marshall, *The Gospel of Luke, NIGTC* (Grand Rapids: Eerdmans, 1978), 430.

Susanna; and many others. These women were helping to support them out of their own means (Lk 8:1–3).

The wording here is important to note. The phrase "with him" (*sun autō*) is a technical phrase in Luke's gospel (cf. Lk 8:38; 9:18; 22:56), indicating much more than mere immediate presence; it indicates discipleship.[13] While Jewish parallels can be found for women supporting rabbis and their disciples out of their own money, property, or foodstuffs, they were not considered disciples of the rabbis. The wording in this passage indicates that these women were themselves disciples of Jesus. These women were called to a ministry that meant traveling with Jesus and the Twelve in order to provide material support for the group.[14] Some of this same group of women followed Jesus[15] up to Jerusalem, where they attended the Crucifixion and were the first ones at the empty tomb after the Resurrection (Lk 23:49, 55; 24:9).

The occurrence of this group of women traveling with Jesus and the Twelve is a remarkable phenomenon. Mary Magdalene would have been considered a social misfit prior to her exorcism. Joanna was a woman from the higher echelons of Jewish social life. Nothing is revealed to us about Susanna's background, yet we note that there were "many other" women along. Ben Witherington notes, "Here Luke gives evidence of how the Gospel breaks down class and economic divisions, as well as social barriers, and reconciles men and women from all walks of life into one community."[16] Women disciples of a great master were an unusual occurrence in first-

---

[13]Cf. Martin Hengel, "Maria Magdalena und die Frauen als Zeugen," *Abraham unser Vater*, Festschrift for O. Michel, ed. O. Betz et al., Arbeiten zur Geschichte des Spätjudentums und Urchristentums 5 (1963) 243–56; Eugene Maly, "Women and the Gospel of Luke," *BThB* 10 (1980): 99–104; Rosalie Ryan, "The Women from Galilee and Discipleship in Luke," *BThB* 15 (2, 1985): 56–59; Ben Witherington III, "On the Road with Mary Magdalene, Joanna, Susanna and Other Disciples: Luke 8:1–3," *ZNW* 70 (1979): 243–48.

[14]Ryan, "Women from Galilee," 57; Witherington, "On the Road," 243–48.

[15]Among those mentioned in Lk 8:1–3 were Mary Magdalene, out of whom were cast seven demons; Joanna, whose husband, Cuza, was Herod's steward; and Susanna. Susanna is not mentioned at the Resurrection scene. Matthew and Mark have *akoloutheō* (Mt 27:55; Mk 15:41), while Luke has *sunakolouthousai* (Lk 23:49), a compound for the technical discipleship word, *akoloutheō*. While we have demonstrated that *akoloutheō* can be used in a sense other than discipleship, when linked with the way in which John says that Mary Magdalene called Jesus "Lord" (Jn 20:2, 13, 18) and Matthew says that they worshiped Jesus after the Resurrection (Mt 28:9), we can see that these women had exercised saving faith in Jesus and so were part of the broader group of disciples.

[16]Ben Witherington, *Women in the Ministry of Jesus: A Study of Jesus' Attitude Toward Women and Their Roles as Reflected in His Earthly Ministry*, SNTSMonograph 51 (Cambridge: Cambridge Univ. Press, 1984), 118.

century Palestine, as even the reaction to Jesus' interaction with the Samaritan woman by early disciples reveals (Jn 4:27). However, these women certainly exhibited the twin characteristics of Jesus' disciples—cost and commitment. While they were not considered members of the circle of the Twelve, they had a significant part in his earthly ministry.

The exact role of the women on this preaching tour is debated. Some suggest that since they were considered disciples, they were also involved in proclamation along with Jesus and the Twelve.[17] This may stretch the context further than is appropriate by making an unwarranted connection between public proclamation and discipleship. Although they had joined Jesus so that they could support the proclamation ministry, it is questionable whether they were themselves involved in public proclamation. On the other hand, it may be unwarranted to imply that these women accompanied Jesus and the Twelve simply to cook and clean for them.[18] Besides the explicit statement that the women "support[ed] them out of their own means" (Lk 8:3), the exact nature of their ministry is uncertain. By including these women within his circle of disciples, Jesus appeared to be breaking several social barriers within Judaism. However, since he did not include them within the circle of the Twelve, he continued to operate within the basic patriarchal matrix of his time. Probably the most that can be stated with certainty is that their roles were redefined but within rather than outside the structure of Jewish society.[19]

We find here in Luke's record of these women who served Jesus and the Twelve another instance of the unique form of discipleship Jesus instituted. Women are called to be disciples and even to serve Jesus in his public proclamation ministry. But the word *serve* (*diakoneō*) should not be understood in the menial sense. It should be taken in the significant sense in which "serving" one another is the essence of discipleship. Luke records a dispute that arose among the Twelve during the Last Supper about which of them was the greatest.

Jesus said to them, "The kings of the Gentiles lord it over them; and those who exercise authority over them call themselves Benefactors.

---

[17]E.g., Susanne Heine, *Women and Early Christianity: A Reappraisal* (Minneapolis: Augsburg, 1988), 60–62.

[18]E.g., Ben Witherington, *Women in the Ministry*, 118.

[19]Cf. Grant R. Osborne, "Women in Jesus' Ministry," *WTJ* 51 (1989): 280; Evelyn and Frank Stagg, *Woman in the Ministry of Jesus* (Philadelphia: Westminster, 1978), 121–23, 225, 228. For one who wrestles with the exact role of the women, see Pheme Perkins, *Jesus As Teacher* (Cambridge: Cambridge Univ. Press, 1990), 33–37.

But you are not to be like that. Instead, the greatest among you should be like the youngest, and the one who rules like the one who serves. For who is greater, the one who is at the table or the one who serves? Is it not the one who is at the table? But I am among you as one who serves. (Lk 22:25–27)

This group of women had already displayed the essence of discipleship as they served Jesus and the Twelve.[20]

The Wider Group of Disciples

Following Jesus around physically was not the normal life of the believer in Jesus' day. Physical following was for service in Jesus' announcement of the kingdom of God. The Twelve, the Seventy (-two), and the group of women from Galilee were called to follow Jesus around so that they could help him in their various ways. But what do we make of the crowds of listeners and even crowds of disciples who appeared periodically around Jesus?

Some would say that only those who followed Jesus around physically were truly disciples. This is the implication of Gerd Theissen's seminal study, when he distinguishes "wandering charismatics" (the disciples) from the "sympathizers" in the local communities.[21] Theissen suggests that both were part of the social organization of the Jesus movement, but the disciples were those who heeded Jesus' radical ethic, and the sympathizers were those who allowed themselves to remain within society and compromise Jesus' radical ethic. However, Theissen overlooks the evidence for a broader group of people around Jesus who were not called to follow Jesus around but who were disciples nonetheless.

Attachment to Jesus in physical proximity—following him around the countryside in his earthly ministry—was not intended for all of his followers.[22] In fact, that privilege was reserved for only a small group. Two examples, the Gerasene demoniac and Joseph of Arimathea, illustrate this point. After the legion of demons was cast out of the Gerasene demoniac, he begged to accompany Jesus. But Jesus told him to go home to tell his family and friends about how much

---

[20]Later the feminine form of the word for disciple, *mathētria*, is used casually as a synonym for "believer" to speak of another individual woman, Dorcas (Ac 9:36).

[21]Gerd Theissen, *Sociology of Early Palestinian Christianity*, trans. John Bowden (Philadelphia: Fortress, 1978), 8–23. Theissen's study has recently been subjected to intense criticism by Richard A. Horsley, *Sociology and the Jesus Movement* (New York: Crossroad, 1989).

[22]Gerhard Kittel, "ἀκολουθέω," *TDNT* 1:214; Schweizer, *Lordship and Discipleship*, 20, n. 1.

God had done for him (Mk 5:18–19; Lk 8:38–39). This man saw the Twelve with Jesus, he understood what many master-disciple relationships were like in Palestine, and he desired to become a disciple like these others. But, as one commentator notes, Jesus had another plan: "The man wishes to follow through with discipleship in the only manner that has been patterned to him. Jesus does not refuse him but rather redirects him. Jesus returns to Jewish Palestine, and this man—a Gentile—is to return to his native place. He is to demonstrate his faith by proclaiming to his fellows what God in Jesus has done for him."[23] Joseph of Arimathea is another example. Here is a person who apparently did not follow Jesus around in his earthly ministry but who was still considered a disciple of Jesus (cf. Mt 27:57; Jn 19:38), even while he continued to serve within the religious establishment of Israel (Mk 15:43; Lk 23:50–51).

But, while following Jesus around physically was intended only for the Twelve and for some of the broader group of disciples, figurative following was required for all. The pattern was set in Jesus' declaration to the crowds, "Anyone who does not carry his cross and follow me cannot be my disciple" (Lk 14:27). Jesus did not expect the crowds to go find a literal cross. The figurative cross stood for dying to their own will and taking up the will of the Father as found in discipleship to Jesus.[24] "Following Jesus" is to be understood in a figurative sense as well, meaning for the crowds to put their decision into action by committing their ways to Jesus' way. All those of the broader assembly of disciples, even though they could not follow Jesus physically, were to follow him in the figurative sense of putting into action their faith commitment to him. William Schrage explains:

> Admission to the inner circle of disciples is neither an indispensable condition of salvation nor an ascetic accomplishment for a religious elite. One can accept the message of the kingdom, repent, and become an adherent of Jesus without entering into intimate association with Him and walking the roads of Palestine with Him. Of course, those who are called cannot remain as they were; they cannot allow themselves to be held captive by the things of this world and hold on to them at all costs. . . . For all, however, the call of Jesus implies readiness for self-denial and renunciation, for risk and suffering.[25]

Figurative following leads naturally to the thought of figurative attachment of disciples to Jesus like branches to a vine (Jn 15), which

---

[23]John Nolland, *Luke 1–9:20, WBC* 35A (Dallas: Word, 1989), 414–15.

[24]Cf. Michael P. Green, "The Meaning of Cross-Bearing," *BS* 140 (1983): 117–33.

[25]Wolfgang Schrage, *The Ethics of the New Testament* (Philadelphia: Fortress, 1988), 50–51.

in turn leads naturally to a favorite Pauline expression of being "in Christ." The figurative sense sets the stage for the church era. Jesus would not be upon the earth for disciples to follow physically, yet, since Jesus would be with his disciples always (cf. Mt 28:19–20), they *could* follow him figuratively, drawing upon his life to become more like him.

THE DISCIPLES GROW TO BECOME LIKE JESUS

We can now see that following Jesus figuratively in discipleship was the normal life of the believer. All disciples were to be attached to Jesus spiritually, to draw their spiritual nurture from him, to learn from him, to become like him. Some disciples, especially the Twelve, were to follow him around physically, which meant that they were joined with him in his earthly ministry of proclaiming the kingdom, and which also meant that they were being trained for their ministry in the church after Jesus had ascended. But figurative following was for all disciples, in which they would grow to become like Jesus.

Inside-out

Masters were highly esteemed by their disciples in the ancient world. As a general principle, whether one was a student in an academic institution, or a follower of a militant rebel, or a devotee of a religious fanatic, the disciple was bound to adopt the lifestyle, teachings, and values of the master because of proximity and intimacy. Jesus recognized that principle: "A disciple is not above his teacher, nor a slave above his master. It is enough for the disciple that he become as his teacher, and the slave as his master" (Mt 10:24–25 NASB).[26] Jesus' disciples would become like him. They would go out with the same message (cf. Mt 4:17 with 10:7), they would exercise the same ministry and compassion (Mt 9:36 with 10:5ff.), they would perform the same religious and social traditions (Mt 12:1–8; Mk 2:23–27), they would belong to the same family of obedience (Mt 12:46–49). Even as Jesus came not to be served but to serve, his disciples would be characterized by the same servanthood (Mt 20:26–28; Mk 10:42–45; Jn 13:12–17). And finally, Jesus' disciples would share the same destiny of suffering that he endured (Mt 10:16–25; Mk 10:38–39).

Analogous to other master-disciple relationships, Jesus' disciples would become like him and carry out the same ministry as he did.

---

[26]Max Gruenewald, "It Is Enough For The Servant To Be Like His Master," *Salo Wittmayer Baron Jubilee* Volume 2, 573–76.

But Jesus' disciples would become like him in a unique way. The spiritual unity that would be established between Jesus and his disciples—Jesus in them and they in Jesus (cf. Jn 17:13–26)—guaranteed a likeness quite unknown in any other kind of discipleship relationship. This spiritual unity looks ahead to the kind of "likeness" that Paul will eventually address, where his greatest desire is to be like Christ, where the ultimate goal of the believer's life is to be conformed to the image of Christ (Ro 8:29).

During the earthly ministry of Jesus, his disciples could see his life and direct their ways to be like him. After Pentecost a spiritual relationship would be established through the indwelling Spirit that would transform the disciple into the image of Christ from the inside-out.

Examples for Believers

The term *disciple* is simply the most common title for a person who has made a commitment of faith to Jesus. Disciples were not called because they were better than other people; they were called as sinners who were in need of salvation and who were transformed by their association with Jesus. Hans Kvalbein flatly declares that "it is basically wrong to think of the 'disciples' as models for some special or 'higher quality' Christians among other Christians."[27] The disciples are never characterized as a higher form of believer. Indeed, the picture painted of them is quite negative at points. Rather, the disciples are examples of the normal process of growth for all Christians.

The Evangelists presented a realistic portrait of the disciples. They had strengths and weaknesses, victories and defeats. Jesus took ordinary men and women and called them to salvation, to service, and to growth in godliness. While the Evangelists unanimously testify to the imperfections of the disciples, both of the larger group and of the Twelve, they also testify to their growth. The realistic portrayal of good and bad traits in the disciples was intended to be an example to the church of how Jesus helped his disciples to grow. What Jesus commanded them, how he helped them to become obedient, they were in turn to teach all those who became disciples from among the nations (cf. Mt 28:19–20). Jesus taught the disciples (Mk 4:10–12), corrected them (Mt 16:5–12), admonished them (Mt 17:19–20), supported them (Lk 22:31–34), comforted them (Jn 20:19–22), and restored them (21:15–19). Jesus held up high

---

[27]Hans Kvalbein, "'Go Therefore and Make Disciples. . .': The Concept of Discipleship in the New Testament," *Themelios* 13 (1988): 48.

standards of discipleship for his followers, but he was right there with them helping them to accomplish those standards. Since a disciple is always becoming more fully a disciple, the process of growth that occurred in their lives is intended as an example and as an encouragement to the church.

At the same time that they were examples of how all believers were to grow, the Twelve, since they were both disciples and apostles, were examples of how Jesus trained the leadership of the church. Peter, in particular, was isolated by the gospel writers because of his leadership role both during the earthly ministry of Jesus and during the early days of the church. During Jesus' earthly ministry, Peter often functioned as spokesman for the Twelve (e.g., Mt 14:28; 15:15; 18:21; 26:35, 40; Mk 8:29; 9:5; 10:28; Jn 6:68). During the days of the early church, Peter fulfilled Jesus' prediction that he would play a foundational role as the rock and holder of the keys of the kingdom of heaven (Mt 16:17–19; cf. Ac 1:8; 2:14ff.; 8:14ff.; 10:34ff.). Yet neither Peter nor the Twelve are exalted as supersaints. They are portrayed as ordinary people whom Jesus called to follow him as disciples and then whom he trained to become leaders of the church. Later, leaders within the churches to which the Evangelists wrote could be greatly encouraged as they read of the process of growth through which Jesus took the Twelve.

Many people today exalt the disciples so highly that the disciples do not seem to be like us; they are exalted as saints, special people with whom we cannot really relate. On the other hand, some people today belittle the disciples (especially Peter) for their failings. One of the most encouraging perspectives that the gospel writers gives us is that Jesus called ordinary men and women who were transformed by their association with Jesus.

Dimensions of Discipleship

Becoming like Jesus, therefore, demanded growth in discipleship. And it required growth in every area of one's life. When the apostle John looked back on his experience of following Jesus, he recorded three marks of discipleship that Jesus said were evidences of whether a person had truly believed, had truly become a disciple. Those marks are abiding in Jesus' word (Jn 8:31–32), loving the brethren (13:34), and bearing fruit (15:8).[28] Those three marks affected the entire life of the disciple. Growth in discipleship should be understood as being synonymous with what we call Christian growth

---

[28]See chap. 12 for a complete discussion of these three marks in the light of John's overall conception of discipleship.

generally. Although he allowed for the differences that would come about as a result of the Resurrection and the coming of the Spirit at Pentecost, Jesus' teaching on discipleship is virtually identical with the rest of the New Testament teaching on sanctification. To grow as a disciple is to grow as a Christian, and vice versa. Jesus understood discipleship as a multidimensional phenomenon. The whole disciple was addressed.

SPIRITUAL LIFE

Throughout church history, the development of "spiritual disciplines" has been seen to be a key to spiritual growth. These "disciplines" are viewed from different perspectives. One way is to view them as "inward disciplines," "outward disciplines," and "corporate disciplines."[29] Another way to view them is as "disciplines of abstinence" and "disciplines of engagement."[30] But the crux of the matter lies in the balance of God's operation in the disciple's life and the disciple's obedience to God's will.

Spirit-produced growth. As a foundation to growth as a disciple, Jesus emphasized that a person must be born anew by the Spirit of God. In one of his earliest recorded conversations, Jesus told Nicodemus that the kind of kingdom life he was inaugurating began through new life brought by the Spirit (Jn 3:1–15). Growth as a disciple is dependent upon regeneration through the Spirit. The Spirit will also produce continual, spontaneous growth from within. Jesus pointed to Pharisaic Jews of the first century and upbraided them for cleansing the outside first (Mt 23:25–28). Jesus emphasized that the heart is the source of what we are on the outside (12:33–37); hence, change needs to occur from the inside-out. Through new life from the Spirit, a change is made in the disciple's heart. Only then does a person receive true spiritual life. Spiritual growth begins, and is sustained, by the work of the Spirit in the disciple's heart.

Continuing to count the cost/bear the cross. We have seen that following Jesus required the would-be disciple to count the cost of what it would take to come after him. It took exchanging the allegiances of this world for allegiance to Jesus alone. Only then

---

[29]"Inward disciplines" are meditation, prayer, fasting, and study. "Outward disciplines" are simplicity, solitude, submission, and service. "Corporate disciplines" are confession, worship, guidance, and celebration. Cf. Richard J. Foster, *Celebration of Discipline: The Path to Spiritual Growth* (San Francisco: Harper & Row, 1978).

[30]"Disciplines of abstinence" are solitude, silence, fasting, frugality, chastity, secrecy, and sacrifice, while "disciplines of engagement" are study, worship, celebration, service, prayer, fellowship, confession, and submission. Cf. Dallas Willard, *The Spirit of the Disciplines: Understanding How God Changes Lives* (San Francisco: Harper & Row, 1988), 156–75.

could Jesus be one's Savior. But Jesus also challenged his disciples to *continue* to count the cost (Mk 8:34–9:1). The gate of entrance to life is narrow, and once entered, one finds that life on the Way is hard (cf. Mt 7:13–14). Disciples must deny themselves, take up their crosses *daily*, and follow Jesus (Lk 9:23).[31] With the addition of "daily" (*kath' hēmeran*) to the cross-bearing proclamation, Luke specifies that Jesus called for daily self-denial, daily carrying one's cross, and daily following in the footsteps of the Master (cf. Lk 9:23; Mk 8:34).[32] Therefore, self-denial, taking up the cross, and following Jesus not only characterize entrance into the Way, but also characterize life on the Way. The reason for this is twofold: (1) It was possible for a person to fool himself or herself and not truly be a part of the Way (e.g., Judas Iscariot). As Jesus saw the movement around him gaining momentum, he could see the mixed nature of the group who called themselves disciples. He challenged them to examine themselves to see whether they were truly giving sole allegiance to Jesus as their Master and Lord. If they were not, they had not really made that step of faith. (2) The same cost that characterized entrance to discipleship was to characterize the life of discipleship. Growth as a disciple came through continually giving allegiance to Jesus and following the will of the Father. Matthew tells us of one "disciple" (Mt 8:22) who was apparently having second thoughts about the life of discipleship that Jesus expected. He wanted to go back home to bury his father. This points back to the harsh demand that Jesus gave to nondisciples about hating one's father and mother before one could become his disciple (Lk 14:26). This "disciple" was on the verge of leaving Jesus. Yes, he wanted to leave for a good cause—burying his father—but Jesus' harsh reply—"Let the dead bury their own dead" (Mt 8:22)— allows us to see that it was simply an excuse to leave the undivided loyalty that Jesus demanded. As one commentator says, "In the life of discipleship, divided loyalties, even when rooted in religion and ancient custom, pose an unacceptable threat to the allegiance due to Jesus alone."[33]

Nurture and prayer. The balance of God's work and the disciple's obedience is illustrated in the need for nurture through Jesus'

---

[31]In Luke the saying is addressed to "all" (Lk 9:23–27) but comes in a discipleship context, as does Matthew (Mt 16:24–28), but both of these sayings have the indefinite "if anyone" (*ei tis*) of Mark, which makes it addressed to the Twelve but giving a principle that is directed toward anyone with discipleship ambitions; cf. D. A. Carson, "Matthew," *EBC*, vol. 8 (Grand Rapids: Zondervan, 1984), 379.

[32]Joseph A. Fitzmyer, *Luke the Theologian: Aspects of His Teaching* (New York: Paulist, 1989), 134.

[33]Jack Dean Kingsbury, "On Following Jesus: The 'Eager' Scribe and the 'Reluctant' Disciple (Matthew 8.18–22)," *NTS* 34 (1988): 56.

teaching and prayer. A definitive objective of Jesus' form of discipleship is that his disciples will know his teaching, which, when obeyed, will set them free from bondage to sin (Jn 8:31–32). While Jesus bore some similarity to other Jewish masters of the first century, his distinctive teachings marked him off from the religious authorities of Israel. Both Matthew and Mark note that in Jesus' earliest teachings, whether in the synagogue or on the mount, "The crowds were amazed at his teaching, because he taught as one who had authority, and not as their teachers of the law" (Mt 7:28–29; cf. Mk 1:22). Jesus brought a new authoritative teaching, the very Word of God. Therefore, knowing Jesus' teachings mark his disciples off from other kinds of followers. Jesus' teachings mark the distinctive boundaries of his form of discipleship.

But knowing these teachings is not enough. Jesus' disciples are called to "obey" or "observe" all that Jesus commanded (Mt 28:19). Jesus' disciples will live different kinds of lives than other kinds of disciples, because they will be obeying the most distinctive Teacher and teachings of history. This is one reason why we should be hesitant to refer to Jesus' "disciples" simply as "learners." Jesus' disciples will know the content of his teachings, but the real difference in their lives will be manifested because they *obey* his teachings. Indeed, in their worldwide mission, Jesus sends the disciples out to make disciples of all nations, which includes "teaching them to obey everything I have commanded you" (Mt v. 20). Jesus' disciples are nurtured in their spiritual lives as they feed upon Jesus' teachings. Obedience to his teachings provides the necessary spiritual exercise.

Prayer had always been a central element of Jewish life. Prayer was a central element in Jesus' life. Jesus prayed before beginning crucial activities of his ministry (Mk 1:35; 6:46). In times of prayer, Jesus communicated with the Father about his earthly ministry (Jn 17:1–5) and honestly wrestled with the Father's will for his life (Mk 14:32–39). Through prayer Jesus supported the disciples in their present and future activities (Jn 17:6–26).

Prayer was also a central element in the spiritual life to which Jesus introduced his disciples (cf. Mt 6:7–15; Lk 11:1–4). The disciples learned to communicate with the Father through prayer. The Father's will was clarified for them in Jesus' teaching, but through prayer they placed themselves in line with the Father's will. Through prayer, the disciples testified to the Father's glorious nature, they asked for his will to come to fruition, they affirmed their dependence upon his daily sustenance, they confessed the need for forgiveness of sin, they avowed the need for harmony among believers, and they sought the Father's guidance through times of temptation. Prayer would also be the way in which the disciples would maintain communication with Jesus once he left them. As they continued to carry out Jesus' work, prayer would join the disciples with Jesus, so that whatever they asked in Jesus' name, he would do (Jn 14:12–14). In the age to come prayer would be a significant way in which the disciples would walk in the presence of Jesus on a moment-by-moment, day-by-day basis (Mt 28:20).

ETHICAL LIFE

Jesus' teachings created the basis for an ethic that would sustain the disciples during his earthly ministry as well as beyond it. From Jesus' discipleship teachings we can discern basic distinctives that form the heart of the disciple's ethical life.[34]

First, Jesus' disciples are to focus on the ultimate ideal. The antitheses of the Sermon on the Mount declared Jesus' radicalization of the Old Testament law for his disciples (5:21–47). The lofty ideal is expressed in his words, "Be perfect, therefore, as your heavenly Father is perfect" (v. 48). No half-way measures are in mind for Jesus' disciples. They are to rely upon the mercy and grace of God in the process, but they are to aim fully for the ideal.

Second, thought and motive are as important as actions. Since the new life of the disciple begins with a work of the Spirit in the heart, righteousness plumbs to the very depths of the human heart. Anger is the essence of murder (Mt 5:21–22), and adultery can be committed in the heart (v. 28). There is no place for pretense or superficiality in the disciple's righteousness.

Third, love is the central theme of the disciple's life. Jesus emphasized, "You have heard that it was said, 'Love your neighbor and hate your enemy.' But I tell you: Love your enemies and pray for those who persecute you, that you may be sons of your Father in heaven" (Mt 5:43–45). Once, when a lawyer asked Jesus what he must do to gain eternal life, Jesus replied:

> "What is written in the Law? . . . How do you read it?"
> He answered: " 'Love the Lord your God with all your heart and with all your soul and with all your strength and with all your mind'; and, 'Love your neighbor as yourself.' "
> "You have answered correctly," Jesus replied. "Do this and you will live." (Lk 10:26–28)

Love is the central theme of the disciple's life and actions.

---

[34]See Everett F. Harrison, *The Apostolic Church* (Grand Rapids: Eerdmans, 1985), 146–47.

Fourth, Jesus' disciples will be called to account for all they do and think. Jesus taught that judgment was an inescapable factor in human existence. It is the factor that will condemn the unbeliever but will also separate out those who have professed discipleship but whose profession is unreal. Jesus said:

> "Not everyone who says to me, 'Lord, Lord,' will enter the kingdom of heaven, but only he who does the will of my Father who is in heaven. Many will say to me on that day, 'Lord, Lord, did we not prophesy in your name, and in your name drive out demons and perform many miracles?' Then I will tell them plainly, 'I never knew you. Away from me, you evildoers!' " (Mt 7:21–23)

COMMUNITY LIFE

Jesus' form of discipleship included a complex balance of individualism and community. We have seen that Jesus' invitation to follow him demanded that an individual count the cost and make a personal decision. Yet the concept of community is everywhere apparent, whether it is the solidarity of the Twelve with the plural term *disciples,* the spiritual family emphasis (Mt 12:46–50), the promise of the church (16:18; 18:17) or the relational responsibilities within the community (ch. 18).

Individualism or community? Which did Jesus promote in his form of discipleship?[35] Many have suggested that Jesus' treatment of the family is a key to understanding his form of discipleship. From Old Testament to New Testament, the earthly family plays a major role in God's program for humankind. The family was established by God, it was protected by the Law, and it was an illustration of God's relationship with his people. God's people were called to be his family, and in many ways the family was the center of covenantal activity. The family was the means through which succeeding generations of individuals were assured of being raised to know the will of God and the importance of community life.[36] Therefore, why

---

[35]Some scholars deny the concept of "community" in Jesus' disciples, whether because they do not seem to function as a community (James D. G. Dunn, *Unity and Diversity in the New Testament,* 2d ed. [London: SCM, 1990], 104–6) or because they do not seem that separated from the social structure of Israel (Richard A. Horsley, *Jesus and the Spiral of Violence* [San Francisco: Harper & Row, 1987], 209–12). However, the disciples may be viewed as a community if we recognize the role for which they were being trained for the future church; cf. Donald Guthrie, *New Testament Theology* (Downers Grove, Ill.: InterVarsity Press, 1981), 706–10; George Eldon Ladd, *A Theology of the New Testament* (Grand Rapids: Eerdmans, 1974), 347.

[36]See Shmuel Safrai, "Home and Family," *The Jewish People in the First Century,* vol. 2; Section One: Compendia Rerum Iudaicarum ad Novum Testamentum (Philadelphia: Fortress, 1976), 728–92.

did Jesus seem to sever this established community when he called
for those who would follow him to "hate" father and mother, wife and
children (Lk 14:26)? What did Jesus intend by harking back to the
prophet Micah when he gave his harsh statement about the sword
and the family?

> "Do not suppose that I have come to bring peace to the earth. I did
> not come to bring peace, but a sword. For I have come to turn

> " 'a man against his father,
>   a daughter against her mother,
> a daughter-in-law against her mother-in-law—
>   a man's enemies will be the members of his own household.' "
>   (Mt 10:34–36; cf. Mic 7:6)

When Jesus gave a challenge to leave family and even to "hate"
father and mother, wife and children (Lk 14:26), he was not calling
for the disruption of the family or rebellion against it. Rather, Jesus
was declaring that *he* must be the primary focus of allegiance, not the
family. By the time of Jesus, the family took such a primary place
within the social life of Judaism that it could determine the direction
of an individual family member's life and could demand unswerving
loyalty.[37] It is evident that Jesus did not intend to sever all earthly
family relationships in that pairs of brothers were called to be among
the Twelve (Mt 4:18–22), Peter maintained a family relationship with
his wife's mother (Mk 1:29–31), and Jesus himself directed the
apostle John to care for Jesus' earthly mother after his death (Jn
19:26–27). Jesus continued commitment toward biblical family
relationships, yet when those relationships competed with giving
priority to him, they were to be "hated." Hans Kvalbein says wisely:

> Jesus' call to his disciples to leave their family and even to "hate" father
> and mother, wife and children (Lk 14:26) is of course no general
> command of unlimited validity. It only has relevance when these
> relationships prevent an absolute obedience to him. It cannot make
> invalid the command of the decalogue: "honour your father and your
> mother", which is confirmed by both Jesus (Mk 10:19) and the apostle
> (Eph 6:2).[38]

When it came to the family, the people of Jesus' day had confounded
the means with the ends. The family was designed to bring
succeeding generations into knowledge of the will of God, yet family
loyalties became so strong that they were in danger of usurping the
will of God. Jesus maintains the earthly family as a high priority, but

---

[37]Cf. W. White, "Family," *ZPEB* 2:496–501; O. J. Baab, "Father," *IDB* 2:245.
[38]Kvalbein, " 'Go Therefore,' " 51.

he shows its ultimate purpose when he says that "whoever does the will of my Father in heaven is my brother and sister and mother" (Mt 12:50).

Jesus called men and women into a deep personal relationship with himself, yet if we focus exclusively on the individual in our studies of discipleship, we run the danger of separating the individual from the community of faith. "This focus on the vertical dimension of discipleship, the individual's own personal call and subsequent relationship with the Lord, can easily lead to selfishness and a lack of concern for others."[39] Jesus called individuals to discipleship, yet responding to that call brought the disciple into a community of faith.

IMPLICATIONS

Becoming like Jesus is a glorious thought! Immediately the great, old hymn comes to mind, "O to Be Like Thee!" The first stanza with chorus goes:

> O to be like Thee! blessed Redeemer,
> This is my constant longing and prayer.
> Gladly I'll forfeit all of earth's treasures, Jesus,
> Thy perfect likeness to wear.
>
> O to be like Thee!
> O to be like Thee, Blessed Redeemer, pure as Thou art!
> Come in Thy sweetness, come in they fullness;
> Stamp Thine own image deep on my heart.

Wonderful expression, isn't it? I do have that longing. But what else comes to my attention is the present state of my life. I am a long way from being like Jesus!

Jesus' disciples were not that much different than us. These men and women were attracted by Jesus' life and by his teachings, yet they knew that their own lives were nothing by comparison. In one of the early encounters, after Peter witnessed Jesus' miraculous work, "He fell down at Jesus' feet, saying, 'Depart from me, for I am a sinful man, O Lord!' " (Lk 5:8 NASB). In the light of Jesus' life, the disciples were only too well aware of their shortcomings.

Therefore, growth was necessary for them. And growth is necessary for us. If I am going to become like Jesus, I have to grow. And I cannot just sing about it in church. I have to grow in my daily life with him.

---

[39] Dennis M. Sweetland, *Our Journey with Jesus. Discipleship According to Mark,* GNS 22 (Wilmington, Del.: Michael Glazier, 1987), 85.

That is why a life-oriented approach to discipleship is so important. Jesus took a small group of disciples with him in the various circumstances of life that he encountered on a day-to-day basis. He was able to provide an example for the disciples in all of the activities of life. In our churches, we gather with other believers away from life, and then we talk about life, strategize how to do better. But the church setting can seem so artificially separated from the rest of life that what we do there appears to be irrelevant to daily life. In our structured discipleship groups, we tend to focus on one dimension of life, the spiritual. But without discussing or demonstrating how the spiritual dimension interrelates with other aspects of life, such as the ethical, physical, relational, social, intellectual, emotional, or psychological dimensions, we can develop a propensity toward dissociating the spiritual dimension from the rest of the person. In our daily lives we tend to be alone, because our careers, families, neighborhoods, or recreational activities isolate us from other believers. We then develop a life that is somewhat different than what it would be if other believers were with us. I do not necessarily mean "sinful." Perhaps "secular" or "a-spiritual" would be better a better way of saying it. Our Sunday life can begin to be much different than the rest of our life.

In following chapters we will interact with these issues more directly. Here I would like to suggest two implications. First, we must develop our walk with Jesus in the real world. Men and women, preachers and laypeople, mature and immature, rich and poor, married and single—we all need to learn how to live with Jesus in the everyday world. He desires to walk with us in every circumstance of every day. We do not have to withdraw from the circumstances of life in order to be his disciples. In his prayer for the disciples on the night before his crucifixion, Jesus said to the Father:

> I have given them your word and the world has hated them, for they are not of the world any more than I am of the world. My prayer is not that you take them out of the world but that you protect them from the evil one. They are not of the world, even as I am not of it. Sanctify them by the truth; your word is truth. As you sent me into the world, I have sent them into the world. (Jn 17:14–18)

Jesus promised to be with the disciples as they went forth into the world with the Great Commission (Mt 28:18–20). As you and I go into the everyday world of work, school, family, and friends, Jesus goes with us.

Individually, we must learn to practice the presence of Jesus. In the first few days of my conversion I was afraid of ridicule for my new-found faith. I had been a vocal (although somewhat ignorant!)

atheist who had taken great pleasure in trying to ridicule people who claimed to be Christians. Now I was a Christian! I was sure that all of my old friends would ridicule me as I walked across that college campus my first morning back. I recollect getting ready for school, talking to Jesus all the time. As I drove my old Volkswagen van, I remember talking to Jesus as though he were sitting in the seat next to me. Going across campus for the first time, I walked with Jesus next to me. As I went into my first class, I even looked for a place with two empty desks so that Jesus could sit next to me! Naive? Innocent? Perhaps. But this was the faith of a new disciple of Jesus. Those early days gave me an understanding of the reality of Jesus on a day-by-day basis as I lived in his presence. Once Jesus ascended, the early disciples were without him physically, but they were with him through prayer, through "practicing the presence of Jesus" on a daily basis. We must learn to open our conscious attention to him anywhere we go, developing a line of communication with him in all circumstances.

It is in the various circumstances of life that Jesus shows us how to be real people. He does not want to take us out of life. He promises to be with us as we go through the problems, the difficulties, the temptations, the testings. Now that we are united to Christ through the indwelling Spirit of God, he works from within to change us, empower us, and encourage us in every circumstance.

The second implication that stands out is the necessity of having other disciples walk with us. Notice how often we find the disciples in a group, whether it is the Twelve, the group of women, or the Seventy being sent out two by two. Very seldom do we find them alone. We need other disciples. Growth in our developing walk with Jesus will be, in part, proportional to our accountability to others. That is what I found with my wife, Lynne, in those early days. Neither one of us knew what it meant to "disciple" anyone, but as we grew in our knowledge of the Word and of each other, we were able to hold each other accountable through the various circumstances of life together. We developed a habit of transparency and of confessing our sins and weaknesses to each another. And we allowed each other appropriate authority over our lives, which meant helping each other to say no to the temptations that came in life, calling each other on the tendency toward phoniness, and keeping each other honest in our walk. I learned and am still learning from that relationship how to develop mutual discipleship relationships with other people, including my daughters, a couple of very close colleagues, and a couple of neighbors and friends—real people, real disciples with whom I am privileged to walk as together we follow Jesus Christ.

Following up:

1. What are the differences between following Jesus literally in the first century versus following him figuratively today?
2. If you had your choice, which would you have preferred, to follow Jesus then or now? Why?
3. What can we do to help develop the growth of disciples today?
4. What role of the women who followed Jesus in the first century would be equivalent for women today?
5. How should we develop a balance of personal discipleship with the community of disciples?

8

The Twelve

Getting focused:

1. What do you know of the twelve disciples? What was their background? Did they know each other before being called to follow Jesus?
2. What characteristics do you think Jesus was looking for in those he chose to be part of the Twelve? How were the Twelve different from other disciples?
3. Were there distinctions among the Twelve? What kind?
4. Why did Jesus choose twelve? Why not more or less?

"I can't wait to get out into the real world!" I have heard these words from students on many different campuses over the years. They are gathered away on a campus among other students, waiting for the day when they can finish their education and get out into the "real world." Where I now teach, some students refer to the campus as the "Biola Bubble." I have also heard many other Christian settings referred to as bubbles. In this sense, a Christian bubble is an artificial environment where we live in full view of the world yet are separated, isolated, insulated from reality. I have heard similar expression given to such settings as colleges, seminaries, Christian conference grounds or retreat centers, Christian service organizations, and even churches.

In most cases, the people who express themselves in this way are venting an admirable desire. By depreciating a "Christian bubble," they may be indicating that they want to get on with life, to live out their faith in the world in order to make a difference among unbelievers. They are eager to put into practice all that they have learned; they cannot wait to live on the cutting edge of life and faith.

I can understand such a desire. In the last chapter we saw how Jesus designed a type of discipleship that was intended to be lived with him in the world. His disciples are not to be *of* the world but are to live with him *in* the world.

On the other hand, by depreciating a so-called bubble, we may indicate that we misunderstand the very purpose of the institutions that can be invaluable in preparing us for life. I will use an analogy from a related experience to explain. I was the squad leader of an airborne infantry squad during most of the year I spent in Vietnam. The last thing I would have wanted was some young guy right off the block coming over to join our squad, with me having to try to teach him combat techniques while we were in the middle of a battle. What he needed was a period of time, in relative peace and safety, where he could be taught all of the skills necessary to make him most effective for his tour of duty in combat.

That training time was the purpose of boot camp. But, interestingly, when I was a drill sergeant I also heard comments about an artificial bubble from the trainees. These trainees were learning skills that were critical for combat readiness, but some of them thought that what they were learning seemed irrelevant. Soon they grew tired of the training. It seemed to them almost as though they were little children again, playing war games like G.I. Joe.

But during the training, I would tell them a story about a trainee who once had the same attitude. This trainee paid little attention to his instruction in map reading. He was sure that he would never be in a position of leadership where he would be the one required to read a map. He was just an enlisted man, and there would always be people above him in rank who would take care of reading the map. But little did he know that only two months after he arrived in Vietnam he would be thrust into a position of leadership. Now he was required to take a group of men out on patrol. On the very first patrol he and his men were ambushed. They got pinned down out in the open while crossing a rice paddy. They needed to call in artillery support to drive off the enemy. That meant that he needed to read his map. He looked at the map, figured out their position and the position of the enemy, and then called in on the radio the coordinates where he wanted the artillery rounds to land. The first round came whistling in over head. But instead of landing three hundred meters away, it landed only fifty meters away! The next rounds were supposed to get closer! Quickly he yelled into the radio, "Cease fire, cease fire!!" He had read his map incorrectly, almost directing the artillery right on top of his men and himself!

That story usually caught my trainees' attention. But what gave it even more impact was when I told them that the one who paid such little attention to map reading, the one who thought that map reading was not necessary for his future role, the one who almost killed himself and the others, was *me!* And now I was their drill sergeant, teaching them, among other things, map reading!

That incident taught me a lesson that has never left me. Institutions—the college campus, the seminary, the Christian conference grounds or training center, and even the local church—have come into existence for the purpose of giving people the time and circumstances in which to become better prepared to live more effective daily lives. The environment that best accomplishes that task is often away from day-to-day activities, where a person can give focused attention to training, or in the case of many conference grounds or retreat centers, where a person can reevaluate and even recover from the hard times of daily life. This training, recovery, and fellowship is also one of the essential functions of the local church on a weekly basis. All too soon, however, time spent in the Christian bubble ends, and a person must go out into the normal activities of life. I often hear from graduates that they wished they would have understood the value of school while they were still there.

We do need to become aware of the potential danger of a Christian bubble. One danger is becoming so comfortable in the bubble that we do not get out of it. This is a problem for many professors and pastors or full-time workers. Another danger is when the training or time spent in the bubble does not adequately prepare us for daily life, when it creates an artificial environment that seems inapplicable to daily life. We are all too well aware of the "mountain-top experience" at the Christian camp which can be lost as soon as we come down from the mountain.

Jesus' twelve disciples were also placed into a bubble of sorts. The four Gospels unanimously witness to a core of twelve disciples who were called by Jesus into a special relationship with him. Those Twelve, in the light of Luke's wording, were called out from among a much larger number of disciples (6:13; 17). Jesus called the Twelve to be with him so that he could give them specialized training for the role of assisting him in his earthly ministry as well as training that would equip them for their future role as apostles after his ascension.[1] They were separated from their occupations, their families, and their regular activities so that for a period of time, somewhere around three years, they could be trained by Jesus.

On some occasions, the sacrifice of separation was felt keenly. Peter, comparing a rich young man's unwillingness to follow Jesus,

---

[1]A. B. Bruce, *The Training of the Twelve*, 1871, reprint (Grand Rapids: Kregel, 1971), 11–12.

pointed to himself and the rest of the Twelve and asked, "We have left everything to follow you! What then will there be for us?" (Mt 19:27). On other occasions, the privilege of being with Jesus offered incredible experiences. When Peter, James, and John were privileged to witness Jesus' transfiguration and the appearance of Moses and Elijah, this mountain-top experience provoked a different reaction from Peter. "Master, it is good for us to be here. Let us put up three shelters—one for you, one for Moses and one for Elijah" (Lk 9:33). Finally, at the end of their time together, Jesus said that they were ready for their future work; whether they appeared ready or not. At the seaside breakfast with some of the assembled disciples who had gone fishing, three times the risen Jesus asked Peter if he loved him. "The third time [Jesus] said to him, 'Simon son of John, do you love me?' Peter was hurt because Jesus asked him the third time, 'Do you love me?' He said, 'Lord, you know all things; you know that I love you.' Jesus said, 'Feed my sheep'" (Jn 21:17).

We can learn much from the Twelve. We have seen their role in the Jesus movement (chap. 6), and we have seen some of the process of discipleship that moved them to become like Jesus (chap. 7). In this chapter we will take a closer look at them as a group, and then we will look briefly at each one individually. Their time in the bubble prepared them for life's greatest challenges. We will all have times in various kinds of bubbles, and we can learn from their example. Just as we are unique individuals, so was each of the Twelve, and the Lord called and developed each one according to his own personal potential. We can learn much from each of the Twelve, because the Lord desires to develop each of us according to our own potential.

GENERAL CHARACTERISTICS

We begin with some observations about general characteristics of the Twelve.

Disciples and Apostles

An important observation often missed in studies of biblical discipleship is the distinction between the call to discipleship and the call to apostleship.[2] In the introduction to the lists of the Twelve,

---

[2]For example, Martin Hengel, *The Charismatic Leader and His Followers*, trans. James Greig (New York: Crossroad, 1981); and Hans Kvalbein, "'Go Therefore and Make Disciples...': The Concept of Discipleship in the New Testament," *Themelios* 13 1988. Hengel (Kvalbein follows Hengel here) rightly understands that the call of the Twelve was "service to the cause of the approaching Kingdom of God," yet since he does not see the distinction between

Luke states that Jesus "called his disciples to him and chose twelve of them, whom he also designated apostles" (Lk 6:13). This is a clue to the role of the Twelve as we see it in the Gospels: not only are they Jesus' disciples (believers), but they are also in training to be his apostles (commissioned representatives). Both terms are applied to the Twelve in the Gospels. As "disciples" the Twelve are set aside as examples of what Jesus accomplishes in believers; as "apostles" the Twelve are set aside as the leaders within the new movement to come, the church.[3]

The Number Twelve

The number Twelve has obvious salvation-historical significance. In the selection of twelve disciples "there is with equal resolution both a backward and a forward look: backward to the ancient constitution of Israel; and at the same time forward to the final form of the Messianic community."[4] The number corresponds with the twelve patriarchs of Israel, the sons of Jacob, from whom the tribes of Israel descended. The number twelve is significant in the transition to the church because the eleven apostles found it important to choose a new apostle, Matthias, to replace Judas Iscariot (Ac 1:15–26).

The Twelve, therefore, symbolize the continuity of salvation-history in God's program, which also means continuity yet discontinuity between Israel and the church. Jesus said to his disciples, "I tell you the truth, at the renewal of all things, when the Son of Man sits on his glorious throne, you who have followed me will also sit on twelve thrones, judging the twelve tribes of Israel" (Mt 19:28). The church has become participants in the great promises of blessing that are foundational to God's total salvation program. Prior to this time those promises had been covenanted only to Abraham and Israel. However, this does not replace Israel nor fulfill her specifically national prophecies. Interestingly, the number twelve becomes important once again in the book of Revelation. The twelve tribes of

the Twelve as disciples and the Twelve as apostles he is forced to say that following Jesus concretely as his disciple cannot be construed as entrance to the kingdom (Hengel, *Charismatic Leader*, 61–62; 73–74). He does acknowledge that other calls in the Gospels must be interpreted as entrance to salvation but says that they are part of a later tradition from the early church (cf. ibid., 62–63). He could avoid this difficulty by recognizing that there is a uniform distinction between the call to the Twelve for apostleship and the general call to discipleship. He himself seems to recognize this later (cf. ibid., 82–83).

[3]Cf. John Nolland, *Luke 1–9:20*, WBC 35A (Dallas: Word, 1989), 270; Ben Witherington III, *The Christology of Jesus* (Minneapolis: Fortress, 1990), 126–31.

[4]Karl H. Rengstorf, "δώδεκα," *TDNT* 2:326.

Israel are sealed for service in the period of tribulation (Rev 7:1–8), and in the new, heavenly Jerusalem the names of the twelve tribes of Israel are inscribed on the gates and the names of the twelve apostles are inscribed on the foundations of the city walls (21:12–14). "Both Israel and the church share in their distinctive phases in God's program as the people of God through whom he will be glorified."[5] In the gathering of twelve disciples, we find the hint that Jesus is indeed the messianic king of Israel who has come to unite the people of God in all ages.[6]

The twelve disciples do not function as a permanent organizational group within the church, however. They are significant in the foundational days of the early church. They appear in the days before Pentecost, and they function as a group in the earliest days after Pentecost. They also emerge to provide leadership for the distribution of food in the dispute between factions of the disciples. Luke records, "So the Twelve gathered all the disciples together and said, 'It would not be right for us to neglect the ministry of the word of God in order to wait on tables. Brothers, choose seven men from among you who are known to be full of the Spirit and wisdom. We will turn this responsibility over to them and will give our attention to prayer and the ministry of the word'" (Ac 6:2–4). From that point on, however, we do not find the title "Twelve" used in the narrative of Acts, nor does the title appear in the Epistles. The title "apostles" appears regularly, showing us that they were active in the early church. Although the Twelve provided continuity in God's salvation-historical program, the absence of the title in the later developing church gives us a clue that they do not provide permanent organizational leadership as a group.[7]

Lists of the Twelve

The following is a chart of the Twelve disciples as they occur in the listings found in the Gospels and Acts.

---

[5]Robert L. Saucy, *The Church in God's Program* (Chicago: Moody, 1972), 82. See also Robert L. Saucy, "Israel and the Church: A Case for Discontinuity," in *Continuity and Discontinuity: Perspectives on the Relationship Between the Old and New Testaments*. Essays in Honor of S. Lewis Johnson, Jr., ed. John S. Feinberg (Westchester, Ill.: Crossway, 1988), 239–59.

[6]Cf. Seán Freyne, *The Twelve: Disciples and Apostles. A Study in the Theology of the First Three Gospels* (London: Sheed & Ward, 1968), 23–48; Bruce, *Training of the Twelve*, 32–33.

[7]Rengstorf, "δώδεκα," 326–28.

Matthew 10:2–4	Mark 3:16–19	Luke 6:13–16	Acts 1:13
Simon, called Peter, first	*Simon, named Peter*	*Simon, named Peter*	*Peter*
Andrew, brother of Peter	James, son of Zebedee	Andrew, brother of Peter	John
James, son of Zebedee	John, brother of James	James	James
John, brother of James	Andrew	John	Andrew
Philip	*Philip*	*Philip*	*Philip*
Bartholomew	Bartholomew	Bartholomew	Thomas
Thomas	Matthew	Matthew	Bartholomew
Matthew, the tax collector	Thomas	Thomas	Matthew
James, son of Alphaeus	*James, son of Alphaeu*	*James, son of Alphaeus*	*James, son of Alphaeuss*
Thaddaeus (or, Lebbaeus)	Thaddaeus	Simon, called the zealot	Simon the zealot
Simon the Cananaean	Simon the Cananaean	Judas, son of James	Judas, son of James
Judas Iscariot the betrayer	Judas Iscariot the betrayer	Judas Iscariot the traitor	

These lists reveal important distinctions within the Twelve. First, the uniformity of the names from list to list reveals the importance of the Twelve in the early church. Only one of the twelve names shows variation: Thaddaeus and/or Judas of James. As will be seen below, this is simply literary preference for referring to the same person.[8] The listing in Acts is the last time the names of the Twelve are given as a group. We do not find a list that includes Matthias nor the later apostle Paul. Second, only Peter, John, and Matthew wrote books included in the New Testament. Although several of the Twelve do not have any personal prominence attached to them in the New Testament, their inclusion in the apostolic band assured them a permanent place of importance in Jesus' earthly ministry and in the early days of the church.

Third, within the Twelve is a recognizable division into groups of four. The first name of each of the groups remains the same in all of the lists (the first, fifth, and ninth places are occupied, respectively, by Peter, Philip, and James of Alphaeus). The order of the names within the groups varies except for the first name. The sequence of

---

[8]See below under Thaddaeus. See also John Nolland, *Luke 1–9:20*, WBC 35A (Dallas: Word, 1989), 265, 271.

the groups is the same in each list. This grouping suggests that the Twelve were organized into smaller units, each with a leader.[9]

Fourth, the first group is composed of those two pairs of brothers who were the first called—Peter, Andrew, James, and John (Mt 4:18–22 par.), commonly called the "inner circle" (however, on some significant occasions only Peter, James, and John accompanied Jesus). This inner circle accompanied Jesus on special occasions such as the healing of Jairus's daughter (Mk 5:37ff. par.) and the Transfiguration (9:2ff. par.). They were the audience of the Olivet Discourse (13:3ff.; Andrew is included) and were with Jesus during his agony in the Garden of Gethsemane (Mt 26:37ff. par.).

Fifth, Matthew's list gives pairings of disciples in the Greek text, which may reflect the commission of Mark 6:7, where Jesus sent the Twelve out two by two.[10] Sixth, Peter occurs first in all of the lists, indicating his place of leadership within the Twelve, while Judas Iscariot always occurs last, except in the list in Acts where he is omitted. Peter regularly functioned as the spokesman for the Twelve (e.g., Mt 14:28; 15:15; 18:21; 26:35, 40; Mk 8:29; 9:5; 10:28; Jn 6:68), and during the days of the early church Peter fulfilled Jesus' prediction that he would play a foundational role as the rock and holder of the keys of the kingdom of heaven (Mt 16:17–19; cf. Acts 1:8; 2:14ff.; 8:14ff.; 10:34ff.). Peter is called "first" (e.g., Mt 10:2) in the sense that he was first among equals (*primus inter pares*) as the leader of the Twelve.

INDIVIDUAL CHARACTERISTICS

In the New Testament the Twelve are normally mentioned as a group with only occasional focus on individuals. For example, Peter is the most familiar of the apostles to the average Christian because his name is mentioned 210 times in the New Testament. The name of Paul is mentioned 162 times. The combined names of all the other apostles occur only 142 times. The Twelve displayed a remarkable personal diversity, including businessmen (Peter, Andrew, James, and John), a tax-collector (Matthew), and a zealous revolutionary (Simon the zealot). Not much is known about the individual lives of the Twelve other than what can be gathered from brief biblical data

---

[9]See Bruce, *Training of the Twelve*, 36ff.; Donald A. Carson, "Matthew," *EBC* (Grand Rapids: Zondervan, 1984), 8:237.

[10]Carson, "Matthew," 237; Robert A. Guelich, *Mark 1–8:26*, *WBC* 34A (Dallas: Word, 1989), 321.

and some statements from the early church fathers. In later church history, inconceivable legends developed about these men.[11]

Simon Peter

Simon, later called Peter by Jesus, was a native of Galilee, where he grew up making his living as a fisherman, along with his father and his brother, Andrew. Since Andrew was originally a disciple of John the Baptist, there is a strong possibility that Peter was as well (cf. Jn. 1:35–40). When Jesus came to be baptized by John the Baptist, Andrew followed Jesus and then went to tell his brother Peter that Jesus was the Messiah. Peter was called to follow Jesus and soon became the most prominent of the disciples, his name always standing first in every listing of the disciples or apostles (Mt 10:2–4; Mk 3:16–19; Lk 6:14–16; Ac 1:13). Jesus gave Simon the Aramaic name *Cephas,* "stone," which is translated *Petros* in Greek, from which we get the English transliteration *Peter.*[12]

Peter was among the inner circle of three around Jesus (Peter, James, and John—cf. Mt 17:1; 26:37; Mk 5:37; 14:33). He was a spokesman for the Twelve in Jesus' lifetime (cf. Mt 16:13–16; Jn 6:66–69) and is called "first" (e.g., Mt 10:2) in the sense that he was first among equals as the leader of the Twelve. Peter appeared with the most forceful personality among the Twelve. He requested to walk on the water to Jesus (Mt 14:28–33), he asked for explanation of parables (15:15), and he stepped forward to give a statement of confession for the Twelve (Jn 6:66–69). But his forceful personality got him into trouble as well. When he presumptuously stepped forward to dissuade Jesus from going to the cross, Peter was held personally culpable for being a Satan-inspired stumbling stone (Mk 8:31–33). Peter was a very real, human disciple. He was caught with conflicting faith and lack of faith (Mt 14:28–31). He could be quite obtuse and foolish in his apprehension of Jesus' ministry (15:15; 17:4; 19:27). He could go from the highest confession to the lowest spiritual perception in one setting, and as a result receive from Jesus the greatest pronouncement or the strongest denouncement. But what has been such an encouragement to many Christians over the

[11]See the bibliography for various studies of the twelve apostles.

[12]See Wilkins, *The Concept of Disciple in Matthew's Gospel,* 174–75; also, Chrys Caragounis, *Peter and The Rock,* BZNW 58 (Berlin/New York: de Gruyter, 1990); Oscar Cullmann, *"Petros," TDNT* 6, trans. G. W. Bromiley (Grand Rapids: Eerdmans, 1968), 100; Oscar Cullmann, *Peter: Disciple—Apostle—Martyr. A Historical and Theological Essay,* 2d ed. (Philadelphia: Westminster, 1962), 19; Joseph Fitzmyer, "Aramaic *Kepha'* and Peter's Name in the New Testament," *To Advance the Gospel* (New York: Crossroad, 1981), 112–13.

years is Peter's resiliency. His infamous night of denials was his darkest night, yet at the Resurrection scene Peter ran and went into the tomb first (Jn 20:1–10).

Peter played a leading role in the early church. The leadership role he was beginning to assume at the time of his great confession (Mt 16:16ff.) was recognized by Jesus and was promised to be extended in the laying of the foundation of the church. This is borne out in the historical record. Jesus appeared to Peter after the Resurrection and gave him special encouragement to feed Jesus' sheep (Jn 21). Peter held a leadership position among the disciples prior to Pentecost (Ac 1:15ff.) and was the leading figure/preacher at Pentecost and beyond (cf. 2:14, 37, 38; 3:4, 6, 12; 4:8; 5:3ff.; 8:14, 18ff.; 9:32ff.; 10:9ff.; 11:2ff.; 12:3ff.; 15:6ff.). Peter, as the representative disciple who gave the first personal declaration of the Messiah's identity, was the apostle in the book of Acts who opened the door of the kingdom to all peoples. Through his authoritative preaching and presence, the kingdom was opened to Jews (Ac 2), Samaritans (Ac 8), and Gentiles (Ac 10).[13] Peter was given a unique function and position in the foundation of the church. Although crucial in New Testament church history, Peter was almost always together with other disciples. Early in Acts he appeared as the recognized leader (Ac 2, 3, 5, 8), but at the Jerusalem council he shared the leadership with James (cf. 15:7–13ff.). Thereafter Peter disappears from the narrative and Paul is the one given special notice for continuing the work of the church. Peter was crucial for his role in the foundation of the church, but he was not the only part of the foundation (cf. Eph 2:19–20; Rev 21:14).

Peter is both a positive and negative example of a disciple, especially in the portrait from Matthew's gospel.[14] He is a very human disciple whom Matthew has presented as a model for all disciples to follow. He is an example of exercising faith (14:28–29), confessing Jesus as Messiah, Son of God (16:16), and learning from Jesus (17:24–27). In even more cases he is the example of what not to do: disciples should not take their eyes off Jesus (14:30), should not be a stumbling block (16:23), should not seek earthly rewards (19:27), and should not deny Jesus (26:69–70). Even with all the highs and lows of Peter's prominence, he is characterized by Matthew as a very real, very human, quite exemplary disciple.

Peter appears in the biblical record as a person of tremendous

---

[13]Even though the Samaritans had "believed" through the preaching of Philip (Ac 8:4–13), it was necessary for Peter and John to go there in order for them to receive the Holy Spirit (vv. 14ff.). Cf. ibid., and Donald Guthrie, *New Testament Theology* (Downers Grove, Ill.: InterVarsity Press, 1981), 714.

[14]See Wilkins, *Concept of Disciple*, 173–216.

personal strengths, but he was not always consistent in the outworking of those strengths. Peter was still a young man when called by the Lord to be his follower. What has been a source of inspiration and encouragement to the church is the way in which we see growth in Peter throughout his life. The Peter who was so forceful in his early years was still forceful later. But the difference is that Peter learned how to be consistently forceful for his Master.

After the Council of Jerusalem Peter's name is dropped from the book of Acts, but he apparently traveled as an apostle with his wife (1Co 9:5), visiting and establishing churches. In his later life he acted as a shepherd to the churches, writing the letters that bear his name. Tradition tells us that he was martyred in Rome about A.D. 65, crucified upside down.

Andrew

Andrew is best known as the brother of Simon Peter. Growing up as a fisherman in Bethsaida, a fishing village on the north shore of the sea of Galilee, Andrew became a disciple of John the Baptist and is the first named person to follow Jesus (cf. Jn. 1:35ff.). Later he and Peter left their fishing business to follow Jesus in his earthly ministry. Andrew was also part of the inner circle around Jesus.

Outside of the listings of the Twelve, Andrew is mentioned on six occasions in the Gospels (Mk 1:16 par.; 1:29; 13:3; Jn 1:40ff.; 6:8; 12:22). John gives the most insight to Andrew, emphasizing his practical faith. Andrew's first encounter with Jesus was revealing. He was concerned enough about his brother that he went to tell him about his encounter with Jesus and then personally introduced Peter to Jesus. Later Andrew brought the boy with the loaves and fishes to Jesus for the feeding of the five thousand (Jn 6:8) and then, with Philip, brought the inquisitive Greeks to Jesus (12:22).

Later church tradition says that Andrew ministered in various places, among them Bithynia, Scythia, Greece, and Ephesus. The apocryphal *Acts of Andrew*[15] says that Andrew was imprisoned and crucified in Achaia on an X-shaped cross (subsequently called St. Andrew's cross).

James (Son of Zebedee)

James and John, the sons of Zebedee, were also from Bethsaida. They were from a family of some wealth and influence, probably

---

[15]Edgar Hennecke, *New Testament Apocrypha*, 2 vols., ed. Wilhelm Schneemelcher (Philadelphia: Westminster, 1963–1965), 2:416–23.

derived from a profitable fishing trade (cf. Mk 1:20; Lk 5:10; Jn 18:15). Their father Zebedee was wealthy enough to employ other fishermen, and their mother was most likely Salome, one of the women who followed Jesus to the cross and the tomb (cf. Mt 27:55–56; Mk 15:40; 16:1) and who helped support Jesus' earthly ministry (Mt 27:55–56; cf. Lk 8:3). This Salome is understood by many to be the one designated as "Jesus' mother's sister," which, if so, would make James and John cousins of Jesus.[16] This would explain the reason why Jesus turned his mother over to John at the crucifixion and would also help explain the seemingly forward nature of James and John's mother requesting a place for her sons in Jesus' kingdom (Mt 20:20–21). James and John were called "Sons of Thunder" (Mk 3:17), quite likely because of their fiery temperament, which may explain their aggressive ambitions (10:35ff.; as well as their mother's! Mt 20:20–21).

Along with Peter, Andrew, and John (all fishing partners—cf. Lk 5:10), James was called to follow Jesus in his earthly ministry (Mk 1:19–20 par.) and became part of the inner circle around Jesus, accompanying Jesus on such significant occasions as the healing of Jairus' daughter (5:37ff. par.), the Transfiguration (5:37ff. par.), the Olivet Discourse (13:3ff.), and the Garden of Gethsemane (Mt 26:37ff. par.). James is later distinguished as the first apostolic martyr, a victim of the sword during the persecution undertaken by Herod Agrippa I (Ac 12:2).

John (Son of Zebedee)

Since John was almost always listed second, he was probably the younger brother of James. From earliest times, the church has identified John as the other disciple who joined Andrew in going after Jesus (Jn 1:35–40).[17] If so, John was also first a disciple of John the Baptist before becoming a disciple of Jesus. Later the two sets of brothers (Peter/Andrew, James/John) were called to follow Jesus, making up his inner circle. As one of the "Sons of thunder" (Mk 3:17), John was a young man zealous for the work and honor of his Lord (9:38–41; Lk 9:51–54).

An unnamed disciple of Jesus, known as "one of them, the disciple whom Jesus loved," occurs only in John's gospel (13:23; 19:26–27;

  · [16]Raymond E. Brown, *The Gospel According to John (xii–xxi)*, AB 29A (Garden City, N.Y.: Doubleday, 1970), 906; Leon Morris, *The Gospel According to John*, NICNT (Grand Rapids: Eerdmans, 1971), 810–11; Carson, "Matthew," 583. Others argue against this relationship; e.g., Rudolph Schnackenburg, *The Gospel According to St. John*, 3 vols. (New York: Crossroad, 1990), 3:276–77.

  [17]Cf. Morris, *Gospel According to John*, 155.

20:2; 21:7, 20; 21:4 [possibly 1:40; 18:15; 19:35]) and is also said to be connected with the authorship of the fourth gospel (Jn 21:20–24). Proposals for the identity of the beloved disciple include: (1) he was not a real person but a symbolic figure; (2) Lazarus; (3) John Mark; (4) an unknown Jerusalem disciple of Jesus connected with the high priest; (5) the apostle John, the son of Zebedee; and (6) disciples of the apostle John. Notwithstanding vigorous scholarly support for the competing proposals, the internal evidence (when considering those disciples particularly close to Jesus at the scenes mentioned) plus the external evidence of statements of early church fathers such as Irenaeus (*Heresies* 3.1.1) and Polycrates (cited in Eusebius, *History* E.3.31.3, also V.24.2f.) weigh most heavily in favor of the apostle John, the son of Zebedee, to be the "beloved disciple."[18]

"The beloved disciple" is the only disciple recorded to have witnessed the Crucifixion. After the Crucifixion he took Jesus' mother into his own home (Jn 19:25–27). He was the first to see the empty tomb and was one of the early leaders of the church, one of those recognized by Paul as a "pillar of the church" (Gal 2:9). After the Jerusalem Council there is no more word of John, but church tradition (especially through Irenaeus) indicates that he was an overseer of the church at Ephesus and the surrounding area. He was exiled to the island of Patmos during the last decade of the first century, coinciding with the persecution of Emperor Domitian. Tradition says that John was the only one of the Twelve to escape martyrdom, living on till nearly the close of the first century.

The fiery John, the disciple whom Jesus loved, was greatly touched by Jesus' love. One of the early church fathers, Jerome, tells a famous story of "blessed John the evangelist," in extreme old age at Ephesus. He used to be carried into the congregation in the arms of his disciples and was unable to say anything except, "Little children, love one another." At last, weary of always hearing him speak these same words they asked, "Master, why do you always say this?" "Because," he replied, "it is the Lord's command, and if this only is done, it is enough."[19]

---

[18]Barrett accepts John as the beloved disciple but has questions as to whether or not he is the author of the gospel; C. K. Barrett, *The Gospel According to St. John: An Introduction with Commentary and Notes on the Greek Text*, 2d ed. (Philadelphia: Westminster, 1978), 100–105. Brown, *John* [*AB*, vol. 29] holds to John as the Beloved Disciple (p. XCVIII), but with later work on the composition of the gospel by disciples of John.

[19]From Jerome's commentary on Gal 6:10, longer version, chap. 6; cited by John R. W. Stott, *The Epistles of John: An Introduction and Commentary, TNTC* (Grand Rapids: Eerdmans, 1964), 49.

Philip

Philip, like Peter, Andrew, James, and John, was from Bethsaida, the fishing village on the north shore of the sea of Galilee (Jn 1:43–44). Philip also may have been a disciple of John the Baptist before Jesus called him. Philip and Andrew often occur together in the listings of the Twelve (Mk 3:18; Ac 1:13—the only two Greek names). In the rare incidents in which they are mentioned by name (Jn 6:8; 12:21–22), we may find a hint that they shared a relationship that probably began in their hometown.

Philip always occurs fifth in the listings of the Twelve, at the head of the second group of four. The synoptics mention him only in the listings, but John's gospel recounts four incidents involving Philip that reveal that he had a clear understanding of Old Testament expectations concerning the Messiah and that he had a missionary heart. Right after he was called to follow Jesus, he brought Nathaniel to Jesus (Jn 1:43–46). Later, when some Greeks went to worship at Jerusalem, they came to Philip with a request. "'Sir,' they said, 'we would like to see Jesus.' Philip went to tell Andrew; Andrew and Philip in turn told Jesus" (12:20–22).

Yet Philip also exhibited defective spiritual insight. He could see only the hopelessness of human resources for feeding the five thousand (Jn 6:5–7). At the Last Supper, when Jesus was giving further insight about his relationship with the Father, Philip said, "Lord, show us the Father and that will be enough for us." Jesus answered: "Don't you know me, Philip, even after I have been among you such a long time? Anyone who has seen me has seen the Father. How can you say, 'Show us the Father'? Don't you believe that I am in the Father, and that the Father is in me?" (Jn 14:8–10).

While later church tradition tended to confuse Philip the apostle with Philip the evangelist (Ac 6:5), Eusebius quotes Polycrates and Papias, second-century bishops, referring to Philip as "one of the twelve apostles," who ministered in Asia Minor and was buried with his two aged virgin daughters in Hierapolis.[20]

Bartholomew

Bartholomew appears in all four lists of the twelve disciples, but he is otherwise unmentioned in the New Testament. Bartholomew is quite likely an Aramaic patronymic [*Bar-Talmai*] for "son of Thola-mi" (cf. LXX Jos 15:14) or "son of Tholomaeus" (cf. Josephus, *Antiq.* 20.5[1.1]), a name found in several forms in the Septuagint and Josephus. From the ninth century onward, Bartholomew generally

---

[20]Eusebius, *History* 3:31; 5:24.

has been identified with Nathanael. This is based on the conjecture that Nathanael is a surname of Bartholomew, so that his full name would have been Nathanael Bar-Tholami (cf. Simon Bar-Jonah). Several factors point in this direction. (1) Since the Synoptic Gospels never mention Nathanael, while John never mentions Bartholomew, the juxtaposition of the names Philip and Bartholomew in the synoptic lists of the Twelve (not in the list in Acts) suggests the close relationship between the two depicted in John 1:43–51. Since study of the apostolic lists indicates pairing and grouping into fours, this suggests that Bartholomew and Philip were companions in the second group headed by Philip. (2) John's gospel treats Nathanael as an apostle. All of the companions of Nathanael are apostles (Jn 1:35–51) and Nathanael appears as a member of a group of apostles (21:1–2). Christ's promise to Nathanael that he would be a witness to the central role of the Son of Man in God's revelation to people, suggests an apostolic function (1:50–51). (3) Since Bartholomew is quite likely a patronymic, its bearer would be expected to have another name as well.

Arguments have been raised against each of the above factors. (1) The juxtaposition of Philip and Bartholomew in the synoptic lists may be fortuitous, because in the Acts list they are not together. (2) Since there is no mention of Nathanael during Jesus' ministry, his interaction with Jesus in John 1:43–51 does not necessarily imply a formal call to apostleship. (3) The name Bartholomew may stand by itself in the apostolic lists as a proper name. It is not necessarily a patronymic. The patronymic is normally expressed in the lists by the Greek genitive, not by the Aramaic *bar*.

If the identification of Bartholomew with Nathanael is correct, Philip brought Bartholomew (Nathanael), a native of Cana of Galilee (Jn 21:2), to acknowledge Jesus as the Messiah (1:45–46). The description of his encounter with Jesus is found in John 1:47–51. A true Israelite, without guile, Nathanael gave a profound declaration of the messianic identity of Jesus. Jesus, in turn, stated that Nathanael would see even greater demonstrations of messianism. If the identification of Bartholomew with Nathanael is incorrect, then we have no other New Testament information about Bartholomew than the four lists. Since the identification of Bartholomew with Nathanael is not conclusive, to assume it without question is to go beyond the evidence. Certainty is unattainable with the present evidence, but to reject categorically the identification is likewise unwarranted.

Traditional stories about Bartholomew abound, but few appear to be trustworthy. According to the "Genealogies of the Twelve Apostles," Bartholomew was of the house of Naphtali, and his name was formerly John but Jesus changed it because of John the son of

Zebedee, the beloved. Eusebius (*History* 5.10.3) reports that Bartholomew preached the Gospel in India and left behind the gospel of Matthew "in the actual Hebrew characters." Traditions also claim that Bartholomew ministered in Armenia, Phrygia, Lycaonia, Mesopotamia, and Persia. Several traditions are also associated with his death. One tradition states that Bartholomew brought the Gospel to India and to Greater Armenia, where he was flayed alive and beheaded. The "Martyrdom of St. Bartholomew" states that he was placed in a sack and cast into the sea.

A few apocryphal works are also traditionally associated with Bartholomew. Jerome, in the preface to his commentary on Matthew, mentions a "Gospel of Bartholomew." Apart from its condemnation by the Decretum Gelasianum we know little about this work. A later work, "The Questions of Bartholomew," extant in five recensions, may be based in part on this earlier work. A Coptic "Book of the Resurrection of Christ by Bartholomew the Apostle" is extant in several fragments. Authentic association of these works with the apostle Bartholomew is highly doubtful.

The Bartholomew of the New Testament is shrouded in the silence of history. His abiding fame resides in his inclusion in the four apostolic listings of Jesus' closest associates.[21]

Thomas

Thomas occurs in the second group of disciples in the listings of the Twelve. "Thomas" is most likely a title or nickname, since it is Aramaic for "twin" (*téômā*) and John calls him "Thomas (called Didymus)" three times (11:16; 20:24; 21:2), Didymus being the Greek word for twin. No conclusive evidence exists for the identity of his twin.

Personal accounts of Thomas' activities appear only in John's gospel (11:16; 14:5; 20:24–29; 21:2). While he is known popularly as "Doubting Thomas" because of his doubt concerning Jesus' resurrection (20:25) and his spiritual imperception of Jesus' destiny (14:5), Thomas is otherwise portrayed in the Gospels as a strong figure. His courage stands out when he urges the other disciples to travel with Jesus to Judea so that they might die with him (11:16), his faithfulness is revealed when he gathers with some of the other disciples in Galilee after the Resurrection (21:2), and his confession of Jesus as Lord and God (20:28) stands as one of the most profound declarations of Jesus' deity in all of Scripture.

---

[21]Michael J. Wilkins, "Bartholomew," *The Anchor Bible Dictionary*, ed. David Noel Freedman, 5 vols. (Garden City, N.Y.: Doubleday, forthcoming).

Church tradition claims that Thomas traveled to the east as a missionary in Parthia and possibly even as far as India.[22] The apocryphal *Acts of Thomas* says that he experienced many trials in India and was finally martyred and buried by his converts. This account appears to be speculative however, because, according to Clement of Alexandria, Thomas died a natural death.[23] Thomas is a favorite figure for later legendary speculation, but these writings are not at all reliable.

Matthew

The lists of the Twelve each place Matthew in the second group of four. The list in Matthew's gospel calls him "Matthew the tax collector," which harks back to the calling of Matthew the tax collector in 9:9. When recounting the call of the tax collector, Mark and Luke refer to him as Levi. Much speculation surrounds the reason for the variation, but most scholars suggest that this tax collector had two names, Matthew Levi, either from birth or from the time of his conversion.[24] The name Levi may be an indication that he was from the tribe of Levi and therefore was familiar with Levitical practices.[25] Mark's record of the calling refers to him as "son of Alphaeus" (Mk 2:14), which some have understood to mean that he was the brother of the apostle "James son of Alphaeus" (cf. 3:18). But since the other pairs of brothers are specified to be brothers and are linked as such, it is unlikely that Matthew Levi and James were brothers.

Matthew Levi was called to follow Jesus while he was sitting in the tax collector's booth. This booth was probably located on one of the main trade highways near Capernaum, collecting tolls for Herod Antipas from the commercial traffic traveling through this area. Matthew immediately followed Jesus and arranged a banquet for Jesus at his home, to which he invited a large crowd of tax collectors

[22]Eusebius, *History* 3:1.1.

[23]Cf. Hennecke and Schneemelcher, *New Testament Apocrypha*, 2:59ff.; 798ff.

[24]E.g., Carson leans toward it being a double name from birth since he does not see any evidence for "Matthew" being a Christian name ("Matthew," 224), while Hagner suggests that the name Matthew was given to Levi after his conversion (Donald Hagner, "Matthew," *ISBE*, rev., 4:280). Some scholars have attempted to show that Levi was not one of the Twelve and therefore different from Matthew, but this is unwarranted speculation since the circumstances of the calling are the same in Matthew and Mark-Luke. For a treatment of the evidence equating Matthew and Levi as one person see R. T. France, *Matthew: Evangelist and Teacher* (Exeter/Grand Rapids: Paternoster/Zondervan, 1989), 66–70.

[25]W. F. Albright and C. S. Mann, *Matthew*, AB 26 (Garden City, N.Y.: Doubleday, 1971), 177–78, 183–84.

and sinners (Lk 5:29–30). Since tax collectors generally were fairly wealthy and were despised by the local populace (cf. Zacchaeus, 19:1–10), Matthew's calling and response were completely out of the ordinary and required nothing short of a miraculous turn-around in this tax collector's life.

Little else is known of Matthew Levi except for the widely attested tradition from the second century on that he was the author of the gospel that now bears his name. As a tax collector he would have been trained in secular scribal techniques, and as a Galilean Jewish Christian he would have been able to interpret the life of Jesus from the perspective of the Old Testament expectations.[26] Eusebius said that Matthew first preached to "Hebrews" and then to "others," including places such as Persia, Parthia, and Syria.[27] The traditions are mixed regarding Matthew's death, with some saying that he died a martyr's death and others saying that he died a natural death.

James (Son of Alphaeus)

James, the son of Alphaeus,[28] is always listed ninth, the head of the third group of disciples. Apart from the inclusion of his name in the four New Testament lists, he is otherwise unmentioned, although he is usually identified with "James the younger," the son of Mary and the brother of Joses (Mk 15:40; cf. Mt 27:56). If so, the designation "younger or less" (Gk. *ho mikros*) distinguishes him from the James the brother of Jesus and James the son of Zebedee as either younger in age, smaller in stature, or less renowned. His mother, Mary, would have been in attendance at the Crucifixion and at the discovery of the empty tomb (Mt 27:56; Mk 15:40; 16:1; Lk 24:10).[29]

Later church tradition says that James was from the house of Gad

---

[26]Cf. R. T. France, *Matthew: Evangelist and Teacher* (Grand Rapids: Zondervan, 1989), 70–74.

[27]Eusebius, *History* 3:24.6.

[28]As mentioned above when discussing the apostle Matthew, although Mark refers to Levi as the "son of Alphaeus" (Mk 2:14), it is unlikely that Matthew-Levi and James were brothers, especially since this James likely has another brother mentioned, Joses, but not Matthew.

[29]Some attempt to equate "Mary the wife of Clopas" (Jn 19:25) with "Mary the mother of James and Joses" (Mt 27:56; Mk 15:40), but then comes the additional difficulty of either arguing that Alphaeus is an alternative form of Clopas or suggesting that James' father had two names, Alphaeus and Clopas. Such a suggestion, although with difficulties, would more easily harmonize the lists of women at the crucifixion in Matthew, Mark, and John, than to suggest that Mary the mother of James and Joses is actually the mother of Jesus (e.g., Carson, "Matthew," 583). Reference to Jesus' mother as "the other Mary" (Mt 27:61; 28:1) seems highly unlikely.

and was stoned by the Jews for preaching Christ. Legend places his burial by the sanctuary in Jerusalem.

Thaddaeus/Judas of James

Thaddaeus (some texts have Lebbaeus or conflations[30]) is mentioned in the third group of disciples by Matthew (10:3) and Mark (3:18), while Luke refers to "Judas son of James" (lit. Judas of James) in his two lists (Lk 6:16; Ac 1:13). The uniformity of the rest of the names from list to list assures us that the Evangelists were quite familiar with the makeup of the Twelve, hence these names appear to refer to the same person. Judas is probably the given name and Thaddaeus is a nickname or place name.[31] The only incident about this person recorded in the New Testament is during Christ's message to the disciples after the Last Supper, when "Judas (not Judas Iscariot) said, 'But, Lord, why do you intend to show yourself to us and not to the world?'" (Jn 14:22).

Many apocryphal stories recount later activities of Judas-Thaddaeus, but the most that can be reliably conjectured is that he ministered in the area of Mesopotamia during the early days of the church era.[32]

Simon the Zealot

This other Simon among the Twelve was known as Simon the Cananaean (Mt 10:4; Mk 3:18 NRSV) or Simon the Zealot (Lk 6:15; Ac 1:13). Cananaean is not to be confused with the place name of a person from Canaan (Canaanite; cf. Mt 15:22) or Cana, but rather is a Greek transliteration of the Aramaic word for "zeal" or "zealot" (*quan'ānā'*). Hence, the Greek word that Luke uses (*zēlōtēs*) is an equivalent of the Aramaic transliteration in Matthew and Luke.[33] The expression indicates that this Simon was a zealous nationalist prior to

[30]Metzger recounts the difficulty of the textual variants, but the agreement of early representatives of Alexandrian, Western Caesarean, and Egyptian witnesses suggests that Thaddaeus (θαδδαῖος) was the original reading; cf. Bruce M. Metzger, *A Textual Commentary on the Greek New Testament*, UBS, 3d ed. (New York: United Bible Societies, 1971), 26.

[31]Carson suggests that Thaddaeus is a nickname, roughly meaning "beloved" (Carson, "Matthew," 239), while Mann suggests that an Aramaic etymology indicates a place name (C. S. Mann, *Mark*, AB 27 [Garden City, N.Y.: Doubleday, 1986], 250). Several suggest that after the name Judas became stigmatized because of Judas Iscariot, Judas the son of James changed his name to Thaddaeus; e.g., Robert H. Mounce, *Matthew*, A Good News Commentary (San Francisco: Harper & Row, 1985), 90.

[32]Cf. Eusebius, *History* 1.13; 2.1.6–8.

[33]Guelich, *Mark*, 163; Carson, "Matthew," 239.

his call to follow Jesus and may indicate some of his on-going temperament. Political-religious revolutionary activity consistently characterized the Jewish populaces' attitude toward Roman oppression and the Jewish religious establishment's compromise. Later the term *zealot* was used to designate the military-political-religious group that was active in guerilla-type warfare in the period leading up to the A.D. 70 destruction of Jerusalem.[34]

Judas Iscariot

Judas Iscariot always occurs last in the listings of the Twelve, and a description is attached to his name that brands him with an infamous stigma as the one who betrayed Jesus (Mt 10:4; Mk 3:19; Lk 6:16; cf. Jn 18:2, 5). He is omitted from the list in Acts. The meaning of the term *Iscariot* is uncertain.[35] Some have suggested that the term derives from the Semitic form of *sicarios*, "a daggar-bearer, bandit, assassin" (cf. Ac 21:38), which would identify Judas as a radical nationalist, similar to Simon the zealot.[36] However, since the Sicarii movement did not come into prominence until the A.D. 50s, it is doubtful that the term would be used of Judas this early.[37] Others suggest that Iscariot is derived from the Aramaic term for "liar," indicating that Judas was "a man of the lie," a betrayer. However, this would cause a redundancy in the descriptions. Others have suggested that the term is a nickname derived from the Hebrew word for "a leather bag," since Judas might have carried the treasury in such a pouch. However, the word for *treasurer* used in the New Testament to designate Judas's responsibility is not the equivalent Greek term.[38] The most widely held view is that "Iscariot" identifies Judas's place of origin, especially since Judas's father is described as "Simon Iscariot" (Jn 6:71; 13:2, 26). This place may be either Kerioth in Moab (cf. Jer 48:24, 41; Am 2:2), Kerioth-Hezron or Hazor located fifteen kilometers south of Hebron in southern Judah (Jos 15:25), or Kartan in Galilee (Jos 21:32), but the specific identity of this place of origin is uncertain.

Nothing firm is known of Judas's early life, but if he came from

---

[34]Cf. Richard A. Horsley and John S. Hanson, *Bandits, Prophets, and Messiahs: Popular Movements at the Time of Jesus* (Minneapolis: Winston, 1985), 190–243.

[35]Besides the listings, see the variant readings and spellings in Jn 6:71; 12:4; 13:2, 26; 14:22.

[36]E.g., Martin Hengel, *The Zealots*, (Edinburgh/Philadelphia: T. & T. Clark/Fortress, 1988), 49–57.

[37]See Horsley and Hanson, *Bandits, Prophets, and Messiahs*, 200–216.

[38]The expression used is *to glōssokomon echōn*. Cf. Leon Morris, *The Gospel According to John*, NICNT (Grand Rapids: Eerdmans, 1971), 578, n. 21.

Kerioth near Hebron, he may have been the only Judean among the Twelve. We do know that Judas was the treasurer for the apostolic band (Jn 12:4–6; 13:29). He is mentioned for the first time in the choosing of the Twelve (Mk 3:19; Lk 6:16), but nothing is said of him in particular until the episode in the last week of Jesus' earthly life at Bethany when Mary anointed Jesus with a vial of expensive ointment. Although some of the other disciples were indignant at the waste of money that could have been given to the poor (cf. Mt 26:8–9; Mk 14:4–5), John alone focuses the blame upon Judas, while including the others in his rebuke (12:4–6; "you have," *echete*, in v. 8 is plural). John points out that Judas's culpability was due to his regular thievery of the apostolic funds (v. 6).

The event for which Judas is known in biblical and historical infamy is his betrayal of Jesus.[39] He was under the direction of Satan (Lk 22:3; Jn 13:2), and his greed, which had prompted him to steal (Jn 12:4–6), may have motivated him to betray Jesus for the paltry sum of thirty pieces of silver, which may have been only a partial payment of the agreed-upon amount (Mt 26:14–16; Mk 14:10–11; Lk 22:3–6). Although Jesus anticipated the betrayal (Jn 6:71; 12:4) and Luke tells of previous plans (Lk 22:3–6), the treacherous act apparently came at the Last Supper as a surprise to all except Jesus (Mt 26:20ff.; Mk 14:17ff.). Securing a band of soldiers from the chief priests and Pharisees (Jn 18:3), Judas led them to where Jesus was alone with the disciples in the Garden of Gethsemane, away from the crowds, and kissed Jesus to identify him for the soldiers (Mt 26:47–56; Mk 14:43–52; Lk 22:47–53; Jn 18:2–12).

When Jesus was officially condemned to death, Judas was filled with remorse and returned the pieces of silver to the priests. Then Judas went and committed suicide (cf. Mt 27:3–10; Ac 1:18–19). Later the priests used the blood money to purchase a burial plot for strangers. After Jesus' ascension Judas was replaced in the circle of the Twelve by Matthias, about whom nothing else is known (Ac 1:26).

Judas must have been a complex individual. Since he was the treasurer for the apostolic band, we may assume that he displayed some positive characteristics that were recognizable by the others, since this office was not usually given to one who was known to be greedy and irresponsible. It was a respected position and probably indicates the degree of esteem in which the Twelve held him.[40]

However, the love of money has contributed to the downfall of more than one person, and Judas appears to have fallen victim to it.

[39]Mt 10:4; 26:25; 27:3; Mk 3:19; Lk 6:15–16; Jn 6:71; 12:4; 13:2; 18:2, 5.
[40]Morris, *John*, 578.

John tells us that Judas's objection to Mary's anointing of Jesus with the costly ointment was not because of his concern for the poor, as Judas claimed, but was instead motivated by greed. Judas had become a thief, pilfering from the treasury funds (Jn 12:6). "Thus to covetousness there is added the trait of deceit."[41]

This leads to the complexity behind Judas's betrayal of Jesus. Why did Judas betray his Master, whom he had faithfully followed and served? Matthew and Mark, in their narrative arrangements, speak of Judas as going away to make arrangements with the chief priests for Jesus' betrayal immediately after the anointing incident. Many things have been suggested as motivating forces behind Judas's betrayal— avarice and love of money; jealousy of the other disciples; disillusionment at the inevitable outcome of the Master's ministry; an enthusiastic intention to force Christ's hand and make him declare himself as Messiah; a bitter, revengeful spirit that arose when his worldly hopes for a place of prominence in the messianic kingdom were crushed. Perhaps they all have some place in the complexity of such an odious betrayal, but underlying all attempts to understand Judas's motivation must be a clear recognition of Judas's spiritual state. While the predetermined plan of God included Judas's betrayal (Jn 6:64, 70–71), what is clear is the place of his own spiritual responsibility for his actions. Jesus' call of Judas to be a disciple and apostle was sincere, and all appearances indicated that Judas had responded sincerely. Yet, as with others who had responded to that call by turning and walking away, Judas never truly believed (v. 64). Inwardly he was always a part of the Devil's corp (v. 70), while on the surface he followed Jesus. It was finally at the end that his true inner nature was revealed as a "son of perdition" (17:12 NASB), a tool of Satan (13:2, 27–30) whose eternal verdict is solemnly declared in Acts 1:25: "This apostolic ministry, which Judas left to go where he belongs." Judas's spiritual state is the true underlying motivation for the betrayal; he who was not truly with Jesus was indeed against him. Ralph Martin vividly declares:

Judas was never really Christ's man. He fell from apostleship, but never (so far as we can tell) had a genuine relationship to the Lord Jesus. So he remained "the son of perdition" who was lost because he was never "saved." His highest title for Christ was "Rabbi" (Mt 26:25), never "Lord." He lives on the stage of Scripture as an awful warning to the uncommitted follower of Jesus who is in his company but does not share his spirit (cf. Ro 8:9b); he leaves the Gospel story "a doomed and

<hr/>

[41]Ralph P. Martin, "Judas Iscariot," *The Illustrated Bible Dictionary*, ed. J. D. Douglas and N. Hillyer, 3 vols. (Leicester/Wheaton: Inter-Varsity/Tyndale House, 1980), 2:830.

damned man" because he chose it so, and God confirmed him in that dreadful choice.[42]

IMPLICATIONS

The Twelve display a remarkable personal diversity and intricacy. Jesus chose those who were friends, business partners, and even those who, in their normal daily circumstances, would have been foes. Although Matthew, as a tax collector, would have been at the opposite end of the political spectrum from Simon, Jesus chose both to be included among his closest associates.[43] Such was the complexity of Jesus' mission, and the measure of his grace, acceptance, and love. Those years spent with Jesus, separated from the normal activities of life, were a crucial time in which they were molded to be like the Master so that they could could carry out his mission of making disciples of all the nations. They were in a bubble of sorts, but that period of time was crucial for their mission.

To talk depreciatingly about a bubble, for many of us in a variety of Christian settings, may be to misunderstand God's purposes. I tell my students:

> You have been called to this school to receive training that is intended to equip you for a life of "combat." Yes, some of you may have come for the wrong reasons: some to escape from life, some just for a good time. And yes, some of us who are your professors can isolate ourselves away here and not truly prepare you for reality. But the fact of the matter is that you need this time here, in relative peace and safety, in order to refine the skills you will need for the rest of your lives. The academic preparation, the spiritual nurture, the maturing process—physiological, emotional, and relational—that you gain will all be used some day (sooner than you think!) to enable you to succeed in the battle out there.

That is why I do not talk about a "Biola Bubble." Rather, I tell my students that we should call it "Biola Bootcamp"! That always gets a chuckle from them, but they immediately begin to understand the parallels. The faculty and the staff are there to provide the kind of environment in which we can equip them most effectively for the real-life battles to be found in the world. They need to learn their skills well because once they go out it is much more difficult to do on-the-job training.

We should also not overlook the times for "live-fire" exercises in which people can get out of the safe environment so that they can test their skills. When I was a drill sergeant in the army I had to teach the

---

[42]Martin, "Judas Iscariot," 2:831.
[43]Cf. Witherington, *Christology of Jesus*, 96–101.

trainees how to "low crawl." The technique is not that difficult, but doing it for long distances is very strenuous. They would try to cheat by getting up on their hands and knees. In order to teach them the necessity for doing it the right way, we would take the trainees out to a firing range at night. There we set up a machine gun firing live ammunition about three feet off the ground. Tracer rounds were included so they could see how low the rounds were to the ground. Then we had all of the trainees "low crawl" across the range under the live rounds. Let me assure you, there was no cheating. They would get so low that they almost went under ground! We should consider the times when we go out of the bubble as live-fire exercises—part-time off-campus jobs, off-campus ministries, short-term missions, and so on. I used to take students out on evangelism projects or to visit cult groups in order for them to try out their skills in real-life settings!

You may not be in an academic setting right now, but we all have our own form of bubble that can be a haven for a while—the weekend church camp; the week-long family camp; the training seminar; the women's, men's, or couple's retreat. I also believe that we should look at the church in this way. The church is there to provide recovery from life in the world, fellowship with other believers, and training for the next foray out into the world. It is possible to live for church to the point where we are trying to escape from the world, but we should see it for one of the most important places of refuge in our lives. Another major bubble in our lives should be our families. I think of my own home as the one sure place of peace and refuge in a world of turmoil. Sometimes I take it too far and exclude others because I enjoy being with my family so much. However, the family, centered on Christ, is a place where Jesus can produce some of the most effective disciples.

We have much to learn from the Twelve and the way our Lord trained them for their life in the world. All of us who are disciples of Jesus Christ are also remarkably diverse, and the relationships that are produced are intricate. We should be encouraged by what the Lord did with their lives. Which of the Twelve do you relate to the most easily? Why? Which one can be an encouragement of what the Lord desires to do in your life? That is where the bubbles come in as well as our individual bubble where we meet with him daily. We should thank God for the various bubbles in our lives. Occasionally the training may seem artificial, but thank God for this time. You may never again have the kind of opportunity you now have to equip yourselves. Do not waste a minute of the opportunity! Soon you may be asked to lead the way for yourself and others, and they are going to rely on your "map-reading" abilities. The way you spend your time will determine whether there will be casualties or victory!

Following up:

1. Which of the Twelve do you relate to the most easily? Why? If Jesus were to pair you up with one of the Twelve as part of sending you out two by two to preach the gospel, who would you have liked most to be paired up with? Who least? Why?
2. Jesus chose a diverse group to form the Twelve. What would have been the difficulties of them working together as a group of leaders? What does it teach us?
3. What kind of leadership example do the Twelve show you?
4. Why do you think the New Testament authors record so little of the activity of most of the Twelve?

PART IV

GOSPEL PORTRAITS
OF DISCIPLESHIP

Students of the four Gospels have long recognized that each presents the record of Jesus' life from a different perspective. Ask most any adult Bible class what portraits of Jesus are found in Matthew, Mark, Luke, and John, respectively, and they will readily indicate that Matthew presents Jesus as the "King," Mark presents him as "Servant," Luke as "True Man," and John as "True God." While variation exists among opinions of Bible scholars as to the exact theological portrait drawn, most would agree that the gospel writers have presented Jesus from differing theological perspectives, depending upon the individual evangelist's background, the needs of the audience, and the leading of the Holy Spirit.

If each gospel has a different perspective about Jesus, we might expect to find different perspectives about his closest companions, the disciples. Such is indeed the case. Each gospel records a unique perspective of Jesus' disciples. Each focuses on distinctive features that help us understand Jesus' purpose in calling and training his disciples.[1]

The scene depicting disciples following Jesus around during his earthly ministry dominates the Gospel panorama. That vision of discipleship demands our attention on a historical as well as personal level. Discipleship can be understood narrowly as a technical discussion of the historical master-disciple relationship. It can also be understood in a broader way as Christian experience and what such a way of life requires, implies, and entails.[2] To understand fully the Gospel portrait of discipleship, one must keep in view (1) the moment within the early life of Jesus in which the challenge of discipleship is given to and lived out by the disciples, and (2) the moment within the church's life when the would-be disciple is tested.[3]

The purpose here is to expose the portraits of the disciples of Jesus as they are found in the four individual gospel records.[4] The

---

[1]Paul D. Hanson, *The People Called: The Growth of Community in the Bible* (San Francisco: Harper & Row, 1986), 430–38.

[2]Fernando F. Segovia, "Introduction: Call and Discipleship—Toward a Re-examination of the Shape and Character of Christian Existence in the New Testament," in *Discipleship in the New Testament*, ed. Fernando F. Segovia (Philadelphia: Fortress, 1985), 2. See also Ernest Best, *Disciples and Discipleship: Studies in the Gospel According to Mark* (Edinburgh: T. & T. Clark), 1–2.

[3]John J. Vincent, "Discipleship and Synoptic Studies," *ThZ* 16 (1960): 464.

[4]The development of this section was helped by research I carried out for a gospel reference volume. See Michael J. Wilkins, "Discipleship," *Dictionary of*

preceding section gave us the broadest angle of Jesus' form of discipleship as seen from the combination of the four Evangelists' perspectives of the Jesus movement (chap. 6), of what it meant to become like Jesus (chap. 7), and of the Twelve (chap. 8). While there will be some overlap from the themes discussed there, our intention in this section is to accentuate the uniqueness of each evangelist's perspective of discipleship. We will also find some overlap from one gospel writer's discussion of discipleship to another. Each evangelist records discipleship material that is common to each. Much of that overlap material was also covered in the preceding section.

In this section we will focus on one particular theme from each gospel that is accentuated more in that gospel account than in any of the others. That theme will provide a convenient way of spotlighting the evangelist's perspective of Jesus' disciples. We will highlight that perspective of each evangelist without attempting an exhaustive analysis. Since entire books have been written about each gospel's portrait of discipleship, we will direct the reader to the resources. Here we will draw only brief sketches.

Each of the Gospels records a unique perspective of Jesus' disciples. Each focuses on distinctive features that help us understand Jesus' form of discipleship. "We have in the four canonical Gospels portraits of Jesus with lines, shadows, colors, and *chiaroscuro* that differ. The Marcan Jesus acts differently from the Lukan Jesus; the Matthean Jesus speaks differently from the Johannine Jesus. Correspondingly, the role of discipleship differs in the four Gospels."[5] Combined, the sketches of the disciples in each gospel give us a well-rounded illustration of what Jesus intended discipleship to mean. As we look at the perspectives of the individual Evangelists, we should try to enter into the thinking and vision of each gospel writer. To do so will provide a challenge for our own lives and will allow us to see Jesus himself more clearly!

Jesus and the Gospels, Joel Green and Scot McKnight, eds., I. Howard Marshall, consulting ed. (Downers Grove, Ill.: InterVarsity Press, 1992).

[5]Joseph A. Fitzmyer, *Luke the Theologian: Aspects of His Teaching* (New York: Paulist, 1989), 118.

9

Matthew: Examples with a Commission

Getting focused:

1. Do you have any "heroes"? Who have they been? What makes a person a hero in your eyes? Is it helpful to have heroes? Why or why not?
2. In what ways are the disciples of Jesus examples of Christian living for us in the present day?
3. Are all disciples called to fulfill the Great Commission of Matthew 28:16–20? Why or why not?
4. Of whom are we called to "make disciples"? What is the process? When is it finished?

Heroes. I grew up with heroes like Lou Gehrig, General Dwight D. Eisenhower, Helen Keller, Jackie Robinson, President Teddy Roosevelt, Davey Crockett, Annie Oakley, and one of my special heroes, Abraham Lincoln. Through books and movies and tales from my story-telling grandfather (who was also one of my childhood heroes!), these men and women became daily heroes to a very impressionable young boy. I knew many of their stories by heart. These were men and women who were larger than life because of their great accomplishments or because of the remarkable legends that developed about them. I stood in awe of their exploits that cast them into the public eye. Here were people I could look up to! Yet, at the same time, these men and women were not that much different from me. I read biographies avidly, which brought to light their common side, their human side, their unfavorable side. Seeing that side made my heroes seem realistic, not that much different from me.

These heroes did wonderful things for me. Stories of their lives allowed me to dream. I experienced with them those escapades and

174

challenges that made them into heroes. I learned to understand that life was bigger than my little neighborhood and my day-to-day activities. Grand causes and great adventures await the dauntless! But perhaps even more importantly, these heroes provided me with an example of how I could make something of my life if I would only put my mind to it. I was challenged by women and men who rose above adversities, above the unfairness of life, and who made their lives count for something worthwhile. Because I knew that these heroes were not perfect, and because I saw the tragic end to some of their lives, I saw how heroes are susceptible to failure. I learned from both their strengths and their weaknesses.

Heroes are realistic people who have responded to the circumstances of life in such a way that they have given single-minded attention to accomplishing an arduous task with courage and nobility. Matthew presents us with those kinds of heroes in his account of the disciples. But the distance between the lives of the disciples and the lives of the people of the modern church often seems much further than the nearly two thousand years that have transpired. The distance is often measured qualitatively by people of the church when they perceive a difference between the kind of lives that the disciples of Jesus lived and the kind of lives that many people of the church live. That qualitative difference has influenced some modern students of the Gospels to posit a two-class or two-tiered system within the followers of Jesus. On the first level are ordinary believers, those who have exercised faith in Jesus. On the second level are those who have been called to be Jesus' disciples. This two-tiered understanding is reflected in the writings and ministry of several diverse students of the New Testament. This perspective has had a far-reaching influence upon the church, because if two levels of believers are reflected in the ministry of Jesus, then two levels should be expected in the church today. This kind of teaching declares that the disciples are examples of what only a few specially committed Christians can become.

Instead, Matthew gives us a picture of disciples who are a realistic display for all Christians. In the development of his story, Matthew reveals disciples who display a normal process of growth. In their response to the call to follow Jesus they embark upon a lifelong adventure that requires single-minded devotion to the Master. But they are not ideal. They have weaknesses and failures. They are simply common folk who respond to Jesus' call and who grow into the role planned for them. They are indeed special people, but Matthew does not idealize them. If Matthew intends to idealize anyone, it is Jesus. Jesus is the central figure of Matthew's gospel.[1] Jesus is the Lord. Jesus is Immanuel, "God with us" (1:23). We could say that Jesus is the "ideal hero" of the story. But the disciples form another type of hero for us in Matthew's gospel. The disciples are those typically human persons with weaknesses, with failings, yet with potential, who respond to Jesus' call and go on to be strategic in God's great work of establishing his kingdom. The disciples provide us an example of realistic people who have responded to the circumstances of life in such a way that they have given single-minded attention to accomplishing their task with courage and nobility. We should not put the disciples into a category that idolizes or idealizes them. They are special in the work to which they were called in the foundation of the church, but they are at the same time simply common people much like us. Such is the stuff of which heroes are made. We can learn much from their example.

MATTHEW'S DISTINCTIVE VIEW OF DISCIPLESHIP

Matthew views the disciples of Jesus from alternating perspectives. At times he specifies that the disciples are with Jesus when the parallels do not (9:19), but at other times he excludes them from being with Jesus when the parallels say that they are present (12:15). At times Matthew purposely projects a very positive attitude about the disciples through including the term *disciples* when it is absent in the parallels (v. 49), but at other times he includes the term in such a way that the disciples are singled out for negative associations not specified in the parallels (26:56). Sometimes Matthew omits reference to the disciples sharing guilt with Peter (Mt 16:23), yet on other occasions they are singled out and specified as sharing in his guilt (14:31). At times it appears that Matthew purposely carries forward the traditional association of the disciples with the apostolic title "the twelve" (10:1), but on other occasions he implies a wider

---

[1]Regardless of how much we may focus upon other characters in the Gospels, the Evangelists are primarily writing a Christological story. Matthew is no exception. For recent discussion of Matthew's Christology, see E. P. Blair, *Jesus in the Gospel of Matthew: A Reappraisal of the Distinctive Elements of Matthew's Christology* (Nashville: Abingdon, 1960); Graham Stanton, "The Origin and Purpose of Matthew's Gospel: Matthean Scholarship from 1945–1980," *Aufstieg und Niedergang der Römischen Welt*, 2, 25, 3, ed. H. Temporini and W. Haase (Berlin: Walter de Gruyter, 1985), 1922–25; Jack Dean Kingsbury, "The Figure of Jesus in Matthew's Story: A Literary-Critical Probe," *JSNT* 21 (1984): 1–36; David Hill, "The Figure of Jesus in Matthew's Story: A Response to Professor Kingsbury's Literary-Critical Probe," *JSNT* 21 (1984): 37–52; Jack Dean Kingsbury, "The Figure of Jesus in Matthew's Story: A Rejoinder to David Hill," *JSNT* 25 (1985): 61–81.

circle of disciples (8:21; 27:57). These alternating perspectives give us special insight into Matthew's distinctive view of discipleship.[2]

The Small Group of Disciples Around Jesus

Matthew and Mark refer to only a small group of Jesus' disciples, differently than Luke and John who refer to a great crowd of Jesus' disciples (cf. Lk 6:17; 10:1; Jn 6:60, 66). Albright and Mann suggest that since Jesus can meet with the disciples in a house (cf. Mt 9:10–19, 28; 13:36ff.) and they can all travel together in a single boat (cf. 8:23; 14:22), Matthew emphasizes that only a small group of disciples would have been able to accompany him.[3]

We saw earlier that in the beginning days of the Jesus movement great crowds, including a large number of disciples, followed Jesus around. Matthew is well aware of this large number of disciples. Examination of parallel passages indicates that on several occasions Matthew focuses only on the Twelve when in Luke and even in Mark there are indications of a much larger group of disciples. Either as an eyewitness or as one privy to the same oral tradition as the other synoptics, Matthew surely would have been aware of a larger number of disciples who had followed Jesus in his earthly ministry.[4] However, in his story Matthew consistently has only a small group of disciples around Jesus.

Disciples, the Twelve, and Apostles

This small group of disciples is closely related to the Twelve. Matthew and Mark tend to identify those individuals called "the disciples" with the titles "the Twelve" and "the apostles." Robert Meye contends, "Mark describes Jesus' ministry consistently with

---

[2]In an earlier study, I undertook an extensive analysis of Matthew's use of the term *disciple* in comparison to the other Evangelists' use. See Michael J. Wilkins, *The Concept of Disciple in Matthew's Gospel: As Reflected in the Use of the Term Μαθητής, NovTSup* 59 (Leiden: E. J. Brill, 1988), 126–72.

[3]W.F. Albright and C.S. Mann, *Matthew*, AB 26 (Garden City, N.Y.: Doubleday, 1971), 76.

[4]E.g., in Matthew's account of the Sermon on the Mount, the disciples come away from the crowds (Mt 5:1), but in Luke's account of the Sermon on the Plain we find "a great multitude of his disciples" (Lk 6:17 NASB); in Matthew's account of the Triumphal Entry a "crowd" is spoken of as going before Jesus (Mt 21:9), yet Luke speaks of a "multitude of the disciples" (Lk 19:37 NASB); Matthew speaks of Jesus summoning the twelve disciples who were also called apostles (Mt 10:1, 2), yet in Mark and Luke's account these apostles were chosen from among numerous other disciples (Mk 3:13–19 and Lk 6:13); Matthew tells of Jesus sending out only the Twelve (Mt 10:5), but Luke speaks of Jesus sending out at another time the Seventy (Lk 10:1).

only the Twelve in view as the disciples of Jesus."[5] Matthew also views Jesus' disciples from this perspective.[6] Mark refers to Jesus' disciples simply as "the Twelve" on at least eleven occasions. Matthew uses "the Twelve" eight times to refer to the disciples but never by itself.[7] As an accepted identification in parallel passages, Matthew can use "the disciples" where Mark has "the Twelve" (Mt 13:10; cf. Mk 4:10; Mt 18:1; cf. Mk 9:35), he can give a narrative reference "to his twelve disciples" (11:1), and he can occasionally complete the title "the Twelve" with "disciples" to form the longer title "the twelve disciples" (cf. 10:1; 20:17; 26:20). Interestingly, only Matthew uses this longer title, "the twelve disciples." R. Pesch indicates that even in the replacement of "Levi" (Mk 2:14) with "Matthew" (Mt 9:9; cf. 10:3), Matthew wants to be sure to emphasize a strict equation of the disciples and the Twelve.[8] In addition to this unique use of the title "the Twelve," Mark and Matthew both use the title "apostles" only once (Mt 10:2; Mk 6:30), in each case referring to the Twelve being sent out on their mission in Palestine. Hence, Matthew makes a very close identification of the term *disciple* with the title "the Twelve," which is immediately connected with the term *apostles*.

While Matthew (and Mark) generally identified the term *disciple* with the title "the Twelve," he did not intend to limit the term *disciple* exclusively to the Twelve. Matthew speaks specifically of

---

[5]Robert P. Meye, *Jesus and the Twelve* (Grand Rapids: Eerdmans, 1968), 210; see also 98–140, 228–30. The majority of modern scholarship accepts the thesis that at least from Mk 3:13 on Mark identified the terms *disciple* and *the Twelve* with one another. Cf. Vincent Taylor, *The Gospel According to St. Mark*, 2d ed., reprint (Grand Rapids: Baker, 1981), 229–30; Rudolf Bultmann, *The History of the Synoptic Tradition*, trans. John Marsh, rev. ed. (New York: Harper & Row, 1963), 344–46; Leonhard Goppelt, *Theology of the New Testament*, trans. John E. Alsup (Grand Rapids: Eerdmans, 1981), 1:210. That this is not a consensus is observed in Martin Hengel, *The Charismatic Leader and His Followers*, trans. James Greig (New York: Crossroad, 1981), 81–82, n. 163.

[6]Ulrich Luz, "Die Jünger im Matthäusevangelium," *ZNW* 62 (1971): 142–43. Georg Strecker, *Der Weg der Gerechtigkeit* (Göttingen: Vandenhoeck & Ruprecht, 1962), 191–98, somewhat differently, sees Matthew making a conscious effort to make the identification complete. An English translation has been made of Luz's work. Cf. Ulrich Luz, "The Disciples in the Gospel According to Matthew," trans. Robert Morgan, *The Interpretation of Matthew*, ed. Graham Stanton, *IRT* 3 (London/Philadelphia: SPCK/Fortress, 1983).

[7]J. Keith Elliott, "*Mathētēs* with a Possessive in the New Testament," *ThZ* 35 (1979): 304. The Matthean lack of the bare title οἱ δώδεκα leads Elliott to conclude that the longer title οἱ δώδεκα μαθηταί is the correct textual reading at 20:17 and 26:203. Cf. Wilkins, *Concept of Disciple*, 228, app. B, n. 1, for a discussion of these texts.

[8]R. Pesch, "Levi-Mätthaus (Mc 2:14/Mt 9:9; 10:3). Ein Beitrag zur Lösung eines alten Problems," *ZNW* 59 (1968): 40–56.

disciples other than the Twelve (Mt 8:21).[9] He indicates a wider circle of disciples who were recipients of Jesus' teaching and who obeyed his radical summons to follow him (10:24–42). Matthew also acknowledges through a related verb the existence of a named disciple other than the Twelve, Joseph of Arimathea (27:57). And the women who were in attendance at Jesus' crucifixion are described with discipleship terms.[10] Matthew generally identifies the disciples with the Twelve, but he does not exclude the existence of other disciples. Unless Matthew states otherwise, he refers to the Twelve when he refers to the disciples, but he does not mean to imply that Jesus has no other disciples.[11]

Disciples, Crowds, and Religious Leaders

Three groups—Jesus' disciples, the crowds, and the Jewish leaders—provide a background for Matthew's story of Jesus. The disciples were Jesus' true followers, true believers. The crowd was the basically neutral group that was the object of Jesus' saving ministry of preaching, teaching, and healing; but as a group the crowd did not exercise faith in him. The Jewish leaders were the antagonists, the ones responsible for Jesus' crucifixion.[12]

The disciples were Jesus' intimate companions during his earthly ministry (Mt 9:19; 14:22) and his fellow workers in the ministry of caring for the crowds (9:36–37; 14:13ff.; 15:32ff.). Jesus held the disciples up to the crowds as an example of his true family—that is, those who did the will of the Father (12:49–50). The "crowd" was a basically neutral, though curious, group who were not attached in a serious way to Jesus and who were at various times either positively or negatively oriented toward him.[13] As Jesus preached, taught, and

---

[9]Cf. Jack Dean Kingsbury, "On Following Jesus: The 'Eager' Scribe and the 'Reluctant' Disciple (Matthew 8.18–22)," *NTS* 34 (1988): 57; Ben Witherington III, *The Christology of Jesus* (Minneapolis: Fortress, 1990); 137–40.

[10]Cf. Michael J. Wilkins, "Named and Unnamed Disciples in Matthew: A Literary/Theological Study," *SBLSP* 30 (Atlanta: Scholars, 1991); Benno Przybylski, *Righteousness in Matthew and His World of Thought*, SNTSMS 41 (Cambridge: Cambridge Univ. Press, 1980), 108–10. Signs of disciples other than the Twelve also occur in Mark (cf. Hengel, *Charismatic Leader*, 81–82, n. 163).

[11]As Kingsbury notes, the term "disciples" where it refers to followers of Jesus, "is synonymous with those who are otherwise familiar to us as the Twelve. . . . In those cases where Matthew employs 'disciple' [otherwise], he regularly makes this clear" (Jack Dean Kingsbury, *The Parables of Jesus in Matthew 13: A Study in Redaction-Criticism* [London: SPCK, 1969], 41).

[12]Jack Dean Kingsbury, "The Developing Conflict Between Jesus and the Jewish Leaders in Matthew's Gospel: A Literary-Critical Study," *CBQ* 49 (1987): 57–73.

[13]T. W. Manson, *The Teaching of Jesus*, 2d ed. (Cambridge: Cambridge Univ. Press, 1935), 19.

healed, the crowd followed him around (e.g., 4:25), but they did not exhibit the twin prerequisites of discipleship: cost and commitment. The crowd followed Jesus only in a literal sense, never in the metaphysical sense of accompaniment as one's disciple.[14] The crowd followed him (4:25), appealed for healing (15:29–31), gave acclaim to him (7:28; 21:9, 10), but at times laughed at him (9:23–25), came to arrest him (26:47), became influenced by the chief priests and elders (27:20), and finally became responsible for the blood of Jesus (27:24).

Jesus' objective was to make disciples from among the crowd. As Jesus taught and preached, the sign of faith was when one came out of the crowd to call Jesus "Lord" (cf. Mt 8:18, 21; 17:14, 15).[15] As an individual came out of the crowd, he or she chose either to exercise faith and become a believer or chose not to believe (cf. Mt 19:16–22). Therefore, the crowd is a neutral group, out of which came those who would either become disciples of Jesus or join the religious leaders in opposing him.

The Disciples Understand Jesus' Teaching

More than any other evangelist, Matthew emphasizes that the essence of true discipleship lies in individuals who understand and obey Jesus' teaching. On at least three occasions Matthew says that the disciples "understand" Jesus' teaching (Mt 13:51; 16:12; 17:13), whereas in parallel passages Mark indicates that the disciples do not understand (Mk 6:52; 8:21; 9:10, 32). Matthew's purpose is different from that of Mark. Mark emphasizes how difficult it was for even the disciples to comprehend the magnitude of Jesus' earthly ministry. Matthew agrees, but he goes on to give a further point: when Jesus teaches, true disciples will understand. Typically, Matthew shows how difficult it is to understand all that is transpiring in Jesus' earthly ministry but then goes on to show that after Jesus has finished teaching, the disciples finally understand.

The disciples and the crowds were at opposite ends of the spiritual-understanding spectrum. On the occasion of the great discourse on the parables of the mystery of the kingdom, Jesus first directed parables to the crowd (Mt 13:1ff.). However, the parables revealed the hard-heartedness of the crowd: they could not under-

---

[14]Jack Dean Kingsbury, "The Verb AKOLOUTHEIN ('To Follow') as an Index of Matthew's View of His Community," *JBL* 97 (1978): 61; Albright and Mann, *Matthew*, 77.

[15]Günther Bornkamm, "End-Expectation and Church in Matthew," in *Tradition and Interpretation in Matthew*, ed. Günther Bornkamm, Gerhard Barth, and Heinz Joachim Held, trans. Percy Scott, 1963, reprint (Philadelphia: Westminster, n.d.), 40–41.

stand (vv. 10–17). As a result, Jesus left the crowd to go into the privacy of the house where the disciples became recipients of his teaching (vv. 10, 36). At the end of Jesus' instruction to his disciples, they indicated that they now understood (v. 51). True disciples will understand Jesus' teaching. Jesus implied that knowing the will of God is found as one learns from him and his embodiment of the will of God (9:13; 11:29). The true disciple is the one who is obedient to the will of God (12:49-50), who learns from Jesus' parables (13:51; 24:32), and who is "discipled" by Jesus in the ways of the kingdom (13:52; 27:57). Some scholars take the contrast between the "understanding" of the disciples in Matthew and the "nonunderstanding" in Mark to mean that Matthew has tried to "idealize" the disciples; that he smooths away anything derogatory about them.[16] Although Matthew does not focus on the disciples' failure (e.g., 8:25; 13:16; 14:31), he does tell of their deficient faith (14:31; 16:8, 22–23; 17:20) and presents negative aspects of the disciples (e.g., 26:8, 56).[17] Instead of idealization, the disciples' "understanding" accentuates Jesus and his teaching.[18]

In the true sense that this is a "gospel," Matthew has incorporated "a paradigmatic history angled to set forth the fulfillment of God's redeeming motive and activity in Jesus."[19] Matthew's angle is especially apparent in his understanding of the relationship between Jesus the Teacher and his disciples. While they should not be relegated to *extras*,[20] the disciples serve a primary purpose in Matthew's gospel of accentuating Jesus in his words and deeds. Matthew's arrangement of his story accentuates Jesus as the effective Teacher of his disciples.[21] Each of the major discourses are directed primarily to the disciples (5:1; 10:1; 13:10, 36; 18:1; 23:1; 24:1–3), and teaching segments are often transformed into explicit discipleship-teaching pericopae by inclusion of the term *disciple*.[22] Matthew

---

[16]T. Francis Glasson, "Anti-Pharisaism in St. Matthew," *JQR* 51 (1960–1961): 136; cf. also Allen, *St. Matthew*, xxxiiii f.; Erich Klostermann, *Das Matthäusevangelium, Handbuch zum Neuen Testament*, 4th ed. (Tübingen: J. C. B. Mohr, 1971), 4:21.

[17]Cf. Grant R. Osborne, *The Resurrection Narratives: A Redactional Study* (Grand Rapids: Baker, 1984), 91, n. 28.

[18]Cf. Trotter, *Understanding and Stumbling*, 282–85.

[19]Ralph P. Martin, *New Testament Foundations: A Guide for Christian Students* (Grand Rapids: Eerdmans, 1975), 1:23.

[20]As does Hans Conzelmann, *Jesus* (Philadelphia: Fortress, 1973), 34.

[21]Cf. Andrew H. Trotter, "Understanding and Stumbling: A Study of the Disciples' Understanding of Jesus and His Teaching in the Gospel of Matthew," Ph.D. diss. (Cambridge Univ., 1987), 280–81; Hengel, *Charismatic Leader*, 79.

[22]8:21, 23; 9:37; 10:42; 12:49; 13:10; 15:23; 16:5; 17:6; 17:10; 18:1; 19:10; 21:20; 24:3; 26:8, 40, 45.

wants us to know that Jesus has come to teach the will of God, and the true disciple is the one who understands and obeys.

MATTHEW'S DEVELOPMENT OF DISCIPLESHIP

Therefore, Matthew focuses on a small group of disciples around Jesus, composed primarily of the Twelve, who are separated from the religious leaders and the crowds because they truly understand and obey Jesus' teaching. What did this perspective of Jesus' disciples mean for the church of Matthew's day, and what does it mean for our own?

With Jesus or Against Him

Some scholars interpret the small group around Jesus as an indication that only a small group of supremely committed individuals were able to become disciples. Gerd Theissen suggests that the incident of the rich young ruler indicates that only through the process of accomplishing a "better righteousness" can one become a disciple. He explains:

> In Matthew, the rich young ruler is first of all asked to observe all the commandments. Only after this is he summoned to become a disciple. His call is put in conditional, rather than apodictic, terms: "If you would be perfect, go, sell what you possess and give to the poor. . ." (Mt. 19.21). There are special rules for those who are perfect. The Didache puts it in a similar way: "If you can bear the whole yoke of the Lord, you will be perfect, but if you cannot, do what you can." (Didache 6.2)[23]

Theissen suggests that traversing a graduated series of norms was necessary to pass from being one who was in sympathy with Jesus to being one who was a fully committed disciple. Hence, only a small group of radically committed individuals were able to become disciples.[24]

Theissen raises an issue that we must be very clear about. He rightly emphasizes the commitment of the disciples to Jesus. But the commitment has to do with obtaining eternal life, not an advanced

---

[23]Gerd Theissen, *Sociology of Early Palestinian Christianity*, trans. John Bowden (Philadelphia: Fortress, 1978), 19.

[24]Ibid., 18–21. This same position was held early in this century by the influential Matthean scholar Benjamin W. Bacon, *Studies in Matthew* (New York: Henry Holt, 1930), 87–89, 240. This is also a widely held view among Catholic scholars: cf. M. L. Held, "Disciples," *New Catholic Encyclopedia* (New York: McGraw-Hill, 1967), 4:895. See also Mark Sheridan, "Disciples and Discipleship in Matthew and Luke," *BThB* 3 (October 1973): 237; Strecker, *Der Weg der Gerechtigkeit*, 191–92.

stage of the Christian life. The rich young ruler whom he cites came with the question, "Teacher, what good thing must I do to get *eternal life*?"(Mt 19:16, italics mine). A person becomes a disciple through a faith commitment to Jesus, not a work commitment. We must be clear about this issue.

Jesus made a sharp distinction between those who would follow him as his disciples: "He who is not with me is against me, and he who does not gather with me scatters" (Mt 12:30).[25] A person is either with Jesus or against him. The disciples made the commitment to be with Jesus. When they confessed Jesus as Lord they became disciples. There is no middle ground. In this statement we find an illustration of the three groups that surrounded Jesus in his earthly ministry: the disciples are with Jesus, the Jewish leaders are against Jesus, and the crowds must make a decision to be either with him or against him.

At first the crowds were amazed at Jesus' teaching (Mt 7:28–29) and miracles (9:8) and received Jesus' compassionate attention (9:35–38; 14:13–14), apparently siding with him. But the crowds increasingly demonstrated hardness of heart (cf. Mt 13:2–3; 10–17; 34–36), until at the end the Jewish leaders persuaded the crowds to ask for the death of Jesus (27:15–25). Only the disciples, his brethren who do the will of God, are "with Jesus" as his followers after the Resurrection (cf. Mt 12:49–50; 28:10, 16).

The disciples are not idealized believers who rise above the masses in the church,[26] or the priestly class in the church serving the lay people.[27] Rather, the disciples are Jesus' true followers, the religious leaders are Jesus' enemies, and the crowd is the mass of people that continues to be the object of Jesus' saving ministry. In his earthly ministry Jesus went to the crowds himself. He preached to them, he taught them, and he healed them. Then he prepared his disciples to go to them (10:5ff.; 14:14–19; 15:29–36). In his ascended ministry Jesus sends the disciples to a larger crowd, the nations, to make disciples of them (28:16–20).

[25]Matthew and Luke (Lk 11:23) record the pronouncement as it is found here. Mark and Luke also have the reverse saying, "The one who is not against us, is for us" (cf. Mk 9:40; Lk 9:50). The saying here is more restrictive.

[26]E.g., Benjamin W. Bacon, *Studies in Matthew* (New York: Henry Holt, 1930), 87–89, 240.

[27]E.g., R. Thysman, *Communauté et directives éthiques: la catéchèse de Matthieu*, Recherches et Synthèses: Section d'exégèse, no. 1 (Gembloux: Duculot, 1974); Paul S. Minear, "The Disciples and the Crowds in the Gospel of Matthew," *AThR* Sup. Ser., 3 (March 1974): 31–32, 40–42; Mark Sheridan, "Disciples and Discipleship in Matthew and Luke," *BThB* 3 (1973): 237ff.

Laity and Leaders

The original disciples are an example for Matthew's church of the way in which Jesus continues to call, teach, and train disciples. As Matthew passed on the story of Jesus and his disciples, he interpreted it to meet the needs of his particular community. This is not to say that Matthew read his own situation back into the historical setting of Jesus and the Twelve; rather, just the opposite. He selected the historical data that best spoke to his audience. He portrayed the disciples as they really were so that they could be an example of what Christ's church should be, although he did not intend an ideal paradigm.[28] Instead of idealization, as we saw earlier the disciples' "understanding" accentuates Jesus and his teaching.[29] Matthew shows both the positive and negative. The positive is to show what will happen to true disciples who fully obey and follow Jesus (especially presented in the discipleship teachings). The negative shows what can happen to disciples who do not identify with Jesus in his obedience to the will of the Father (fleeing, Mt 26:56; sleeping, 26:40, 45; brash boldness, v. 35). Portrayed both positively and negatively (15:23; 16:5–12; 17:6, 7; 17:16–20; 19:13–15), the disciples become examples of imperfect followers of Jesus who are taught and who advance to understanding and solidarity with Jesus.[30] And, as an example, they become a very practical and realistic display of what one must be to be called a disciple (28:16–20).

Actually, the Twelve are examples for both laity and leaders in the church (Mt 4:18–22; 10:1–2). The word *disciple* brings to mind a follower of Jesus, a person who stands as a figure of the believer, one with whom the church in general can identify. The word *twelve* brings to mind the historical figures who were part of the unrepeatable group who functioned in the role of apostles in the early church. The Twelve perform dual roles of believer and leader, of disciple and apostle. Matthew combined leadership emphasis with their normal role as Christians.[31] While only a small group responded to the call to enter through the narrow gate to eternal life (7:13–14), once they entered, all were privy to the forthcoming Passion (16:21) and to

[28]Cf. Osborne, *Resurrection Narratives*, 91, n. 28.

[29]Cf. Trotter, *Understanding and Stumbling*, 282–85.

[30]Cf. Jack Dean Kingsbury, "On Following Jesus: The 'Eager' Scribe and the 'Reluctant' Disciple (Matthew 8.18–22)," *NTS* 34 (1988): 57.

[31]Cf. Andrew T. Lincoln, "Matthew—A Story for Teachers?" *The Bible in Three Dimensions: Essays in Celebration of Forty Years of Biblical Studies in the University of Sheffield*, ed. David J. A. Clines, Stephen E. Fowl, Stanley E. Porter, *JSOT* Sup 87 (Sheffield: Sheffield Academic Press, 1990), 105–6.

Jesus' innermost plans concerning the kingdom (13:10ff., 36ff.).[32] Such privilege is accorded to all true believers.

Simon Peter: First Among Equals

Even as the disciples function in Matthew's gospel as an example, both positively and negatively, of what it means to be a disciple, so also the portrait of Simon Peter in Matthew's gospel provides a personalized example of discipleship for Matthew's church.[33] Matthew focuses on Jesus, who calls, instructs, and sends disciples out to make more of what he has made them to be. But the disciples are a nameless, faceless, collective unity. Matthew often intentionally omits reference to specifically named disciples (e.g., Mt 20:20–28; 24:3; 26:37) or categories in the disciples (e.g., 24:1; 26:18, 19) in order to present the disciples as a unified, nameless group. This Matthean tendency is in line with what Conzelmann states is the tradition's tendency to view the disciples as a collective unity,[34] but interestingly, Matthew stresses this even more so than Mark.

Against this backdrop of a nameless, faceless group of disciples, Peter stands out starkly because he is the only named disciple who is emphasized. Matthew brings Peter into more prominence—both positively and negatively[35]—than the other evangelists. Peter functions exemplarily in much the same way as does the group of disciples. While Matthew concentrates on the disciples as an exemplary group, Peter is seen as a "typical" individual.[36] In his strengths and in his weaknesses he can be an example to Matthew's church, so Matthew accentuates the truly human element in Peter. The church would find much in common with Peter's typically human characteristics. He is much like any ordinary believer with his highs and lows, and he, therefore, becomes an example from whom the church can learn.

This is also the case for the leaders of Matthew's church. Peter is always cast in the Gospels as the leader of the disciples. But it is a leadership from within: Peter is first among equals. Therefore, Peter

---

[32]Albright and Mann, *Matthew*, 77.

[33]See Wilkins, *Concept of Disciple*, chap. 5; cf. Oscar Cullmann, *Peter: Disciple—Apostle—Martyr. A Historical and Theological Essay*, trans. Floyd V. Filson, 2d ed. (Philadelphia: Westminster, 1962); Chrys Caragounis, *Peter and The Rock*, BZNW 58 (Berlin/New York: de Gruyter, 1990).

[34]Hans Conzelmann, *History of Primitive Christianity*, trans. John E. Steely (Nashville: Abingdon, 1973), 149.

[35]Positively—e.g., Mt 16:15–19; negatively—e.g., Mt 16:23. Matthew omits "seeing disciples" found in Mk 8:33.

[36]Cf. Jack Dean Kingsbury, "The Figure of Peter in Matthew's Gospel as a Theological Problem," *JBL* 98 (1979): 78.

can function as an example for the leaders of Matthew's church. Even as Peter had success and failure as a leader, so the leaders of the church can learn from Peter's experiences. Several of the questions or responses to Jesus voiced on behalf of the disciples by Peter were issues that still speak to the church of Matthew's day (e.g., Mt 15:15; 17:24–25; 18:21).[37]

The church as a whole can identify with the group of disciples, while the individual believer and individual leader within the church can learn from Peter. As Jesus instructs Peter, instruction is provided for the church. The focus is on Jesus who promised Peter, "I will build my church." Jesus had called him, corrected him, and instructed him. As Jesus worked with and through Peter, so he would do with the church.

Ambassadors of the Great Commission

Jesus' training and teaching time with his followers in the earthly ministry resulted in the kind of disciple and the definition of disciple that he desired. In the Great Commission he said that his disciples were to make more of what he had made of them. The Commission encapsulates Jesus' purpose for coming to earth. In addition, the placement of the Commission at the conclusion of Matthew's gospel has long been recognized as an indication of Matthew's overall purpose for writing his gospel.[38] It is especially crucial for our understanding of the role of the disciples in Matthew's gospel. As the risen Jesus meets with those disciples who have been with him in his earthly ministry, now called "the eleven disciples" (28:16), he declares, "All authority in heaven and on earth has been given to me. Therefore go and make disciples of all nations, baptizing them in the name of the Father and of the Son and of the Holy Spirit, and teaching them to obey everything I have commanded you. And surely I am with you always, to the very end of the age" (vv. 18–20).

This commissioning points once again to the uniqueness of Jesus' form of discipleship. Jesus' call was at the same time an invitation to salvation and a summons to service. Understood within the broader biblical concept of "calling,"[39] Jesus summoned his disciples in a way similar to the way God called Israel to be the blessed people and to be a blessing for others. Even as Israel was not called solely to be

---

[37]Cf. J. Andrew Overman, *Matthew's Gospel and Formative Judaism: The Social World of the Matthean Community* (Minneapolis: Fortress, 1990), 126–40.

[38]For recent discussion, see B. Rod Doyle, "Matthew's Intention as Discerned by His Structure," *Revue Biblique* 95 (1, 1988): 34–54; David R. Bauer, *The Structure of Matthew's Gospel* (Sheffield: Almond, 1988).

[39]See chap. 6 for our discussion of biblical "calling."

God's people and to enjoy his blessing but were in turn to be the source of blessing to all the nations of the earth, so also when Jesus issued his call it meant both a call to enter into a discipleship relationship with him and to become fellow workers with him in the kingdom. Men and women were called into a relationship with Jesus that secured their own salvation and secured the ongoing proclamation of the Good News. While some passages seem to emphasize one element more than the other, Jesus' call to follow him—whether it was the Twelve or the broader group of disciples[40]—meant that those who responded would join him in both the blessings of the Gospel message and the future proclamation of the Gospel message. Jesus told the disciples: "I no longer call you servants, because a servant does not know his master's business. Instead, I have called you friends, for everything that I learned from my Father I have made known to you. You did not choose me, but I chose you and appointed you to go and bear fruit—fruit that will last" (Jn 15:15–16).

Jesus spent his earthly ministry teaching and training his disciples; now he sent them out to make more of what he had made of them. In the use of the full title "the eleven disciples" (Mt 28:16), Matthew addresses the solidarity of the church with the Commission, while at the same time he acknowledges the leadership role of the apostolic circle. As "the Eleven" these followers have a unique role in the foundation of the church and in salvation history (19:28). As "disciples" they represent all those who have entered into eternal life (v. 29). Therefore, as "the Eleven" the injunction of the Great Commission is given to those who have a leadership role in the church, but as "disciples" they are a paradigm for all disciples. Hence, in their role as "the eleven disciples" the Great Commission is the obligation of all believers.[41]

Jesus committed his earthly ministry to making disciples within Israel (cf. Jn 4:1). In his ascended ministry he commissions his disciples to "make disciples" among the nations (Mt 28:16–20). The obvious meaning of "making disciples" is to proclaim the Gospel message among those who have not yet received forgiveness of sins. Luke gives us insight to the meaning of the commission from his record of another postresurrection appearance of Jesus. Just before his ascension, Jesus spent time clarifying for the disciples the

---

[40]Luke, especially, allows us to see the involvement of the broader circle of disciples in Jesus' earthly mission. In the ministry of the Seventy (10:1–20) and the women who accompanied Jesus (8:1–3), Luke shows that disciples other than the Twelve went on missions with Jesus.

[41]Cf. also Donald A. Carson, "Matthew," *EBC* (Grand Rapids: Zondervan, 1984), 8:596.

relationship of his earthly ministry and his ascended ministry. Luke tells us:

> Then he opened their minds so they could understand the Scriptures. He told them, "This is what is written: The Christ will suffer and rise from the dead on the third day, and repentance and forgiveness of sins will be preached in his name to all nations, beginning at Jerusalem. You are witnesses of these things" (Lk 24:45–48; cf. Jn 20:21–23).

Combining Luke's insights with Matthew's, we see that "making disciples" is accomplished through preaching repentance and forgiveness of sins in Jesus' name. In other words, becoming a disciple is accomplished by a person turning to Christ for the forgiveness of his or her sins—that is, receiving salvation.

Who is the object of this "preaching" in Luke's account and "making disciples" in Matthew's account? In both it is "all nations" (*panta ta ethnē*). All nations, now including both the Gentiles and Jews, receive the opportunity to become Jesus' disciples. Although some suggest that "all nations" means only "Gentiles," not the "Jews," since Matthew invariably refers only to Gentiles by this title,[42] most recognize that Matthew's overall intention is to include the Jews. The full expression "all nations" is used four times in Matthew in settings that more naturally include all peoples, even Jews (here and in 24:9, 14; 25:32). Most importantly, we can see that in the Great Commission Matthew returns to the universal theme of the introductory verse to his gospel (1:1). There the blessings promised through Abraham to all people of the earth (Ge 12:3) are said now to be fulfilled in Jesus the Messiah. When the original covenant promise to Abraham is reiterated in Genesis 18:18; 22:18, the Septuagint uses the same words found in Matthew 28:19: "all nations." Matthew's purpose has been to show how Jesus is the Messiah of all peoples. His theme of universal salvation through Jesus (e.g., Mt 1:1; 2:1–12; 4:15–16; 8:5–13; 10:18; 13:38; 24:14; et al.) thus climaxes this gospel in the command to "make disciples of all nations."[43] When we see Matthew's commission to make disciples of "all nations" in the light of Luke's commission, that "repentance and forgiveness of sins will be preached in [Jesus'] name to all nations, beginning at Jerusalem" (Lk 24:47), we understand that

---

[42]E.g., Stephen Hre Kio, "Understanding and Translating 'Nations' in Mt 28:19," *The Bible Translator* 41 (2, 1990), 230–39; Douglas R. A. Hare, *The Theme of Jewish Persecution of Christians in the Gospel According to St. Matthew* (Cambridge: Cambridge Univ. Press), 1967.

[43]Alfred Plummer, *An Exegetical Commentary on the Gospel According to St. Matthew*, 1915, reprint (Grand Rapids: Baker, 1982), 430; Carson, "Matthew," 596.

Jesus' ministry in Israel was to be the beginning point of what would be later a universal offer of salvation to all the peoples of the earth.[44]

The command to make disciples of all nations finds remarkable verbal fulfillment in the activities of the early church as the apostles went from Jerusalem to Judea to Samaria and to the ends of the earth proclaiming the message of Jesus and making disciples. Luke tells us that when going through the pagan city Derbe in Asia Minor, Paul and Barnabas "preached the good news in that city and won a large number of disciples. Then they returned to Lystra, Iconium and Antioch, strengthening the disciples and encouraging them to remain true to the faith" (Ac 14:21–22). In the early church, to believe in the Gospel message was to become a disciple (cf. Ac 4:32 with 6:2). Men and women were called into a relationship with Jesus that secured their own salvation and secured the ongoing proclamation of the Good News. Whereas isolationaries such as the people of Qumran resolved to withdraw from "the company of the unjust men," Jesus and his movement went to work both within Israel and to the uttermost parts of the earth.[45]

But Jesus' Great Commission implies more than securing salvation as Jesus' disciple. It also includes the process of growth as a disciple.[46] As Jesus addressed the disciples and commanded them to "make disciples of all the nations," he told them to make more of what he had made of them. The process would not be exactly the same as what Jesus did with them because the circumstances after Pentecost would change the process.[47] However, the process would be similar in many ways. Specifically, the process of growth is implied in the phrases, "baptizing them in the name of the Father and of the Son and of the Holy Spirit, and teaching them to obey everything that I have commanded you" (Mt 28:19–20 NRSV). As a person responds to the invitation to come out of the nations to start life as a disciple, she or he begins the life of discipleship through baptism and through obedience to Jesus' teaching. "Baptizing" describes the activity by which the new disciple identifies with Jesus, and "teaching" introduces the activities by which the new

---

[44]Cf. Joseph A. Fitzmyer, *The Gospel According to Luke (X-XXIV)*, AB 28A (Garden City, N.Y.: Doubleday, 1985), 1583–84.

[45]Max Wilcox, "Jesus in the Light of His Jewish Environment," *Aufstieg und Niedergang der Römischen Welt*, 2, 25, 1, ed. H. Temporini and W. Haase (Berlin: Walter de Gruyter, 1982), 169.

[46]Grant R. Osborne, *The Resurrection Narratives: A Redactional Study* (Grand Rapids: Baker, 1984), 91. Matthean contextual usage points to this conclusion, rather than theologizing based on the occurrence of the transitive verb; cf. the note in Moisés Silva, "New Lexical Semitisms?" *ZNW* 69 (1978): 256, n. 9.

[47]See our discussion of the process after Pentecost in chap. 13 on Acts.

disciple grows in discipleship.[48] We should note that the process of growth does not include only instruction. Growth in discipleship is accomplished as the new disciple is obedient to what Jesus commanded. Obedience was the hallmark of Jesus' disciples, as we see in an incident in Jesus' earthly ministry. "Pointing to his disciples, he said, 'Here are my mother and my brothers. For whoever does the will of my Father in heaven is my brother and sister and mother'" (Mt 12:49–50). H. N. Ridderbos says succinctly: "The apostles had to teach people to obey all that Jesus commanded them during his ministry on earth. Their listeners had to be brought under his commandments so that they could show by their lives that they really belong to him. That is the final purpose of the preaching of the gospel."[49]

Therefore, Matthew's gospel is intended, at least in part, as a resource tool to help Jesus' disciples in their task of making and developing future disciples. We have seen that Matthew points to Jesus to be the supreme Lord and Teacher of the disciples. Although the disciples were still susceptible to incomprehension and misunderstanding in his earthly ministry, Matthew emphasizes that Jesus' teaching brought them understanding and obedience. That same understanding and obedience will continue to be the hallmark of disciples in the ongoing age. Matthew's gospel is readily usable for this purpose, because the growth process of discipleship is comprised in large part of teaching new disciples to obey all that Jesus had commanded the original disciples. Since all of the major discourses in Matthew are directed to the disciples, and since most of Jesus' sayings in Matthew are directed to the disciples as discipleship teachings, Matthew's gospel is a handy resource of discipleship teaching. The goal of the believers' life of faith is thereby made clear: Jesus' disciples are called, trained, and commissioned to "make disciples of all nations." Matthew has constructed a gospel that will equip the disciples in this task of making and developing future disciples. Wolfgang Trilling notes that the instruction to be given to the new converts

> must contain all that Jesus had commanded his disciples. It is given in this gospel, especially in the great discourses. They are precepts of the Master, instructions about true discipleship, and about the way to fulfill

---

[48]Richard DeRidder, *Discipling the Nations* (Grand Rapids: Baker, 1975), 190. For a recent discussion of the meaning of baptism as "adherence," see William B. Badke, "Was Jesus a Disciple of John?" *Evangelical Quarterly* 62 (3, 1990): 195–204.

[49]H. N. Ridderbos, *Matthew*, Bible Student's Commentary, trans. Ray Togtman (Grand Rapids: Zondervan, 1987), 555–56.

the true will of God. They contain the "way of righteousness" ([Mt] 21:32). Nothing may be suppressed and nothing added, nothing may be watered down or given a new meaning. This is solemnly confirmed by the risen Lord.[50]

Jesus concludes the Commission with the crucial element of discipleship: the presence of the Master. "And surely I am with you always, to the very end of the age" (Mt 28:20). Jesus is present as the new disciple is baptized and is taught to observe all that Jesus commanded. Both those obeying the command and those responding are comforted by the awareness that the risen Jesus will continue to fashion all his disciples. The Master is always present for his disciples to follow.

IMPLICATIONS

The heroes I looked up to as a boy offered me a challenge for life. The disciples of Jesus offer me a challenge for life and eternity. They were courageous men and women who obeyed Jesus' summons to leave the broad gate and easy way of first-century, status-quo religiosity in order to enter in through the narrow gate and embark on the way that leads to eternal life.

I doubt that the Twelve would be happy with me calling them heroes. They knew their own weaknesses all too well. They knew that it was only through the presence of Jesus, the will of the Father, and the power of his Spirit that they would be transformed and would later transform the world. They were ordinary men who responded to the call of Jesus and who grew in discipleship as they obeyed the Master's instructions. By focusing on the Twelve, Matthew emphasized the solidarity of all believers with Jesus' disciples. Those first disciples were an example for all believers. All those who are with Jesus—that is, those who have become believers—are disciples who can grow as did the Twelve. The implications of this for the church today are significant. I would suggest at least the following.

First, Matthew intends for his readers to understand that the Christian life is equivalent to being with Jesus as his disciple. This means that conversion—not a later point of commitment or a process of spiritual growth—marks the beginning point of discipleship. Degrees of maturity will be realized as one traverses the discipleship path, but all true believers are disciples on that path. Therefore, evangelism is the starting point for making disciples. Jesus said that

---

[50]Wolfgang Trilling, *The Gospel According to St. Matthew*, 2 vols., New Testament for Spiritual Reading, ed. John L. McKenzie (New York: Crossroad, 1981), 2:270.

we are to make disciples of all "nations," not of those who are already believers. Those "with Jesus" as his disciples are small in number in comparison to the nations of the world. Jesus declared that those who enter into the narrow gate to salvation and discipleship are relatively few in comparison to those who reject the message. That was the case in Jesus' day, and it will continue to be so today.

The second implication of Matthew's perspective is that discipleship teaching is directed to all believers. Matthew intends his readers to identify with Jesus' disciples as they are being instructed by him. The term *disciple* links the believer in the church with Jesus' intimate followers. Although uniqueness accrues to the historical situation of Jesus' ministry, the process through which Jesus took his disciples is an example of the process through which Jesus takes believers/disciples today. We need to challenge the people of the church to see themselves as disciples of Jesus if they acknowledge him as Savior. There is a subtle impression among many believers that discipleship training is directed only toward those who are more committed than the average believer or toward those who are in positions of leadership, or else it is only for those who are in professional ministry. Obedience to Jesus' teaching is the heart of discipleship training, and discipleship training is the calling for all believers.

Third, Matthew intends for his readers to recognize that distinctions among disciples are related to function, not to spiritual standing or commitment. The Twelve were both disciples and apostles at the same time. They were disciples by way of belief in Jesus as Messiah. They were apostles by way of their calling to a particular function of leadership and ministry. The same principle holds today. All believers must recognize that they are disciples through belief in Jesus as Savior. We must also recognize that God designates some disciples to be leaders within the church. Three issues stem from this point. (1) Believers within the church are equal as disciples. Two classes or levels of Christians is an artificial creation that destroys the priesthood of all believers by perpetuating a false dichotomy between more- and less-committed Christians, or between clergy and laity. We must be careful to recognize that we are all equal as believers, but there are distinctions of function. (2) Disciples who have been called to leadership do so as disciples/leaders. The disciple/leader is always equal with other believers. Peter acted as a leader among equals. We must do the same. (3) We must be as careful as possible to distinguish when the Twelve are being used as examples for all believers and when they are being used as examples for leaders.

We must understand the genuine humanness of the disciples if we are to understand the necessity of growth in discipleship. Christians often idealize the disciples to the detriment of truly understanding them as examples of discipleship. If we idealize them, we cannot see how the Lord brought about growth in their lives, and we cannot see how they can be examples for us.

The awareness of their own sinfulness and imperfections probably would have made the Twelve reluctant to point out their own accomplishments. They would rather that I point to Jesus. And I will, even as did the apostle Paul when he said, "Follow my example, as I follow the example of Christ" (1Co 11:1). Paul was not less humble than the Twelve. He simply acknowledged the necessity of human examples now that Jesus has ascended. As we look to the disciples in Matthew's gospel, we can equally say, "Follow their example, as they follow Christ."

As I have studied the lives of the disciples over these many years, they have become my heroes. They are men and women who followed Jesus in his earthly life to the farthest reaches of the world in order to preach the Good News. They are my heroes, but Jesus is my Savior and Lord. I pray that we look to the disciples as examples of what Jesus desires to accomplish through us today. May we have the courage to follow that example and to provide an example for those who watch our lives, for we may be someone else's hero!

Following up:

1. Who are the "nations" for whom you are responsible to "make disciples"?
2. What is the best way of carrying out the Great Commission? How should the church be involved?

10

Mark: Servants of the Redemptive Servant

Getting focused:

1. Which teachings of Jesus did the disciples have the most trouble understanding?
2. Which of Jesus' teachings do you think are the most difficult for us to understand and obey today?
3. What is the meaning of "greatness"? How would you go about becoming a "great" man or woman of God?

The *Back to the Future* movie series was a smash success because it brilliantly played back and forth between the realities of the present, the past, and the future. It allowed the viewer to move back and forth in time, evaluating present values and activities against those of other times. I saw only the first episode, but the incongruous picture of a skateboarder astounding people from an earlier generation still amuses me. The popularity of the movies demonstrated the fascination people have with the impact of the past on the present, and the present on the future.

Learning from the past while adapting to the present, has always been a difficult issue. Yet it is a recognized necessity. Parents and grandparents forewarn younger generations with stories from their past that are designed to instill "good old-fashioned values" in the younger generation. The younger generation appeals to older generations to "become more contemporary" and to not "live in the past."

The Evangelists all lived with that tension. Mark, in particular, wanted to make the past story of Jesus so alive for his readers that their present lives would be affected. The Evangelists were people of their own times who wanted the past to be relevant to contemporary

194

concerns. Mark compels his readers, then and now, to consider Jesus a truly contemporary figure.

Mark transports us back into the first century to walk with Jesus under Palestinian skies, to hear him preach and teach, to watch him perform miracles, to see him in disputation with the religious leaders, and to witness the reactions of people to him. The person who reads Mark's gospel is challenged to move back and forth between the first century and the present day, viewing the message and ministry of Jesus in its original context so that it may speak clearly to the present circumstances of life. Mark's gospel is the most basic proclamation of Jesus' message and ministry. It commences with the declaration, "The beginning of the gospel about Jesus Christ, the Son of God" (Mk 1:1), and from that opening declaration of purpose, shows, in rapid-fire sequence, the message and ministry of Jesus as it developed in the first century.

MARK'S DISTINCTIVE VIEW OF DISCIPLESHIP

Mark also gives us a basic portrait of Jesus' disciples as they walk with Jesus.[1] Here we gain insight to what it must have been like to have encountered Jesus, to have experienced his authoritative call, to watch in amazement as he drove out demons, healed lepers, and calmed the stormy sea. Through Mark's narrative we understand the disciples' excitement as Jesus becomes the center of a popular movement, we appreciate their astonishment as he feeds the multitudes, and we sympathize when the messianic triumph of Palm Sunday turns to fear as Jesus is led away from the Garden of Gethsemane as a political prisoner.

Experiencing Jesus

The simplicity of Mark's treatment of Jesus and his disciples is the clue to understanding the portrait he draws for us. Mark writes to people who need to experience the stark reality of Jesus, who need to have their lives touched and challenged by his message and his ministry. Mark wants us to experience anew what the disciples experienced as they walked with Jesus. People of the church face the danger of being too familiar with Jesus: we have heard about him in church, we have read four different gospel accounts of his life, we

---

[1]For a succinct overview of Mark's perspective of discipleship, see Demetrios Trakatellis, "'Ακολούθει μοι/Follow Me' (Mk 2:14): Discipleship and Priesthood," *GOThR* 30 (3, 1985): 271–85. For the most complete recent scholarly overview, see C. Clifton Black, *The Disciples According to Mark: Markan Redaction in Current Debate*, JSNTSup 27 (Sheffield: JSOT, 1989).

have even seen movies of his life on television or at the theater. That familiarity with Jesus can reduce him to the level of our preconceptions or to a stereotyped figure. The disciples of the first century were continually having to make mental and spiritual adjustments to Jesus as he revealed himself and his purposes to them. He took them to the cutting edge of faith where sometimes they triumphed, other times they faltered, and still other times they completely misunderstood. Mark wants us to experience that same stark reality of experiencing Jesus, yet he wants us to learn from the original disciples' example of faith.[2]

The Difficulty of Understanding Jesus' Message and Ministry

Mark's portrait of the disciples is perhaps the most ambiguous among the gospel accounts. On the one hand, the disciples receive a positive treatment. They are introduced as being specially selected and commissioned with authority by Jesus (1:16–20; 3:13–19a) to hear the secrets of the kingdom (4:10–12) and to promote his ministry (3:14–15; 6:7–13, 35–44). Empowered by Jesus for ministry in Israel, the disciples do as Jesus does: they preach, heal, and cast out demons. On the other hand, the disciples are painted with unflattering colors. Although enlightened by God and empowered by Jesus, the disciples show themselves to be uncomprehending. They do not understand parabolic teaching (4:13; 7:17–18), do not understand the true identity of Jesus as the Son of God in the calming of the sea (4:35–41; 6:45–52), and do not understand Jesus' potential to feed the multitudes miraculously (6:34–44; 8:1–10). The disciples do not truly understand the nature of Jesus' ministry or teaching (8:14–21), which in essence involves the way to the cross (8:31–33; 9:30–32) through servanthood (10:35–45). This incomprehension eventually leads Judas to betray Jesus (14:43–46), the disciples to forsake him (v. 50), and Peter to deny him (14:54, 66–72).

MARK'S DEVELOPMENT OF DISCIPLESHIP

Through the development of his plot, Mark contrasts two fundamentally opposing points of view concerning Jesus' Gospel message. These opposing points of view are thinking the things of God and thinking the things of humankind (cf. 8:33).

---

[2]Cf. Christopher D. Marshall, *Faith As a Theme in Mark's Narrative*, SNTMS 64 (Cambridge: Cambridge Univ. Press, 1989).

"Thinking the Things of God"

The disciples' response to Jesus is a major portion of the plot. The disciples had been specially called to follow Jesus and to respond to him as the one effectively proclaiming the Gospel of God. They were given the mystery of the kingdom; they experienced in their own lives God's redeeming activity. Privy to special instruction, they were even empowered to act in Jesus' name to preach the Gospel, to heal, to cast out demons, and to teach. Yet, on the other hand, they misunderstood. They became confused and afraid. When adversity set in, the disciples reflected little faith and hardness of heart. This confusion ate away at their fundamental perception of who Jesus was, as well as at the implications of Jesus' identity for the life of discipleship.[3]

Thus Mark deals with a fact of history: During Jesus' earthly life the disciples did not completely understand him. Mark uses the historical disciples to show his readers how difficult it is to grasp the mystery of Jesus and the Cross. Although Jesus has come as God's promised, Spirit-anointed, royal Son to herald and inaugurate the kingdom, Mark writes to correct those who would look to the glory of the final consummation of the kingdom instead of its vulnerable beginnings. The kingdom is here in hidden fashion, and Jesus the Messiah, Son of God (1:1), must be understood in terms of suffering and the Cross (8:31–33; 9:30–32; 10:32–34).

The Greatness of Servanthood

Jesus' pivotal pronouncement in Mark 10:45 underscores the depth of incongruity between Jesus' and the disciples' understanding of life and ministry: "For even the Son of Man did not come to be served, but to serve, and to give his life as a ransom for many." The issue centers on servanthood, a concept not expected by the disciples. This passage is important for us to examine because it is the key to understanding Jesus' perspective of discipleship. By comprehending the essence of *Jesus' ministry* as servanthood, the disciples will comprehend the essence of discipleship as servanthood,[4] including their motivation, position, ambition, expectations, and example (note the crucial placement of the servanthood passages, 9:33–37[5] and 10:35–45, within the larger discipleship section, 8:27–10:45).

---

[3]Robert A. Guelich, *Mark 1–8:26*, WBC 34A (Dallas: Word, 1989), xxiii, xxv, xlii.

[4]Cf. Jack Dean Kingsbury, *Conflict in Mark: Jesus, Authorities, and Disciples* (Minneapolis: Fortress, 1989), 112–17.

[5]The term *servant* (*diakonos*) does not occur in the parallels in Mt 18:1–5 or Lk 9:46–48.

When Jesus gave his third prediction of the Crucifixion (Mk 10:32–34), he revealed that his purpose in coming to earth was to go to the cross. Throughout his life he knew that what waited for him was the suffering of the cross. Immediately after giving this prediction, James and John come to ask if they can sit with Jesus, one on the right, and the other on the left, when he enters into his glory. This seems like an incredibly inappropriate question to be asking since Jesus has just told them of his future suffering! Jesus points out their confusion when he says, "You don't know what you are asking." The ensuing interaction further indicates that they did not really understand Jesus' destiny (cf. vv. 38–39).

James and John had only a fuzzy idea of what Jesus' suffering was going to be. What they seemed to be focusing on was not the suffering, but the glory and the greatness beyond the cross. They rightly understood that when Jesus was raised from the dead he was going to enter into glory. And for them, that was what mattered.

This was not the first time that the disciples had been concerned about such things. Earlier Mark tells us that they had been caught by Jesus arguing about who was the greatest (cf. 9:33–37). The disciples had something deep within their nature, which, when focused in the wrong direction, lead them to go contrary to the will and work of God. It may be referred to as the "ambition of greatness." James and John were motivated by the ambition of greatness. Even if greatness must come through sacrifice and suffering, the reward is worth it. As they heard Jesus talking about the cross, they must have understood him to mean that pain (the cross) was worth the gain (glory). And they are willing here to make that sacrifice, to suffer that pain, if only they could gain the position of glory at Jesus' right and left side in his kingdom. Along with the other disciples, James and John thought that Jesus was going to establish an earthly kingdom, and they rightly understood that the disciples would have places of authority in this kingdom. Isn't that what the other kingdoms had? But what they did not realize was that Jesus' kingdom was to be different than the typical earthly kingdom, and, therefore, Jesus' special people were to be of a completely different sort than important people in the other types of kingdoms.

What happened here is that James and John misunderstood Jesus' motivation in going to the cross. Yes, Jesus will enter into glory. Yes, he will establish his kingdom. Yes, he will sit on the throne as King. But that is not his ultimate motivation. His motivation is not *self*-centered, it is *other*-centered (cf. Mk 10:42–45). Jesus did not go to the cross just so that he could enter into glory. He came from glory! Jesus went to the cross and gave his life so that others could experience redemption. The climax to this section (vv. 35–45) comes in verse 45: "For even the Son of Man did not come to be served, but to serve, and to give his life as a ransom for many." In the kingdom of God humble service is the rule, and Jesus is the perfect example of it, especially in his redemptive mission. The phrase "did not come to be served, but to serve" describes Jesus' incarnate life. He did not come as a potentate whose every personal whim was to be catered to by groveling servants; instead he came as a servant himself. And his coming issued in giving his life as a "ransom for many."[6]

What is Mark's intent in his portrayal of the disciple? Several recent studies have emphasized primarily the negative aspects. Often those who focus solely on the negative aspects see the Twelve simply as literary figures who represent a faction of the church against which the evangelist polemicizes. A common approach is to point to the incomprehension of the disciples as evidence that they were opposed to Jesus and his program. Mark's audience was to recognize the failings of the disciples and be warned of their opponents within the church.[7]

Looking at both the positive and negative features of the disciples allows us to see that Mark has a pastoral motivation: although Mark has the highest regard for the disciples, he uses their failures to instruct his community.[8] Mark points to the difficulty the disciples had understanding Jesus' message and ministry. Jesus did not fit within the expectations and stereotypes of the disciples, and therefore they had difficulty understanding him. Mark uses the historical disciples to show his readers how difficult it is to grasp the mystery of Jesus and the Cross. Those passages that stress the incomprehension

---

[6]Walter W. Wessel, "Mark," *EBC* (Grand Rapids: Zondervan, 1985), 8:720–21.

[7]E.g., Joseph Tyson, "The Blindness of the Disciples in Mark," *JBL* 80 (1961) 261–68; Christopher Tuckett, ed., *The Messianic Secret, IRT* 1 (Philadelphia/London: Fortress/SPCK, 1983), 35–43; Theodore John Weeden, Sr., *Mark—Traditions in Conflict* (Philadelphia: Fortress, 1971); Etienne Trocmé, *The Formation of the Gospel According to Mark*, trans. Pamela Gaughan (Philadelphia: Westminster, 1975); and especially Werner Heinz Kelber, "Conclusion: From Passion Narrative to Gospel," *The Passion in Mark: Studies on Mark 14–16*, ed. Werner Heinz Kelber (Philadelphia: Fortress, 1976), 153–80; and ibid., "The Hour of the Son of Man and the Temptation of the Disciples (Mark 14:32–42)," 41–60; Werner Heinz Kelber, "Mark 14:32–42: Gethsemane. Passion Christology and Discipleship Failure," *ZNW* 63 (1972): 166–87; Werner Heinz Kelber, *Mark's Story of Jesus* (Philadelphia: Fortress, 1979).

[8]E.g., Robert P. Meye, *Jesus and the Twelve: Discipleship and Revelation in Mark's Gospel* (Grand Rapids: Eerdmans, 1968); Ernest Best, *Following Jesus: Discipleship in the Gospel of Mark, JSNTSup* 4 (Sheffield: Univ. of Sheffield, 1981); Ernest Best, *Disciples and Discipleship: Studies in the Gospel According to Mark* (Edinburgh: T. & T. Clark, 1986); Camille Focant, "L'Incompréhension des Disciples dans le deuxième Evangile," *Revue Biblique* 82 (1985): 161–85; Frank J. Matera, "The Incomprehension of the Disciples and Peter's Confession (Mark 6:14–8:30)," *Biblica* 70 (2, 1989): 153–72.

of the disciples instruct Mark's church about the necessity of thinking the thoughts of God rather than the thoughts of humans (e.g., 8:33). The Resurrection scene provides fulfillment of Jesus' predictions (9:9; 14:28) and obligates the reader to project reconciliation of the disciples and Peter with Jesus since they would see him in Galilee just as he had told them (16:7).[9] The summons to Galilee provides the assurance that Peter and the disciples, in spite of denying and forsaking Jesus, have not been rejected by the risen Lord.[10] The evangelist points to the obtuseness of the disciples to instruct his readers about the meaning of authentic discipleship, i.e., selfless servanthood.

The disciple who is privileged to be a member of Jesus' kingdom is a servant, which means thinking God's thoughts (8:31–33), pursuing the life of the cross (vv. 34–38) through the message (9:1–8) and example of Jesus (vv. 9–32), and hence, rejecting status (vv. 33–37), exclusivism (9:38–10:16), and the treasures of this world (10:17–31). The disciples in Mark's gospel are privileged members of the kingdom of God, and their incomprehension comes from their worldly expectations. Discipleship teaching directs them to think God's way, the way of suffering and the Cross through servanthood.

IMPLICATIONS

The implications for Mark's church and for the church today are powerful. Because of the pride and self-centeredness that govern our fallen world, the world's standard of "greatness" often becomes one of the central, driving motivations of life. Think of that little maxim— "No pain, no gain." If no pain is experienced in a workout, no gain is experienced in the growth of pushing muscles to new capacities. If no pain of sacrifice is experienced in a diet, no gain of lost weight will be realized. If no pain of discipline is experienced in going to school, no gain of a new position on the job can be experienced. If we do not endure the pain of saving now, we will not gain enough money to take that wonderful vacation later.

"No pain, no gain" is a true maxim. But Jesus told his disciples, and he tells us now, that it is not the only, nor even the highest, motivation. Jesus did not go to the cross just so that he could enter into glory. Remember, he came from glory! Jesus went to the cross so

---

[9]Cf. Kingsbury, *Conflict in Mark*, 112–17.

[10]William L. Lane, *The Gospel According to Mark*, NICNT (Grand Rapids: Eerdmans, 1974), 589–92; Augustine Stock, *Call to Discipleship: A Literary Study of Mark's Gospel*, Good News Studies 1 (Wilmington, Del.: Michael Glazier, 1982).

that others could gain release from sin. He went to the cross so that others could gain eternal life, abundant life right now. Jesus says, "Yes, pain will produce gain; yes, I will gain the kingdom, but that is not my highest motivation, that is not the heart of what I am doing. I am not here for glory. I am here to give all that I am for others so that they can gain real life." Jesus did not go to the cross for his own glory. He went to the cross so that you and I can sit here with our sins forgiven and eternal life now ours. A higher motivation for Jesus' life was "My pain, others' gain."

If our sacrifice in this life is directed only toward our own gain, our own future comfort, it is a gain that becomes increasingly self-centered, and increasingly empty of meaning. James and John learned that greatness in the kingdom of God is not a matter of power, position, accomplishment, or recognition. Greatness involves taking the place of a servant and seeking the best of those around us. Our own personal sacrifice has meaning and purpose if it is directed toward the gain of others.

I hasten to add that this does not mean that all ambition is bad. Ambition is bad when it is greedy, when it hurts and uses people, when it exalts self over others, when it is prideful. James and John were ambitious people. They wanted to make something of life, they wanted to be significant, they wanted to be of great use in the kingdom of God. Those are strengths when focused in the right way, and that means hitching ambition to selfless servanthood. James' and John's strength was their greatest weakness when it was greedy and selfish. When it was selflessly directed toward servanthood their ambitious nature was used by God in powerful ways. John's ambitious drive, when properly focused, was used to guide and nurture the early church in Jerusalem and later in Asia Minor. James' zeal resulted for him in being the first apostle to suffer martyrdom, a turning point in the courage of the church.

The reason that this kind of servanthood is possible is because of Jesus' work of servanthood in ransoming us. He has paid the price for our release. He has released us from (1) the penalty for sin (cf. "The wages of sin is death, but the free gift of God is eternal life in Christ Jesus our Lord," Ro 6:23 NASB) and from (2) the power of sin over us who are prideful and self-centeredly motivated. Especially in this context the motivation of self-serving greatness is broken through redemption, and we are enabled to focus on others in servanthood. Mark shows us that even as Jesus was the redemptive servant, authentic discipleship entails selfless servanthood.

It will be difficult for us to grasp fully Jesus' ministry and message because of our cultural biases, our self-centered motivations, and our human weaknesses. Disciples should always stand in awe of the ministry and message of Jesus because they are so different from our ways. But for those who respond to Jesus' call, we have the assurance that he will never reject us. He desires to be the Master who walks before us today even as he did with the disciples of the first century.

Following up:

1. Why does Mark emphasize so strongly the fact that the Twelve consistently did not understand Jesus' message or ministry?
2. How can we train Christians to "think the things of God"?
3. Is "servanthood" a popular vocation in the present age? Why? Why would Jesus want his followers to be servants?
4. How did Jesus model servanthood for the disciples? How can we be servants today?

11

Luke: Followers
on the Costly Way

Getting focused:

1. Why does Luke describe the Christian life as "the Way" (cf. Ac 19:8–9)? How does that concept fit with the biblical idea of discipleship?
2. When Jesus said that a person could not be his disciple unless he "'hated father and mother, wife and children, brothers and sisters—yes, even his own life,'" what did he mean? What does that mean for you?

Ralph Carmichael wrote a beautiful melody several years ago. It used to be quite popular at camp fire sings because it challenged people to consider the results of having a personal encounter with Jesus. After the verses speak of the majesty of God stamped upon nature and the incident of Jesus entering history, a refrain asks, "What is that to me?" The chorus answers:

What is that to me?
'Til by faith I met Him face to face
  And I felt the wonder of His grace,
Then I knew that He was more than just a God who didn't care,
  Who lived away out there,
And now He walks beside me day by day,
  Ever watching o'er me lest I stray,
Helping me to find that narrow way,
  He's everything to me.

As with many of these hauntingly nostalgic camp songs, the words speak more than many who sing them avow. The chorus testifies that the personal experience of the grace of God sets a person onto the narrow way of following Jesus day by day. The phrase "He's

203

everything to me" may be sung nonchalantly by some, but those words actually claim an attachment to Jesus that radicalizes every aspect of a person's life. This is an intense claim, but Jesus called for that kind of faith commitment when a person undertook to follow him into the new life of salvation.

I remember well my own conversion. As I listened to the Gospel message I knew that making a decision to become a Christian was all or nothing. If Jesus truly was who he said he was—that he was the Son of God who had come to earth to show people the way to life— then it was either true or not true. There was no middle ground. And my response had no middle ground. I either became a Christian, which meant all I was, or else I didn't become a Christian, which meant turning away from it entirely. This decision for Christ was the central issue of life. He was either my God, or he wasn't. I had no interest in "religion." I did not, and still do not, like religious rituals. This issue—Jesus being God—had to do with life. It had to do with how I lived my life. If he was truly God, then I was a fool for not listening to him about the meaning of life, about how I was to direct my life's energies, about living out the day-to-day activities of my life. If he was not God, then I was a fool to try to pretend religiously that he was.

I grew up in churches where many families drove through the "magic tunnel" as they got to church. Families could be at each other's throats, they could be mean and hateful, they could be treating each other cruelly, yet upon entering the church parking lot it was as though they drove through a magic tunnel and everyone became a completely different person—loving, kind, and happy! I think that we have all experienced some of that, because the Evil One seems to work overtime on Sunday morning, trying to keep us out of sorts so that we cannot worship with a pure heart! However, some of those who drive through "magic tunnels" reveal a deeper problem—the problem of religiosity. This is a problem of those who attend church because they are attempting to "earn" salvation by good works, of those who do not have a personal relationship with Jesus Christ yet are cultural Christians who have grown up going to church as the "right thing to do" while their heart is far from the living God.

The step-father that I had in my early childhood could be a very mean person (not the step-father I have now, who is a wonderful, godly man!). Some of the earliest recollections of my childhood are waking up at night and hearing my mother being hit and slapped around by my step-father, seeing her getting knocked to the ground, and hearing her crying out in pain. My mom is an incredibly strong person. But her strength is not physical strength; it is the strength of character, of determination, of faith. She had tuberculosis of the bone as a child and spent months in a full body cast as she healed from surgeries on her diseased hip. To this day she has a slight limp, yet it has never slowed her down! She is a strong, courageous person. But my step-father, for some mean reason, liked to ridicule her. When they would have an argument, he would lift up her skirt, point to her disfigured hip, laugh, and call her "cripple." Yet this same step-father was often a leader in the different churches we attended. He would be one person during the week but a different person as soon as we arrived at church.

I left church in my early teens. My mom was not happy with that decision, but she knew my personal struggle. I came to the realization that much of what I saw was religious game playing. I did not want that. I went off in my own directions, trying to find happiness and meaning. But because I was so young, I usually settled for self-indulgent pleasure seeking. Through some of the experiences I have described in earlier chapters, I became a very unhappy, bitter young man. I hit the bottom of life's direction. I realized that I was as phony and as much of a game player as many of those whom I criticized in church. In the blackness of my own heart I came to know that I was really no different than my early step-father, even though I may not have acted like him on the outside.

It was then that I came in contact with Jesus. As I listened to his message, I knew that he was calling me to follow him as my God. It meant giving all that I was to him. This was no flip decision. It was no simple prayer to gain some kind of "life insurance." It meant giving my life to Jesus. I struggled with that all-or-nothing decision for several months. Finally, convinced that Jesus truly was God, I gave myself to him. I had counted the cost of what it meant to have Jesus as my God, and I was ready to follow him.

Naturally, my life turned around. I was following Jesus every day, and I was listening to what he said about life. I had a direction to follow and a purpose for life. I spent time with other believers who helped me to know Jesus better. Some things naturally went by the wayside. The day I became a Christian I gave up drugs and the way of life that drugs represented—the lifestyle, the philosophies, the musical expressions of reality—for they had been my "god." That very first day I exchanged my "god" of drugs for the God of the universe, Jesus Christ. Other things went by the wayside in due time. For example, I had a foul mouth back then. As I began to understand the purity of life Jesus provided, I was enabled by his Spirit to control my swearing. My wife still looks at that as a major miracle! I was not becoming religious; I was becoming a true human being as God had intended me to be from creation. I was living life in the way it was intended to be lived. The Christian life is life as God created it to be lived.

To this day, that time of considering the implications of Jesus being my God remains as the determining criterion of life. I certainly have much growing yet to do. And I still have areas of life that must be brought into line with Jesus' goals for me. Yet my first decision set the direction for how I would live my life. Jesus is either God, or he is not. If he is God, then I am a fool for not living in relationship with him as my God. If he is not God, then I am a fool for trying to pretend religiously that he is. The decision is all-important. The cost of the decision is one's entire life.

Luke, the beloved physician, who is so tender in his portrayal of people and events surrounding Jesus' life, presents one of the harshest delineations of what authentic discipleship to Jesus means. Luke is the only evangelist to continue his story beyond the Resurrection into the early church, allowing us to see the outworkings of discipleship in the Christian era. He recognizes that a long path lies beyond one's initial commitment, a path that will be marked by Spirit-filled victory for the church but will also be marked by apostasy, persecution, and martyrdom. Truly, Luke allows us to see that responding to the call to follow Jesus is the beginning point that leads onto the path of the Christian life. Because of this historical perspective, Luke, more than any other evangelist, emphasizes the cost that Jesus' disciples must make in following after him. That cost involves seemingly impossible demands for entrance into discipleship, such as taking up the cross, hating family and one's own life in this world, not looking back, or selling all one owns. It is a cost that ultimately means one's own life, sounding intriguingly similar to Paul's statement, "You are not your own; you were bought at a price. Therefore, honor God with your body" (1Co 6:19b–20).

Responding to the call to follow Jesus is no flip decision, no fad dedication. Neither is it for the half-hearted or the faint-hearted. Following Jesus means committing one's life to the Master and his Way. As we do so, his Spirit provides the courage, the strength, and the endurance necessary to make it to the end of the Way.

LUKE'S DISTINCTIVE VIEW OF DISCIPLESHIP

Detecting Luke's portrait of the disciples must come from a thorough study of his gospel itself, but that portrait comes more sharply into focus when we compare discipleship teaching in his gospel with that found in the other Gospels, especially the synoptics. Also, since Luke's gospel is volume one of two volumes, Luke-Acts, we will gain a more comprehensive perspective of his portrait by comparing discipleship teaching in his gospel with that found in Acts.

The picture of the disciples in Luke's gospel bears many similarities to those found in Matthew and Mark, but differences occur as well. The most notable differences are as follows.[1]

1. Luke gives a unique account of the calling of Jesus' first followers. Matthew and Mark record an incident in which Jesus walks along the sea of Galilee, sees Peter, Andrew, James, and John, and calls them to follow him, which they did immediately (Mt 4:18–22; Mk 1:16–20). Luke, instead, records the incident of Peter going out into the boat with Jesus, bringing in a miraculous catch of fish, and confessing his sinfulness in the light of Jesus' evident divine authority. Then the brothers left everything to follow Jesus (Lk 5:1–11).

2. Luke mentions a large number of disciples never revealed in Matthew or Mark but recognized by John (Jn 6:60–66). Luke reveals that the Twelve were chosen to be apostles from out of a much larger number of disciples (Lk 6:13, 17). He also notes that at the triumphal entry a large crowd, including Pharisees, observed the entry (19:39), while *a large crowd of disciples* participated in the celebration (19:37–39).

3. Luke alone tells us that Jesus not only sent out the Twelve on a missionary excursion (cf. Mt 10:5ff.; Mk 6:6b–13; Lk 9:1–6), but also sent out seventy (-two) (Lk 10:1–16). Whether the Seventy illustrate a mission to the seventy Gentile nations (Ge 10), are representative of the elders of ancient Israel (Ex 24:1; Nu 11:25), or suggest a supplanting of the ruling Sanhedrin, they indicate that Jesus had many disciples besides the Twelve whom he trained and used in his earthly ministry.[2]

4. Luke also tells of a preaching tour through Galilee in which Jesus took "with him" the Twelve and several women who had been healed by Jesus and who were contributing to the support of Jesus and the Twelve out of their own means (8:1–3). Among those women were Mary Magdalene, out of whom were cast seven demons; Joanna, whose husband, Cuza, was Herod's steward; Susanna; and many

---

[1]Cf. Joseph A. Fitzmyer, *Luke the Theologian: Aspects of His Teaching* (New York: Paulist, 1989), 123–28; Dennis M. Sweetland, *Our Journey with Jesus: Discipleship According to Luke-Acts* (Collegeville, Minn.: Michael Glazier, 1990); Mark Sheridan, "Disciples and Discipleship in Matthew and Luke," *BThB* 3 (1973): 235–55.

[2]Cf. E. Earle Ellis, *The Gospel of Luke*, NCB, rev. ed. (London/Grand Rapids: Marshall, Morgan & Scott/Eerdmans, 1974), 156–57.

others. The wording indicates that these women were themselves disciples of Jesus.[3]

5. Luke reveals a tenderness toward Peter's denials not found in the other Gospels. Not only does Luke tell of the spiritual conflict involving Satan sifting Peter, but the scandal of Peter's denials is somewhat tempered by Jesus' prayer for Peter and the hint of his future role of strengthening the other disciples (22:31–34).

6. While Luke does not include the devastating statement that all the disciples left Jesus and fled at the betrayal scene at Gethsemane (cf. Mt 26:56; Mk 14:50; Lk 22:53–54), he does mention that all those knowing Jesus were with the women from Galilee at the Crucifixion (cf. Mt 27:55–56; Mk 15:40–41; Lk 23:49). The phrase "all those knowing him" refers to Jesus' friends, not his relatives (cf. Lk 2:44), indicating that some of his followers were at the Crucifixion (cf. Jn 19:26).[4] The phrase "all those knowing him" is masculine plural (*pantes hoi gnōstoi*). Combined with mention of "the women who had followed him from Galilee," the phrase indicates that there were both men and women followers of Jesus who witnessed the Crucifixion.[5]

An important light is thrown on Luke's portrait of discipleship when we compare the Gospel of Luke with Acts. In Acts the word *disciple* (Ac 6:1–2, 7; 9:10, 26; 11:26; 14:21–22; 15:10; 16:1) is used as a synonym for "believers in Christ." For example, "all the believers" (4:32) is a synonymous expression for "all the disciples" (6:2). Disciples were all those who confessed Jesus as Savior, those who later were called "Christians" (11:26; 26:28), or "saints" (9:13, 32, 41), or "the sect of the Nazarenes" (24:5). Luke's use of the term *disciple* in his gospel foreshadows the use in Acts. Since "a large crowd of his disciples" (Lk 6:13, 17a) is distinguished from "a great number of people" (v. 17b), Luke wants his readers to know that Jesus had a great following of people who were his disciples, who were not just part of the crowd (6:13; 8:9; 9:54; 10:23; 11:1; 14:26; 19:37, 39). These disciples were convinced believers in Jesus, in contrast to the crowds, who could be termed "the curious."[6] However, this broader group of disciples were not apostles (6:13). The Twelve continued to act as the focal point to represent

---

[3]E.g., "with him" [*sun autō*] expresses discipleship in Luke's gospel; cf. Lk 8:38; 9:18; 22:56. See chap. 7, "Becoming Like Jesus."

[4]I. Howard Marshall, *The Gospel of Luke: A Commentary on the Greek Text*, NIGTC (Grand Rapids: Eerdmans, 1978), 877.

[5]Ibid., Marshall notes that *gnōstoi* is normally neuter in Luke.

[6]Cf. Charles H. Talbert, "Discipleship in Luke-Acts," in *Discipleship in the New Testament*, ed. Fernando F. Segovia (Philadelphia: Fortress, 1985), 62.

discipleship, but Luke wants his readers to know that a much larger group of disciples were followers of the Master as well.[7]

LUKE'S DEVELOPMENT OF DISCIPLESHIP

An important point Luke allows us to see is that there were concentric circles of disciples around Jesus during his public ministry. In the inner circle were the two sets of brothers (Peter and Andrew, James and John). Then came the circle of the Twelve. After the circle of the Twelve came a circle of colaborers, including the Seventy (-two) and the women who ministered to Jesus. Then came a circle that included the multitude of disciples, people who were committed believers. Outside this last circle of disciples came the large crowds of people who were curious about Jesus and his activities but who were not yet believers. All of this is very important to help us understand Luke's unique perspective of discipleship.

Followers on the Way

One of Jesus' favorite metaphors describing entrance to eternal life was a variation on the concept of a "door" (*thura*) or "gate" (*pulē*).[8] In one of the best-known expositions of this metaphor (Jn 10:1–17), Jesus declares that he is the gate (*thura*) to the sheepfold, into which a person goes to be saved, to find abundant life (Jn 10:9–10). Here Jesus emphasizes that a person can find salvation only through him and that after entering through Jesus the gate, the person ventures forth into abundant life.[9] In another well-known saying, Jesus contrasts the wide gate and broad/easy way that leads to destruction with the narrow gate (*pulē*) and narrow/difficult way that leads to life (Mt 7:13–14). An important point Jesus makes here is that the door comes first, before the way. What this means is that a person does not walk a narrow way in order to gain access to the door to life; that would be a system of works. Rather, a person comes through the door to salvation, i.e., Jesus, which then opens onto the narrow path of life shared with Jesus, i.e., discipleship.[10]

---

[7]John Nolland, *Luke 1–9:20*, WBC 35A (Dallas: Word, 1989), 246.

[8]Interestingly, Mark does not record this metaphor, while each of the other Evangelists do, indicating a strong witness to the metaphor in the early tradition; cf. Marshall, *Gospel of Luke*, 563; Barnabas Lindars, *The Gospel of John*, NCB (London/Grand Rapids: Marshall, Morgan & Scott/Eerdmans, 1972), 352–55; W. D. Davies and Dale C. Allison, Jr., *The Gospel According to Saint Matthew*, ICC (Edinburgh: T. & T. Clark, 1988), 1:695.

[9]Cf. Lindars, *John*, 359–60.

[10]For a discussion of this distinction, see Donald A. Carson, "Matthew," *EBC* (Grand Rapids: Zondervan, 1984), 8:189–90.

Luke, both in his gospel and in Acts, also records this metaphorical expression of the narrow door (*thura*) through which people must enter in order to gain salvation (Lk 13:23–24; Ac 14:27). On one occasion an unknown person came to Jesus and asked, "Lord, are only a few people going to be saved?" Jesus responded with the door metaphor, saying, "Make every effort to enter through the narrow door, because many, I tell you, will try to enter and will not be able to" (Lk 13:23–24). Although many disciples confessed Jesus as Savior, in the light of the general crowds of people who had not made a decision, even the large number of disciples were only a few. Those who enter through the narrow gate are ushered into salvation, bringing into view the central theme of Luke's portrait of discipleship: *Disciples of Jesus are followers on the Way.*

Both in his gospel and in Acts, Luke emphasizes that entrance into the Way of salvation and discipleship is found through faith alone (Lk 7:50; 8:48; 13:22–30; 17:19; cf. Ac 10:43; 13:38–39; 16:31).[11] Salvation itself is "the Way" (*hē hodos*), a pattern of life revealed by God. As the believer enters the narrow gate to salvation, he or she is introduced to the Way of discipleship, a pattern of life following Jesus. Thus people must enter into and stride along that Way in the footsteps of the Master.[12] Luke's geographical perspective, with Jerusalem the center, concentrates on Jesus as he journeys to Jerusalem for the Passion (Lk 9:51), the disciples traveling with him along the road (v. 57). This idea of salvation as "the Way" leads in time to calling the community of disciples in Acts "the Way" (Ac 9:2; 19:9, 23; 22:4; 24:14, 22), an early designation or title for those known as "the church."

The Costly Way

Although Jesus graciously holds open the door of faith to the curious seekers who wish to follow him, he also declares that true faith for those who wish to enter and walk on the Way with him is costly. The theme of "counting the cost" provides a primary color for Luke's overall portrait of discipleship (e.g., 9:57–62; 18:24–30). A

---

[11]See I. Howard Marshall, *Luke: Historian and Theologian,* 3d ed. (Exeter: Paternoster, 1988), 188–215; Joseph A. Fitzmyer, *The Gospel According to Luke (I–IX): Introduction, Translation, and Notes, AB* (Garden City, N.Y.: Doubleday, 1981), 28:235–37; Fitzmyer, *Luke the Theologian,* 130–31.

[12]Fitzmyer, *Luke the Theologian,* 134–35; cf. Ernest Best, *Following Jesus: Discipleship in the Gospel of Mark, JSNTSup* 4 (Sheffield: Univ. of Sheffield, 1981), 246ff. Fitzmyer notes that Luke plays on the compounds of the word *way* (*hodos*) and aspects of "the way." Jesus has entered on that course (*eisodos,* Ac 13:24); he moves along it (*poreuesthai,* passim); and he heads for its outcome (*exodos,* the transit to the Father, Lk 9:31) (*Luke the Theologian,* 134–35).

distinctive "cost" was necessary for those who received the call to follow Jesus and join him in traveling around on his mission of publicly proclaiming that the kingdom of God was at hand. Those who received this call were especially the Twelve but presumably also the Seventy (Lk 10) who were sent out on a preaching mission, and the women who traveled with Jesus and the Twelve on a preaching mission (8:1–3).

The call to "count the cost" was not just for those called to service. This call was extended to all who would come after Jesus. It was given to individuals and to the crowds of people who had not yet made a decision to enter into eternal life.[13] Positively, to count the cost meant to recognize that love for God was at the center of faith.[14] A key passage is Luke 10:25–37, where an expert in the law came to Jesus asking about obtaining eternal life. When Jesus asked him what was written in the law, the lawyer rightly understood that to obtain eternal life one's heart, soul, mind, and strength must be focused on loving God and one's neighbor as oneself. But what does it really mean to love God and neighbor? Jesus did not leave such important issues as an abstract concept—he regularly brought abstracts into the realm of the concrete. Here he indicated that the practical demonstration of love for God and neighbor was found in showing mercy to one's neighbor. If this lawyer would obtain eternal life, he must go and do likewise (v. 37).

Negatively, to count the cost meant to recognize that one entered into the life of discipleship through detachment from competing allegiances and through giving personal allegiance to Jesus as Master.[15] A key passage is Luke 14:25–33, in which Jesus addresses the crowds about the conditions of entrance into discipleship. The crowds were coming to Jesus but had not yet made a commitment to him. Before they make such a commitment, Jesus gives a threefold challenge, indicating that they must count the cost of such a commitment. Luke records the incident in some detail.

> Large crowds were traveling with Jesus, and turning to them he said: "If anyone comes to me and does not hate his father and mother, his wife and children, his brothers and sisters—yes, even his own life—he cannot be my disciple. And anyone who does not carry his cross and follow me cannot be my disciple.

[13]Wolfgang Schrage, *The Ethics of the New Testament* (Philadelphia: Fortress, 1988), 51.

[14]Cf. Marshall, *Gospel of Luke*, 443.

[15]Cf. Charles H. Talbert, "Discipleship in Luke-Acts," in *Discipleship in the New Testament*, ed. Fernando F. Segovia (Philadelphia: Fortress, 1985), 62.

"Suppose one of you wants to build a tower. Will he not first sit down and estimate the cost to see if he has enough money to complete it? For if he lays the foundation and is not able to finish it, everyone who sees it will ridicule him, saying, 'This fellow began to build and was not able to finish.'

"Or suppose a king is about to go to war against another king. Will he not first sit down and consider whether he is able with ten thousand men to oppose the one coming against him with twenty thousand? If he is not able, he will send a delegation while the other is still a long way off and will ask for terms of peace. In the same way, any of you who does not give up everything he has cannot be my disciple."

The costly way is understood most clearly by looking at the threefold repeated refrain in verses 26, 27, 33—". . . cannot be my disciple." Here Jesus describes the cost of discipleship in terms of allegiance to family, self-will, and one's all.

FAMILY

First, Jesus says, "If anyone comes to me and does not hate his father and mother, his wife and children, his brothers and sisters—yes, even his own life—he cannot be my disciple" (Lk 14:26). Following Jesus as his disciple was not what the people might expect. Following Jesus meant to put him in such a place of prominence in one's life that, if any other commitment dared to usurp the place of Jesus, one must "hate" it. Nothing else must be a substitute for Jesus as the focus of allegiance: neither family (14:26), nor wealth (12:13–21; 16:10–13, 14–15, 19–31), nor one's own life (14:26), nor anything at all (v. 33). Entrance into the way of discipleship meant entering the narrow gate to salvation (13:22–30) to follow after Jesus alone (9:23; 14:27). This must have been a shock to the crowd, because prophetic figures regularly gathered large crowds around them. Jesus instead halted the enthusiastic crowd by his challenge to count the cost. Jesus' form of discipleship is radically different than other forms, demanding that the "would-be follower" give him preeminence as Master.

Luke 14:26 obviously cannot mean literal hatred, because Jesus commanded his followers to love even their enemies (6:27), because he cared for his own mother (Jn 19:26–27), and because he would not go contrary to Old Testament commands to honor one's father and mother (Ex 20:12).[16] Rather, "hate" here may mean something like loving less (cf. Ge 29:31, 33; Dt 21:15), indicating the necessity of the preeminence of love for God in comparison to all other love

---

[16]Cf. Robert H. Stein, *Difficult Passages in the New Testament: Interpreting Puzzling Texts in the Gospels and Epistles* (Grand Rapids: Baker, 1990), 172.

relationships,[17] or it may point to the separation that must come when loyalties of this world attempt to keep a person from following after Jesus (cf. Lk 8:20ff.; 9:59–62), or, similarly, it may point to the necessity of subordinating everything, even one's own being, to one's commitment to Jesus (cf. Lk 16:13; also 9:59–62).[18] We saw earlier that the family played a major role in the life of Judaism, to the point where it could determine the direction of an individual family member's life. Within first-century Judaism, the accepted ideal was marrying and building up a family. Shmuel Safrai concludes, "The sages saw in the family not only the fulfillment of a divine commandment but also the basis for social life, and they tried to invest family life with an aura of holiness."[19] Jesus did not call for a disruption of the family or for rebellion against it; rather he declared that he, not the family, must be the primary focus of allegiance. We can see that Jesus did not mean to sever all family relationships, because he called pairs of brothers to be among the Twelve (Mt 4:18–22); he had the highest regard for marriage, condemning adultery and prohibiting divorce except in cases of unchastity (Mt 5:27–32; 19:3–9); he allowed Peter to maintain a family relationship with at least his wife's mother (Mk 1:29–31); and he directed the apostle John to care for his (Jesus') mother after his death (Jn 19:26–27). Jesus supported biblical family relationships, yet when they were a hindrance to following him, they were to be "hated."[20] Therefore one enters into the life of discipleship through giving allegiance to Jesus as one's God and Master, not allowing anything else to hinder that allegiance.[21]

SELF

Second, Jesus says, "And anyone who does not carry his cross and follow me cannot be my disciple" (Lk 14:27). Jesus knew the heart of those whom he called to follow him. He wanted people whose faith was singularly focused upon him. Some who took up following him

---

[17]Leon Morris, *The Gospel According to St. Luke* (Grand Rapids: Eerdmans, 1974), 235–36.

[18]Ellis, *Luke*, 195.

[19]Shmuel Safrai, "Home and Family," *The Jewish People in the First Century*, vol. 2, Section One: Compendia Rerum Iudaicarum ad Novum Testamentum (Philadelphia: Fortress, 1976), 728–92.

[20]Cf. W. White, "Family," *ZPEB* 2:496–501; O. J. Baab, "Father," *IDB* 2:245. For a rather critically slanted perspective, but with some of the same conclusions, see Richard A. Horsley, *Jesus and the Spiral of Violence* (San Francisco: Harper & Row, 1987), 231–45.

[21]Cf. Charles H. Talbert, "Discipleship in Luke-Acts," in *Discipleship in the New Testament*, ed. Fernando F. Segovia (Philadelphia: Fortress, 1985), 62; Donald Guthrie, *New Testament Theology* (Downers Grove, Ill.: InterVarsity Press, 1981), 422.

turned out not to be true believers (e.g., Jn 6:60–66). Therefore, Jesus consistently called people to count the cost of his form of disciple-ship, which essentially meant the cost of one's life. The full principle is found in the saying found earlier in Luke's gospel.

> Then he said to them all: "If anyone would come after me, he must deny himself and take up his cross daily and follow me. For whoever wants to save his life will lose it, but whoever loses his life for me will save it. What good is it for a man to gain the whole world, and yet lose or forfeit his very self? If anyone is ashamed of me and my words, the Son of Man will be ashamed of him when he comes in his glory and in the glory of the Father and of the holy angels." (9:23–26)

This "cost" saying comes in a setting where Jesus offers eternal life through the Gospel message; notice that Jesus spoke to all. Denying one's self, bearing one's cross, and following Jesus is the same as the cost one must count in following Jesus in discipleship (Lk 14:27). The entire expression must be understood in the context of Jesus' prediction of his going to the cross. The cross, while a terrible symbol of suffering and shame, was the Father's will for Jesus' life. Going to the cross was the purpose for which Jesus came to earth. In Gethsemane prior to his crucifixion Jesus affirmed to the Father his willingness to go to the cross, because "not my will, but yours be done" (22:42). To come after Jesus means to deny one's own will for one's life, to take up the Father's will, and to follow Jesus as an outward demonstration of one's faith. It is a symbol of submission to God's will for our lives.[22] On an occasion when his earthly mother and brothers were wanting to speak to him, Jesus made clear the relationship of those who heard his call to discipleship. "Pointing to his disciples, he said, 'Here are my mother and my brothers. For whoever does the will of my Father in heaven is my brother and sister and mother'" (Mt 12:49–50). Following Jesus in discipleship was the expression of doing the will of the Father.

Even as Jesus came to earth not to do his own will but the will of the Father, and that will for his life was going to the cross (Lk 22:42), so each person must imitate Christ by denying his or her own will, taking up the Father's will, and following Jesus (cf. 9:23). The imagery of the cross necessarily implies considering as well the suffering that will accompany following Jesus.[23]

---

[22]Cf. Michael P. Green, "The Meaning of Cross-Bearing," *BS* 140 (1983): 117–33. Cf. also Johannes Schneider, "σταυρός," *TDNT* 7:577–79; Schrage, *Ethics of the New Testament*, 51.

[23]Cf. Marshall, *Gospel of Luke*, 593; Ellis, *Luke*, 195; David P. Seccombe, "Take Up Your Cross," in *God Who Is Rich in Mercy: Essays Presented to D. B.*

The switch of tense in the saying, from the aorist imperative to the present imperative, has been seen by some grammarians as significant. Nigel Turner indicates that the first two admonitions—"deny oneself, take up one's cross"—which are aorist imperatives, give commands to commence some action, while the third admonition—"follow me"—gives a command to do something constantly, to continue to do it. Here it would mean, "Let him deny himself [at once, aorist imperative] and take up his cross [at once, aorist imperative] and follow me [continually, present imperative]." Denying self and taking up the cross is a decision, once and for all, but following is a continuous discipline.[24] This is the distinction between the decision of salvation and the continuous practice of following Jesus.

ONE'S ALL

Third, in this extended statement to the crowd, Jesus gives two parables that emphasize the necessity of a person counting the cost of what following him will entail (Lk 14:28–32). On the one hand, Jesus likens it to a person who sits down before building a tower to consider what it will cost so that he is not ridiculed for failing to have enough to finish (vv. 28–30). On the other hand, Jesus likens it to a king who must calculate the necessary strength of his army before going into battle (vv. 31–32). The lesson of the two parables is made clear in verse 33: "In the same way, any of you who does not give up everything he has cannot be my disciple." These words condemn all half-heartedness. Jesus' words play on the thought of the two parables in an intriguing manner. The parables emphasize the complete dedication of resources one must make in order to complete a task or win a battle. The discipleship saying emphasizes the complete dedication of oneself that a person must make to Jesus. There seems to be a twofold teaching. First, when looking ahead at the long path of discipleship, one must recognize that complete dedication is required for the long haul. Those who are only half-hearted will abandon the task. Second, when a person gives away the right of ownership to all one has, he or she is utterly dependent upon Jesus to supply the necessary resources to accomplish the tasks to which Jesus calls his disciples. That Jesus is not here asking the crowds to give away everything in order to become disciples is

Knox, ed. Peter T. O'Brien and David G. Peterson (Homebush, Australia: Anzea, 1986), 145–48.

[24]Nigel Turner, *Syntax,* vol. 3 of *A Grammar of New Testament Greek* by James Hope Moulton (Edinburgh: T. & T. Clark, 1963), 76. Cf. also H. E. Dana and Julius R. Mantey, *A Manual Grammar of the Greek New Testament,* rev. ed. (New York: Macmillan, 1957), 300.

recognized by the fact that other followers continued to retain possessions (e.g., Peter and Andrew retained a house after their calling [Mk 1:29]; Joseph of Arimathea was a wealthy disciple [Mt 27:57; Lk 23:50–53]; and the women followers supported Jesus out of their own possessions [*huparontōn*, Lk 8:1–3, the same participle found here in Lk 14:33]). Walter Liefeld remarks:

> Here, in contrast to the cares of the rich young ruler (18:22), Jesus does not say a disciple should sell all his possessions and give everything away. His thought probably is that of abandonment of things, yielding up the right of ownership, rather than outright disposal of them. The disciple of Jesus may be given the use of things in trust, as a stewardship, but they are no longer his own. The present tense ["give up," *apotassetai*] implies that what Jesus requires in relation to possessions is a continual attitude of abandonment.[25]

Possessions all too often become one's source of security, one's badge of self-worth, one's means of personal power. Jesus commands his followers to find their security, self-worth, and power in him. They must count the cost of what such a wholehearted commitment to Jesus requires.[26]

If a person desires to become a disciple of Jesus, it will cost much in terms of undivided allegiance to Jesus as God (Lk 14:26), in terms of denial of one's own will for the sake of taking up the will of God (v. 27) and in terms of abandonment of personal resourcefulness for the resources one obtains as a disciple of Jesus (v. 33). Nothing else must be a substitute for Jesus as the focus of allegiance: neither family (v. 26), nor wealth (12:13–21; 16:10–13, 14–15, 19–31), nor one's own life (14:26), nor anything at all (v. 33). Entrance into the way of discipleship means entering the narrow gate to salvation (13:22–30) to follow after Jesus alone (9:23; 14:27).

Personalized Cost and Cross

How paradoxical it is that the gift of eternal life comes through counting the cost of following Jesus! Yet this is seen clearly in the incident surrounding a rich young man who came to Jesus seeking how he might inherit eternal life. Although the young man could declare confidently that he had kept the commandments from his youth, Jesus said that he lacked one thing:

---

[25]Walter L. Liefeld, "Luke," *EBC* (Grand Rapids: Zondervan, 1984), 8:980.
[26]Norval Geldenhuys, *Commentary on the Gospel of Luke*, *NICNT* (Grand Rapids: Eerdmans, 1951), 398–99.

"Sell everything you have and give to the poor, and you will have treasure in heaven. Then come, follow me."

When he heard this, he became very sad, because he was a man of great wealth. Jesus looked at him and said, "How hard it is for the rich to enter the kingdom of God! Indeed, it is easier for a camel to go through the eye of a needle than for a rich man to enter the kingdom of God" (Lk 18:22–25).

Mark adds the additional, tragic detail that this rich young man "went away sad" (10:22). This young man was not being told to go earn his salvation or to buy it by almsgiving. Rather, his heart was being tested by Jesus, for Jesus knew his priorities. Although he had a form of religious motivation, his wealth was a higher priority than following Jesus. Jesus was trying to help this young man overcome his wealth centeredness.[27]

The temptation to substitute wealth for trust in God is also demonstrated in the parable of the rich fool (Lk 12:13–21). Wealth, with the accompanying power and prestige, can easily become one's god, one's source of security, hope, and self-esteem. Jesus put this young man to the test, trying to get him to see that his wealth was what was keeping him from God. But as was sadly revealed, this young man could not let go of the central place wealth had in his life. Hence, he could not find true treasure, the treasure of eternal life by following Jesus in discipleship. His faith was in wealth, not in Jesus.

Undivided loyalty to Jesus, which can be defined as love for God, is at the center of faith.[28] A lawyer who came to Jesus rightly understood that to obtain eternal life one's heart, soul, mind, and strength must be focused on loving God, and that the practical demonstration of love for God is loving one's neighbor as oneself (Cf. Lk 10:25–37). Love for God and neighbor is the evidence that one has made unqualified commitment to Jesus and his Way.

These "cost and cross" passages are some of the most difficult in Scripture to understand rightly. They have given rise to polarized theological positions that are somewhat artificial. Many of the difficulties would be resolved if we would see that the call by Jesus to count the cost and bear the cross are calls for allegiance to him as one's God. He is not at that moment calling people to clean up every area of their lives before making a decision to follow him. The cost of each person's cross was personalized in keeping with the inclinations

----

[27]Cf. Guthrie, *New Testament Theology*, 422; contra Zane C. Hodges, *Absolutely Free: A Biblical Reply to Lordship Salvation* (Grand Rapids/Dallas: Zondervan/Redención Viva, 1989), 181–90. Hodges' theological agenda causes him to overlook completely the point of the interaction with the ruler and the ensuing interaction with the disciples and Peter.

[28]Cf. Marshall, *Gospel of Luke*, 443.

of the heart of the individual and the will of the Father. Although the rich young ruler was called to give up his riches, Nicodemus and Joseph of Arimathea, who became disciples of Jesus sometime during his earthly ministry (cf. Jn 3:1–14; 19:38–42), remained within the religious establishment and retained their wealth. When demonstration of their faith and allegiance to Jesus was required, they came forward to claim the body of Jesus (Mt 27:57–60). Although they were wealthy individuals, apparently wealth was not the same kind of personal "god" that it was for the rich young ruler.[29] Joseph of Arimathea and Nicodemus used their wealth and influence to supply a new tomb for the crucified Jesus to occupy until his resurrection.

Each person must count the cost of allegiance to Jesus, but that cost is personalized by Jesus to each individual. "The call to give up everything for the sake of the one precious pearl is addressed to all (Mt 13:45–46), but the either/or and the break with familiar and customary rules of conduct, indeed the nature of adherence and cause of Jesus and thus the presence of the kingdom of God, obviously takes on different forms for different people."[30] Jesus knows the heart of each one whom he calls, but the cost remains for each. The "cost" of discipleship is one's life. As the apostle Paul would say later, "I have been crucified with Christ; and it is no longer I who live, but Christ lives in me; and the life which I now live in the flesh I live by faith in the Son of God, who loved me, and delivered Himself up for me" (Gal 2:20 NASB).

Traveling Along the Way

Discipleship begins through entrance to the Way of salvation; discipleship advances as one travels along the Way. Luke reveals to us that self-denial, taking up the cross, and following Jesus not only characterize entrance into the Way but also characterize life on the Way. The Lukan account of the cross-bearing proclamation specifies that denial of one's own will and taking up of the Father's will to follow the Master is something that must occur on a daily basis (cf. Lk 9:23; Mk 8:34). Jesus' life is continually set before the disciples as the example of the life that is given over to fulfilling the will of God. Therefore, the blessed life on the Way is the one that hears and obeys the Word of God (Lk 11:27–28). Not all who walk on the Way truly belong to the Way. External statements of commitment must be judged by the fruit of one's life (6:43–49; 19:11–27). That fruit consists, at least in part, in loving and doing good to others (6:17–36),

---

[29] Cf. Guthrie, *New Testament Theology*, 422.
[30] Schrage, *Ethics of the New Testament*, 51.

proper stewardship of material possessions (6:35; 8:3), servanthood (22:24–30), prayer (10:2; 11:1; 18:1–8), and testimony to the Way (9:1–6; 10:1–12, 17–20; 12:8–12; 14:23–24; 24:44–49).

In Mark's gospel the cross saying is given to an audience composed of both the crowds and the disciples (Mk 8:34–38), and in Matthew's gospel the saying is given to an audience composed of only disciples (Mt 16:24–28). We should note, therefore, that there is a point of examining oneself even after making a commitment for salvation. During Jesus' earthly ministry there was a developing understanding among the disciples of who he was. We must remember that not all who called themselves his disciples at the beginning correctly understood that Jesus was a different sort of messianic Deliverer than some of them hoped for or expected. Many of Jesus' disciples turned away when he more clearly revealed himself (cf. Jn 6:60–66). Even the Twelve came to firmer recognition of his messianic identity and purposes than they had when they first started following him, and one of the Twelve turned out not to be a true believer (cf. vv. 70–71). When Jesus gave the cross-bearing saying to those who were already disciples, it was intended to make them examine themselves to see whether they actually knew what their decision entailed. The way of the cross would eventually involve much more than the initial decision. "Jesus did not permit any compromise. Those who were ashamed of him now, the Son of man would be ashamed of in the coming of the kingdom (Mk 8:38)."[31]

IMPLICATIONS

Luke accents the cost that disciples must make in following Jesus on the Way. Jesus' seemingly harsh demands for entrance into discipleship—such as taking up the cross, hating family and one's own life in this world, not looking back, and selling all one owns—have long been difficult to reconcile with his gracious invitation. When understood within the context of the first-century social/religious setting, those demands allow us to see that Jesus was calling for a distinct form of discipleship. Becoming Jesus' disciple was not a vocational change, not a political attachment, not even a new stirring of God. Rather, this was a decision of whether one would follow Jesus as the Way to eternal life. Any other attachment, whether familial or religious or economic, was substituting another "god" for Jesus. Both entrance to the Way and life on the Way are through following Jesus in discipleship. While Luke concentrated on this portrait of discipleship, he was not alone in this emphasis. The

---

[31]Guthrie, *New Testament Theology*, 422.

apostle John also emphasized life with Jesus as the true Way. John records that Jesus said, "I am the way and the truth and the life. No one comes to the Father except through me" (Jn 14:6). The apostle Paul emphatically declared, "For to me, to live is Christ and to die is gain" (Php 1:21).

The life of the disciple may be summed up in Luke's perspective as a person who has given his or her allegiance to Jesus as Savior, who has been ushered into the Way of walking with Jesus as Master, and who is being transformed into the likeness of the Master through obedience to his Word. Jesus calls for a radical commitment to him that will ultimately produce change in a person's life. He offers salvation solely by grace, but the door to salvation is narrow (13:23–24)—as narrow as Jesus: allegiance to Jesus alone as Savior, allegiance to Jesus' will for life, and allegiance to identification with Jesus.

Jesus understands the heart of individuals and calls for personalized external actions that will declare the state of the heart. The actions of the rich young ruler in clinging to his wealth were an indication that his wealth was a higher priority than faith in Jesus for eternal life (Lk 18:18–25). The actions of Zacchaeus the tax collector in giving up his wealth was an indication that salvation had come to this lost sinner (19:1–10). What must be declared emphatically is that in both of these cases the work of God is in view. Even though the rich young ruler turned away from salvation because of his love for money, he could have done as Jesus directed him to do. The power of God can accomplish what is seemingly impossible for man (cf. Lk 18:26–27).[32] Zacchaeus's response of generosity was not prompted by his religious pursuit of salvation; rather, Jesus came to seek and to save Zacchaeus. Giving up his wealth was simply an indication that Zacchaeus had responded to Jesus with the same kind of faith that characterized all true people of faith, such as Abraham (cf. 19:9–10).[33] External actions are an indication of a heart that is rightly directed toward Jesus, and those actions are accomplished by the inner working of God in response to faith.

We can see the interplay of faith and actions clearly in these passages from Luke, but we often have difficulty seeing how they should work in our own experience. When we try to apply Jesus' challenge to count the cost, we often struggle with going to extremes. Some people emphasize counting the cost so strongly that they have been accused of advocating "works salvation." Some people who do not include any challenge to count the cost have been accused of

---

[32]Cf. Liefeld, "Luke," 1004.
[33]Cf. Ellis, *Luke*, 220; Liefeld, "Luke," 1007–8.

advocating "easy-believism." Somehow we must find Jesus' balance, a balance in which we clearly establish that salvation is received by faith alone through grace, yet at the same time we clearly establish that attachments of this world cannot be substitute "gods" for Jesus.

I recently observed some young people who struggled with this balance. One incident occurred on a study tour in Israel when I met three young Palestinians who had become Christians. One of them shared with us how he had been rejected by his family because he had become a Christian. Another was living as a vagabond because his family disowned him when he made known his commitment to Jesus. The third shared that he had not yet told his family that he had become a Christian because he was certain that one of his brothers would kill him for disgracing the family heritage. He knew that the day would soon come when he could no longer keep his faith secret, and it would likely be a matter of choosing eternal life over earthly life. These young men were forced to count the cost of family allegiance over against allegiance to Jesus. Their decision to receive Christ as Savior was by faith, but it was indeed a costly faith.

An opposite incident occurred here in the United States. A young lady became very active in a local church and made a profession of faith in Jesus. Her mother belongs to the Jehovah's Witnesses cult and soon began making life very difficult for the young lady. She made her feel guilty, made her feel that she was rejecting her mother. Finally the young lady succumbed to the pressure and left the church to become active in the Jehovah's Witnesses group with her mother. This young lady counted the cost of allegiance to her family over against allegiance to Jesus and chose to leave Jesus.

In neither of these examples can we know absolutely their hearts. But their actions are a demonstration of the faith response of their hearts.

We saw earlier that Matthew intends his readers to understand that the Christian life is equivalent to being "with Jesus" as his disciple. This means that conversion marks the beginning point of discipleship, not a later point of commitment or a process of spiritual growth. Degrees of maturity will be realized as one traverses the discipleship path, but all true believers are disciples on that path. Therefore, evangelism is the starting point for making disciples. Jesus said that we are to make disciples of all "nations," not to make disciples of those who are already believers. With Luke's additional insights, we can see that prospective converts must somehow be challenged to count the cost of the life of discipleship. We need to be clear in our evangelistic presentations to clarify this point. Those "with Jesus" as his disciples are small in number in comparison to the world. Jesus declared that those who enter into the narrow gate to salvation and discipleship are relatively few in comparison to those who reject the message. That was the case in Jesus' day, and it will continue to be so today. Jesus' Way is the way of the cross, a way that is the calling for all believers.

Therefore, the time of conversion is a significant moment for considering the hardships that lie ahead. Jesus revealed in many places that persecution would come to the early disciples. Our study of discipleship will allow us to look at the early church in Acts and the apostolic fathers, where persecution and martyrdom were the regular lot of Jesus' disciples. To claim the name of Jesus as Savior meant that one would surely experience persecution for the sake of the Name. This is an unmistakable illustration of Jesus' teaching on counting the cost of discipleship. Counting the cost not only meant the cost of what becoming a disciple meant but also the cost of what the life of discipleship might entail. In the parables of counting the cost of discipleship, Jesus plainly pointed out the cost of what completing the process of discipleship would take (Lk 14:28–33). Jesus wanted people to recognize that discipleship was not simply the moment of conversion; it included the life that would follow. We will see that it is this ongoing life that the apostles and apostolic fathers emphasized. Ignatius, in particular, emphasized that the closer he came to the time of completing his life, the closer he was to being a completed disciple.[34]

The same principle of costly faith must characterize not only the initial step of faith but also the ongoing life of faith. We all face many distractions that could keep us from Jesus. Many of those distractions are attempts to create an identity allegiance with the things of the world instead of an allegiance with Jesus. Christians exercise costly faith by continuing to find their personal identity as disciples of Jesus who walk with him in the world. We are tempted to substitute many things for Jesus, often things which are the antithesis of discipleship. Sometimes they can be good things, such as career or community service, which provide us with such prestige or acclaim that we sacrifice our identity as a disciple of Jesus for them.

We know all too well that the things of the world can cause us to lose sight of Jesus, but we need to recognize that things of Christianity can also occupy the place that Jesus should have. As a professor in a Christian school and as a pastor of evangelical churches, I have sometimes been too occupied with things that promote *me* or the *institution*, not necessarily *Jesus*. Whether it is the

---

[34]Cf. chap. 16, "Apostolic Fathers: Martyrs for the Name." See also Demetrios Trakatellis, "'Ακολούθει μοι/Follow Me' (Mk 2:14): Discipleship and Priesthood," *GOThR* 30 (3, 1985): 283, 285.

number of books I write, or the acclaim I receive for my work, or the numbers of people that hear me speak, I can be tempted to find my identity in these things rather than simply in being a disciple of Jesus who walks with him in this world. As I did in my first response to Jesus, I must do today. I must count the cost, and then I must daily take up my cross and follow Jesus. C. S. Lewis recognized that Jesus' call to count the cost meant that we were putting our lives into his hands so that he can perform the task of making us completely into his image. Lewis tries to explain this from Jesus' standpoint, declaring:

> That is why He warned people to "count the cost" before becoming Christians. "Make no mistake," He says, "if you let Me, I will make you perfect. The moment you put yourself in My hands, that is what you are in for. Nothing less, or other, than that. You have free will, and if you choose, you can push Me away. But if you do not push Me away, understand that I am going to see this job through. Whatever suffering it may cost you in your earthly life, whatever inconceivable purification it may cost you after death, whatever it costs Me, I will never rest, nor let you rest, until you are literally perfect—until My Father can say without reservation that he is well pleased with you, as he said he was well pleased with Me. This I can do and will do. But I will not do anything less."[35]

These are tough words, but being a disciple of Jesus is only for the tough, those who have counted the cost for real life, eternal life, life with the living Master.

Following up:
1. Why did Jesus give some requirements for entrance to discipleship to some people and different requirements to others?
2. What are some "idols" or "gods" in people's hearts today that might stand in opposition to a "would-be" disciple following Jesus unreservedly? How would you present the Gospel to such a person?
3. What is the significance of the concentric circles of disciples for our ministries today?

---

[35]C. S. Lewis, *Mere Christianity* (New York: Macmillan, 1960), 158.

12

John: Believers
Marked by Jesus

Getting focused:

1. What is "true belief" as opposed to "false belief"? How can we tell the difference between them?
2. Is it possible for someone to believe in Jesus and not be a true disciple? Why or why not?
3. In what way(s) is a Christian different from other people? What would people point to in your life that would mark you as a Christian? What are the most important characteristics of a true Christian?

One of my closest friends (and surfing partner!) and I have had a mutual accountability relationship for more than ten years. Ken and I are as different as day and night when it comes to profession and personality. He is a vice-president in his company, living in the rough and tumble world of international corporate life, with a gregarious, outgoing, and spontaneous personality. I live in the subtle and stretching world of academia, and I tend to be a bit of a loner, somewhat quiet and restrained, although my wife and Ken have been working at getting me out of myself for several years! Ken and I are quite different, yet we meet almost every Saturday morning at 6:30 to surf together, to challenge each other in our personal walk with God, to encourage each other in our family lives, and to support each other in our diverse professional lives. We have shared this relationship since we were involved in a college ministry together more than ten years ago.

When Ken graduated from college, he immediately got a job in his family's business learning the ways of corporate life. Ken had been an extremely dedicated young Christian in college. He wanted to bring that same dedication into the business world. During one of our talks together, I asked him what his goals were for his business career. I've never forgotten his response. He said, "Mike, I'm not in the business world simply to maintain the world system. I'm going to try to do an excellent job, but what I'm really here for is to influence the business world for Jesus. I'm here to tell people about Jesus and to try to let them see that he is real in my life." Those are lofty sounding goals for a young Christian working in a non-Christian company in a non-Christian industry! Yet as I have watched Ken over the years, I have seen him remain unswerving in his commitment to those goals.

Ken is a prime example of the kind of discipleship that John portrays for us in his gospel. John's cosmic perspective views Jesus coming into the world to save people from the wickedness of this age. He draws a striking contrast between those people who truly believe in Jesus for salvation and those who do not. That contrast is displayed visibly in his disciples. Jesus' disciples are the living demonstration to the world that true belief in Jesus makes a difference in a person's life. That is really what Ken is all about. He goes out every day into the rough and tumble of the business world, and his life is evidence that true belief in Jesus for salvation makes a difference in our everyday lives.

At the center of discipleship, at the center of Jesus' purposes for you and me, is the word "life." When Jesus explained to the Jews his reason for coming to earth, he said, "I have come that they may have *life*, and have it to the full" (Jn 10:10, italics mine). Jesus came to bring a life that is different than the life we received at physical birth. At birth we received physical life; that life which we have in common with the rest of creation. But Jesus came to offer us something far different; he came to offer us spiritual life. We need to be very clear about this, because the life that Jesus offers is what brings meaning and purpose. His kind of life is what makes a difference in our day-to-day existence.

Last summer my family and I drove down to the tip of Baja California, Mexico. We drove through a thousand miles of desert roads to get to some beautiful surf spots near Cabo San Lucas. While there I met an intriguing young man. He was about thirty years old and owned a surf shop in a magnificent location called Costa Azul, "Blue Coast." As we sat in an open-air cafe on a hill overlooking this beautiful coastal scene, he told me that in his young life he had traveled over much of the world trying to find the "good life." He had settled in this beautiful location where he has his own tropical paradise. But as we talked he looked at me and said, "Mike, I know that there's still something missing. This "good life" hasn't brought me what I was looking for."

What a contrast between Ken and this young man. It is the very contrast that John draws for us: the contrast between belief and unbelief, the contrast between disciples and nondisciples, the contrast between life and death. John draws a clear line between types of belief and types of disciples. Only true belief makes true disciples, and John allows us to see that inner belief will cause such a radical change that the external life will bear evidence of that belief. The true disciple's life will bear evidence of belief by abiding in Jesus' words, loving other disciples, and bearing fruit.

JOHN'S DISTINCTIVE VIEW OF DISCIPLESHIP

Recent scholarly studies of the meaning and nature of discipleship from the Johannine perspective, while employing a variety of exegetical methodologies, have arrived at general agreement concerning three fundamental aspects of discipleship within John's gospel.[1]

First, the central characteristic of the disciple is belief or acceptance of Jesus' claims vis-á-vis the Father.[2] The disciples, particularly the Twelve (Jn 6:67, 70; 13:18; 15:16, 19; cf. 6:64, 66), are characteristically those who, from the beginning, recognize, acclaim, and believe Jesus for who he truly is (1:41, 45, 49; 6:69; 13:13; 20:28–31; 21:7, 12b). "Jesus' disciples" appear for the first time in John's gospel at the beginning of his public ministry, at the wedding at Cana (2:2). Jesus performs his first public miracle, changing the water into wine, after which John says, "This beginning of His signs Jesus did in Cana of Galilee, and manifested His glory, and His disciples believed in Him" (Jn 2:11 NASB). This is the first hint of John's purpose for writing his Gospel, which he states explicitly in the latter portions of this gospel. There John declares, "Jesus did many other miraculous signs in the presence of his disciples, which are not recorded in this book. But these are written that you may believe that Jesus is the Christ,

---

[1]Cf. Fernando F. Segovia, " 'Peace I Leave with You; My Peace I Give to You': Discipleship in the Fourth Gospel," *Discipleship in the New Testament*, ed. Fernando F. Segovia (Philadelphia: Fortress, 1985); R. Moreno Jiménez, "El discípulo de Jesucristo, según el evangelio de S. Juan," *EstBib* 30 (1971): 269–311; Rudolf Schnackenburg, "Excursus 17: The Disciples, The Community and the Church in the Gospel of John," in *The Gospel According to St. John*, 3 vols., *HTKNT* 4 (New York: Crossroad, 1990), 3:203–17; M. de Jonge, "The Fourth Gospel: The Book of the Disciples," in *Jesus: Stranger from Heaven and Son of God. Jesus Christ and the Christians in Johannine Perspective*, SBLSBS 11 (Missoula, Mont.: Scholars, 1977), 1–27; R. E. Brown, *The Community of the Beloved Disciple: The Life, Loves, and Hates of an Individual Church in New Testament Times* (New York: Paulist, 1979), 25–28.

[2]Segovia, "Discipleship in the Fourth Gospel," 90.

the Son of God, and that by believing you may have life in his name" (20:30–31). Through the performance of miraculous signs, Jesus manifested his glory and revealed his true nature. When people truly recognized him as the Messiah, the Son of God, and believed in him, they received eternal life. From beginning to end, John emphasizes that recognition, acclaim, and belief in Jesus are the central characteristics of a disciple of Jesus.[3]

However, second, this belief is portrayed as necessitating and undergoing a process of gradual understanding and perception.[4] The disciples lack complete understanding of "the hour" of Jesus' ministry,[5] but through his ministry and teaching (Jn 6:67–71; 9:2–7; 11:1–45), the Resurrection appearances (20:8–21), and the reception of the Spirit (vv. 19–23), the disciples ultimately comprehend Jesus' full status as the Son of God. True belief accords with recognition and understanding. As they walked with Jesus, seeing his ministry, hearing his teaching, witnessing his resurrection, and receiving his Spirit, the disciples increasingly recognized and understood him for who he truly was, with a corresponding growth in their belief in him. But this does not imply that their earlier belief was defective; John clearly identifies those who exercise defective belief (e.g., 2:23–24). Rather, true belief grows and matures with increasing recognition and understanding of Jesus' identity.[6]

Third, John draws a sustained and deliberate contrast between believers and unbelievers, between disciples and nondisciples. The nondisciple, the unbeliever, is a part of the unbelieving "world." Although by definition "the world" as a category includes anyone who is actively hostile to God, in the Johannine narrative (and "farewell discourse") "the world" becomes practically synonymous with the category "the Jews," thus giving rise to a very specific contrast between the believing disciples and the unbelieving Jews.[7] John's penchant for contrasts is nowhere more evident than here. Jesus' disciples truly believe, marking them off from those who do not believe, who belong to the world, who have rejected him, who ultimately will be responsible for his death.

---

[3]C. K. Barrett, *The Gospel According to St. John: An Introduction with Commentary and Notes on the Greek Text*, 2d ed. (Philadelphia: Westminster, 1978), 193–94.

[4]Segovia, "Discipleship in the Fourth Gospel," 90, 92.

[5]Jn 2:21–22; 4:27, 33; 6:60; 9:2; 10:6; 11:8, 11–15; 12:16; 13:36; 14:5, 8, 22; 16:17–18.

[6]Barnabas Lindars, *The Gospel of John*, NCB (London/Grand Rapids: Marshall, Morgan & Scott/Eerdmans, 1972), 131–32; Barrett, *John*, 77, 81, 201.

[7]See Jn 1:10c–11; 3:19; 7:4, 7; 8:23; 12:31; 14:17, 19, 22, 27, 30, 31; 18:36. Donald Guthrie, *New Testament Theology* (Downers Grove, Ill: InterVarsity Press, 1981), 132–33; Segovia, "Discipleship in the Fourth Gospel," 90–91.

JOHN'S DEVELOPMENT OF DISCIPLESHIP

John clearly accentuates belief as the center of discipleship. Just as clearly, John accentuates belief as the characteristic that distinguishes true and false disciples, and he also accentuates belief as the center of the development of discipleship.

Defective Belief

The disciples' belief differs qualitatively from others who observed Jesus' signs and heard his teaching and believed but whose belief was defective. A festival crowd in Jerusalem at the beginning of Jesus' ministry observed signs he performed and believed in him. Yet Jesus would not entrust himself to them (Jn 2:23–25), recognizing in them a failure to believe adequately. Raymond Brown explains:

> The reaction described here is intermediary. It is better than the hostile blindness of "the Jews" in the temple scene, but it is not equal to the faith of the disciples at Cana in 2:11 who are brought through the sign to see Jesus' glory. Here at Jerusalem there is a willingness to see the sign and be convinced by it, but all that is seen through the sign is that Jesus is a wonder-worker.[8]

Another incident is even more striking. During the discourse in which Jesus described himself as the Bread of Life, he said that true life is found in eating his flesh and drinking his blood (Jn 6:51–58). John tells us that many of Jesus' disciples found this teaching particularly hard to accept (v. 60). Such a hard saying may indeed produce confusion, but Jesus revealed to them the real problem: "'The Spirit gives life; the flesh counts for nothing. The words I have spoken to you are spirit and they are life. Yet there are some of you who do not believe.' For Jesus had known from the beginning which of them did not believe and who would betray him" (vv. 63–64). Apparently these disciples had confessed to believe, but Jesus knew their hearts from the beginning; they had never truly believed. Now their unbelief was evidenced in their actions. They had difficulty understanding Jesus' teaching because they were fleshly, not empowered by the Spirit. Perhaps they were even causing division among the disciples. Tragically, their unbelief is evidenced when John says, "From this time many of his disciples turned back and no longer followed him" (v. 66). These disciples apparently were following Jesus because he was an exciting new miracle worker and teacher, and as in John 2:23–25, Jesus recognized that they did not truly

---

[8]Raymond E. Brown, *The Gospel According to John (i–xii): Introduction, Translation, and Notes, AB,* 2d ed. (Garden City, N.Y.: Doubleday, 1966), 29:127.

believe. They had made some kind of a commitment to Jesus, but their later actions displayed their unbelief.[9]

Marks of True Belief

Once this group of Jesus' disciples turned away, Jesus turned to the Twelve and asked, "You do not want to leave too, do you?" (Jn 6:67). Simon Peter stepped forward as spokesman for the Twelve to give a clear statement of what it meant for them to follow Jesus. Peter asserted, "Lord, to whom shall we go? You have the words of eternal life. We believe and know that you are the Holy One of God" (vv. 68–69). Through believing in Jesus, the Twelve had come to "know" Jesus, i.e., they had entered into a personal relationship with him. While some of the wider circle of disciples had displayed their unbelief through leaving Jesus, Peter's confession was the example of true belief, the example of one who had claimed Jesus' words as the truth concerning eternal life. Simon Peter gave the example of one who had confessed Jesus as his God.[10] Therefore, the true disciple of Jesus is one who professes to believe on him for eternal life. To believe truly is to pass beyond mere curiosity and to become convinced of the truth of Jesus' words for the meaning and purpose of life.

However, even among the Twelve there was one whom Jesus knew did not truly believe: Judas Iscariot (cf. Jn 6:64, 70–71). Simply confessing to believe (2:23–24), simply following Jesus around (6:66), simply claiming to be a disciple of Jesus (vv. 60–66), is not necessarily proof that a person has true belief. John provides a historical reminiscence of the early days of the Jesus movement when a variety of types of people gathered around Jesus in order to become his disciples.[11] Each had their own religious/sociological expectations of what they wanted from Jesus. They each had different ideas of what it meant to be a disciple, often far different from Jesus' intention. For example, after the feeding of the five thousand, the crowd wanted to make Jesus their King. John says, "After the people saw the miraculous sign that Jesus did, they began to say, 'Surely this is the Prophet who is to come into the world.' Jesus, knowing that they intended to come and make him king by force, withdrew again to a mountain by himself" (vv. 14–15). This difference between the people's expectations of what they wanted from Jesus and what Jesus

---

[9]Cf. Schnackenburg, *John*, 2:70–75; Leon Morris, *The Gospel According to John*, NICNT (Grand Rapids: Eerdmans, 1971), 381–87; cf. also 335–37.

[10]Cf. Morris, *John*, 390 and n. 159.

[11]Brown, *John*, 98.

came to accomplish in his earthly ministry, caused a division in those who followed Jesus. Jesus asserted what his form of discipleship entailed.

After the group of disciples abandoned Jesus (Jn 6:66), a type of sifting took place in Jesus' ministry. At first there was a large group of disciples who attached themselves to him at will, but then Jesus began to challenge those following him to examine themselves to see whether they were his type of disciple. Instead of abandoning the master-disciple model because of the misunderstanding of the people, Jesus delineated the nature of his form of discipleship. This involved testing the reality of the disciples' belief. John records three marks of discipleship that Jesus said will be evident in the observable life of the disciple who has truly believed. The true disciple-believer will be characterized by these evidences. In the end, the false disciple-false believer will be known by the absence of these evidences (e.g., Judas Iscariot). True inner belief will cause such a radical change that the external life will bear evidence of that belief.

Abiding in Jesus' Words

The first mark of the true disciple is "abiding in Jesus' word." John records, "Jesus therefore was saying to those Jews who had believed him, 'If you abide in My word, then you are truly disciples of Mine; and you shall know the truth, and the truth shall make you free'" (Jn 8:31–32 NASB). Although some suggest that these Jews exercised true belief in Jesus,[12] the majority of commentators recognize that the ensuing context—which gives no indication that different groups of people are in view[13]—points to a severely defective belief: these Jews needed to be set free from sin (cf. v. 32 with vv. 33–36), they are seeking to kill him (v. 37), their Father is the Devil (vv. 42–44), they do not believe Jesus (vv. 45–46), they are not of God (v. 47), they accuse Jesus of having a demon (vv. 48–52), and they try to stone Jesus (v. 59).[14]

---

[12]E.g., Richard C. Lenski, *The Interpretation of Saint John's Gospel* (Columbus, Ohio: Lutheran Book Concern, 1942), 626–28.

[13]Brown, *John*, 354ff.; Hendriksen, *John*, 50–52; Morris, *John*, 455; Merrill C. Tenney, "John," *EBC* 9 (Grand Rapids: Zondervan, 1981), 94–95.

[14]Cf. C. K. Barrett, *The Gospel of John and Judaism* (Philadelphia: Fortress, 1975), 74; John H. Bernard, *A Critical and Exegetical Commentary on the Gospel According to Saint John*, 2 vols., ICC (Edinburgh: T. & T. Clark, 1928), 1:305; Brown, *John*, 362; F. Godet, *Commentary on the Gospel of John*, trans. Timothy Dwight, 2 vols. (New York: Funk and Wagnalls, 1886), 2:105; William Hendriksen, *Exposition of the Gospel According to John*, 1953, reprint (Grand Rapids: Baker, 1975), 52; Lindars, *John*, 323–24; Morris, *John*, 454; Tenney, "John," 94–95.

In ordinary Johannine usage, the expression "the Jews" signifies "those who are hostile to Jesus."[15] The phrase "the Jews who had believed him,"[16] is an intentional contradiction in terms for effect. They were still really Jews—with their messianic aspirations of the nation—but they were part of Jesus' adversaries. As such, they did not believe in Jesus as the Son of God. They only put some kind of credence in his Word.[17] If they abide, or continue, or remain in his Word, it will be to them a revelation of Jesus and it will assert its power. This will result in their salvation as they are freed by its truth (cf. v. 32).[18] The third-class conditional statement ("If you abide in My word," NASB) indicates that their future loyalty to Jesus' word will prove the reality of their present profession of belief. The conclusion of the future condition is put in the present tense ("you are truly disciples of Mine;" NASB) to indicate that the proof of what they now claim will be exhibited in their abiding or nonabiding. "Continuance in the word proves the sincerity or insincerity of the profession. It is the acid test of life."[19]

These Jews were not true believers. They may have believed that Jesus was a national deliverer, or they may have simply respected him as a prominent teacher. However, they were in need of salvation, true belief, not more commitment. They believed in only a shallow sense, merely giving credence to his Word. But now Christ put them to the test. True belief would be proven by the evidence of abiding in

---

[15]Brown, *John*, 362; Lindars, *John*, 323–24.

[16]Some commentators make much of the difference of construction between Jn 8:30 ("believed in him" *pisteuō eis* + accusative) and 8:31 ("had believed him," *pisteuō* + dative), suggesting that the former indicates true belief while the latter indicates false belief (e.g., Lindars, *John*, 324; B. F. Westcott, *The Gospel According to Saint John*, 1881, reprint [Grand Rapids: Eerdmans, 1975], 132–33). However, while the use of the simple dative does often indicate simple credence rather than trust in a person, John does not appear to put much difference between the two constructions. The reason for the change of construction is problematic. In this instance, the context indicates the same people are in view in vv. 30–31, even if the Jews in v. 31 are only a portion of the larger group in v. 30. Also, we should not overlook the fact that *pisteuō eis* + accusative is used of a defective faith (cf. Jn 2:23–24). Hence, the construction in v. 30 may simply be a general statement to indicate persons who believe, while the construction in v. 31 may focus on a certain segment of those believers in v. 30, those who definitely had defective faith. However, the construction in v. 30 cannot be considered an indication that all had true belief, because it includes those in v. 31 (cf. Morris, *John*, 455, n. 61, and Additional Note E, pp. 335ff.; Hendricksen, *John*, 2:50–52; Brown, *John*, 354–55; Schnackenberg, *John*, 2:204–5; Tenney, "John," 94–95).

[17]Barrett, *John*, 344.

[18]Lindars, *John*, 324; William Milligan and William F. Moulton, *Commentary on the Gospel of Saint John* (Edinburgh: T. & T. Clark, 1898), 106.

[19]Archibald T. Robertson, *The Fourth Gospel*, vol. 5, *Word Pictures in the New Testament* (Nashville: Broadman, 1932), 149.

his Word. Then they would be set free from sin and live as true disciples.

"Abiding" means to "remain in the sphere of existence," which is here Jesus' Word. This means to pass beyond mere curiosity and to become convinced of the truth of Jesus' words for the meaning and purpose of life, as Peter had declared (cf. Jn 6:66–69). These Jews did not see Jesus as possessing the sole truth. They only partially followed, partially believed (cf. 8:23–24). True belief means to live in the truth of Jesus' Word about every area of life. Jesus' true disciples hear his word, claim it, and obey it as their standard of truth for all of life. This sets them free from sin (v. 34) to live life as the Father intended it for them (vv. 36–40).

Therefore, Jesus is not here calling for a higher form of commitment from true believers in order for them to become disciples. A person does not abide in the Word in order to become a disciple. Rather, a person becomes a disciple through true belief, and the reality of that belief is proven through abiding or remaining in Jesus' Word of truth. These Jews had defective faith, similar to those who believed defectively in John 2:23–25.

Jesus was sifting out false believers from true believers. He did so by challenging them to look at their own lives as evidence of whether or not they were true believers. And it worked! At the end of the discourse they showed their true colors by turning against him when he declared his eternal deity (Jn 8:57–59).[20] True discipleship, true belief, will be evidenced by abiding in Jesus' words. The evidence of true belief is seen in disciples who cling to Jesus' Word as the truth for life. True disciples are free from bondage to sin through Jesus' liberating Word.

Loving one another

Love for each other, as Jesus has loved them, is the second identifying mark of true disciple-believers. During the Upper Room Discourse on his final night with the disciples, Jesus said, "A new command I give you: Love one another. As I have loved you, so you must love one another. By this all men will know that you are my disciples, if you love one another" (Jn 13:34–35). The conditional statement (v. 35, "By this all men will know that you are my disciples, if you love one another") contributes two important elements to the meaning of discipleship in John. The first is that the disciples' love is in contrast with that of the unsaved world. All those who are not disciples will see that brotherly love is a distinctive

---

[20]Cf. Morris, *John*, 472–74; Lindars, *John*, 335–36.

characteristic of Jesus' disciples.[21] This spectacle of love was a witness to the world and was treated as such by the early church fathers. The early church father Tertullian said:

> The heathen are wont to exclaim with wonder,
> "See how these Christians love one another,"
> for they hate one another;
> "and how they are ready to die for one another,"
> for they are ready to kill one another.[22]

This love is the outward manifestation of the love that only Christ can exert once he dwells in a believer's heart. The world cannot know this love in its own experience. Therefore the world will immediately recognize and know that, because of their love, it is to Christ and to no one else that the disciples belong.[23] As such, this love becomes a revelation to the world of the reality of belief and the change that Jesus makes in the life of the believer.[24] The love the disciples exhibit toward one another is contrasted with the world.

Second, this love is to be exhibited by all disciples. If the contrast is between the world and the disciples, this does not leave any other options. Love is not a standard by which a superior believer is measured above a lesser believer. Rather, love is the standard by which a true believer is set apart from the world. This love is the mark of the true believer in general, not a special class of believers. Nothing in nature can bring about this love. It is not something that can be feigned; rather it is that which only those born of God can and must experience. It is a test which the conditional statement "If you have love for one another" (*ean* and the subjunctive) expects to be met.[25] Love is the criterion by which the believer can know that he or she has ceased to belong to the old world. Hence, "mutual love is the proof of Christian discipleship, and its evident token."[26]

Bearing fruit

The third mark of the disciple, the true believer, is bearing fruit. Jesus states, "By this is My Father glorified, that you bear much fruit, and so prove to be My disciples" (Jn 15:8 NASB). The true believer-disciple will bear fruit, because true attachment to the Vine brings

[21]James H. Charlesworth, ed., *John and Qumran* (London: Chapman, 1972), 159.

[22]Cited in Westcott, *John*, 198.

[23]Hendriksen, *John*, 253–54.

[24]Charles A. Dodd, *The Interpretation of the Fourth Gospel* (Cambridge: Cambridge Univ. Press, 1958), 405.

[25]Lenski, *John*, 962.

[26]Barrett, *John*, 452–53.

true life to the branch. The professing believer who is either falsely attached (v. 2) or unattached (v. 4) to Jesus will not bear fruit, because fruit-producing life from the Vine cannot enter the branch without proper attachment. Eventually, non-fruit-bearing branches will be cast into the fire (v. 6), a consistent picture of the final destiny of unbelievers.[27]

The second part of John 15:8 is important for this study, especially when we focus on the clause beginning with "that" (*hina*). The KJV renders it, "Herein is my Father glorified, that ye bear much fruit; so shall ye be my disciples." Some have interpreted this to mean that disciples are more committed than average believers. For example, one commentator states that "the highest aspiration of all is to become 'a disciple'" and then quotes another who says, "True discipleship is hardly begun until the earthly life is near its end and the fruit hangs thick and ripe upon the branches of the vine."[28] An extreme of this view appeared among the church fathers, where only those who tasted the blood of martyrdom were considered true disciples.[29]

Among the majority of the early church fathers and among modern commentators, the rendering given by the NASB above and the NIV— "This is to my Father's glory, that you bear much fruit, showing yourselves to be my disciples" (Jn 15:8)—discloses the majority interpretation. Raymond Brown, for example, says, "The sense is not that when the hearers bear fruit, they will become his disciples, but that in bearing fruit they show they are disciples. Becoming or being a disciple is the same as being or remaining in Jesus."[30] The sense is that "discipleship is not static, but a growing and developing way of

---

[27]J. Carl Laney, "Abiding Is Believing: The Analogy of the Vine in John 15:1–6," *BS* 146 (1989): 55–66.

[28]Bernard, *John*, 2:483; citing Swete.

[29]Cf. chap. 16, where I discuss some of the early church fathers' attitudes toward discipleship. Cf. also William F. Arndt and F. Wilbur Gingrich, trans. and eds., *A Greek-English Lexicon of the New Testament and Other Early Christian Literature*, 1957, reprint (Chicago: Univ. of Chicago Press, 1974), 487.

[30]Brown, *John*, 2:662–63. While this verse has a number of problems associated with it, especially establishing the reference of ἐν τούτῳ ("in this"), and the reference of ἵνα ("that"), the only problem that affects this study (and that only peripherally) is deciding the reference and original reading of *ginomai*. Was it *genēsthe* (a second aorist middle subjunctive) or *genēsesthe* (a future middle indicative)? While the majority of commentators prefer the future indicative reading, they also point out that it does not materially affect the interpretation (e.g., Barrett, *John*, 475; Bernard, *John*, 2:483; Brown, *John*, 2:662; Godet, *John*, 2:297; Hendriksen, *John*, 302; Lindars, *John*, 490; Morris, *John*, 672; Robertson, *Fourth Gospel*, 259). This gives a somewhat independent sense to the phrase, rather than being governed strictly by the *hina* clause.

life. Always the true disciple is becoming more fully a disciple."[31] Bishop Westcott states, "Something is always wanting to the completeness of discipleship. A Christian never 'is,' but always 'is becoming' a Christian. And it is by his fruitfulness that he vindicates his claim to the name."[32]

John emphasizes here that fruit bearing is the outward and visible sign of a believer-disciple. This should be connected with the thoughts of John 8:31 and 13:34–35. As people abide in Jesus' Word of truth for salvation, they become disciples. These new disciples then characteristically continue to abide in Jesus' Word for every area of life. They are touched by the love of Jesus to such an extent that they will love other disciples, and because they are attached to Jesus, his life will flow into them, producing fruit.[33]

IMPLICATIONS

John clearly demonstrates that belief in Jesus for salvation is what produces disciples. He is equally clear that disciples bear the marks of Jesus' life upon their lives as evidence of true discipleship. The reason for this is because of the new birth to which John pointed at the very beginning of Jesus' ministry, in his interaction with Nicodemus (Jn 3:1ff.). Disciples of Jesus are not merely people who have followed Jesus around and are learning from him. No! Disciples of Jesus have entered into a new life that causes radical transformations.

The apostle John wrote this gospel near the end of his life, after many years of reflection upon his time with Jesus, both walking with him in his earthly ministry and walking with him in his ascended ministry. When we compare John's gospel with his epistles, we see that John wants us to know that belief in Jesus produces a radically new life. John wants the church to grab hold of this truth and let it transform us. Over the past several years I have listened carefully to John's message of discipleship, and I have become convinced that my personal life and ministry need to be characterized by John's message.

True Belief Produces Disciples of Jesus

We need to heed carefully Jesus' message that true belief in Jesus for salvation produces disciples of Jesus. From the moment I

---

[31]Morris, *John,* 672–73.

[32]Westcott, *John,* 219.

[33]Most commentators make this kind of connection of Jn 8:31; 13:34–35; and 15:8; e.g., Barrett, *John,* 475; Brown, *John,* 662–63; Tenney, "John," 153; Robertson, *Fourth Gospel,* 259.

received Jesus as my Savior, I became his disciple. I was ushered into this new life solely through the grace of God, and the life that began through faith continues through faith. Jesus called me to follow him. When I obeyed, it set the pattern for my entire life. He made me into a disciple, and he continues to cause me to grow as I am obedient to him. This is especially evident when we look at the three marks of a disciple in John's gospel. Each mark is initiated originally by God through the new birth. Each becomes more and more evident through God's activity in the life of the disciple as he or she continues by faith to follow Jesus' example.

Abiding in Jesus' Liberating Word

True discipleship, true belief, will be evidenced by abiding in Jesus' words. The evidence of true belief is seen in disciples who cling to Jesus' word as the truth for every area of life. As they hear the truth, they live it out (abide), which will eventually be evidenced in their lives. True disciples are free from bondage to sin through Jesus' liberating Word.

True discipleship begins with abiding in Jesus' Word about eternal life, resulting in salvation. But notice that abiding in Jesus' Word also becomes the standard for all of life. Knowing the truth about Jesus broke the bonds of sin concerning eternal life, but knowing the truth from Jesus about every other area of life breaks the bonds of sin there as well. When we know the truth, it means that we claim it internally, and then it will work from the inside to the out to be our value system of life.

An important example for us is the issue of "success." What is our definition of success? The world around us has various definitions, and the tragedy is that the world's standards of success tend to hold us prisoner. That is why in the 1960s so many tried to escape, to find freedom from the rat race of worldly pursuits of success. But for Christians, instead of running away, as so many did in the sixties generation, or instead of buying into the world's standards, as so many have now done in the yuppie generation, to abide in Jesus' Word means to find our definition of success in him—that is, we find our sense of success, of worth, in what he says is of true value.[34] We could summarize it by saying, "Seek first the kingdom of God and his righteousness."

---

[34]Notice the contrast of external evidences of Jesus' statement of "success" or "value" in Mt 6: vv. 16–18—religion; vv. 19–21—treasure; vv. 22–23—focus of value; v. 24—money; vv. 25–33 priorities: Seek first his kingdom and his righteousness.

The choice of value begins on the inside and then works to the outside. As we choose to obey Jesus' Word about any area of life, the choice breaks the bond that sin has around us in that area, because we now know what the truth is. Sin (pride of life) will try to tell us that if we get such and such a position, then we are a success. Jesus says that such positions are secondary: the definitive position is being his disciple. As we choose to value being his disciple over anything else, then positions in the world can be put into proper perspective. We can then be used as means to the end of being salt in the world.

Another example is the issue of self-image. Sin tries to sell us various lies about ourself, but to abide in Jesus means to live with what he says about us: God loves us and we are his special creatures who will be fulfilled only when we are in right relationship with him.

Loving with Jesus' Love

In the early church love was a distinguishing mark. The church experienced persecution and alienation from the world, and this suffering did not produce conflict or fear in the church. Rather, such suffering resulted in a fellowship of love. It was this love that the world noticed and that caused the church to stand out. The church's love was something that the world had never seen before. The love of disciples for each other showed how they really were Jesus' disciples and not of the world.

What makes this love possible? First, through regeneration a change has been made in the heart of the believer by God's love which now impels the believer to love (cf. 1 Jn 4:17–21). Second, the regenerate heart now has an endless source of love from God by which it can continually pour forth love (see especially 4:12–16, 19–21). If the person does not love, that person shows that he or she does not know God. It was God's love that brought us life, and it is his love in us that guarantees that we will love one another.

The whole world wants this love. On the radio, in magazines, in discussions of solving world problems, inevitably the word *love* surfaces. God designed us to love. But the great tragedy of humankind is that we are self-centered and prideful. We want our own way, and if our way is hindered by someone else, we cannot truly love that person. God's life in our life is what breaks the self-centeredness and pride. Self-centeredness and pride are never completely eradicated in this life, but God promises that we will be able to control them so that we can place others' needs before our own. That is what love is all about.

Bearing the Fruit of Jesus' Life

When I was a little boy, I loved to spend time on my grandparents' farm. They had a large fruit-tree orchard where I learned to care for the trees in the various seasons of the year. Irrigating, fertilizing, pruning, thinning out crops, harvesting; all of these had to come in their own time. I learned how to nurture and care for the trees so that they could produce the most fruit. There was, however, one thing I could not do. I could not make them grow fruit. Fruit was a result of the natural life of the tree, and the kind of fruit was always in accord with the kind of tree. If the tree was alive, at the same time every year it produced fruit; my job was to nurture the life of the tree. If the tree was a peach tree, it would naturally produce peaches, not pears.

By the use of the branch analogy, Jesus allows us to see that when we have new life, we will bear fruit as a natural result of that life, and the kind of fruit will be in keeping with this new life. Only dead branches do not bear fruit. My personal responsibility is to nurture myself on the Word, drink of the Living Water, bask in the Son, and be protected from the elements of the world through the fellowship of others who have life. My responsibility in ministry is to nurture and care for other "fruit trees" by providing the right environment for fruit to be produced. What is the kind of fruit that will be produced? First, the fruit of the Spirit, those characteristics of the Spirit which as a whole will be evidenced in true believers (Gal 5:22–26). Second, new converts produced by God through the disciple (Jn 4:34-38; 15:16). And third, righteousness and good works which are produced by God through the person who has received new life in Christ (Php 1:11; Col 1:10).

The Ministry of Discipleship

Through my years in pastoral and teaching ministries, I have come to focus on these truths from John's teaching on discipleship as the focal point for all that I do. Discipleship is, therefore, not one thing that I do; rather, discipleship summarizes all the activities of my personal, family, and church life. Personally, I see myself as a disciple of Jesus above all else. I see my responsibilities in my family as promoting mutual discipleship. And I see discipleship not as one program of the church, but as summarizing the goal of the church.

How? First, regeneration must be emphasized. We must recognize that when people are saved they become new creatures. When a person is saved God has placed in her or him new life. From that point a person has become a new person, a disciple of Jesus. This is the foundation for my personal, family, or church ministry.

Second, from that foundation the life of discipleship is built upon three pillars. The first pillar comes from Jesus' teaching on abiding in his Word. We must provide opportunity for people to hear God's Word, we must help them to understand how it can be claimed as their own truth for life, and then we must show them how and encourage them to live it out. Proper placement of the first pillar allows proper placement of the next two pillars.

The second pillar is loving other disciples. We must exemplify love in our personal and corporate lives, and we must provide a setting in our homes and churches where love is nurtured, where it is central in our relationships, and where it is reflected in all of our activities. People do not really know how to love with God's love until they become his new creatures. We must help them to understand and to experience his love. Then we must share that love in our relationships and structure our activities so that it can be expressed toward each other. The wonderful perspective that John gives us is that this love will naturally result because of the love of God that now permeates our lives!

The third pillar is bearing fruit. When we help people to understand the workings of the Spirit and show them how to be filled with the Spirit, the fruit of the Spirit will be produced naturally in the individual disciple as well as in the life of the church. As we allow Jesus' heart for the lost to characterize our heart, we will be compelled to be involved in the world, carrying the message and ministry of Jesus to a lost world so that God can produce the fruit of conversion through us. And as the righteousness and life of Jesus become increasingly central in our priorities, the Spirit of God will cause us to become like him in our personal and corporate righteousness and in our personal and corporate service toward others.

As we can see, John's teaching on discipleship becomes a powerful model for stucturing our personal life, our family life, and our life of ministry to the church. Yes, we can take our eyes off of Jesus and fail, or deny him, or reject his leading. So did the early disciples. But John tells us that those who truly believed never stopped being disciples. Jesus restored them. One of the most beautiful portraits of this restoration is found in the final chapter of John's gospel. There we see Jesus appearing to the disciples after their failure, after his resurrection, after they gathered in Galilee. Peter, the leader of the Twelve, the one who publicly denied Jesus, is the focal point for Jesus' loving restoration. Jesus' final directive? "Follow me!" (Jn 21:22). John is realistic. As new creatures in Christ, we will grope and stumble through this fallen world, yet Jesus our Lord and Master goes before us to show us the way, to pick us up when we fall, and to encourage us on to new levels of growth in discipleship.

Following up:

1. If the apostle John were to visit your church this week, what evidence would he find that the members of your congregation are truly abiding in Jesus' Word, loving each other, and bearing fruit?
2. What could you point to in your own life of these three evidences of discipleship?
3. Do you think that discipleship is more of an event or a process? Explain.
4. What do you see as the key elements/stages of that event or process?

PART V

DISCIPLESHIP IN THE EARLY CHURCH

13

Acts: The Community
of Faith

Getting focused:

1. From the following passages, develop a "theology of discipleship in Acts" (i.e., who are disciples, what does a disciple do, what is entailed in discipleship?). What else is needed in order to develop such a theology? (Ac 6:1, 2, 7; 9:1, 10, 19, 26, 36, 38; 11:26, 29; 13:52; 14:20, 21, 22, 28; 15:10; 16:1; 18:23, 27; 19:9, 30; 20:1, 30; 21:4, 16).
2. Which is more important to the concept of biblical discipleship: individual or community relationships? What is the connection between "disciples" and the "church" in the book of Acts?
3. How do you explain the following occurrences of the word *disciple* in the context of its usage and the overall context of Acts? (Ac 9:25; 19:1)
4. What other terms might be used as near synonyms for *disciple* in the book of Acts?

The idea of discipleship brings to the minds of many people a one-on-one relationship with Jesus. They believe, "I am a disciple of Jesus, and to grow in discipleship means to develop that relationship by becoming more like him." That certainly is an important truth, because we can see many situations in the Gospels where Jesus called individuals to follow him, serve him, and grow in relationship with him (e.g., Peter, Andrew, John, James, Matthew, Zacchaeus, etc.). One of the great truths of the Christian faith that attracted me to it so many years ago was the claim that God in Jesus had come to earth to offer and establish a personal relationship with individuals. I eagerly responded to that offer and entered into a personal discipleship relationship with Jesus that has been at the center of my daily life ever since then.

However, pushed to an extreme, as with so many truths, individual discipleship often overshadows an equally important biblical truth, the idea of "community."[1] From the earliest times of the biblical record, God called his people to community, whether in the early patriarchal families, in the wandering people of Israel, in the kingdom of Israel, in the group of Twelve, or in the church.[2] Jesus did indeed call men and women into a deep personal relationship with himself, yet if we focus exclusively on the individual in our growth in discipleship, we run the danger of separating the individual from the community of faith. One-on-one discipleship pushed too far can easily develop into the kind of unhealthy independency that marks twentieth-century culture.[3] That kind of unhealthy individualism deceives us into separating ourselves from others, it encourages us to pride ourselves on not needing anyone, and it makes us reluctant to have anyone need us. David Gill has wisely said:

> We must have the *community to support and correct our discipleship in the world.* This seems so obvious, but our practice is so frequently individualistic. Christian discipleship is not for Lone Rangers (though in all fairness, even the masked man had Tonto as his sidekick). We must resist the individualism of our culture and cultivate deep and strong relationships with others. The challenges we face are formidable; without community they become impossible.[4]

"The challenges we face are formidable; without community they become impossible." Do we really believe that statement? I know that in my younger years I didn't. Whether it was cultural back-

[1]"Community" is a concept that is difficult to define. However, as James Dunn recognizes, this term, somewhat better than related terms (e.g., "congregation" or "sect"), implies two essential ingredients: relations and structured organization; cf. James D. G. Dunn, *Unity and Diversity in the New Testament: An Inquiry into the Character of Earliest Christianity,* 2d ed. (London/Philadelphia: SCM/Trinity, 1990), 398, n. 2a. See the "Implications" section in this chapter.

[2]The initiation and development of Israel and the church as a called community is extensively documented in the study of Paul D. Hanson, *The People Called: The Growth of Community in the Bible* (San Francisco: Harper & Row, 1986).

[3]Gerhard Lohfink gives a powerful account of the heritage of liberal theological "individualism" in Germany in this century, which in turn has affected secular German society. That account is equally applicable to Europe in general, North America, industrialized Asian society, the emerging third world, and, indeed, much of twentieth-century culture as a whole; see Gerhard Lohfink, *Jesus and Community: The Social Dimension of Christian Faith* (Philadelphia: Fortress, 1984), 1–5.

[4]David W. Gill, *The Opening of the Christian Mind: Taking Every Thought Captive to Christ* (Downers Grove, Ill.: InterVarsity Press, 1989), 135–36.

ground, my own particular environment, or my own prideful independency, I preferred to walk alone, to need no one, and to have no
one need me. In my early years right out of high school I gloried in
my independency, my ability to make it on my own through life. My
theme was Simon and Garfunkel's song "I Am a Rock, I Am an
Island."

The one person who made a dent in my individual independency
in those early days was my older brother, Bill. There were three of us
brothers. I was in the middle, with two years separating me from both
my younger and older brothers. At various times of our growing up
years the three of us rotated as "best friends." At other times we
fought like crazy. All in all, I look back on our times together and
realize that we had a wonderful thing going as brothers.

At times my younger brother, Tim, and I were best of friends. He
was an excellent athlete, and he loved baseball and football like I did.
We were constantly playing ball together with the other kids in the
neighborhood. We had a great deal in common, so we were extremely
close.

At other times, Bill and I were the best of friends. In my late teen
years various circumstances combined so that Bill and I became very
close. We played different sports together, we worked different jobs
together, we got into all kinds of trouble together (neither of us was a
Christian then!). Our closeness as brothers and friends finally
culminated in us enlisting in the army together on a "buddy
program," both of us volunteering for Airborne Infantry-Ranger
training. We knew that we would end up going to Vietnam, but we
knew that as we went through training together we would be able to
rely on each other when we got into combat.

However, just before we were to leave for basic training, we got
into another one of our famous fights. This was an intense one, and I
had a violent temper. On this occasion I got so mad that I decided I
did not need Bill or anyone else, so that night I called my mom, said
good-bye to her on the roadside, and left for the army all by myself.
As we always did, Bill and I later made up and laughed at our stupid
fight, but this time my independency had resulted in setting a course
from which I could not return. As I went through that year of training
by myself, I became more and more independent. In fact, I became
more and more proud of the fact that I could make it alone.

I received orders for Vietnam in 1968. That year in combat was a
major turning point in my life. It broke down my cocky self-
sufficiency as I realized that in order to come back alive I needed the
other men in my squad. As I became the squad leader, I suddenly
came to realize that those other men needed to rely on me. I retained
my individualism, but I came to understand the necessity of

community like never before. "The challenges we faced were formidable; without community they became impossible."

When I returned from Vietnam, Bill and I were stationed together at Fort Bragg, North Carolina, and he invited me to live with him and his wife, Susie. That was an important year together; the love and friendship Bill and Susie continually shared with me was vitally important as I readjusted to normal life. Soon after I left them I became a Christian, and I realized that as we had together talked and tried to figure out ourselves and the world, they had been significant support persons on my road to becoming a disciple of Jesus.

But my story about Bill does not end there. Now it was his turn for independency to lead him down a rocky road. Something caused Bill to snap, and he came home from a trip where he had been visiting friends and announced to us in the family that he was leaving. I will never forget his words: "I've been thinking about other people all my life [we think we've been around so long when we're twenty-five!]; it's time that I started thinking about myself." So Bill left. He left his wife, turned away from our family, left his schooling, gave up on his promising career as an architect, turned his back on the Lord, and went off to pursue his independency and his own pleasure. He traveled all over the world and pursued activities and philosophies and pleasures that finally ended, after fifteen years, at a dead end.

Three years ago I got a phone call from Bill. It was a phone call that was full of pain and horror. Bill had just been diagnosed as having AIDS. As Bill swiftly succumbed to the disease over the next two years, I went to visit him several times where he lived near our family in another state. One time I had not seen him for a few months, and as the door opened in response to my knock, I saw standing before me a skinny old man, bent over, walking with a cane, shuffling along, almost bald. It was Bill. Bill had been six-feet-three-inches tall and had weighed about 180 pounds. He had been an outstanding athlete, great looking, and in marvelous shape. But now the disease had ravaged him.

A few weeks later I got a call from my mom saying that I should fly to see Bill as soon as possible because the doctors did not think that he would live long. I found Bill in an AIDS hospice house, where I spent most of that weekend with him. The disease had completely devastated him now. He lay in the bed, unable to move, barely able to speak, looking like a figure from a Nazi concentration camp. What Bill endured was horrible. Just before I left to fly home, our family gathered around his bed, together for the last time.

Bill asked to say good-bye to me alone, and as the others left, he gasped out to me, "Arch my neck." I thought that he wanted to be placed in a different position, so I reached around to put my hand under his head. As I did, he screamed out from the pain of movement but grasped my arm and in a weak, tear-filled voice said, "Mike, hold me." As I held Bill in my arms we both cried and cried like I don't believe either of us ever had before. And then, in his whisper of a voice, he said to me, "Mike, thank you for loving me. Thank you for being here when I needed you. I've had the two best brothers, the best family, a person could have."

I left then, and my mother called the next day to say that Bill had died. He had slipped into a coma after I left and never regained consciousness.

I have learned through my family the absolute necessity of community. "The challenges we face are formidable; without community they become impossible." I needed Bill, but my own independency caused me to turn my back on him as he later did with us. We made our mistakes. But when challenges became so overwhelming that it was impossible to make it alone, our family community provided the strength, courage, and love necessary to endure the darkest moments of our existence.

That is why individual disciples must function as a community, the family of God. The disciples spent three years with Jesus as they obeyed his call, listened to his teaching, and witnessed his ministry. At the end of their training came the darkest moment of their experience, Jesus' trial and crucifixion. As they huddled in the Upper Room in the shadow of the empty cross, all they had hoped for appeared lost; all they had endured appeared to have been in vain; all they had sacrificed appeared to be wasted. Where was their Master? Who would lead the way now?

But out of the darkness came the brightness of a new hope—the Resurrection—and a new creation—the church. Jesus' followers now embarked upon a dimension of their discipleship journey to which Jesus had pointed but which they had only dimly perceived. The small band of disciples around Jesus during the darkest moments exploded to thousands in Jerusalem within days of Pentecost and soon became countless throughout the Roman world. The disciples were now empowered by the Holy Spirit to proclaim boldly in the remotest parts of the earth the Gospel message that Jesus had inaugurated in Israel. And these disciples were now joined together to form the church, the body of their risen Master, Jesus Christ. Jesus called individuals to discipleship, yet responding to that call brought disciples into a community of faith.

Luke is the only evangelist to extend his story from the time of Jesus' earthly ministry to the time of his ascended ministry. As Luke continues his story from the Gospel to the book of Acts, he allows us to see the crucial necessity of the community for discipleship. Jesus no longer was with his disciples physically, yet he promised to be with them always (Mt 28:20). Through the Spirit, the community would now provide the fellowship, encouragement, edification, and mutuality necessary for following the Master in the new era.

LUKE'S DISTINCTIVE VIEW OF DISCIPLESHIP IN ACTS

Luke's portrait of the disciples in Acts extends many of the same sketches begun in his gospel, yet the portrait is unique in that it is colored by the dawning of the age of the church. To understand fully the portrait of discipleship in Acts, we must draw upon our previous examination of Luke's gospel, because the gospel foreshadows the post-Easter situation. "A proper reading of Acts rather requires using Luke as a commentary on it, while a correct interpretation of Luke necessitates employing Acts as a commentary on it."[5]

Disciples As a Referent[6] for "Believers," "Those of the Way," "Christians"

The word *disciples* appears for the first time in Acts when Luke declares that in the early days following Pentecost "the number of disciples was increasing" (6:1). In like manner, Luke declares that as the word of God increased, the number of disciples multiplied, included among them a great many priests who became "obedient to the faith" (6:7).[7] Prior to this, Luke used the expression "those who believed" to indicate those who had professed faith in Jesus (cf. 2:44; 4:32; 5:14). Luke thereby draws a parallel between the expressions

---

[5]Charles H. Talbert, "Discipleship in Luke-Acts," in *Discipleship in the New Testament,* ed. Fernando F. Segovia (Philadelphia: Fortress, 1985), 62.

[6]Cotterell and Turner say, "The *referent* of a word or expression in an utterance is the *thing in the world which is intentionally signified by that word or expression.*" The intended "thing in the world" signified by "disciples" is the person or persons who are also called "believers," "those of the Way," "Christians." Peter Cotterell and Max Turner, *Linguistics and Biblical Interpretation* (Downers Grove, Ill.: InterVarsity Press, 1989), 84. "Referent" is preferred to "synonym" for the sake of linguistic clarity; see Johannes P. Louw and Eugene A. Nida, eds., *Greek Lexicon of the New Testament: Based on Semantic Domains,* 2 vols. (New York: United Bible Societies, 1988), 1:15–20.

[7]There is some difficulty as to whether "faith" should be considered in an objective or subjective sense, but in either case it is stressed that faith played an integral part in the increase of the disciples; cf. F. F. Bruce, *The Acts of the Apostles: The Greek Text with Introduction and Commentary,* 3d ed. (Grand Rapids: Eerdmans, 1990), 185; R. C. H. Lenski, *The Interpretation of the Acts of the Apostles* (Columbus, Ohio: Wartburg, 1944), 248; I. Howard Marshall, *The Acts of the Apostles: An Introduction and Commentary,* TNTC (Leicester/Grand Rapids: Inter-Varsity/Eerdmans, 1980), 128; Karl H. Rengstorf, "μαθητής," *TDNT* 4:458.

"those who believe" and "the disciples." This is similar to the use in Luke's gospel, where we noted that the word *disciple* designated a believer in Jesus.[8] Throughout the book of Acts, *disciples* is a title for those who have placed their faith in Jesus and are now followers of Jesus, converts.[9] That the term *disciple* was still used makes it clear that continuity is maintained between those who followed Jesus during his earthly ministry and those of the postresurrection church.[10]

A similar use is found elsewhere. A record of the activities of the early church equated the "disciples" with "the Way" (Ac 9:1–2), i.e., those who believed in Jesus as Messiah, later to be called "Christians."[11] In Acts 9 Luke records the persecution of the Palestinian disciples by Saul of Tarsus (v. 1), Saul's Damascus road experience, and Saul's encounter with the disciples in Damascus (vv. 1, 10, 19). When the new convert attempted to become a part of the disciples (v. 26), the Jerusalem Christians were afraid of him, "not believing that he really was a disciple."[12] The question was whether Paul was a true believer or a "secret agent" attempting to infiltrate the ranks of the disciples. But Barnabas vouched for the genuineness of Saul's conversion, and Saul became an accepted member of the disciples.[13]

Luke's unconstrained use of *disciple* as a referent for "believer" is also displayed in the incident surrounding Tabitha (Gk. *Dorcas*) in Joppa. Here we have the only New Testament example of the feminine form of disciple, *mathētria*, a word that occurs in secular Hellenistic and later Christian literature.[14] Luke simply calls Tabitha a "disciple" as a designation of her faith in Christ (Ac 9:36), paralleling the use of the masculine form to describe the general body of believers in Joppa as "the disciples," *hoi mathētai* (v. 38).

---

[8]See chap. 11 on Luke, above; e.g., a great crowd of Jesus' disciples (Lk 6:13, 17) were those who were convinced believers in Jesus' messiahship, whereas "a large crowd of his disciples" (v. 17) were those who could be termed "the curious." Cf. also Talbert, "Discipleship in Luke-Acts," 62.

[9]Cf. Ac 6:1, 2, 7; 9:1, 10, 19, 26, 36, 38; 11:26, 29; 13:52; 14:20, 21, 22, 28; 15:10; 16:1; 18:23, 27; 19:9, 30; 20:1, 30; 21:4, 16. There is virtually no argument among commentators about this meaning of "disciple" (μαθητής) in Acts: i.e., synonymous with "believer in Jesus." See, e.g., Bruce, *Acts of the Apostles*, 180; Ernst Haenchen, *The Acts of the Apostles: A Commentary* (Philadelphia: Westminster, 1971), 260, n. 1; Richard N. Longenecker, "The Acts of the Apostles," *EBC* (Grand Rapids: Zondervan, 1981), 9:493; Rengstorf, "μαθητής" 458; Talbert, "Discipleship in Luke-Acts," 62; David John Williams, *Acts, A Good News Commentary* (San Francisco: Harper & Row, 1985), 102.

[10]Williams, *Acts*, 102.

[11]Marshall, *Acts*, 168–69.

[12]. . . μή πιστεύοντες ὅτι ἐστιν μαθητής.

[13]Bruce, *Acts of the Apostles*, 205; Rengstorf, "μαθητής," 458.

[14]μαθήτρια. Cf. Bruce, *Acts of the Apostles*, 248; Haenchen, *Acts of the Apostles*, 338–39, n. 1. See also the chapter below on the postapostolic church.

Although the term *mathētēs* is masculine in form and generally refers to men, it is neutral as to sex distinction and thus includes women when used to designate a group of people of mixed sex who are all followers of Jesus (e.g., 6:1).[15] Therefore, Luke's use of the feminine form here strongly reiterates the fact that women as well as men were disciples of Jesus.

Instructively, the first time the word *Christian* occurs in Scripture, it is associated with the word *disciples:* "The disciples were called Christians first at Antioch" (Ac 11:26). Again, *disciple* is simply a referent for "believer," and here, "Christian." The name Christian must have originated within the Gentile population.[16] In the large metropolis of Antioch, with its many competing cults and mystery religions, those who spoke so much about *Christos* were soon called *Christianoi,* Christ's people. The term then distinguished the "disciples" from unconverted Gentiles as well as from Judaism. While the occurrence of the term in Acts 11:26 indicates, at the very least, the recognition by Gentiles that believers in Christ were an entity separate from both pagan Gentiles and Judaism, the other two occurrences in the New Testament probably indicate that elements of contempt (26:28) and hostility (1Pe 4:16) were attached to the term *Christian* by the early use of those outside of the church. There is no New Testament evidence that *Christian* was commonly used as a self-designation by the early church. Luke's anachronistic reflection in Acts 11:26 implies that the common term for Jesus' followers at the time of the origin of the word *Christian* was *disciples* (*mathētai*), with other terms used interchangeably by the church, such as *believers* (*hoi pisteuontes; hoi pistoi*) (Ac 5:14; 10:45; Ro 1:16; 1Ti 6:2), *brothers/sisters* (*adelphos/adelphē*) (Ac 6:3; Jas 2:15), and *saints* (*hoi hagioi*) (Ac 9:13; 1Co 1:2).[17]

This common use of the word *disciples* to indicate Jesus' followers recurs throughout the book of Acts. Luke simply includes the term

[15]Louw and Nida, *Greek Lexicon,* 1:471.

[16]The infinitive χρηματίσαι (*chrēmastisai*) has been interpreted to mean that the disciples first "bore the title" Christians in Antioch, suggesting that the term was coined by the church to give expression to their own self-consciousness in the new age of Messiah. But Haenchen has demonstrated that, while possible, usage in Philo and Josephus shows that the infinitive should be rendered "were called," indicating that the name was coined by those outside of the church (Haenchen, *Acts of the Apostles,* 367–68, n. 3). Of those outside, the Jews were not likely to have referred to the disciples as Christians, *followers of Christos,* the Messiah, since this would have validated Jesus' claim to that title (see the disputed passage in Josephus where *Christos* and *Christianoi* are used in this manner [*Antiq.* 18:63–64]). The Jews instead referred to the disciples of Jesus as "the Nazarene sect" (Ac 24:5).

[17]Cf. Michael J. Wilkins, "Christian," *The Anchor Bible Dictionary,* ed. David Noel Freedman, 5 vols. (Garden City, N.Y.: Doubleday, forthcoming).

disciples to indicate believers in distinction from unbelievers. For example, in spite of persecution from the Jews and Gentiles in the regions of Pisidian Antioch and Lystra, "the disciples were filled with joy and with the Holy Spirit" (Ac 13:52) and "the disciples had gathered around" the apostles (14:20). Luke summarized the missionary ministry of Paul and Barnabas among the Gentiles in Derbe as "preaching the good news" and "won a large number of disciples," and their pastoral ministry among the believers in Lystra and Iconium as "strengthening the disciples and encouraging them to remain true to the faith" (vv. 21, 22). When Luke records Paul and Barnabas's visit to "the church" in Antioch (v. 27), he makes a synonymously parallel reference to the same group of people by saying that Paul and Barnabas "stayed there a long time with the disciples" (v. 28). Peter's defense of Christians' liberty from the legalistic regulations of Judaism was made merely on behalf of "disciples" (15:10). Timothy's identity as a believer is expressed simply by the title *disciple* (16:1). Paul's apostolic ministry in the region of Galatia and Phrygia included "strengthening all the disciples" (18:23). When Apollos wanted to go to Achaia, the "brothers" of Ephesus wrote to the "disciples" there to welcome him (v. 27). In contrast to the people in the synagogue in Ephesus who spoke evil of the Way, the "disciples" went with Paul to be instructed in the school of Tyrannus (19:9). It was the "disciples" of Ephesus who tried to protect Paul from the Ephesian assembly (19:30) and to whom Paul gave exhortation before leaving for Macedonia (20:1). Later Paul addressed the Ephesian elders about their responsibilites for protecting the "flock," which is equivalent with the "disciples" (cf. 20:28–30). When Paul and his companions landed at Tyre, they looked up the "disciples" to stay with them, similar to when landing at Ptolemais they looked up the "brothers" and stayed with them, and similar to when on the way to Jerusalem some of the "disciples" from Ceasarea accompanied them in order to introduce them to Mnason, "one of the early disciples," with whom they were to stay (cf. 21:4, 7, 16).

As in Luke's gospel, in Acts the expressions "those who believe" and "the disciples" designate an equivalent group of people.[18]

THE EXCEPTIONS?

Although virtually all scholars acknowledge that the word *disciple* normally occurs in Acts as a referent for "believer," two significant

---

[18]Note the statement by Gould, "It is evident that to St. Luke τῶν πιστευσάντων and τῶν μαθητῶν were equivalent expressions" (George P. Gould, "Disciple," *Dictionary of Christ and the Gospels*, ed. James Hastings [New York: Scribners, 1906], 1:457).

passages may be exceptions to this usage. Of the twenty-eight occurrences of the word *disciple* in Acts,[19] only 9:25 and 19:1ff. show some variation in the use of the term.

Acts 9:25

An intriguing use of the term *disciple* occurs in Acts 9:25, where Luke's narrative speaks of "Saul and his disciples." The Jews were plotting against the newly converted Saul, watching the gates to see that he did not escape from them, and then Luke says, "but his disciples took him by night, and let him down through an opening in the wall, lowering him in a large basket" (Ac 9:25 NASB). What does Luke mean by saying that these are Saul's disciples?[20] This intriguing phenomenon has caused much controversy. Some commentators suggest that Saul, a recognized rabbi, had disciples of his own in the rabbinic tradition (cf. Mt 22:16; Mk 2:18) who had accompanied him to Damascus. These rabbinic disciples had now also become converts to Christianity, and they helped Saul to escape from the Jews. If so, this is the only time that Luke uses "disciples" in Acts to refer to rabbinic disciples. Other commentators conclude that Saul's preaching in Damascus and the surrounding area had been fruitful and that "his disciples" were those people from the Damascus region who had been converted under his preaching and who were now gathered around Saul as their spiritual leader.[21] If so, this is the only time in Acts (or the New Testament?) that an individual Christian is said to have personal disciples. Several commentators declare that such a relationship is impossible in New Testament usage and instead contend that a later, minor, variant textual reading reflects Luke's original text. This reading substitutes "him" (accusative *auton*) for "his" (genitive *autou*), concluding that Luke says, "The disciples took him." These commentators contend that since it is out of keeping with the normal meaning of disciple in Acts to refer to any individual Christian having personal disciples, and since "the

---

[19]Μαθητής occurs twenty-eight times in Acts, fewer than in any of the Gospels; cf. Robert Morgenthaler, *Statistik Des Neutestamentlichen Wortschatzes* (Frankfurt Am Main: Gotthelf-Verlag Zurich, 1958), 118.

[20]The NIV obscures the issues by translating μαθηταί as "followers": "But his followers took him by night and lowered him in a basket through an opening in the wall" (Ac 9:25).

[21]F. F. Bruce, *Commentary on the Book of Acts: The English Text with Introduction, Exposition and Notes,* NICNT (Grand Rapids: Eerdmans, 1954), 204; Homer A. Kent, Jr., *Jerusalem to Rome* (Grand Rapids: Baker, 1972), 85; Lenski, *Acts,* 373; Longenecker, "Acts," 377; Rengstorf, "μαθητής," 459; J. Rawson Lumby, *The Acts of the Apostles,* Cambridge Greek Testament for Schools and Colleges (Cambridge: Cambridge Univ. Press, 1894), 201.

disciples" is used absolutely in vv. 19 and 26, Luke would not have written "his disciples."[22]

The variant reading is appealing because it seems to solve a difficulty, but the motivation appears unnecessarily harmonistic. Although we have observed that Luke normally uses "disciple" to be a referent for "believer," it may be begging the question to force the use here to conform to Luke's usage elsewhere. Since "his disciples" is the harder reading,[23] there is a high probability that it is the original reading. If so, our understanding of the discipleship phenomena must be adjusted. Luke apparently indicates that Saul had a positive response to his early preaching, and "his disciples" were those who were converted under Saul's preaching and who were being helped by Saul in their Christian growth.

Therefore, the disciples in Acts 9:25 are believers, similar to Lukan usage elsewhere in Acts; but uniquely in Lukan (and possibly New Testament) usage in Acts, they are converts gathered around a spiritual mentor.

Acts 19:1ff.

Another intriguing use of the term *disciple* occurs in Acts 19:1, where Paul is said to have found certain "disciples" when he arrived in Ephesus. The problem is that they do not appear to be Christians but instead followers of John the Baptist. Commentators have discussed this passage at length and are about evenly divided. One view is that these "disciples" are actually Christians but are imperfectly instructed.[24] Another view suggests that since these people had only received John's baptism, they were disciples of John the Baptist, hence, not Christians. They may have accepted John's baptism and then called themselves his disciples, but they were unaware of John's full teaching (e.g., concerning the Spirit) and were

---

[22]E.g., Bruce M. Metzger, ed., *A Textual Commentary on the Greek New Testament: A Companion Volume to the UBS Greek New Testament*, 3d ed. (Philadelphia: UBS, 1971), 366; Haenchen, *Acts of the Apostles*, 332, n. 3; Marshall, *Acts*, 174–75, n. 1; William Kelly, *An Exposition of the Acts of the Apostles*, 3d ed. (London: Hammond, 1952), 136, n.; Johannes Munck, *The Acts of the Apostles*, AB 31, rev. William F. Albright and C. S. Mann (Garden City, N.Y.: Doubleday, 1967), 85; Williams, *Acts*, 161.

[23]"His disciples" is the harder reading. We can more easily account for the change to "him" ($\alpha \dot{\upsilon} \tau \acute{o} \nu$) through scribal emendation than to conceive of a scribe changing the text to "his" ($\alpha \dot{\upsilon} \tau o \hat{\upsilon}$).

[24]This appears to be the conclusion of Bruce, *Acts of the Apostles*, 406, and his earlier English commentary, *Commentary on the Book of Acts*, 352. Cf. also Haenchen, *Acts of the Apostles*, 552–57. A novel view, which may not gather many followers, suggests that Jesus baptized these disciples into John's baptism, see Jerome Murphy-O'Connor, "John the Baptist and Jesus: History and Hypotheses," *NTS* 36 (1990): 367–68.

unaware that Jesus was the fulfilment of John's message.[25] Still another view proposes that these people were neither Jesus' disciples nor John the Baptist's, but only appeared to be Jesus' disciples. Luke has told the story from the viewpoint of the principal actor: Paul had met some people who appeared to him to be disciples, but because he had some doubts about their Christian status, he examined their claims more carefully. Luke is not saying that they were disciples but is describing how they appeared to Paul when he first arrived. They were people who had learned (imperfectly!) of John's teaching while they were living in Ephesus, who had been baptized into John's baptism, and who were now claiming (falsely) to be Christians.[26]

If these people were true believers in Jesus (the first view), then they really were "disciples" of Jesus, although imperfectly instructed. This would make the occurrence of the term here similar to the prior usage in Acts. Perhaps a parallel could be drawn between these disciples and the disciples early in the Jesus movement who had attached themselves to Jesus without fully understanding his form of discipleship (e.g., Jn 6:66; 8:31).

If these people were John's disciples (the second view), then Luke uses the term here in the general sense to indicate a follower of a great master or teacher other than Jesus. This is in line with the evidence found in the Gospels where we discovered other disciples of John the Baptist (e.g., Mk 2:18; Jn 1:35). This would be an exception to Luke's normal usage in Acts but would be quite in line with common Hellenistic usage.[27]

On the other hand, if these people were not truly Jesus' disciples nor John's, but were only apparently disciples of Jesus (the third view), adherents of John who attached themselves to the Christian

---

[25]E.g., Rengstorf, "$\mu\alpha\theta\eta\tau\acute{\eta}\varsigma$," 456–57; Heinrich August Wilhelm Meyer, *A Critical and Exegetical Handbook to the Acts of the Apostles* (New York: Funk and Wagnalls, 1983), 364–65.

[26]E.g., Marshall, *Acts*, 305–6; Homer A. Kent, Jr., *Jerusalem to Rome* (Grand Rapids: Baker, 1972), 150.

[27]Several commentators suggest that since Luke's normal use of "disciple" means "Christian" he cannot deviate from this. E.g., Haenchen, *Acts of the Apostles*, 552–57. Cf. Lake, who says that these "disciples" must be Christians because in Acts $\mu\alpha\theta\eta\tau\acute{\eta}\varsigma$ is always so used (Kirsopp Lake, *Additional Notes to the Commentary*, vol. 5, *The Acts of the Apostles: The Beginnings of Christianity*, reprint [Grand Rapids: Baker, 1966], 237). Alford agrees with this, adding that they could not have merely been disciples of John, because of the use of $\mu\alpha\theta\eta\tau\acute{\eta}\varsigma$, which can bear no other meaning than that of "believing on the Lord Jesus"; Henry Alford, ed., "The Acts of the Apostles," vol. 2, *The Greek New Testament*, reprint (Chicago: Moody, 1958), 193. But surely this is begging the question. Luke was no doubt aware of the secular use of $\mu\alpha\theta\eta\tau\acute{\eta}\varsigma$ to designate followers of masters other than Jesus and could have used it in that way here, even though the normal use of the term in Acts is to designate *believers in Jesus*.

movement before Paul's arrival, then Luke simply describes them from Paul's perspective, and, hence, uses the term here in line with his use elsewhere in Acts to designate "believers in Jesus," even though they were perceived incorrectly to be believers.

This is a difficult problem. Bruce says, "Whether they were disciples of John or of Jesus, how and where they received instruction must be a matter of speculation."[28] Since our purpose here is not to explore this problem fully, we can only make two observations on its relevance to our study: (1) These disciples are obviously not "Christians" in the full sense understood by Luke in Acts since they have not, up to this incident, participated in the experience of the Holy Spirit (Ac 19:1–3, 6). (2) These disciples, because they have been baptized into John's baptism, are rightly to be considered followers of John. The unqualified use of "disciple," however, makes it unlikely that the author was intending the expression to mean "disciple of John the Baptist."[29]

In the light of these two observations, a modification of the third view seems most likely. These "disciples" had been baptized into John's baptism, attaching themselves to John's message. However, they were very ill-informed of John's message since they were not aware of the Holy Spirit (Ac 19:2), which was an important part of John's earliest message (cf. Mt 3:11). Nonetheless, they called themselves disciples of John. When the Jesus movement began to make itself felt in the surrounding area, these disciples of John identified with the Jesus movement, since it apparently was related to their understanding of John's ministry. So these disciples attached themselves to the Jesus movement, calling themselves Jesus' disciples, even though they were unaware of the real distinction between John and Jesus. However, when Paul arrived on the scene, he was able to discern a deficiency in their understanding and belief. Upon questioning them, it came to light that they were not truly believers, hence, not truly Jesus' disciples. As they came to a fuller understanding of the Christian message, they believed. As a sign of their newfound faith, the Holy Spirit came upon them and they became a part of the community of true disciples, the church.[30]

These "disciples" are like those in Jesus' earthly ministry who had first become followers of John, but when they heard of Jesus they followed after him. As they attached themselves to the Jesus

---

[28]Bruce, *Acts of the Apostles*, 406. See this source for a bibliography of some of the more important studies and views of this problem.

[29]Marshall, *Acts*, 305.

[30]A similar incident occurs with regard to Apollos in the preceding narrative (Ac 18:23–28). The problem of Apollos is similar yet different as well.

movement, they were called his "disciples" even though it was later discovered that there were some who were not true believers and who had no real commitment to him (e.g., Jn 6:66; 8:31). The "disciples" in Acts 19:1ff. appear to have undergone a similar experience. They were calling themselves "Christians" or "disciples," although they were unclear of the real distinction between John and Jesus and had no real commitment to him.[31] Because of their initial, outward appearance as those who called themselves followers of John and Jesus, Luke calls them disciples, meaning "believers in Jesus." This is consistent with Luke's use elsewhere in Acts, although it was discovered later that they had a faulty understanding of both John's and Jesus' message and were not true disciples/believers until they believed.

For Luke in Acts, the simple use of the term *disciple* indicates a confessing believer in Jesus as Messiah.

Disciples As "the Church"

Significantly, although Luke draws an equation between the expressions "those who believe" and "the disciples," he makes it clear that with the coming of Pentecost a new era for discipleship had been inaugurated. One of the most significant features for us to recognize is that the word *disciples* is used in the book of Acts to describe the post-Easter believers intimately associated together as the new community of faith, the church.[32]

In his very first contextual use of the term in Acts, Luke indicates that *disciples* are united as a distinct community of faith. After Luke observed that the "disciples were increasing in number," he next described them as being banded together as a "congregation of the disciples" (Ac 6:2 NASB; *plēthos tōn mathētōn*). The word rendered *congregation, plēthos,* is found with two meanings in Acts: it can mean "a crowd, a large number of persons" (e.g., 2:6), or it can mean "the full assembly." The latter is intended in Acts 6:2. The "congregation of disciples" refers to the collective assembly of believers in Jerusalem. This is especially striking when compared to the occurrence of the same phrase in Luke 19:37, where Luke uses it in the first sense, to refer to the "crowd" of disciples who gathered to witness Jesus' entry into Jerusalem on Palm Sunday.[33] By connecting

---

[31]This is similar to the view of Longenecker, "Acts," *EBC* 9:493.

[32]Robert P. Meye, "Disciple," *The International Standard Bible Encyclopedia,* ed. Geoffrey W. Bromiley, rev. ed. (Grand Rapids: Eerdmans, 1979), 1:948.

[33]Cf. Joseph A. Fitzmyer, *The Gospel According to Luke (x-xxiv): Introduction, Translation, and Notes, AB* 28A (Garden City, N.Y.: Doubleday, 1985), 1250; I.

plēthos with "disciples" in Acts 6:2, Luke has now made the expression "the congregation of disciples" equivalent to such expressions as "the congregation of those who believed" (Ac 4:32 NASB), "the congregation" (Ac 6:5; 15:12, 30 NASB), and "the church" (5:11 NASB; 7:38 NASB; 8:1; et al.).[34]

The word *church* occurs only twice in the Gospels, both in Matthew's gospel, when Jesus speaks prophetically of the future community of believers (Mt 16:18; 18:17). Soon after the Pentecostal experience of the indwelling Spirit of God, the word *church* (*ekklēsia*) appears in the Lukan narrative of Acts to designate the community of faith (cf. Ac 5:11). George Ladd says:

> Strictly speaking the *ekklēsia* was born at Pentecost when the Holy Spirit was poured out upon the small circle of Jewish disciples of Jesus, constituting them the nucleus of Christ's body. The disciples before Pentecost should be considered only the embryo church. The *ekklēsia* is not to be viewed simply as a human fellowship, bound together by a common religious belief and experience. It is this, but it is more than this: it is the creation of God through the Holy Spirit. Therefore there is and can be properly only one *ekklēsia*.[35]

The church, then, is God's new creation into which are brought by the Spirit all converts, whether Jews, Samaritans, or Gentiles (cf. Ac 1:8).[36] However, even though there is only one church, the body of Christ, *ekklēsia* is also used to refer to the assembly of Christians in a locale, whether in Jerusalem, Antioch (Ac 11:26; 13:1; 14:27; 15:3; 15:30), Syria and Celicia (15:41), South Galatia (14:23), or in Ephesus (20:17, 28). Luke emphasizes that "disciples" are those who believe in Jesus as the Christ, those who are now associated together in the new creation, the church. The assembly of converts is called the "church" (*ekklēsia*) or "congregation" (*plēthos*), while individuals within the church are referred to as "believers" (e.g., Ac 2:44; 4:32), "brothers" (e.g., Ac 15:1, 3, 32–33, 36, 40; 16:2, 40; et al.), or "disciples" (e.g., Ac 6:1, 2, 7; 9:1, 10, 19, 26, 36, 38; 11:26, 29; 13:52; et al.).[37]

The fact that the term *disciple* was still used makes it clear that continuity is maintained between those who followed Jesus during his earthly ministry and those of the post-Resurrection church.

Howard Marshall, *The Gospel of Luke, NIGTC* (Grand Rapids: Eerdmans, 1978), 714.

[34]Bruce, *Acts of the Apostles*, 63, 159, 182; Williams, *Acts*, 106.

[35]George Eldon Ladd, *A Theology of the New Testament* (Grand Rapids: Eerdmans, 1974), 347. This, essentially, is also the view of Dunn, *Unity and Diversity*, 104–6.

[36]Cf. Ladd, *Theology of the New Testament*, 342–47.

[37]Bruce, *Acts of the Apostles*, 63.

Therefore, the essence of the form of discipleship that Jesus initiated continues into the church. However, discipleship for the new community of faith will be different from the age when Jesus walked physically with his disciples in Palestine.[38]

Disciple and Disciples

Another important observation that leads to our understanding of the disciples as the "community of faith" is the distinction between the use of the singular *disciple* and the plural *disciples*. The singular form *disciple* never occurs in Mark, but it is frequent in John, where it always refers to a particular person, usually the "disciple whom Jesus loved" (cf. Jn 9:28; 18:15, 16; 19:26–28; 20:2–4, 8; 21:7, 20, 23, 24). The singular occurs in Matthew and Luke only on Jesus' lips, where it is used in teachings about the nature of discipleship (Mt 10:24, 25, 42; Lk 6:40; 14:26, 27, 33). The singular occurs only five times in Acts, where it always refers to a particular person (Ac 9:10, 26; 16:1; 21:16; in 9:36 we have the singular feminine noun).

Throughout the Gospels and Acts the plural form *disciples* is normally used. The singular form designates an individual who professes to believe in and follow Jesus.[39] That the plural form is normally used expresses an important point: individual disciples are always seen in conjunction with the community of disciples, whether as Jesus' intimate companions or as the church. Hence, discipleship is a concept that normally occurs within the context of the community. With the inception of the church in Acts, that community is the church.

Disciples and Apostles

Another crucial feature to observe in Luke's perspective of discipleship in Acts is his distinction between the terms *disciple* and *apostle*. The word *apostle* (Heb. *shaliach;* Gk. *apostolos*) has received considerable scholarly attention in the past century, with the renewed conviction that the biblical meaning indicates an individual sent with the authority to represent the message and person of the sender.[40] In the Gospels we have seen that Jesus chose,

---

[38]Williams, *Acts,* 102.

[39]We should note that Judas is called one of Jesus' disciples (Jn 12:4). Here is an individual who professes but who is not a true believer. See the discussion of Judas in chap. 8, "The Twelve."

[40]A recent survey of research is undertaken by Francis H. Agnew, "The Origin of the New Testament Apostle-Concept," *JBL* 105 (1986): 75–96. In addition,

from among the large number of his disciples, twelve whom he called "apostles," who were then sent out on a mission among Israel (cf. Mt 10:2; Mk 6:30; Lk 6:13; 9:10). This select group continued to be called primarily "disciples," the title that indicated their commonality with other believers, but increasingly they were called "the Twelve," the title that indicated their distinctiveness as Jesus' most intimate companions. On a few other occasions in the Gospels (only in Luke) they were designated "the apostles," a title that was patently equivalent with these twelve disciples who were being prepared for their special role in the future church (cf. Lk 17:5 with 17:1; 9:10; 22:14; 24:10).[41]

When we come to the book of Acts a startling phenomenon occurs: the Twelve as a group are never specifically referred to as "disciples"; they are always emphasized to be "apostles."[42] From the very first mention of the Twelve in Acts, Luke calls them "apostles" (Ac 1:2). Luke now focuses upon the Twelve as the leaders of the new community. In the broad sense, the Twelve are of course numbered among the disciples because they are a part of the community of believers (e.g., Ac 9:26). However, when Luke wants to specify the smaller group of leaders, he calls them "apostles" (whether the Twelve or Barnabas or Paul; e.g., 1:2, 26; 2:37; 14:4, 14; et al.). Later other terms for leaders are used, such as *elders* (*presbuteroi;* Ac 11:30; 21:17, 18), and *guardians* charged "to shepherd" the flock (*episkopoi . . . poimanein,* Ac 20:28, NIV "keep watch").[43] But for Luke the "twelve apostles" have a unique role in salvation history. In them is a backward look at the ancient constitution of Israel and a forward look to the final form of the messianic community: the Twelve were chosen from among the larger group of disciples for a special role in founding the church (cf. also Mt 19:28; Eph 2:20).[44]

Linked with our discussion of the term *disciple,* this discussion of the term *apostle* once again demonstrates that in distinction from

refer to the standard studies in Karl H. Rengstorf, "ἀπόστολος," *TDNT* 1:69–75; and Colin Brown and Dietrich Müller, "Apostle/ἀποστέλλω," *NIDNTT* 1:126–37.

[41]See the discussion in Colin Brown, "Apostleship in Luke-Acts," *NIDNTT* 1:135–37. Cf. also Donald Guthrie, *New Testament Theology* (Downers Grove, Ill.: InterVarsity Press, 1981), 707–8.

[42]This phenomenon is observed simply through looking up the terms *disciples, apostles,* and *Twelve* in context by using a Greek concordance; e.g., "μαθητής, δἀπόστολος, δώδεκα," *The Englishman's Greek Concordance of the New Testament,* 9th ed. (Grand Rapids: Zondervan, 1960), 468. I have already discussed every occurrence of the term above; cf. "Disciples" as a referent for "believers," "those of the Way," "Christians."

[43]Bruce, *Acts of the Apostles,* 62–63.

[44]Cf. Seán Freyne, *The Twelve: Disciples and Apostles. A Study in the Theology of the First Three Gospels* (London: Sheed & Ward, 1968), 23–48; Dunn, *Unity and Diversity,* 108–9; Karl H. Rengstorf, "Δώδεκα," *TDNT* 2:326.

apostle the term *disciple* in Acts is simply a term that designates "Christians." Paul Helm succinctly emphasizes the essence of what it is to be a disciple in Acts when he says:

> The term *disciple* is used in the Book of Acts to describe believers, those who confess Christ (6:1, 2, 7; 9:36; 11:26). Though they have not been directly called by Christ himself, such disciples are called by Christ's Spirit through the message delivered by the first disciples; disciples called later are not in any sense inferior to the first disciples, even though they are less privileged [*since they have not been able to walk with Jesus in his earthly ministry*].[45]

Disciples are those who confess Jesus as Savior and Lord. Apostles are those who have been called from among the disciples in order to be the leaders of the community of disciples, the church.

DISCIPLESHIP TRANSITIONS TO ACTS

We see now that the book of Acts is similar to, yet distinct from, the Gospels in the way that it perceives "disciples." Life in the days of the church would be similar to, yet very different from, life in the days when Jesus walked with his followers through Palestine.[46] Although in his earthly ministry Jesus attempted to prepare his disciples for the new era, it was such a radical departure from their apparent expectations that they still needed transitional equipping to prepare them. Therefore, in their vulnerable, post-Resurrection condition, the disciples received from Jesus final instructions for forty days which centered their attention upon principles that would serve them during the new era.

Luke's record of Jesus' final ministry to the disciples in that period between his resurrection and ascension displays principles that would direct the activities of disciples in the age of community (Ac 1:6–11). We can see continuity between the principles enunciated

---

[45]Paul Helm, "Disciple," *Baker Encyclopedia of the Bible,* ed. Walter A. Elwell, 2 vols. (Grand Rapids: Baker, 1988), 630, my clarification.

[46]Many scholars have attempted to account for the continuity/discontinuity phenomenon of the disciples' pre- and post-Pentecost experience by employing different sociological or theological categories; e.g., the complex relationship between unity and diversity, rule of faith and monarchial episcopacy, ministry and authority, as discussed by Dunn, *Unity and Diversity,* 103ff.; or the bewilderment forced upon the disciples in the theory of cognitive dissonance by John G. Gager, *Kingdom and Community: The Social World of Early Christianity* (Englewood Cliffs, N.J.: Prentice-Hall, 1975), 37ff.; or the continuity/discontinuity displayed between the Old Testament and New Testament which often forces the Gospels' characters into a kind of "never-never land," as exemplified in John S. Feinberg, ed., *Continuity and Discontinuity: Perspectives on the Relationship Between the Old and New Testaments,* Essays in Honor of S. Lewis Johnson, Jr. (Westchester, Ill.: Crossway, 1988).

here and the discipleship principles initiated by Jesus in his earthly ministry, yet we can see that the new age requires a new application of those principles. Paraphrased, we may see Jesus' final ministry articulated in the following exhortations.[47] First, focus on the teachings of Jesus for living out the meaning of life (vv. 1–3). Second, actualize the unity of community brought by the Spirit (vv. 4–5). Third, be a witness to the good news of Jesus in the power of the Spirit (vv. 6–8). Fourth, let the absence of Jesus be an incentive to hopefulness until his return (vv. 9–11).

The Teachings of Jesus for Living Out the Meaning of Life

The first exhortation that will enable Jesus' disciples to make the transition from the period of the Gospels to the period of the church is "focus on the teachings of Jesus for living out the meaning of life" (see Ac 1:1–3).

Jesus' teachings are the foundation of the discipleship life of the new community. Jesus specifically stated that a major aspect of growth in the life of discipleship was through obedience to all that Jesus had commanded the disciples during his earthly ministry (Mt 28:20). In the intervening forty days between his resurrection and ascension, he gave final instructions about the kingdom life that the disciples would experience in the age after his ascension (Ac 1:1–3). All that Jesus had taught on the subject of discipleship during his life and during this intervening period provide the basis for discipleship during the age of the church. Everett Harrison says, "In the eyes of the early church, led as it was by men who had companied with Jesus, the identification of a person as a disciple carried with it the implication that he or she had embraced the costs as well as the benefits of being a follower of the Lord Jesus."[48] The Twelve had a leadership role in passing on the teaching of Jesus. The expression "devoted themselves to the apostles' teaching" (cf. Ac 2:42) indicated the means by which Jesus' teaching to them could be passed on to the new disciples of the church.

Given this principle, however, we should recognize that the issue of continuity/discontinuity affects discipleship teaching between the

---

[47]The form of these exhortations was in part stimulated by Harold E. Dollar, "A Biblical-Missiological Exploration of the Cross-Cultural Dimensions in Luke-Acts" (unpublished Ph.D. diss., Fuller Theological Seminary, 1990), 75–76. See also a discussion of "continuity/discontinuity" in discipleship studies, see A. Boyd Luter, Jr., "A New Testament Theology of Discipling" (unpublished Th.D. diss., Dallas Theological Seminary, 1985), 85–89.

[48]Everett F. Harrison, *The Apostolic Church* (Grand Rapids: Eerdmans, 1985), 143.

Gospels and Acts. Specifically, three different categories of disciple-ship teaching must be observed. First, certain teachings were addressed to the disciples primarily with reference to their life with Jesus in his earthly ministry. On occasion the disciples were given teaching that was intended to equip them for the specific circumstances of Jesus' earthly ministry, not for the circumstances of the church.[49] It takes a great deal of patience to identify those disciple-ship teachings that had relevance only for the time of Jesus' earthly ministry, but it is vitally important to do so. However, we must also suggest that principles of discipleship may be derived from these teachings, even though the specifics may be transcended.

An illustration of this category of discipleship teachings is found in the discourse Jesus gave to the disciples prior to their short missionary outreach in Israel (cf. Mt 10). We find there injunctions that have special reference to that trip only. For example, the command "Do not go in the way of the Gentiles, and do not enter any city of the Samaritans; but rather go to the lost sheep of the house of Israel" (Mt 10:5–6 NASB) had special salvation-historical significance only for the time of Jesus' earthly ministry. That command was not carried over to the church. Jesus, in Acts 1:8, specifically counter-manded that injunction by sending the disciples to Jerusalem, Judea, Samaria, and the uttermost parts of the earth, including to the Gentiles. Other injunctions given in the first part of the discourse in Matthew 10, such as not taking bag or tunic or sandals, etc. (Mt 10:10), should also be seen as relevant only for the time of the disciples' short missionary journey in Israel during Jesus' earthly ministry. D. A. Carson comments, "In vv. 5–16, all Jesus' instructions neatly fit the situation of the Twelve during Jesus' public ministry."[50]

However, careful examination of Jesus' missionary discourse reveals that Jesus not only gave directives to govern the mission in Israel (Mt 10:5–15), but he also gave directives in the future tense to govern their future worldwide missionary travels after Pentecost (Mt 10:16–23). Carson continues, "But vv. 17–22 clearly envisage a far more extensive ministry—even to kings and Gentiles. The persecu-tion described does not fit the period of the first apostolic ministry but looks beyond it to times of major conflict long after Pentecost."[51] Further, following teaching he gave about the worldwide mission,

---

[49]See Walter C. Kaiser, Jr., "Legitimate Hermeneutics," *Inerrancy*, ed. Norman L. Geisler (Grand Rapids: Zondervan, 1980), 139ff.

[50]D. A. Carson, "Matthew," *EBC*, ed. Frank E. Gaebelein (Grand Rapids: Zondervan, 1984), 8:241.

[51]Carson, "Matthew," 241.

Jesus gave general discipleship teaching that is relevant for both ages, pre- and post-Pentecost (Mt 10:24–42).

Therefore, in this one discourse we find some discipleship instruction that has relevance only during the earthly ministry of Jesus (Mt 10:5–15), some discipleship instruction that has relevance for future witness beyond Pentecost (vv. 16–23), and general discipleship principles for all ages (vv. 24–42). Carson concludes:

> Therefore it is surely not unnatural for Jesus to treat this commission of the Twelve as both an explicit short-term itinerary and a paradigm of the longer mission stretching into the years ahead. For the latter, the Twelve need further instruction beyond those needed for the immediate tour, which they must see as in part an exercise anticipating something more. In this sense the Twelve become a paradigm for other disciples in their post-Pentecost witness, a point Matthew understands (cf. 28:18–20); and in this sense he intends that Matthew 10 should also speak to his readers.[52]

We must be careful in our analysis of the biblical text to distinguish between those discipleship teachings that were intended for the disciples while they were with Jesus during his earthly ministry and those intended for the time beyond Pentecost. Only in doing so will we accurately appropriate Jesus' discipleship teachings.

Another more general example includes the occasions when Jesus admonished the disciples not to reveal his messianic identity (e.g., Mt 16:20; Mk 9:9). This silence was necessary because of the misconceptions that could be raised in the minds of the Jewish populace. Jesus understood that the expectations of what the people wanted in a Messiah and what he came to accomplish were often quite different, so he wanted to reveal his identity in his own way, without risking misunderstanding. Therefore, he warned the disciples on several occasions not to reveal certain phenomena about himself. But that silence is not the same in the latter part of his ministry as in the first, and we do not find the admonition to silence repeated in Acts. We must be careful to distinguish those discipleship teachings that are intended for instruction about the circumstances of Jesus' earthly ministry.

The second category of discipleship teachings include instructions or statements that were directed toward the Twelve with special reference to their foundational leadership role in the church. The Twelve had a special salvation-historical role in founding the church, and part of their training by Jesus was directed toward that specific role. Some of these discipleship teachings may be used in principle as examples for leaders in the church today, but we must be careful to

---

[52]Ibid., 242.

heed the salvation-historical distinctiveness of some teaching directed toward the Twelve.[53]

An example of this category of discipleship teaching is the famous
interplay between Peter and Jesus near Caesarea Philippi. After
Peter made his confession of Jesus' messianic identity, Jesus said of
Peter:

> Blessed are you, Simon son of Jonah, for this was not revealed to you by
> man, but by my Father in heaven. And I tell you that you are Peter, and
> on this rock I will build my church, and the gates of Hades will not
> overcome it. I will give you the keys of the kingdom of heaven;
> whatever you bind on earth will be bound in heaven, and whatever you
> loose on earth will be loosed in heaven. (Mt 16:17–19)

Many misunderstandings of this passage could be avoided if interpreters would recognize that Jesus was here declaring Peter's unique
role in salvation history in the establishment of the church. This is
seen clearly by the use of personal pronouns and verbs in the second
person singular throughout the passage (e.g., "I will give *you*," v. 19,
soi . . . "whatever *you bind*," *dēsēs*). That which is said to Peter
personally here is unfolded in his unique role in opening the door of
the kingdom to Jews (Ac 2), Samaritans (Ac 8), and Gentiles (Ac 10).
Once Peter utilized the "keys" to open the door to these people-
groups, he fulfilled his unique role and gradually passed from the
scene of Acts.[54] We must carefully observe the unique role of the
Twelve, while not taking their role too far by saying more of them
than Jesus does.[55]

At the same time, we must carefully observe where some of the
teaching directed toward the Twelve may have application for
leaders of the church and for disciples in general. For example, this
same interplay between Jesus and Peter includes a statement about
"forgiving sins" (Mt 16:19) which is repeated in the other "church"
context in Matthew's gospel (18:18). The saying is addressed to the
disciples generally in this context (cf. v. 1), hence the saying Jesus
gave to Peter about forgiving sins is also intended for disciples

---

[53]Cf. Dunn, *Unity and Diversity,* 108–9; F. F. Bruce, *Peter, Stephen, James
and John: Studies in Non-Pauline Christianity* (Grand Rapids: Eerdmans, 1979),
15.

[54]I have discussed this passage in full elsewhere, showing Peter's specific role
as delineated by Jesus here. See Michael J. Wilkins, *The Concept of Disciple in
Matthew's Gospel: As Reflected in the Use of the Term* Μαθητής, NovTSup 59
(Leiden: E. J. Brill, 1988), 185–98. See also Oscar Cullmann, *Peter: Disciple—
Apostle—Martyr. A Historical and Theological Essay,* trans. Floyd V. Filson, 2d
ed. (Philadelphia: Westminster, 1962); Chrys Caragounis, *Peter and The Rock,*
BZNW 58 (Berlin/New York: de Gruyter, 1990).

[55]For example, this passage does not saying anything about "papal succession"
from Peter or even about his personal role beyond utilizing the keys.

generally. In addition, a similar statement about forgiving sins is made by Jesus to the assembled disciples in the Upper Room after the Resurrection (Jn 20:23).

Therefore, a second category of discipleship teachings shows special relevance for the Twelve in the foundational role in the church. Those teachings must be clearly distinguished from general teachings intended for all believers.

The third category includes those discipleship teachings that are directed toward all disciples, both pre- and post-Pentecost. This category includes the majority of Jesus' discipleship teachings. We can say generally that those teachings that are not excluded by the first and second categories are included in the third. But even here it is vitally important to observe our guiding principle of walking through the Gospels beginning with the left foot, the foot that recognizes the first-century historical setting of all teachings.[56] Even general discipleship teachings directed toward all disciples will naturally be conditioned by the social/historical circumstances of the first century. Nonetheless, disciples of the church should feel confident to apply this third category of Jesus' discipleship teachings to themselves today.

This matter becomes extremely important. After we analyze Jesus' discipleship teachings to sift those that are historically related to Jesus' earthly ministry, and those that are given to the Twelve in their salvation-historical roles, we end up with a body of discipleship teaching designed to guide the lives of believers in the church today. These clarifications move us much closer to heeding what Jesus said in the Great Commission. Those who have become disciples are to be taught to observe all that Jesus commanded in his earthly ministry (Mt 28:18–20).

The Unity of Community Brought by the Spirit

The second exhortation that will enable Jesus' disciples to make the transition from the period of the Gospels to the period of the church is to "actualize the unity of community brought by the Spirit" (see Ac 1:4–5).

From the opening chapters of the book of Acts, it is apparent that the Holy Spirit is to play a major role with the disciples in the days ahead. While the disciples have had the privilege of walking with Jesus personally, because of the incarnational limitations of Jesus' earthly ministry (e.g., he could not physically be in more than one place at a time), not all of the disciples had the same degree of

---

[56]Please refer back to chap. 2, where we discussed this principle.

privilege. We saw earlier that within the broad grouping of Jesus' followers there were concentric circles around him. The Twelve were privileged to be with Jesus almost constantly during his earthly ministry. Within the Twelve an inner group enjoyed the privilege of being with Jesus alone on some special occasions. Some women who traveled with Jesus and the Twelve for a period of time enjoyed the privilege of supporting their material needs (Lk 8:1–3). The Seventy were trained by Jesus for the privilege of being sent out on a short missionary journey in Israel (Lk 10:1ff.). The large numbers of disciples, some of whom were privileged to follow Jesus around for a while, mostly were not called to that privilege. But now, with the coming of the Spirit, each disciple had the privilege of the indwelling Spirit and also had the privilege of being brought together as one community in the Spirit. Jesus foretold this transition brought about by the Spirit on his final night with the disciples before he went to the cross. In John's account of that final night, we have a magnificent record of Jesus' teaching on the Holy Spirit's activity in the coming age.

Briefly summarized, that teaching included the promise that the Spirit, who had been with the disciples, would now be in them (Jn 14:17). He would teach them all things, and bring to their remembrance all that Jesus had said to them (v. 26). He would not only bear witness to Jesus, but would also assist the disciples to bear witness to Jesus (15:26–27). The Spirit, who would be the disciples' personal Helper in the coming time of persecution (16:1–7), would in turn convict the world of sin, righteousness, and judgement (vv. 8–11). The disciples would not be without help in understanding the truth, because the Spirit would guide them into all truth (v. 13) and would disclose Jesus words to them, which would in turn glorify Jesus (vv. 13–15). Once Jesus ascended, he sent the Spirit to provide the power, the guidance, the comfort, the presence of God necessary for fulfilling the Great Commission and for transforming disciples into the image of Christ. As F. F. Bruce has said, "The church . . . is the organ of the Spirit in the world. It is he who animates, empowers, and directs this society of the disciples of Jesus."[57]

This age of the Spirit does not shut off the age when Jesus was with them. Rather, the Spirit causes a transition to be made from the kind of discipleship relationship the disciples had with the earthly Jesus to a discipleship relationship with the ascended Jesus. To anticipate Paul's metaphor of the body, the church is now the community of disciples who are brought together by the Spirit as Christ's body (1Co

---

[57]Bruce, *Acts of the Apostles*, 61.

12:12–13), enjoying an unhindered, loving fellowship with him through the Spirit (Eph 1:22–23; 5:23–32).

Witness to the Good News of Jesus in the Power of the Spirit

The third exhortation that will enable Jesus' disciples to make the transition from the period of the Gospels to the period of the church is to "be a witness to the good news of Jesus in the power of the Spirit" (see Ac 1:6–8).

In the preparation period before the Ascension, Jesus focused the disciples' attention on their role in the coming age: "But you will receive power when the Holy Spirit comes on you; and you will be my witnesses in Jerusalem, and in all Judea and Samaria, and to the ends of the earth." (Ac 1:8). In this account, Luke has once again recorded an important transition from the role of the disciples with Jesus to their role in the new era. While he does not mention the church in this passage, "In addressing the disciples Luke is addressing the church that comes into existence by the coming of the Holy Spirit. Mission creates the church and defines the essence of the church."[58] Jesus sent the disciples out on short missionary trips in Israel during his time with them (e.g., Mt 10:5–15; Lk 9:1–6; 10:1–20), but he had also pointed ahead to a future time when their witness would extend to the nations (Mt 10:5–23, esp. v. 18). Witnessing to the gospel of Jesus Christ became one of the clearest objectives of the early church. We trace this activity from Pentecost through the end of Acts, among Jews in Jerusalem and Judea (Ac 2–7), among Samaritans (Ac 8), and among Gentiles of the nations (Ac 10–28).

We note an important illustration of this witnessing transition in the activities of Paul and Barnabas while they were on a preaching trip through Asia Minor during the first missionary journey. Arriving in Derbe, "They preached the good news in that city and won a large number of disciples. Then they returned to Lystra, Iconium and Antioch, strengthening the disciples and encouraging them to remain true to the faith" (Ac 14:21–22). Here Luke summarizes the missionary ministry of Paul and Barnabas among the Gentiles in Derbe as preaching the Gospel and making many disciples, and then summarizes their pastoral ministry among the believers in Lystra and Iconium as strengthening the souls of the disciples and encouraging them to continue in the faith.

Both of these ministries illustrate the church's fulfillment of Jesus' commands. When Luke described the missionary activities among unbelievers, he used the same verb that Matthew used when

---

[58]Dollar, "Biblical-Missiological Exploration," 75.

recording Jesus' Great Commission, i.e., "make disciples" (*mathēteuō*, cf. Ac 14:21 with Mt 28:19). Outside of the three times that the verb occurs in Matthew's gospel (13:52; 27:57; 28:19), it is found in the New Testament only here. Luke's wording makes a direct, verbal connection with the Great Commission, because preaching the Gospel to the heathen results in "having made disciples."[59] Also, when Luke described Barnabas and Paul's pastoral ministry among believers, he said that they strengthened the souls of the "disciples" with the admonition "continue in the faith." Luke's wording suggests a connection with the discipleship process outlined by Jesus in the Great Commission, because "strengthening the souls of the disciples" and "encouraging them to remain in the faith" implies the kind of "teaching them to observe all I commanded you" that Jesus gave as the ongoing process of growth in discipleship.[60] Further, the activity of the church helping these converts "continue in the faith" is similar to Jesus' statement that the mark of true disciples is that they hold to his teaching (Jn 8:31). As these new converts continue in the faith, they demonstrate that they are truly Jesus' disciples.[61] The activities of the church in making disciples of unbelievers and then facilitating the growth of believers is an illustration of what Jesus intended by the Great Commission (Mt 28:18–20).

The early church's faithfulness to their mission of bearing witness to Jesus in the power of the Spirit is an important link that fulfills their missionary preparation in the Gospels (e.g., Mt 10:5–23), the Great Commission (28:18-20), and Jesus' preascension declaration (Ac 1:8).

The Absence of Jesus Is an Incentive to Hopefulness Until His Return

The fourth exhortation enabling Jesus' disciples to make the transition from the period of the Gospels to the period of the church

---

[59]Cf. Archibald T. Robertson, *The Acts of the Apostles*, vol. 3, *Word Pictures in the New Testament* (Nashville: Broadman, 1930), 160–61: "Paul and Barnabas were literally here obeying the command of Jesus in discipling people in this heathen city." See also Everett F. Harrison, *Acts: The Expanding Church* (Chicago: Moody, 1975), 224–25; Richard D. Calenberg, "The New Testament Doctrine of Discipleship" (unpublished Th.D. diss., Grace Theological Seminary, 1981), 201; Bruce, *Acts of the Apostles*, 325.

[60]See Boyd A. Luter, "Discipleship and the Church," *BS* 137 (1980): 270.

[61]Rengstorf, "μαθητής," 458–59. See also R. C. H. Lenski, *The Interpretation of the Acts of the Apostles* (Columbus, Ohio: Wartburg, 1944), 584: "A good beginning is a great achievement, but a good continuation is its normal and essential result. Conversion must pass on to preservation."

is to "let the absence of Jesus be an incentive to hopefulness until his return" (see Ac 1:9–11).

As Jesus' followers watched him lifted up out of their sight into heaven, they were introduced to life as they would now know it: life without Jesus' physical presence. But suddenly two angels in dazzling white garments appeared to announce to them that Jesus would someday return in the same manner in which he had been taken from them. Within days these disciples who had been faltering and failing at Gethsemene and Golgotha were transformed into bold and determined leaders of the church. They seem to have found themselves. The casual observer of this contrast might conclude that it is advantageous for the believer not to have the immediate presence of the Lord. But to reason in this way is to misapprehend what was actually occurring in the lives of these disciples. They did not suddenly muster their own boldness and determination. Rather, the disciples were ushered into a new dimension of life in which God changed them from the inside out.[62]

What brought this change? Several elements. Jesus had promised to be with the disciples as they represented him in the world (Mt 28:20). He had promised that he would be in them and that they would be in him as their very life (Jn 14:20). The greater works that he promised they would do once he left them (v. 12) would be accomplished because of the regenerating, energizing, comforting presence of the Holy Spirit, whom he promised to send to be with them (vv. 16–17). The time for the actualization of those promises was at hand. With the advent of the Spirit at Pentecost, transformation occurred in the lives of these disciples, a transformation that is promised for each person who names the name of Christ and receives his indwelling Spirit. Harrison says, "The new creation is indeed new, different, infinitely superior to the old. It is the very life of God lived out in a human context by the indwelling Christ. If the Lord Jesus is not seen in his people, it is because they have failed to appropriate him and make him their Lord."[63]

Yes, the days without Jesus' physical presence made necessary a transition in the disciples' lives, yet hope sprang from Jesus' promises to them. Even as Jesus had promised to return to be with them (Jn 14:1–3), the two angels reaffirmed that promise (Ac 1:10–11). Jesus' absence confirmed the presence of his Spirit, which in turn was an incentive to hopeful anticipation of Jesus' return.

---

[62]Harrison, *Apostolic Church*, 144.
[63]Ibid.

IMPLICATIONS

Jesus called individuals to follow him. Those individuals came to Jesus from a variety of backgrounds and exhibited a diversity of temperaments and personalities. Jesus was the challenging element that brought them together, the cohesive factor that held them together, and the dynamic vision that pressed them together toward new horizons. The unity of the Twelve and the cohesiveness of the larger movement of disciples was ultimately attributable only to Jesus. We should have expected to see that cohesiveness dissolve once Jesus left them to return to the Father. We should have expected their individualism to again dominate the unity. Instead, the reverse occurred. The disciples became even more unified, more cohesive. They became a community.

The disciples were a community only in embryo during the time when they followed Jesus physically. They were a movement held together loosely by their common commitment to Jesus, but they did not have to operate as a community. The disciples could simply look to Jesus for direction, they could ask him questions about their purpose, they could allow him to make their decisions for them. They did not have to display a great deal of commitment to one another, nor did they have to exhibit much mutuality of service or function. Indeed, quite often their individuality tended to put them at odds with one another. Jesus himself held them together by his physical presence. But now Jesus was gone. What brought them together to form them into a community?

A "community" necessarily manifests two essential ingredients: relations (of mutual acceptance, forgiveness, and service) and structured organization (with clear boundaries and demarcation of function).[64] When the Holy Spirit came upon the disciples at Pentecost he formed them into a clearly discernible entity, the body of Christ. A body demarcates its members according to function, which Paul later described as gifts of the Spirit (1Co 12:4–31). Through the coming of the Spirit, the disciples were formed into a structured organization, the body of Christ. As one body, the disciples were now committed to one another more than ever before. In his earthly time with the disciples, Jesus had taught them the principles of mutual acceptance, forgiveness, and service. Now in the new community of faith, the Spirit impelled the disciples to demonstrate those principles in their relations with one another. From the earliest days following Pentecost, the disciples began to function as a community.[65]

---

[64]Dunn, *Unity and Diversity*, 398, n. 2a.

[65]See Dennis M. Sweetland, *Our Journey with Jesus: Discipleship According to Luke-Acts* (Collegeville, Minn.: Michael Glazier, 1990), 126–69.

Therefore, the book of Acts is determinative for our understanding of the transition the disciples made to this age in which we now live. Our study of the disciples in Acts reveals important implications for our understanding of discipleship in this age. Charles Talbert suggests that two important components interact in Acts to give us the clearest Lukan view of discipleship: "On the one hand, discipleship consists of being molded by a tradition, being empowered by an experience, and being a participant in a community. On the other hand, it involves both a way to walk and a mission to fulfill."[66] Such is what we find in the community of faith in Acts, and such is what becomes our model for today.

The Discipleship Community

Acts gives us the latest chronological, biblical definition of the term *disciple* as it was used in the church. Disciples are all those who have believed on Jesus for salvation, whether men or women; whether Jew, Samaritan, or Gentile; whether active in leadership or simply an individual in the church. We have seen in those "disciples" whom Paul found in Ephesus (Ac 19:1) that profession of belief and/or association with the community implies, but does not guarantee, the reality of belief. True belief is the essence of the true disciple.

Further, Acts allows us to see that the term *disciple* indicates much more than its earliest Greek usage, "learners." While disciples are indeed actively involved in learning from the apostles' teaching, in Acts the "learner" element in the actual term *disciple* is only minimally apparent. The word *disciple* most naturally designates a "follower who has committed his/her faith for salvation to Jesus." Other synonyms for this follower help round out the picture. He or she is a "believer," a "saint," a "Christian," a "brother or sister" in Christ.

The church therefore is a community of disciples composed of all those who have believed on Jesus for salvation. In our day we have lost that perspective. Often people of the church feel as though discipleship is optional, that perhaps it is only for those who are extremely committed, or else it is for those who have been called to leadership or ministry. We must regain the perspective of Acts: To believe on Jesus draws a person into community, a community that defines its expectations, responsibilities, and privileges in terms of discipleship.[67]

---

[66]Talbert, "Discipleship in Luke-Acts," 62.

[67]For a helpful emphasis upon the concept of the church as a community of disciples, see Avery Dulles, *A Church to Believe In: Discipleship and the*

Leadership and Mutuality

Acts also indicates the relationship of "disciples" to various leadership terms. For example, all apostles were disciples, but not all disciples were apostles. In other words, all apostles were believers, but not all believers were chosen for a role as an apostle. The apostles were chosen out from among the rest of the disciples for a leadership role among the disciples. Further, the term *apostles* had a special connotation to indicate the Twelve who were salvation-historically significant in the foundation of the church. Other individuals were called apostles (e.g., Paul and Barnabas), but the term was not broadly used for leadership positions in local churches. Other terms such as *elder, bishop,* and *pastor* came to designate the leadership of local churches. Therefore, the book of Acts allows us to see that leaders were significant in the new community of faith.

However, we must also emphasize the delicate balance that every leader must maintain. At the same time that a leader has been called to exercise a particular role of leadership, he or she is also called to carry out the role of follower. Since every leader is also a disciple, the leader must remember that he or she continues to be a follower of the Master, Jesus. Donald Guthrie forcefully addresses the issue of leadership balanced with discipleship.

> Jesus expressly criticized those who sought positions of superiority and he inculcated humility as a more desirable quality (Mt 18:1ff.; Mk 9:33f. Lk 9:46f.). He also criticized the use of status titles like "Rabbi", since he maintained that his disciples were all brethren who had the same teacher, i.e., himself (Mt 23:8). He linked with "Rabbi", the title of "father" and "master." The greatest among his group of followers were those willing to be servants (*douloi*) utterly obedient to their master's wishes. The only privilege that could be claimed by any of the disciples was the privilege of service and sacrifice (such as taking up a cross).[68]

When equality of discipleship is displayed, the mutuality of the community is emphasized. Indeed, since we all are disciples of one Master, mutuality in our discipleship relationships must be a high priority. We must be committed to the growth of one another as equals. Later this concept would be emphasized in the Epistles and in church tradition as "the priesthood of all believers."

I remember the impact this truth made upon my wife and me in our first pastorate. I was young, right out of seminary, and I took my

---

Dynamics of Freedom (New York, 1982). See also Seán Freyne, *The Twelve,* 23–48.

[68]Donald Guthrie, *New Testament Theology* (Downers Grove, Ill.: InterVarsity Press, 1981), 708–9.

role of pastor quite seriously. God had called us to shepherd the sheep, feed the flock, and to guard them from wolves and encourage them to grow and serve. My role consumed me, becoming the most prominent factor in my own view of myself. In fact, I took my role of leadership so seriously that I lost sight of the other equally important truth: I was a follower of Jesus, his disciple, and in that sense, a fellow disciple with the other believers of the church. I had taken my role so seriously that I began to take myself too seriously! What a liberating experience it was to begin balancing my leadership role with my discipleship role. I could release the responsibility for the leadership of the church to the Head, Jesus; I could rely on him to lead me; I could share my leadership role with other leaders; and I could see myself once more as simply one of the people, a fellow disciple. By doing this, Jesus was exalted, leadership was shared, oneness was established in the body, and the stature of all believers was set at the same level.

Leadership must be balanced with mutual discipleship. Avery Dulles balances them in this way:

> Discipleship applies in different forms and degrees to different individuals, each of whom lives out a personal relationship to Christ as Lord. In a particular way, those called to public ministry in the community must practice discipleship so that, with Paul, they may be able to say "Be imitators of me, as I am of Christ" (1 Cor 11:1 [NRSV]). Although they never replace Christ as the "one Master" (Mt 23:10), their personal assimilation of his outlook by study, prayer, and self-denial enables them to form others in the Christian life.[69]

Practices of the Community

Perhaps the single, most important development of discipleship illustrated in the book of Acts is the establishment of the community of disciples, the church. The community is what focuses the life of discipleship, provides the opportunities for growth in discipleship, and creates the environment for reproducing new generations of disciples. "Discipleship" in this age is intimately associated with the church. Acknowledging the distinctiveness of Jesus' earthly ministry, we also recognize that what Jesus began through his disciples was intended to be brought into full realization in the new community of faith, the church. After that first great sermon of Peter on Pentecost, the practices of the early believers marked an important connection with Jesus' Great Commission. In the Commission, the imperative

---

[69]Avery Dulles, "Discipleship," *The Encyclopedia of Religion*, Mircea Eliade, ed. (New York: Macmillan, 1987), 4:361–64.

"make disciples" was followed by two participles that indicated the process of discipleship that must ensue, "Baptizing them in the name of the Father and of the Son and of the Holy Spirit, and teaching them to obey everything I have commanded you" (Mt 28:19–20). After Peter's sermon, Luke records, "Those who accepted his message were baptized, and about three thousand were added to their number that day. They devoted themselves to the apostles' teaching and to the fellowship, to the breaking of bread and to prayer" (Ac 2:41–42). The practice of the early church was directly in line with Jesus' commission. Their baptism marked their identification with Christ and with his body. Then Luke mentions four things that came to mark the practices of the church: they were devoted to the apostles' teaching, to fellowship, to the breaking of bread, and to prayer. These practices are the beginning point in which Luke "depicts the church as an alternative community within and distinct from Jewish society."[70]

APOSTLES' TEACHING

The "apostles' teaching" refers to "a body of material considered authoritative because it was the message about Jesus of Nazareth proclaimed by accredited apostles."[71] Here the apostles directly fulfilled Jesus' commission, "teaching them to obey everything I have commanded you." The apostles were committing all that they knew of Jesus and his teachings to these new disciples.

A definitive objective of Jesus' form of discipleship was that his disciples would obey his teachings. While Jesus bore some similarity to other Jewish masters of the first century, his distinctive teachings marked him off from the religious authorities of Israel (cf. Mt 7:28–29). Therefore, knowing Jesus' teachings would mark his disciples off from other kinds of followers. Jesus' teachings (and the subsequent teachings of the apostles) marked the distinctive boundaries of Christian discipleship. But knowing these teachings was not enough. Jesus' disciples were called to "obey" or "observe" all that Jesus commanded (28:20). Jesus' disciples will live different kinds of lives than other kinds of disciples because they will be obeying the most distinctive Teacher and teachings of history. This is one reason why we should be hesitant to refer to Jesus' "disciples" simply as "learners." Jesus' disciples will know the content of his teachings,

---

[70]Gerhard A. Krodel, *Acts*, Augsburg Commentary on the New Testament (Minneapolis: Augsburg, 1986), 92. See also Sweetland, *Our Journey with Jesus*, 170–97.

[71]Longenecker, "Acts," 289.

but the real difference in their lives will be manifested because they obey his teachings.

On the practical level, then, disciples of Jesus must know Jesus' Word, and they must live it out in their daily world. This is where the community of disciples is crucial. The gifts of the Spirit must be exercised for the Word to be properly dispensed to other disciples. This includes those who have been gifted as teachers, who have the responsibility for delivering and making relevant Jesus' teachings. The community of disciples is also crucial for encouraging and stimulating one another to obey Jesus' teachings, to live them out in everyday life.

Our individualism often keeps us in isolation from other disciples because we do not place ourselves in relationship with others who can help us to know Jesus' teachings more effectively. On the other hand, if our community is not clearly attuned through the teaching of Jesus to know God's purposes for the community in the world, we can create artificial situations where we gather away from real life, resulting in our removal from everyday life.

The community of disciples will exercise the gifts of the Spirit, which will most effectively communicate the teachings of Jesus to one another and will encourage and stimulate each other to obey those teachings in the real situations of life.

FELLOWSHIP

Another important practice to which the early church was devoted was "fellowship." Here is the first occurrence in the New Testament of the word that is so significant in the life of the church, *koinōnia*. Although the early believers still maintained contact in the early days with the institutions of Judaism, they were soon marked off by their own distinct fellowship.[72]

Fellowship means "sharing in, partaking in, something or someone." Williams suggests that "in this context we should understand the implied object to be God. God was present, and the whole community shared in his Spirit. Despite their differences and difficulties (cf. 5:1–11; 6:1–7; 11:1–18; 15:1–21), this common bond held them together."[73] This is the beginning of the kind of fellowship that would eliminate social barriers, provide practical togetherness in

---

[72]I emphasize this in distinction from those who are so eager to find a socioeconomic base within Judaism for the Jesus movement and the early church that they virtually eliminate the distinctiveness of the community of disciples; cf. e.g., Richard A. Horsley, *Jesus and the Spiral of Violence: Popular Jewish Resistance in Roman Palestine* (San Francisco: Harper & Row, 1987), 209–12, 231ff.

[73]Williams, *Acts,* 39.

building up the church, demonstrate immediate concern for the needs of the community, illustrate to the world the kind of compassion and deliverance that God offers for humanity, and exercise those "one anothers" that became the heart of the functioning church.[74]

We really do need one another. Although we each have personal fellowship with our Master, Jesus, we are a part of a fellowship that is known as the body of Christ. We cannot function in isolation from one another if Christ's purposes for our lives are going to be accomplished. Intimacy of fellowship with God and his people is the natural expression of Jesus' disciples.

BREAKING OF BREAD

The early community of believers was also devoted to the "breaking of bread." The meaning of this practice has been debated. Placed as it is between "fellowship" and "prayers," it carries a sacred flavor, quite likely indicating the Lord's Supper.[75] The significance of this practice of the early church is summed up primarily in the command of Jesus, "Do this in remembrance of me" (Lk 22:19; 1Co 11:24–25). The act of breaking bread provided a memorial of Christ and his redemptive death. But based upon a common participation in Christ and his salvation, Robert Saucy suggests that "there is also in the Lord's supper a communion of believers in the unity of his body (1 Cor 10:16)."[76] We remember that Jesus said to his disciples in the Upper Room on that last fateful night:

> "My children, I will be with you only a little longer. You will look for me, and just as I told the Jews, so I tell you now: Where I am going, you cannot come.
>
> "A new command I give you: Love one another. As I have loved you, so you must love one another. By this all men will know that you are my disciples, if you love one another." (Jn 13:33–35)

PRAYERS

Luke next reveals that the community was devoted to "the prayers," another expression of the *koinōnia*.[77] Prayer had always been a central element of Jewish life. It had been a central element in the spiritual life to which Jesus introduced his disciples (cf. Lk 11:1–4), and it also now became a central element of the new community of faith. These converts, from the very beginning,

---

[74]See Gerhard Lohfink, *Jesus and Community: The Social Dimension of Christian Faith* (Philadelphia: Fortress, 1984), 75–147; Gene A. Getz, *Sharpening the Focus of the Church* (Chicago: Moody, 1974), 112–17.

[75]Longenecker, "Acts," 289–90.

[76]Robert L. Saucy, *The Church in God's Program* (Chicago: Moody, 1972), 216.

[77]Bruce, *Acts of the Apostles*, 132.

gathered together to pray as a new community. The primary reference of the prayers in which the community took part is probably to their appointed seasons for united prayer within the new community, although we know that they attended the public Jewish prayers as well (cf. Ac 3:1).[78]

> The use of the definite article suggests a particular reference. . . , either to specific prayers or to times of prayer, corresponding, perhaps, to the regular Jewish prayers. . . . But in any case, prayer, whether formal (cf. 3:1; 22:17; Luke 24:53) or informal (cf. 4:24), whether at fixed times or as occasion demanded, was of the very warp and wool of their lives. It was integral to the whole forward thrust of the church, and in Luke's eyes at least, the vitality of the church was a measure of the reality of their prayers (cf. v. 47).[79]

From my own earliest days as a Christian, prayer has occupied a most prominent place. In my early days I saw prayer from two perspectives that have not really changed much over the intervening years. In the first place, prayer is the time for me simply to talk to my Lord. Reading the Bible is where God talks to me, and prayer is the time when I can open up to him. What a special privilege for me to be able to talk personally to the God of the universe! Second, prayer is the way in which I learned to walk in the presence of Jesus on a moment-by-moment, day-by-day basis. Those first few weeks and days following my conversion were an exercise of the real faith of a new disciple of Jesus. They gave me an understanding of the reality of Jesus on a day-by-day basis as I lived in his presence. The early disciples were without Jesus physically, but they were with Jesus through prayer, through "practicing the presence of Jesus" on a daily basis.

We continue to have a special oneness with Jesus individually (Mt 28:20), through his presence in our hearts (Eph 3:17), and through the Spirit (Ro 8:10–11). We also have a special oneness with him as we gather together with other believers (Mt 18:20). We find in these practices of the early church—devoted to the apostles' teaching, fellowship, breaking of bread, and prayer—the four essential elements in the religious practice of the Christian church.[80] The early church built on the life of faith that had been developed in their Jewish practices, but discipleship to the risen Jesus gave a distinctive flavor to this spiritual life. We see here the essential ingredients of

---

[78]Bruce, *Commentary on the Book of Acts,* 79–80; Marshall, *Acts,* 83.
[79]Williams, *Acts,* 39.
[80]Marshall, *Acts,* 83.

the way in which the new community sustained their life of discipleship.[81]

Methodology of Discipleship

Finally, what methods were used in the process of discipleship? Did the early church continue to practice what they did with Jesus? Or did they develop a new methodology of discipleship for the age of the church? This is important for us as well, because we need to know what method we should employ in the process of discipleship.

Some look to Jesus' methodology, suggesting that the process he initiated provides the primary model for all later discipleship methodologies, even down to such details as the length of time Jesus spent with the Twelve. Some note that since Jesus interacted primarily with individual disciples and the small band of Twelve disciples, the logical conclusion for us is that the discipleship process necessitates one-on-one relationships or small groups. Those who look primarily to Jesus say that the early church simply carried out what Jesus had begun with the original disciples. Therefore, we should look to Jesus for the process of discipleship and discipling that we employ today.[82]

Others note that since Jesus' ascension in Acts initiated the life of the church, the former relationship of the disciples with Jesus has no relevance for the age of the church; hence, the church now supplies the ingredients necessary for growth as disciples. They suggest that the discipling process Jesus employed is completely different from what we see in Acts and the Epistles, that the process employed by Jesus was confined to his day, and that the early church developed an entirely different discipling process. Therefore, since we belong to the church age, we should look to the early church for our model.[83]

These suggestions are poles apart, creating an unnecessary dichotomy. Those people who create such dichotomous methodological models tend to focus too much on the distinctiveness of either age rather than on the continuity between Jesus and the church. We have observed enough transitions from the time when Jesus was with the

---

[81]Harrison, *Apostolic Church,* 144.

[82]An example of this approach is found in Carl Wilson, *With Christ in the School of Disciple Building: A Study of Christ's Method of Building Disciples* (Grand Rapids: Zondervan, 1976), especially 60–75. This is essentially the approach of the classic study by A. B. Bruce, *The Training of the Twelve.*

[83]An example of this emphasis is found in Lawrence O. Richards, *A Practical Theology of Spirituality* (Grand Rapids: Zondervan, 1987), 228–29. Another example, but which radically dichotomizes the ages even more so, is Dunn, *Unity and Diversity,* 104–23.

disciples on earth in the Gospels to the time of the church in Acts to realize that the discipling process in either time period will be similar to, yet different from, one another.[84]

The primary point for us to keep in mind is that discipling today is always undertaken as an outgrowth of the life of the church, whereas prior to Pentecost it occurred with Jesus personally. Let me clarify those points. When we say that the discipling process today is always undertaken as an outgrowth of the life of the church, we emphasize the church as the body of Christ, with the local church as the particular tool employed in the process. We may go so far as to say that in many ways discipleship is the overall goal of the church, including evangelism, nurturing, fellowship, leadership, worship, etc. Since all believers are disciples, and believers constitute the church, all that we do in the church is somehow related to discipleship and discipling. When we say that prior to Pentecost the discipling process occurred with Jesus personally, we simply emphasize that Jesus is no longer physically on earth with his disciples. But through the Spirit and his body, the church, Jesus continues to minister to his disciples. Circumstances changed dramatically with the ascension of Jesus and Pentecost, hence the disciples had to adjust to the new circumstances.[85]

The difference in methodology often comes down to the issue of the actual form the discipleship process takes, for example, whether in a small group like Jesus chose to be with him or the church setting as in Acts. Once again, these suggestions are overly dichotomous. When we look at the records of either the Gospels or Acts, we can find evidence of several different types of settings where Jesus and the church promoted the growth of disciples. This implies that we should utilize the kind of setting that most effectively contributes to the growth of disciples.

These settings will include one-on-one relationships such as Jesus carried with his followers and as we see exhibited in relationships between members of the early church (e.g., Barnabas and Saul/Paul). Jesus called all people to him personally, whether within his earthly

---

[84]For a rousing emphasis on methodological change to the church but which also attempts to see relevance from Jesus' example, see Luter, "A New Testament Theology of Discipling," passim, and in summary, 222–28.

[85]For a recent attempt to develop a practical methodology that includes both Jesus' and the church's age, see Bill Hull, *The Disciple Making Church* (Old Tappan, N.J.: Revell, 1990). In his earlier book (*Jesus Christ Disciplemaker: Rediscovering Jesus' Strategy for Building His Church* [Colorado Springs: NavPress, 1984]), Hull seemed to go more to the extreme of imitating Jesus' method, but now he is attempting to include much more of the church's methods as distilled from Acts and the Epistles.

ministry or in the church age, and that personal relationship is at the heart of discipleship today.

Discipleship methodology also includes mentor relationships such as Jesus had with the Twelve and such as we can see exhibited in the church (e.g., Paul and "his disciples," the apostles and the early converts, Ac 6).

Furthermore, discipleship methodology also includes small groups for ministry support and specialized interest growth such as Jesus had with the inner circle within the Twelve and such as we see in the relationship developed between the pillars of the church at Jerusalem, the ongoing group of the Twelve, and the missionary endeavors of Paul, Barnabas, Silas, Timothy, and others.

Finally, discipleship methodology includes "mutuality." Jesus' disciples were called to accept one another and to serve one another. They did not seem to understand that concept fully within his lifetime. Jesus continues to call us to that same discipleship concept today, both within the local and universal community of faith.

As we study the record of the Gospels and Acts, we must be prepared to challenge the self-centered individualism of our day and to recognize that Jesus calls us to community. We need each other. The challenges we face in our lives as disciples of Jesus are formidable; without community they become impossible.

Following up:

1. In the book of Acts, Luke records that the disciples in Antioch were so closely associated with Christ that they came to be called "Christ-ians." If an impartial observer decided to nickname the disciples of Jesus in your town today, what might they be called?
2. In many "discipleship" movements in the church today, it is common to define discipleship as a one-to-one or small-group teaching relationship between a mature believer and a more recent convert.
   a. Does this definition fit Luke's description of discipleship in Acts? Why or why not?
   b. Is it biblical for a Christian to be called a "disciple" of anyone other than Jesus? Explain.
   c. Is there some other term that would better describe such a one-to-one or small-group context?
3. What "discipling" methodologies have helped you grow the most as a Christian? Why? What are you doing to help others grow?
4. How has the ministry of the Holy Spirit been emphasized in your personal discipleship journey?

14

Disappearing Disciples?

Getting focused:

1. Open your Bible to a favorite or best-known passage in the Epistles that teaches discipleship. What marks that passage out as a "discipleship" passage?
2. Is it possible to be a disciple of Jesus even though he is not present physically for you to follow? What is your reasoning?

Sometimes I like to be a bit mischievous with my students! One little ruse that inevitably gets their attention comes out of my classes on discipleship. After we have spent considerable time studying the concept of discipleship in the Gospels and Acts, I start a class session by asking the students to turn to their favorite discipleship passage in the Epistles. They are to tell me what that passage teaches about discipleship. The students volunteer a variety of passages and thoughts, especially taken from verses like 2 Timothy 2:2, where the student will say that discipleship means training future disciplers. Another student may suggest Colossians 2:6–7, where discipleship means commitment to personal growth. Usually one student will offer 1 Thessalonians 2:9–12, where discipleship is understood to be witnessing and follow-up. Another may propose Ephesians 4:11–13, where discipleship indicates mutual ministry. Invariably one student will say that Philippians 3:8–11 declares discipleship to mean the entire Christian life!

Then I ask the students to identify what in the passage marks it out as a "discipleship" passage. "Does the word *disciple* or *discipleship* occur in the passage?" I ask. "No? But then why do you call it a discipleship passage?" For a moment they're confused, but then inevitably someone responds, "Well, the *word* isn't found, but the *idea* is there." I continue to toy with them a bit, pressing them to show me a passage where the actual word occurs. "The passages you cite certainly *may* teach discipleship, but so that we are more certain, give me a passage that specifically mentions the word." They scramble furiously through the Epistles looking for the elusive word *disciple*.

Finally I let them in on my little ruse. "The word *disciple* does not occur in the Epistles, nor in Revelation!" Some look stricken, others confused, some impatient because I toyed with them (some of you reading this may even now be experiencing some of those emotions!). Others have that wise, knowing look because they sneaked a peek at the concordance in the back of their Bible. Aside from having a bit of fun, and certainly getting their attention, this exercise makes three important points.

First, although most of the students were convinced that the Epistles teach discipleship, they had not realized that the words *disciple* and *discipleship* do not occur. Most of them had even read books or heard messages expounding discipleship in the Epistles, yet they had failed to realize the absence of the terms.

Second, in order for a particular passage that does not have disciple terminology to be labeled as "discipleship," a verbal or conceptual link must be made with passages elsewhere in Scripture that explicitly teach discipleship. We have already seen an example of this point in our study in Acts. There we saw that the church could be described as a "discipleship community" because we established connections between the terms *believers, disciples, congregation of disciples,* and *church.*

Third, a variety of themes rightly may be described as discipleship (e.g., "leadership training," "personal growth commitment," "evangelistic outreach," "ministry training"), yet the full concept of discipleship is broader than any one of these particular themes. Discipleship can be understood in a narrow sense to speak of specific master-disciple relationships, yet it is also understood in a broader sense to speak of Christian life in general—what such a way of life requires, implies, and entails.[1]

In this chapter and the next we will undertake two primary studies. First, in this chapter we will examine the curious absence of the term *disciple* in the Epistles. What are the reasons for that absence? Does

---

[1]We discussed this definition in chap. 2. The distinction between these two senses are offered by Fernando F. Segovia, "Introduction: Call and Discipleship—Toward a Re-examination of the Shape and Character of Christian Existence in the New Testament," in *Discipleship in the New Testament,* ed. Fernando F. Segovia (Philadelphia: Fortress, 1985), 2.

it matter? If the term *disciple* is absent, does that mean that the writers of the Epistles did not advocate discipleship? Second, in the next chapter we will examine the evidence for the concept of discipleship in other terms, teachings, and metaphors that may provide vital connections with the concept of discipleship in the Gospels.

THE CURIOUS ABSENCE OF *DISCIPLES* IN THE EPISTLES

Matthew, Mark, Luke, and John agree that the word *disciple* (*mathētēs*) is the most appropriate word to designate those who responded to Jesus' call and claims.[2] In the Gospels *disciple* is the most common label for the followers of Jesus, and in Acts it is the common universal label for believers in the risen and ascended Jesus. Jesus' training and teaching time with his followers in the earthly ministry resulted in the kind of disciple and definition of disciple that he desired. In the Great Commission he said that his disciples were to make more of what he had made of them. He would be the risen Lord of all his disciples, promising to be with them always. Sheridan states succinctly, "Matthew sees the age which Jesus inaugurated going on and the disciples are charged to continue the preaching and teaching of Jesus. As Jesus made disciples, they too are to make disciples, but not for themselves. Jesus remains with them as their one Teacher."[3] Therefore, when we come to the Epistles and to the book of Revelation, it is a great surprise to note that the word *disciple* is absent. While many scholars think the absence is only a curiosity, others have made much of this phenomenon.

Cultural Avoidance

Some suggest that, while the word *mathētēs* was appropriate to use in Jewish circles, when the church spread into the Hellenistic world, it would not have been appropriate. They suggest that the term implied, in common Greek usage, a student from one of the philosophical schools. Therefore, the writers of the Epistles avoided it since they did not want to give rise to the idea that Christianity was

---

[2]Μαθητής occurs 231 times in the Gospels and 28 times in Acts; cf. Robert Morgenthaler, *Statistik Des Neutestamentlichen Wortschatzes* (Frankfurt Am Main: Gotthelf-Verlag Zurich, 1958), 118.

[3]Mark Sheridan, "Disciples and Discipleship in Matthew and Luke," *BThB* 3 (1973): 242.

simply a philosophical movement.[4] For this reason, the word *disciple* did not make its way into the church in the Greek-speaking world and declined in usage in primitive Christianity.[5]

Several problems arise with this suggestion. First, although *mathētēs* could refer to Greek philosophical students, it was not a technical term reserved for this usage. Not only were several other terms also used to designate philosophical students, but *mathētēs* had a much broader use in common, religious, and philosophical circles.[6]

Second, in the narrative of Acts Luke allows us to see that the term was used commonly to designate Christian believers in Hellenistic Asia Minor (cf. Ac 14:20, 21, 22, 28; 16:1; 18:23; 19:1, 9, 30; 20:1, 30) and in Achaia, the heart of Greece (Ac 18:27). There was no inherent meaning in the term *mathētēs* that made it inappropriate for use by converts from Greek-speaking circles. Other terms used in Christianity had different connotations in secular Greek circles than in Christian (e.g., word = *logos;* love = *agape;* fellowship = *koinōnia*), but Christians did not eliminate their usage. Indeed, Christians often sought to use common terms as bridges to other cultures. One of the positive gains in the application of modern linguistics to biblical studies is the emphasis that words must be understood in their context, whether written or spoken.[7]

Third, Jesus spent much time refining the definition of his form of discipleship within Judaism because he used the same terminology that the Jews did (e.g., *talmidh*). Apparently the same phenomenon occurred in Greek circles. *Mathētēs* had a broad enough common meaning that the Christian community was able to use the word without being misunderstood and could then clarify its distinctive form of discipleship in relationship to Jesus.

---

[4]Karl H. Rengstorf, "μαθητής," *TDNT* 4:459; Carl W. Wilson, *With Christ in the School of Disciple Building* (Grand Rapids: Zondervan, 1976), 51.

[5]Sheridan, "Disciples and Discipleship," 239.

[6]See chap. 4, previously. For an extensive analysis of the use of μαθητής in classical and Hellenistic writings, see Michael J. Wilkins, *The Concept of Disciple in Matthew's Gospel: As Reflected in the Use of the Term Μαθητής,* NovTSup 59 (Leiden: E. J. Brill, 1988), 11–42.

[7]A common error in imprecise "word studies" is to force one historical definition of a term into all contexts. Modern lexicological and semantical analysis has revolutionized such studies, demonstrating how words often have broad *contextual concepts.* The classic work by James Barr, *The Semantics of Biblical Language* (Oxford: Oxford Univ. Press, 1961), has been followed by such works as G. B. Caird, *The Language and Imagery of the Bible* (Philadelphia: Westminster, 1980); J. P. Louw, *Semantics of New Testament Greek, SBLSS* (Philadelphia: Fortress, 1982); Moisés Silva, *Biblical Words and Their Meaning: An Introduction to Lexical Semantics* (Grand Rapids: Zondervan, 1983); Peter Cotterell and Max Turner, *Linguistics and Biblical Interpretation* (Downers Grove, Ill.: InterVarsity Press, 1989).

According to the record of Acts, *mathētēs* was used to designate Christians on all three of Paul's missionary journeys, all throughout the primary missionary extension of the church on Hellenistic soil. The reason for the absence of *mathētēs* cannot be attributed to inappropriateness in Hellenistic circles.

Associations with the Historical Jesus

Some suggest that *mathētēs* dropped out of use because it was so vitally connected with following Jesus in his earthly ministry that in his absence the term became less appropriate to describe the believer's relationship with the risen Lord.[8] Since various relationships that the historical Jesus enjoyed with his disciples could not be sustained after his ascension, those terms that described relationships not appropriate to the age of the church were dropped from common vocabulary. Robert Meye suggests that "the uniqueness of the pre-Easter community of disciples has left its imprint on the New Testament, with the result that the specific language of discipleship did not become the standard way of describing those who believed in Jesus after Easter."[9] The relationship of the Master with his followers stands out as especially prominent. Gerald Hawthorne notices the striking absence of the words *follow* and *followers* (*akoloutheō*) from the Epistles and Revelation (occurring only in Rev 14:4; 19:4), along with the absence of *mathētēs* (*disciple*). He surmises that the writers of the Epistles saw in the words *disciple* and *follower* a relationship no longer possible in the new era without the historical Jesus and so dropped them from their vocabulary. This was so that the requirements of the disciples of the earthly Jesus, such as leaving one's trade, father and mother, and others, would not be universalized to be made general requirements. With the Lord risen and ascended, it would not be possible to "follow" him in that literal sense.[10]

This explanation offers a helpful perspective, although it overstates both the literal sense of "following" and the absence of discipleship terminology from the early church. A figurative sense of "following in

---

[8]This approach is taken from a conservative point of view and from an extremely critical point of view. These viewpoints are quite different in their perspective. For the conservative viewpoint, see Gerald F. Hawthorne, "Disciple," *ZPEB* 2:130; R. J. Knowling, "The Acts of the Apostles," *The Expositor's Greek Testament,* ed. W. R. Nicoll, vol. 2, reprint (Grand Rapids: Eerdmans, 1974), 164. For the critical viewpoint, see Kirsopp Lake, *Additional Notes to the Commentary,* vol. 5, *The Acts of the Apostles: The Beginnings of Christianity,* reprint (Grand Rapids: Baker, 1966), 376.

[9]Robert P. Meye, "Disciple," *The International Standard Bible Encyclopedia,* gen. ed. Geoffrey W. Bromiley, rev. ed. (Grand Rapids: Eerdmans, 1979), 1:948.

[10]Hawthorne, "Disciple," 130.

discipleship" must also be recognized in the term *akoloutheō*, even in the days of Jesus' earthly sojourn. There was both a universal and a specific form of the call for leaving one's past attachments. The universal, figurative form of the call signified giving allegiance to Jesus alone for salvation. The specific, literal form of the call was only for those (especially the Twelve) who were to join with Jesus in traveling through Israel on his public ministry.[11] Suggesting that the early church dropped discipleship terminology because it was so intimately connected with the historical Jesus also overstates the evidence. In a classic passage that draws directly upon reminiscences from Jesus' earthly ministry, the apostle Peter uses a compound form of "follow" (*epakoloutheō*): "To this you were called, because Christ suffered for you, leaving you an example, that you should follow in his steps" (1Pe 2:21). Long after the Ascension, the book of Acts continues to describe those who believe in Jesus as "disciples." In Luke's chronology, believers were called "disciples" at least twenty years after the ascension, well after the date of the establishment of every known church represented in the Epistles. Therefore, we have strong evidence that believers, most of whom would never have had any contact with Jesus in his earthly ministry, continued to identify themselves as Jesus' disciples long after he had ascended. Further, one of the most prominent terms for Christians in the writings of Ignatius, the overseer of the church at Antioch, is *disciple*, indicating that believers continued to identify themselves as Jesus' followers into the second century.

While this explanation overstates the evidence, it touches on an important element of the curious absence of the term *mathētēs:* the relationship with Jesus was seen by the church in a different light after the Ascension. The following explanation follows up on that element.

Transition to Other Terms

A widespread explanation for the absence of disciple terminology says that other terms, more appropriate to the post-Ascension conditions, replaced *disciple* within the Christian community. Although *disciple* was still an important term in Acts for describing the relationship of believers to Jesus, a transition to other terms began to occur. These other terms expressed more appropriately the relationship of believers to the risen Lord, to each other, and to society.[12] One

---

[11]See chap. 6 previously related to the Jesus movement; cf. also Gerhard Kittel, "ἀκολουθέω," *TDNT* 1:214.

[12]This explanation has enjoyed a widespread and long following. Cf. William Sanday, *Inspiration* (London: Longmans, Green, 1893), 289; Alfred Plummer,

term that naturally expressed the new relationship with the risen Lord was *believers* (*hoi pisteuontes*, Ac 5:14; *hoi pistoi*, 10:45). Among other names used to describe the relation of believers to the risen Lord in Acts are those "who belonged to the Way" (e.g., 9:2) and "Christians" (11:26; 26:28). Names that indicated the relationship of disciples to one another became very prominent, especially the terms *brothers* and *sisters* (*adelphoi, adelphē*), which expressed the spiritual family nature of the new community (e.g., 1:15–16). Where *mathētēs* does not occur after 21:16, *brothers* comes into use to designate those of the community (e.g., 21:7, 17, 20; 28:14–21). An expression that designated the believers' sacred calling and their relationship to society was *saints* (*hoi hagioi;* 9:13, 32, 41 NASB; 26:10).

Therefore, this explanation suggests that in Acts *mathētēs* was going out of use and other terms were coming into use. In line with this, the Epistles reflect day-to-day concerns of the post-Resurrection community. Jesus said that mutual discipleship implied a new family relation of brothers and sisters (e.g., Mt 12:46–50; 23:8), and the church now experienced that relationship under their risen Lord. Terms that addressed their shared oneness in Christ, such as *brethren* or *saints*, should be expected in the Epistles rather than *disciples*, which speaks of following the historical Jesus. We should therefore expect Paul, for example, to address his letters to brothers/sisters, the saints, his beloved ones in the church.

This explanation has merit, especially since we can see a transition in Acts in the way in which the early church referred to themselves. What cannot be decided conclusively is whether or not the term *disciple* was completely dropped from Christian circles. The first two explanations stress the fact that it was dropped from usage. The last explanation stresses that other terms that more accurately described the believers' relationships began to be used more frequently. This last explanation does not necessarily demand that the term dropped from common usage; it simply stresses that its absence from the Epistles and Revelation may be explained by the adoption of words more expressive of the state of affairs addressed in that genre of literature. The Gospels and Acts are narrative material, describing in third person the actions of Jesus and his followers as he prepared them to carry his Gospel into the world. The Epistles are letters to churches written in the first person to fellow believers addressed in the second person, describing relationships with an ascended Lord, with a community of faith, and with an alien society. The Revelation

---

"Disciple," *Dictionary of the Apostolic Church,* ed. James Hastings (New York: Scribner, 1915), 1:301.

is a vision narrating the activities of the glorified Lord who brings judgment on the earth before his return in triumph. The genre of literature reflects the terms most appropriate to describe Jesus and his followers.

The absence of *mathētēs* from the Epistles remains a curiosity, but the above three explanations are helpful. The least likely is the first, because *mathētēs* does not appear to have been avoided on the basis of inherently antithetical usage between secular Greek-speaking communities and the church. More likely is a combination of the second and third. *Mathētēs* continued to be an appropriate word to designate adherents to the Master, but since he was no longer present to follow around, other terms came naturally into use to describe the relationships of these disciples to their risen Lord, to the community, and to society.[13] This would be the case in the Epistles and Revelation especially, where the subject matter is the risen Lord, where mutual affairs of believers in the church are addressed, and where the church must define its interface with society. However, we do not see strong evidence that the term *disciple* was actually dropped from usage. The chronology of usage in Acts in the very places where the churches of the Epistles and Revelation were located overlaps the origin and development of these churches.[14] The converts in these areas were readily and casually called disciples for quite some time, even well into the second century.[15]

Therefore, the absence of the word *disciple* in the Epistles and Revelation is most likely attributable to the general circumstances of the age and the nature of the literature, which makes it a phenomenon similar to that found in the Old Testament. With this in mind, we can now turn our attention in the next chapter to the question of whether the *concept of discipleship* occurs in the Epistles or not.

IMPLICATIONS

This chapter was dedicated to examining a curious feature of the New Testament: the surprising absence of the word *disciple* from the Epistles and Revelation. I have suggested that it was not avoided but

---

[13]This is a widespread conclusion among many scholars. E.g., Avery Dulles, "Discipleship," *The Encyclopedia of Religion*, ed. Mircea Eliade (New York: Macmillan, 1987), 4:361–64; Charles H. Talbert, "Discipleship in Luke-Acts," in *Discipleship in the New Testament*, ed. Fernando F. Segovia (Philadelphia: Fortress, 1985), 62.

[14]Possible exceptions are Romans and Hebrews. Romans was not covered in Paul's journeys but does overlap in chronology. Hebrews appears to overlap in chronology, but the author and location of addressees are problematic.

[15]In chap. 16 we will discuss that phenomenon as we examine discipleship in the apostolic fathers of the late first and early second centuries A.D.

rather that other words were used that were more appropriate to the topics addressed in this literature. Our own experience is probably similar. If we were to record our conversations with one another during a normal day, we would probably find that we seldomly refer to each other as disciples. We refer to each other more commonly as believers, Christians, and brothers and sisters in Christ.

However, we have also found that the narrative of the book of Acts, which overlaps in chronology the Epistolary literature, abundantly labels the believers of the early church as disciples. When the word *disciple* was used in Acts it brought to mind an intimate discipleship association of believers with their Master, the risen Lord whom they could follow even in the new days of the church.

I am afraid that we have lost some of that flavor. When we hear people speak of discipleship today, what is usually implied are relationships among believers. That certainly is not wrong, because the Great Commission's mandate to "make disciples" implies that disciples will be involved in the process of making other disciples. But I do think that we should emphasize more strongly the fact that discipleship today, as in the Gospels and as in the early church of Acts, primarily indicates a disciple's intimate relationship with his or her living Master. The Great Commission emphasizes that those who become disciples are disciples of Jesus. Only in a secondary manner do they have a discipleship relationship with other disciples. Jesus is with us always as the Master of his disciples.

The reality of an intimate discipleship relationship with our risen Lord must not disappear from the mind-set of the modern Christian. We should recognize that different historical circumstances from the period of the Gospels to the church will cause us to look differently at our relationship with the Lord and with each other. But this should motivate us to explore the teachings of the Epistles more carefully to see how it was that the apostles communicated the concept of discipleship to believers in their churches. Most of those believers had never seen Jesus physically. Yet the apostles brought him to life through their experiences and their teachings, thereby equipping the believers with the means necessary to be disciples of Jesus in the age beyond the empty tomb. In that sense, our situation is not much different from that of the early church. We also need to learn from the apostles what it means to be a disciple in the present day. That is the subject of the next chapter.

Following up:

1. Which reason appears to you to be the best explanation for the curious absence of the word *disciple* from the Epistles?

2. If you were to try to label a *disciple* by another term that does occur in the Epistles, what would you use? What other expressions in the Epistles approximate the concept of discipleship?
3. When you think of "discipleship," which comes to mind first, a one-to-one relationship with another believer or a personal relationship with Jesus Christ? In what ways can you enhance your own awareness of Jesus' presence as your Master on a more moment-by-moment basis?

15

The Epistles: Disciples
in Other Words

Getting focused:

1. Is discipleship to be found in the Epistles, even though the word
   disciple is missing? Explain by giving examples from the biblical
   text.
2. From the following passages, develop an understanding of discipleship as it relates to the concepts of imitation and example. I.e.,
   what does it mean to imitate others? What does it mean to use
   someone else as an example (cf. Lk 6:40; 1Co 11:1; Eph 5:1; 1Th
   1:6; Heb 6:12).
3. Is it appropriate for us to use Jesus as an example for our lives?
   Why or why not? If so, in what ways?

Jesus had left his disciples. But before he left them, he had
comforted them with the promise of his Spirit. He had promised to be
with them forever. He had promised to dwell in their hearts. But
Jesus was no longer there for his disciples to see, to walk with, to
follow as Master. What would discipleship be like in the days that
stretched out beyond them? What would it mean to be a disciple of
Jesus in the days when he was not with them—not with them to
teach them personally, not with them to correct them, not with them
to encourage them, not with them to point the right way?

These were the new days, the new dilemmas, the new crises that
faced the fledgling group of disciples whose Master was no longer
with them physically. For some of the disciples, this at first created a
stumbling block of faith. Thomas, well-known as "doubting Thomas,"
had difficulty accepting the news of the risen Jesus. When he finally
saw Jesus physically, he confessed, "My Lord and my God" (Jn
20:28), one of the most profound declarations of Jesus' deity in

Scripture. But Jesus avowed that the kind of faith that would be needed in the days to come was the kind that would believe while not seeing. "Then Jesus told him, 'Because you have seen me, you have believed; blessed are those who have not seen and yet have believed'" (v. 29).

Because our situation is so similar, we understand the situation of those disciples as they faced a new age when Jesus would not be with them physically. For some of us, the fact that Jesus is not here physically for us to follow is a major stumbling block of faith. For some of us this means the blossoming of a real life of faith following our Master in the day-to-day activities of life.

That real life of faith is portrayed for us vividly in a classic book written nearly a hundred years ago called *In His Steps*. Written by Charles Sheldon, this book is about a pastor and his congregation in a small midwest town. It looks at life by asking the hard question, "What would Jesus do in this situation?" Sheldon traced what would happen in the lives of believers who asked that question in the middle of various circumstances they faced in their normal lives. What would Jesus do when confronted by the temptation to cheat in business? What would Jesus do when faced with the hard choice of whether to compromise one's convictions in the face of peer pressure? What would Jesus do when forced to choose between the path of religious popularity, which could be found through preaching what parishioners wanted to hear, and the path of social ostracism that would result from proclaiming the Gospel of Jesus Christ? What would Jesus do when faced with the choice between helping the needy and finding more personal comfort? Although the book has received criticism,[1] it has presented the church with the same kind of challenge that Jesus gave to his followers in the Gospel and the same kind of challenge that the apostles gave in the Epistles. Discipleship means to follow Jesus and become like him—like him not only in church, but like him in the everyday circumstances of life. Sheldon understood rightly that Jesus is our example and that we are to walk in his steps.

The apostle Peter understood this concept clearly. He gave his readers an example of how to handle suffering in their working situations. The example is Jesus. Peter writes, "But if you suffer for

---

[1]Some questions have been raised about the appropriateness of posing such polarized "either-or" ethical decisions. Some questions have been raised about the appropriateness of trying to follow the example of the God-Man who lived in a completely different culture nearly two thousand years ago. Some questions have been raised about the author's understanding of "salvation by grace." In spite of some perceived weaknesses, Sheldon has influenced millions of people through this novel.

doing good and you endure it, this is commendable before God. To this you were called, because Christ suffered for you, leaving you an example, that you should follow in his steps" (1Pe 2:20–21). The final words, "in his steps," are the words that originally influenced Charles Sheldon to write his book.

We are well aware that our Master is not here for us to follow around physically. Yet in the example and teaching he provided in the Gospels, Jesus still leads the way in our world today. Peter and the other apostles had walked with Jesus in his earthly ministry, and the passion of their ministry was to bring Jesus alive in the hearts and lives of those around them. That is the meaning of discipleship.

But what of those who had not been able to follow Jesus in his earthly ministry? Could they say that they followed Jesus' example? The apostle Paul was one who did not follow Jesus in his earthly ministry, yet he followed Jesus' example and called believers to follow Jesus as well. Paul wrote to the Thessalonians, "You became imitators of us and of the Lord; in spite of severe suffering, you welcomed the message with the joy given by the Holy Spirit. And so you became a model to all the believers in Macedonia and Achaia" (1Th 1:6–7). Later he wrote, "Follow my example, as I follow the example of Christ" (1Co 11:1).

It is this kind of language that compels us to respond with a resounding yes to the question of whether or not the concept of discipleship is present in the Epistles. "One may conclude that despite Paul's lack of association with Jesus in the days of his flesh, nevertheless, by his teaching and by his example he wonderfully possessed the mind of Christ in the matter of discipleship, even though the word *disciple* does not appear in his writings."[2] The consensus in the history of the church—ancient and modern—is that the concept of discipleship is apparent everywhere in the New Testament, from Matthew through Revelation. While scholars' emphases and methods of inquiry vary, virtually all scholars agree that the concept of discipleship is present everywhere in the New Testament in related terminology, teachings, and metaphors.[3]

Therefore, throughout the New Testament we have expressions of discipleship to help us walk with Jesus in our day. We now turn to the Epistles to clarify the relationship between expressions of

[2]Everett F. Harrison, *The Apostolic Church* (Grand Rapids: Eerdmans, 1985), 143.

[3]E.g., Avery Dulles, "Discipleship," *The Encyclopedia of Religion,* ed. Mircea Eliade (New York: Macmillan, 1987), 4:361–64; Harrison, *Apostolic Church,* 143; Paul Helm, "Disciple," *Baker Encyclopedia of the Bible,* gen. ed. Walter A. Elwell (Grand Rapids: Baker, 1988), 630; Boyd A. Luter, "Discipleship and the Church," *BS* 137 (1980): 267ff.

discipleship prior to and following the Cross and also to clarify the meaning of discipleship expressions in the Epistles for our day.

EVIDENCE FOR THE CONCEPT OF DISCIPLESHIP

For those of us on this side of the Cross, a certain amount of restatement of the Gospel's expression of discipleship is necessary. In the terminology, teachings, and metaphorical language of the Epistles and Revelation, the apostles give a restatement of discipleship for our day. As we now look at select examples, we will see the same fullness and richness of discipleship found in the Gospels and Acts expressed in the life of the church. This variety of expression is evidence of the richness of the idea of discipleship in the full New Testament conception.

Related Discipleship Terminology

The language of discipleship is naturally connected with the relationship developed between the Master and his disciples. The primary purpose here is to provide links between those called "disciples" in the Gospels and those who are called by other terms in the Epistles and Revelation. We will look at two particular kinds of discipleship terminology that bridge the period from the Gospels to the Epistles. First, some terms directly link the time from the Gospels to the Epistles and Revelation, e.g., *believers, brothers/sisters, servants,* and *church.* Second, some terms refer to the same people in Acts and the Epistles and Revelation: e.g., *saints,* and *Christians.* Although these latter terms are not used to refer to the disciples in the Gospels, they are common referents for the disciples in Acts. These two kinds of discipleship terminology provide a link between those who are called disciples in the Gospels and Acts and who are called other terms in the Acts and Epistles.

BELIEVERS

In Christian history *believer*[4] is one of the most common terms used to designate individuals who have "believed" in Jesus Christ as their Savior and Lord. In response to the Philippian jailer's query, "What must I do to be saved?" Paul and Silas replied, "Believe in the Lord Jesus, and you will be saved" (Ac 16:30–31). For the early church, one phrase that naturally expressed their new relationship

---

[4]For a more extended discussion and bibliography of this topic see Michael J. Wilkins, "Belief/Believers (NT)," *Anchor Bible Dictionary,* 5 vols. (Garden City, N.Y.: Doubleday, forthcoming).

with the risen Lord was *believers* (*hoi pisteuontes, hoi pistoi*).[5] Since they could no longer physically follow Jesus, the early church focused on "belief" as one of the chief characteristics of their relationship with him in the new age.

This transition is recognized in the conclusion to the Gospel of John. Thomas, who had followed Jesus around as his disciple, gave a great confession upon seeing the risen Lord (Jesus is "Lord and God"), but Jesus pronounced blessing on those who would believe without seeing (Jn 20:24–29). Paul also recognized "belief" to be the chief characteristic of the new age. In the oft-disputed phrase where Paul says that he no longer knows Christ "according to the flesh" (2Co 5:16 NASB), he decries his former "worldly" attitude toward Jesus, which has now passed away by being "in Christ."[6] The transition from "disciple" to "believer" indicates how the church understood the connection between the historical Jesus and the risen Christ: the follower of Jesus has passed from being a "disciple" who follows Jesus around in a physical sense to being a "believer" who is a new creation in Christ (2Co 5:17).

Paul also expands the focus from "belief in Jesus" to "belief in the truth" (2Th 2:13), which for him essentially means belief in all that which comprises apostolic Christianity. Elsewhere the noun *faith* (*pistis*) has an additional objective nuance, "belief," and means simply "Christianity" (1Ti 4:1, 6; Tit 1:4).[7] Hence, the true believer is one who, although he or she can now no longer physically follow Jesus around, focuses his or her belief on the reality of a risen Lord and Savior, exercises personal faith unto salvation, and is characterized by a lifestyle consistent with apostolic teaching concerning the Christian life. This is truly a continuation of the concept of discipleship that Jesus taught in his earthly ministry.

---

[5]New Testament Greek does not have a separate noun for the word *believers*. Rather, "believers" is the rendering given by various translations for (1) substantival participial constructions formed from the verb "believe" (*hoi pisteuontes*, e.g., Ac 5:14; Ro 1:16; 1Th 1:7; 2:10; cf. Shepherd of Hermas, *Similitudes* 9.19.1–2) or (2) substantives formed from the adjective "faithful, reliable" (*hoi pistoi*, Ac 10:45; 2Co 6:15; 1Ti 6:2).

[6]Ralph P. Martin, *Reconciliation: A Study of Paul's Theology* (Atlanta: John Knox, 1981), 56–60.

[7]Donald Guthrie, *New Testament Theology* (Downers Grove, Ill.: InterVarsity Press, 1981), 593–94. Cf. Rudolf Bultmann, *Theology of the New Testament*, trans. Kendrick Grobel, one-vol. ed. (New York: Scribner, 1951, 1955), 90; and Rudolf Bultmann, "Πιστεύς," *TDNT* 6:1968.

BROTHERS/SISTERS

The words *brother* (*adelphos*) and *sister* (*adelphē*) have a long and varied history of physical and figurative use.[8] *Adelphos* was used originally for a physical brother and *adelphē* for a physical sister, but *adelphos* could also be used for other relatives as well (e.g., Ge 29:12ff. LXX). The figurative use of the term arose naturally within the nation of Israel because the twelve tribes were descended from the twelve sons of Jacob. This is seen clearly in Ps 22:22[23] where "brothers" are in parallelism with the "congregation" and are equivalent with the descendants of Jacob/Israel in the following verse (v. 23[24]). A related feature is found in the use of the terms *son* and *brother* in the picture of God's relationship to his people (e.g., Hos 1:10–2:1[2:1–3]).

Judaism also used *brother* with both a physical and figurative sense. The term designates physical relationships (4Mc 9:23; 10:3, 15; 13:19, 27) and also the brotherhood established by covenant fellowship (1Mc 12:10, 17). The compound term *love of the brethren* also occurs (*philadelphia;* cf. 4Mc 13:23, 26; 14:1). Josephus uses *adelphos* figuratively to speak of relationships between members of the Essenes (*Wars* 2.122), and in the Qumran texts *brother* is a common term to designate the relationship between members of the community. Indeed, brotherhood was significant for the community because they saw themselves as the true remnant of Israel, the true people of God.[9] The Hebrew term *habher* ("companion, brother"), although used to designate scholars, was also used to describe the associates of the Pharisaic sect during the Second Temple Period up to the time of Jesus.[10]

As was true with the history of the terms, so also is true of their use in the New Testament: *adelphos/adelphē* designate both physical and figurative brothers/sisters. The most famous physical relationships in the New Testament are Peter and his brother Andrew (Mk 1:16), John

---

[8]For a more extended discussion and bibliography of this topic see Michael J. Wilkins, "Brother/Brotherhood (NT)," *Anchor Bible Dictionary*, 5 vols. (Garden City, N.Y.: Doubleday, forthcoming).

[9]Ephraim E. Urbach, *The Sages: Their Concepts and Beliefs*, trans. Israel Abrahams, 2 vols., 2d ed. (Jerusalem: Magnes, 1979), 584–85; Othmar Schilling, "Amt und Nachfolge im Alten Testament und in Qumran," *Volk Gottes: zum Kirchenverständnis der Katholischen, Evangelischen, und Anglikanischen Theologie. Festgabe für Josef Höer,* ed. Remigius Bäumer and Heimo Dolch (Freiberg: Herder, 1967), 211–12.

[10]Wilkins, *Concept of Disciple*, 123; M. Aberbach, *The Relations Between Master and Disciple in the Talmudic Age*, ed. H. J. Zimmels, J. Rabbinowitz, and I. Finestein, *Jew's College Publications New Series*, no. 3 (London: Soncino, 1967), 1:19–20; Emil Schürer, *The History of the Jewish People in the Age of Jesus Christ (175 B.C.–A.D. 135)*, rev. and ed. Geza Vermes, Fergus Millar, and Matthew Black, rev. ed. (Edinburgh: T. & T. Clark, 1979) 2:583–89.

and his brother James (Mk 1:19), Lazarus the brother of the sisters Mary and Martha (Jn 11:1–2), and the brothers and sisters of Jesus (cf. Mk 3:31–35; 6:3). The Old Testament figurative use is carried over to the New Testament when the apostles address Jews as "brothers" (Ac 2:29; 3:17; 7:2; 13:15, 26, 38; 22:1; 23:1ff.; 28:17), and are themselves addressed in the same way (2:37).

But the terms come to have a distinctive emphasis in the New Testament. In Matthew 12:46–50 Jesus gave a definition of those who would be his spiritual brothers and sisters. While his physical mother and brothers waited outside to see him, Jesus stretched out his hand toward his disciples and said: "Here are my mother and my brothers. For whoever does the will of my Father in heaven is my brother and sister and mother" (vv. 49–50). With this definition Jesus declared that spiritual union in the family of God takes precedence over national or blood-family lines (cf. also Lk 14:26). Here Jesus unites discipleship with a familial emphasis.

The early church understood the family nature of the new community. *Adelphos* was one of the first terms for their self-designation (cf. Ac 1:15, 16; 6:3). The decision of the apostolic council explicitly applied the term to Gentile Christians, giving them assurance that they were also part of the family of God (15:23). In 1 Corinthians 5:11 Paul calls the immoral person who postures as a believer a so-called brother, and he calls the Judaizers who attempted to bring believers into bondage to law "false brothers" (*pseudadelphoi*; 2Co 11:26; Gal 2:4).

But the family relationship is not merely figurative. It is based on a spiritual birth. Jesus is the only-begotten, firstborn, beloved Son of God, and through faith in him believers are born into a new life (2Co 5:17; 1Pe 1:3–5) where they are called Jesus' brothers (Ro 8:29; Heb 2:11ff.). To believe in Jesus as the Christ causes one to be born of God, and to love marks the relationship of the members of the family (1Jn 5:1–2). The derivative term *adelphotes* (found only in 1Pe 2:17; 5:9) conceives of a brotherhood of believers throughout the world. Members of the brotherhood are urged to exercise brotherly love toward one another (*philadelphos* only in 1Pe 3:8; *philadelphia* in Ro 12:10; 1Th 4:9; Heb 13:1; 1Pe 1:22; 2Pe 1:7). Indeed, love is to be so characteristic of the believer's relationships that to hate one's brother is to give evidence that one does not love God (1Jn 4:19–21), which means that one is not truly a member of the family of God.

Jesus' true brothers and sisters in his public ministry were his disciples. This family aspect of discipleship is clearly carried over into the Epistles, where the church is composed of brothers and sisters who have entered into this family of God through the new birth.

SERVANTS

In the terms for "servant" (variations in the use of *diakonos* and *doulos*), Jesus expressed the role that he came to perform in service of the Father for the sake of humankind. Likewise, in those terms Jesus declared the role that his disciples must perform in service of him for the sake of each other and the kingdom of God (e.g., Mk 10:42–45; Lk 22:24–27). We saw in our previous discussion of Mark's gospel that Mark especially focuses on this crucial aspect of discipleship.

In the Epistles the terms for "servant" have special significance for those who have been set aside for a particular ministry. For example, Paul regularly refers to himself as a servant of Christ (Ro 1:1, *doulos*; Col 1:23, *diakonos*) in his role as apostle. However, as important as are particular ministries, the writers of the Epistles continue to emphasize with Jesus that all members of the community of faith are servants. Especially by the use of the term *doulos*, which carries an even stronger connotation of indebtedness than does *diakonos*, the writers of the Epistles declare that Christians have an obligation to servanthood.[11] Christians have been set free from slavery to sin through the service of Jesus Christ in order to serve God, one another, and one's neighbor. Peter says flatly, "Live as free men, but do not use your freedom as a cover-up for evil; live as servants of God. Show proper respect to everyone: Love the brotherhood of believers, fear God, honor the king" (1Pe 2:16–17). Paul echoes this theme: "But thanks be to God that, though you used to be slaves to sin, you wholeheartedly obeyed the form of teaching to which you were entrusted. You have been set free from sin and have become slaves to righteousness" (Ro 6:17–18).

Jesus, who emptied himself and came in the form of a servant (Php 2:7, *doulos*) in order to give his life as a ransom for many (Mk 10:45), has set men and women free from bondage to sin so that they in turn might become servants of Christ in this world. That striking discipleship theme resounds clearly throughout the New Testament.

CHURCH

A term that clearly marks a transition from discipleship in the Gospels to the Epistles is the word *church*. We discussed this concept in some length in our discussion of Acts, so here we will only make a few observations.

The word *church* occurred only twice in the Gospels, where Jesus spoke to his disciples of their future role in the establishment and

---

[11]Rudolf Tuente, "Slave, δοῦλος," *NIDNTT* 3:592–98. Cf. Klaus Hess, "Serve, δικονέω," *NIDNTT* 3:544–49.

discipline of the church (Mt 16:18; 18:17). In Acts the phrase "community of disciples" is another expression for "the church." In the Epistles the word *church* is the term that designates all believers universally who now comprise the body of Christ, and it is also the term that designates the local expression of the body. The word *church* is a term that provides direct continuity between believers in the Gospels, the Acts, and the Epistles. As such, it declares a direct link between discipleship in the time of the historical Jesus, the early church, and the Epistles.

In his Great Commission mandate to "make disciples of all nations," Jesus not only provided salvation from judgment, but he also provided through conversion the all-embracing transformation of life. New disciples are gathered into the church, where the process of comprehensive discipleship is lived out. This transformation of life through the process of comprehensive discipleship is often neglected by the church. Discipleship is not just a limited program within the church. Discipleship is the life of the church. Since the true church is composed only of disciples, the overall activities of the church are to provide for the care, training, and mission of the disciples as they follow Jesus in this world. The purpose and mission of the church, therefore, must be understood in terms of comprehensive discipleship.[12]

CHRISTIANS

Although "Christian"[13] is the most common name used today to designate followers of Jesus Christ, it occurs only three times in the New Testament: Acts 11:26; 26:28; 1 Peter 4:16. Most scholars agree that the formation of this term is Latin in origin, and we find the Latin name *Christianus*[14] (pl. *Christiani*) in Tacitus, Suetonius, and Pliny the Younger. A common practice of the first century for identifying adherents was to attach the termination *-ianus* (pl. *-iani*) to the name of the leader or master (e.g., *Pompeiani, Augustiani, Ceasariani*). Hellenistic practice early paralleled this by attaching *-ianos* (pl. *-ianoi*) to the name of a leader or master (e.g., *Herodianoi*, Mt 22:16; Mk 3:6; 12:13; Josephus, *Antiq.* 14.15.10). Hence, whether in Latin (*Christianus*) or in Greek (*Christianos*), the term is formed from

---

[12]This note is sounded urgently in the classic work by Herman Ridderbos, *The Coming of the Kingdom*, trans. H. de Jongste, ed. Ramond O. Zorn (Philadelphia: Presbyterian and Reformed, 1962), 373–75; 395, n. 125.

[13]For a more extended discussion and bibliography of this topic see Michael J. Wilkins, "Christian," *Anchor Bible Dictionary*, 5 vols. (Garden City, N.Y.: Doubleday, forthcoming).

[14]This name is a second declension masculine Latin noun.

Christ and indicates Christ's adherents: those who belong to, or are devoted to, Christ.

The origin of the term *Christian,* according to Acts 11:26, was in Antioch, dating in the Lukan chronology somewhere between A.D. 40 and 44. Luke says, "The disciples were called Christians first at Antioch." The wording indicates that the name was coined by those outside of the church.[15] Of those outside, the Jews were not likely to have referred to the disciples as Christians, *followers of Christos,* the Messiah, since this would have validated Jesus' claim to that title.[16] The Jews instead referred to the disciples of Jesus as "the Nazarene sect" (Ac 24:5). Hence, the name Christian must have originated within the Gentile population of Antioch. In the large metropolis of Antioch, with its many competing cults and mystery religions, those who spoke so much about *Christos* were soon called *Christianoi,* Christ's people. The term would have then distinguished the disciples from unconverted Gentiles as well as from Judaism.

The reason for the origin of the name is problematic. The term *Christianoi* may have been coined by the Antiochian governor's staff to indicate official Roman registry. Or the use of the term may have been intended satirically by the Antiochian people to mock those who believed in Jesus as Messiah, paralleling the mockery directed toward the *Augustiani,* the official enthusiasts of Nero.[17] Or, more likely, the term may have arisen generally among the populace as a slang term to indicate those who were followers of their God *Christos* and who were regarded as a sort of mystery fellowship.[18] The name *Christos,* Messiah, meant nothing special to the Gentiles, sounding more like a second personal name for Jesus than a religious title.

While the occurrence of the term in Acts 11:26 indicates, at the very least, the recognition by Gentiles that believers in Christ were an entity separate from both pagan Gentiles and Judaism, the other two occurrences in the New Testament possibly indicate that an element of contempt (Ac 26:28) and hostility (1Pe 4:16) was attached to the term by the early use of those outside of the church. There is no New Testament evidence that the term was commonly used as a self-designation by the early church.

Christianos appears for the first time as a self-designation in *Didache* 12:4 and is commonly used by Ignatius for a member of the

---

[15]Ernst Haenchen, *The Acts of the Apostles: A Commentary,* trans. R. McL. Wilson (Philadelphia: Westminster, 1971), 367–68, n. 3.

[16]See the disputed passage in Josephus where *Christos* and *Christianoi* are used in this manner: *Antiq.* 18.63–64.

[17]Harold B. Mattingly, "The Origin of the Name *Christiani,*" *JTS* 9 (1958): 26–37.

[18]Walter Grundmann, "Χριστός, Χριστιανός," *TDNT* 9:537.

believing community (late first–early second century), but the name does not occur in abundance elsewhere in the writings of the early church fathers. In the middle of the second century, Polycarp calls himself a *Christianos* (*Ep.* 10.1; 12.1), and in the Apologists the term was used as a self-characterization of one who followed Christ into the death of martyrdom. The reason for the scarcity of the term in the early church fathers may be found in a letter by the Roman governor Pliny the Younger to Emperor Trajan (c. A.D. 112). Those accused of believing in Jesus Christ were asked whether or not they were "Christians." If they admitted to the name, they were put to death; or if they were Roman citizens, they were sent to Rome for trial (*Letters* 10. 96). In the days of persecution of the early church the use of the term was dangerous because it clearly marked the church in the minds of the Romans as believing in a god who was in opposition to the emperor. Nonetheless, within the church, honor was associated with those who suffered while they bore the name of their Messiah, since suffering as a Christian glorifies God (cf. 1Pe 4:16).

The relationship Jesus established with his disciples was one relatively unknown in discipleship relationships of antiquity. With the coming of the Cross Jesus declared that their relationship was a friendship.[19]

> My command is this: Love each other as I have loved you. Greater love has no one than this, that he lay down his life for his friends. You are my friends if you do what I command. I no longer call you servants, because a servant does not know his master's business. Instead, I have called you friends, for everything that I learned from my Father I have made known to you. You did not choose me, but I chose you and appointed you to go and bear fruit–fruit that will last. Then the Father will give you whatever you ask in my name. This is my command: Love each other. (Jn 15:12–17)

Jesus' disciples were now friends with Jesus and therefore friends with one another. The distinctions that marked certain persons of community were only for the sake of serving each other and their Lord. As such they followed his example and were called Christians, "little Christs." Discipleship is the Christian life.

Related Teachings on the Discipleship Life

Discipleship teachings that Jesus emphasized to his disciples are certainly not absent in the Epistles and Revelation. They are filled

---

[19]Interestingly, Socrates preferred to call his followers "friends" but did not want them to be called his "disciples."

out and enriched by the apostles. Even Paul, who did not have an association with Jesus in the days of his flesh, nevertheless showed by the teachings of his letters and by the example of his life that he possessed the mind of Christ in the matter of discipleship.[20]

FOLLOWING JESUS

When Jesus' disciples followed him in his earthly ministry, he gave them his example to follow (Jn 12:26). Likewise, Peter exhorted those in the church to look at Jesus' example and to follow in his steps (1Pe 2:21), even as Paul affirmed to the Thessalonian believers, "You became imitators of us and of the Lord" (1Th 1:6). The author of the book of Hebrews pointed to the path of the race set before his readers and exhorted them, "Let us fix our eyes on Jesus, the author and perfecter of our faith." He challenged them to "consider him" as their example in suffering, obedience, and glorification (Heb 12:2–3). The apostle John in the Revelation saw a vision of the 144,000 saints, pure and undefiled, who are said to "follow the Lamb wherever he goes" (Rev 14:4).

BEARING THE CROSS

One of the hallmarks of a disciple was obeying Jesus' summons to "deny himself and take up his cross and follow me" (Mk 8:34). Obedience to that summons brought a person into a relationship with Christ as Savior, but the principle of self-denial, daily cross-bearing, and following Christ also characterized the on-going, daily life of discipleship (Lk 9:23). Especially through the teachings of Paul the church learned that all believers have in fact died together with Christ in his crucifixion (Gal 2:20). This cocrucifixion is the God-appointed way for his people to realize what Jesus called for— namely, death to sin and self.[21] All that remains in order to make it a working principle of life in the present day is the appropriation of its power (Ro 8:13). "As Paul put the matter in Romans 6, we must first of all *know* that we died and rose again with Christ, then thoughtfully *reckon* on this as a fact of utmost importance, and finally, *present* ourselves and all our redeemed powers to God for his use."[22]

MARKS OF DISCIPLESHIP

Jesus declared that his disciples would believe in such a way that their new life would manifest itself in the three crucial marks of a

---

[20]Everett F. Harrison, *The Apostolic Church* (Grand Rapids: Eerdmans, 1985), 143.

[21]Michael P. Green, "The Meaning of Cross-Bearing," *BS* 140 (1983): 123.

[22]Harrison, *Apostolic Church*, 143.

disciple: abiding in his words (Jn 8:31–32), loving other disciples (13:34–35), and bearing fruit (15:8). The apostles echo these very marks of belief when they give assurance to the church of the kind of true faith that will mark believers off from the unbelieving world and from false teachers.

Abiding in Jesus' words. John declares that the individual who says he believes in Jesus as Savior will evidence that belief clearly by abiding in Jesus' words. "We know that we have come to know him if we obey his commands. The man who says, 'I know him,' but does not do what he commands is a liar, and the truth is not in him. But if anyone obeys his word, God's love is truly made complete in him. This is how we know we are in him: Whoever claims to live in him must walk as Jesus did" (1Jn 2:3–6; cf. 3:24; 4:13–15; 2Jn 9).

Loving other disciples. One of John's major emphases is on love, as we might expect from "the disciple whom Jesus loved." John's emphasis on love harks back to Jesus' emphasis. The true believer will love because he or she has been born of God, whose very nature is love. The true believer now has an endless supply of love from God, who is infinite love. Love for other believers is an evidence that a person loves God. As John tells us in his first epistle,

> God is love. Whoever lives in love lives in God, and God in him. . . .
> We love because he first loved us. If anyone says, "I love God," yet hates his brother, he is a liar. For anyone who does not love his brother, whom he has seen, cannot love God, whom he has not seen. And he has given us this command: Whoever loves God must also love his brother. (1Jn 4:16b, 19–21)

As in the time when Jesus' disciples walked with him in his earthly ministry, disciples in the present day will love even as Jesus loved.

Bearing fruit. In the war between the Spirit and flesh, Paul points to the deeds of the flesh, saying that those who live according to them will not inherit the kingdom of God. But, in contrast, those who have the Spirit bear the fruit of the Spirit (Gal 5:18–23).[23] Even as Jesus said that it was absolutely necessary for the disciples to abide in him in order to bear fruit (Jn 15:5), so Paul prays that the believers will be "filled with the fruit of righteousness that comes through Jesus Christ" (Php 1:11) and "that you may live a life worthy of the Lord and may please him in every way: bearing fruit in every good work, growing in the knowledge of God" (Col 1:10).

---

[23]For a fascinating discussion of this "war" between the Spirit and flesh as a war between believers and unbelievers, see Walter O. Russell, "Paul's Use of Σάρξ and Πνεῦμα in Galatians 5–6, in light of the argument of Galatians," (unpublished Ph.D. diss., Westminster Theological Seminary, 1991), passim, but esp. chap. 5.

LIGHT OF THE WORLD

When Jesus came into the world, he was the light who brought the enlightenment of new life (Jn 1:6–10; 8:12). Jesus exhorted his disciples to be separate from the world yet to continue to be light and salt (Mt 5:13–16). John reiterated that teaching: true life is found in walking in the light. "God is light; in him there is no darkness at all. If we claim to have fellowship with him yet walk in the darkness, we lie and do not live by the truth. But if we walk in the light, as he is in the light, we have fellowship with one another, and the blood of Jesus, his Son, purifies us from all sin" (1Jn 1:5–7). Paul also carried on this theme by speaking of Christians as lights in a dark world.

> For you were once darkness, but now you are light in the Lord. Live as children of light (for the fruit of the light consists in all goodness, righteousness and truth) and find out what pleases the Lord. Have nothing to do with the fruitless deeds of darkness, but rather expose them. For it is shameful even to mention what the disobedient do in secret. But everything exposed by the light becomes visible, for it is light that makes everything visible. (Eph 5:8–14; cf. 1Th 5:6)

PRAYER

Jesus was a person of prayer, and he taught his disciples to pray (Lk 11:1–4). The apostles insisted on the need for continual prayer (1Th 5:17). They practiced prayer themselves (Col 1:9) and called for prayer for other believers (Jas 5:13, 16), church leaders (Eph 6:19), and government leaders (1Ti 2:1–2). Paul followed Jesus' example by becoming a person of prayer and teaching others to pray. He wrote:

> And pray in the Spirit on all occasions with all kinds of prayers and requests. With this in mind, be alert and always keep on praying for all the saints. Pray also for me, that whenever I open my mouth, words may be given me so that I will fearlessly make known the mystery of the gospel, for which I am an ambassador in chains. Pray that I may declare it fearlessly, as I should. (Eph 6:18–20; cf. 1Th 5:17)

PATTERN OF RIGHTEOUSNESS

Christ is the pattern for righteous obedience and is the fulfillment of the Law (Mt 3:15). Those who follow him in the kingdom fulfill the Law and have a righteousness that surpasses the scribes and Pharisees (Mt 5:17–20). Those who respond to Jesus' call to discipleship fulfill the Law by loving the Lord God and their neighbor (Mt 19:16–22). Paul says that Christ has brought an end to the Law's power so that in Christ we might bear fruit (Ro 7:4), that those who are now in Christ are slaves of righteousness (chap. 6), and that love now fulfills the Law (13:9).

Related Metaphors for the Discipleship Community

In addition to terms and teachings that are related to discipleship, several metaphors found in the Epistles hark back to discipleship metaphors of the Gospels.

WALKING

The figurative use of "walking" was a favorite Old Testament expression to describe those who conducted their lives in accordance with God's ways. Those who responded to Jesus' invitation entered into the Way of following him. The apostle John reiterates this theme. "We know that we have come to know him if we obey his commands. The man who says, 'I know him,' but does not do what he commands is a liar, and the truth is not in him. But if anyone obeys his word, God's love is truly made complete in him. This is how we know we are in him: Whoever claims to live in him must walk as Jesus did" (1Jn 2:3–6).

Paul inherits this perspective, because one of his favorite metaphors is "walking with God." Apart from a few occurrences in John's letters, the figurative use of "walking" is unique to Paul in the Epistles. The expression indicates how a person "lives" or conducts himself or herself in relationship to God and others. The summary of Paul's theme is found in the statement, "But I say, walk by the Spirit, and you will not carry out the desire of the flesh" (Gal 5:16 NASB). This defines Paul's concept of the Christian life.[24] In Paul's view, one's manner of walking is an expression of his or her entire life. Hans Dieter Betz declares Paul's perspective as follows:

> A human being must and always does choose between ways of life as they are presented in history and culture. For ancient man, ways of life are more than "styles of life": they are not only different in their outward appearance, but their different appearance is the result of different underlying and determining factors. . . . Therefore, the way of life of human beings determines the quality of their life.[25]

For Paul, one's manner of "walk" is closely tied to the challenge to follow the example God has provided in Jesus Christ. "Therefore be imitators of God, as beloved children; and walk in love, just as Christ also loved you, and gave Himself up for us, an offering and a sacrifice to God as a fragrant aroma" (Eph 5:1–2 NASB).

---

[24]Richard N. Longenecker, *Galatians*, WBC 41 (Dallas: Word, 1990), 244.

[25]Hans Dieter Betz, *Galatians: A Commentary on Paul's Letter to the Churches in Galatia*, Hermeneia (Philadelphia: Fortress, 1979), 277.

SHEPHERD AND SHEEP

Jesus described himself as the door through which his sheep, the disciples, come into the pasture to find salvation. His sheep know his voice and obey it, and he will lay down his life for them (Jn 10:7–18). The author of Hebrews alludes to this relationship Jesus had with the disciples when he recollects how God, "Through the blood of the eternal covenant brought back from the dead our Lord Jesus, that great Shepherd of the sheep" (Heb 13:20). Peter points to Jesus as the Chief Shepherd who will dispense rewards to the elders who shepherd the flock, the church (1Pe 5:2–4).

BRANCHES

As Christ said that disciples are branches who abide in him, the Vine (Jn 15:1–11), so one of Paul's favorite metaphors is being "in Christ" (2 Co 5:17). Paul depicts the Christian as engrafted into the death and resurrection of Jesus. Dying to sin, the baptized are freed from slavery and brought into the glorious freedom of God's children. Paul sees the whole Christian life as a recapitulation of the existence of Jesus and hence as an exercise of what other authors call discipleship. The humility and obedience of Jesus in his incarnation and crucifixion, according to Paul, are a model for all Christians (Php 2:5–10). We are to imitate God as he gave himself to us in Christ (Eph 5:1–2). Paul, who consciously imitates Christ, proposes himself, together with Christ, as an example to be imitated by his converts (1Co 11:1; cf. 1Co 4:16; Php 3:17; 1Th 1:6; 2Th 3:7, 9).[26]

IMITATION

The term *imitator* (*mimētēs*) is an important link between the disciples of Jesus in the Gospels and the believers of the early church.[27] Although the word *disciple* is curiously absent from the Epistles, W. Michaelis's conclusion is representative of recent scholarship: the disciple and the imitator are one and the same.[28] The nouns *imitator*[29] and *fellow imitator* (*summimetes*, Php 3:17) are always joined in the New Testament with the verb *be, become* and

---

[26]Dulles, "Discipleship," 364.

[27]For a more extended discussion and bibliography of this topic, see Michael J. Wilkins, "Imitate/Imitators (NT)," *Anchor Bible Dictionary*, 5 vols. (Garden City, N.Y.: Doubleday, forthcoming).

[28]W. Michaelis, "μιμέομαι, μιμητής, συμμιμητής," *TDNT* 4:673. Cf. also, Hans Dieter Betz, *Nachfolge und Nachahmung Jesu Christi im Neuen Testament*, BHT 37 (Tübingen: J. C. B. Mohr/Siebeck, 1967), 42–43; Anselm Schulz, *Nachfolgen und Nachahmen: Studien über das Verhältnis der neutestamentlichen Jüngerschaft zur urchristlichen Vorbildethik*. SANT 6 (Munich: Kösel, 1962), 332–35.

[29]*Mimētēs*, 1Co 4:16; 11:1; Eph 5:1; 1Th 1:6; 2:14; Heb 6:12.

are thus similar in meaning to the simple verb *imitate*.[30] Related concepts are found in the use of *type, example* (*tupos*), which occurs in several contexts with "imitation" terms.[31]

In classical and Hellenistic Greek, "imitate/imitator" designates (1) the simple act of mimicking what one sees another doing, (2) the joy of following and emulating another, and (3) representing reality in artistic activities (e.g., theater, painting, sculpture, poetry). Used in a derogatory manner the terms indicate weak and unoriginal copying. In Platonic cosmology the present world is the visible, imperfect copy (*mimēma*) of the invisible archetype in the higher world of Ideas; therefore, "to imitate God" indicates ontological development—not an ethical personal decision.[32] In the mystery religions cultic and magical imitation of God becomes a central focus.[33]

While the word group is absent from the canonical Septuagint, imitation of exemplary men and women is prominent in Jewish literature.[34] In the pseudepigrapha, "imitate/imitator" also indicates imitation of God (*Test. Ash.* 4:3) and his characteristics (*Aristeas* 188, 210, 280–81). Philo regularly uses *mimēma* for the Platonic cosmological idea of original and copy (*De op. mund.* 3.877), and uses *mimeomai* for imitation of a model, including man (*Vit. Mos.* 1.158) and God (e.g., *Decal.* 111; *Leg. All.* 1.48; *De op. mund.* 26.79). Josephus does not speak of the imitation of God but does use the terms for conscious imitation of the qualities or acts of others (*mimeomai, Antiq.* 12.241; *mimētēs, Antiq.* 8.315).

Imitating human objects. The concept of "imitation" in New Testament usage calls believers to imitate other believers, Christ, and God. Human objects are those given most numerously for imitation. Human imitation ranges from simple comparison with the conduct of other believers (1Th 2:14) to presentation of examples of conduct to imitate (Php 3:17; 2Th 3:7, 9; Heb 6:12; 13:7). Paul gives himself as an example for imitation (1Co 4:16; 11:1; Php 3:17; 2Th 3:7, 9), but he does not hold himself up as the ideal of mature perfection. On one occasion he deliberately confesses his own imperfection before he gives the call to imitate him (cf. Php 3:13, 17). Imitation of Paul's ways (1Co 4:16–17) should bring believers to an

[30]*Mimeomai*, 2Th 3:7, 9; Heb 13:7; 3Jn 11.

[31]E.g., Php 3:17; 1Th 1:7; 2Th 3:9, "example" (*hupogrammos*, cf. 1 Pe 1:21), and the adverbial forms "just as" (*kathōs*, 2Co 1:5) and "like" (*hōs*, Lk 6:40).

[32]Karl F. Morrison, *The Mimetic Tradition of Reform in the West* (Princeton, N.J.: Princeton, 1982), 3–31.

[33]Betz, *Nachfolge und Nachahmung Jesu Christi*, 48–84.

[34]E.g., 4Mc 9:32; 13:9; *TBen* 4:1; Sir 44–50; 1Mc 2:49ff., esp. v. 61.

appropriate understanding of the message of the Cross and its implications for their life as a community.[35]

Imitating God and Christ. Human objects, therefore, ultimately point to Christ. Twice Paul calls for his readers to imitate himself, but at the same time he names Christ as the final object of their imitation (1Co 11:1; 1Th 1:6). Only in Ephesians 5:1 are believers called to be imitators of God, but even here the example given is Christ: his forgiveness, love, and sacrificial service (Eph 4: 32; 5:2). Christ is the incarnate example of God for believers to emulate in their daily experience.[36]

The theme of imitation was pressed too far in later church tradition. There a distinction was made between discipleship and imitation. Discipleship meant following after Christ, whereas imitation meant replicating Christlike qualities. Following after Christ was seen as a category of faith and obedience that was stimulated by the grace of God, whereas imitation assumed the accomplishments of the dedicated person, the saint.[37] The New Testament does not make this distinction. Although certain aspects of Christ's earthly life are held up as examples for the believer to follow (e.g., suffering, 1Th 1:6; cf. 1Pe 2:21: *hupogrammos*), this does not imply self-justification through emulating his works, nor does it mean reduplicating some specific acts of Jesus' public ministry.[38] The New Testament use of "imitation" has a unique ethical dimension that stresses the contrast between the "indicative" and the "imperative" in the Christian life. Participation in Christ's death and resurrection (the indicative which makes the believer a new creature in Christ [2Co 5:17]) is constituted in the life of the believer here and now by obedience to the imperatival call to imitation.[39]

IMPLICATIONS

This brief overview of discipleship terminology, teachings, and metaphors demonstrates how the work Jesus began with his disciples

[35]Boykin Sanders, "Imitating Paul: 1 Cor 4:16," *HTR* 74 (1981): 363.

[36]H. H. Henrix, "Von der Nachahmung Gottes. Heiligkeit und Heiligsein im biblischen und jüdischen Denken," *Erbe und Auftrag* 65 (3, 1989): 177–87.

[37]Cf. Hans von Campenhousen, *Die Idee des Martyriums in der alten Kirche*, 2d ed. (Göttingen: Vandenhoeck & Ruprecht, 1964). This distinction is still seen in scholarly studies under the German technical terms *Nachfolge* (following after Christ) and *Nachahmung* (replicating Christlike qualities). E.g., cf. also, Hans Dieter Betz, *Nachfolge und Nachahmung Jesu Christi im Neuen Testament*, BHT 37 (Tübingen: J. C. B. Mohr/Siebeck, 1967); Anselm Schulz, *Nachfolgen und Nachahmen: Studien über das Verhältnis der neutestamentlichen Jüngerschaft zur urchristlichen Vorbildethik*, SANT 6 (Munich: Kösel, 1962).

[38]Hans Kvalbein, "'Go Therefore and Make Disciples. . .': The Concept of Discipleship in the New Testament," *Themelios* 13 (1988): 50.

[39]John B. Webster, "The Imitation of Christ," *TB* 37 (1985): 106.

in his earthly ministry was transferred to the age of the church. Jesus continues to disciple his people through the church. The writers of the Epistles draw upon the rich heritage of discipleship concepts from Jesus' ministry and communicate them in a powerful way for this age when the church is united with Christ as his body.

Life with the risen Christ in the church is indeed different from life with the earthly Jesus. However, this survey demonstrates the continuity that the New Testament writers understood between both phases of his ministry. We saw in the discussion of continuity/discontinuity in discipleship methodology from the Gospels to Acts that some scholars suggest that the age of the church requires a completely new form of discipleship. For example, one suggests, "The old relationship of a single teacher, superior to his little cluster of devoted followers, is ended. The training process implicit in the term discipleship is replaced by another."[40] The strength of this argument lies in its emphasis on the change in relationship that did occur when Jesus ascended. However, to suggest that discipleship is to be defined simply by the picture of "a single teacher, superior to his little cluster of devoted followers" is to overlook the defining process through which the concept went in Jesus' ministry. Jesus' disciples were not just like the Jewish form of rabbinical student. The form of discipleship Jesus intended for his disciples was unique, and it was not intended only for the time when they could follow him physically; it was also intended for the time when they would gather as the church.[41] Discipleship as a concept is much more expansive than merely certain terms.[42] While *disciple* and *follow* naturally contribute to and describe the concept of discipleship, other related terms, teachings, and images are important as well.[43] Those discussed

---

[40]Lawrence O. Richards, *A Practical Theology of Spirituality* (Grand Rapids: Zondervan, 1987), 228.

[41]Like some other scholars, Richards dichotomizes the ages of Jesus' earthly ministry and the church. Richards' proposal has three basic difficulties. I have addressed these difficulties in earlier chapters. First, he commits the common error of placing too much emphasis upon parallels between the rabbinic form of discipleship and Jesus' form (see chaps. 5, 6, and 7). Second, he does not emphasize enough the distinctive progression in discipleship as initiated and developed by Jesus throughout his ministry and into the church (see chaps. 6 and 7). Third, he does not recognize the continuity/discontinuity tension between the period of the Gospels and the early church (see chap. 13).

[42]This is a common error of imprecise "word studies"; *concepts* have a broad contributing source. See our earlier chapters, especially 2–6.

[43]Richards has an excellent approach to the present-day process of discipleship (cf. *Practical Theology of Spirituality*, 228–29). He emphasizes, especially, the family and body concepts, which we have demonstrated are a continuation of themes Jesus initiated in his earthly ministry.

in this chapter are some of the ways Jesus provided continuity between his earthly and ascended ministries among his people.

Following in Jesus' steps is a wonderful picture that Peter uses to encourage his readers in the middle of difficult daily circumstances. Peter, who followed in the physical steps of the Master, exhorts us all to continue to follow him: "To this you were called, because Christ suffered for you, leaving you an example, that you should follow in his steps" (1Pe 2:21).

Following up:

1. Which term, teaching, or metaphor is most significant for you in seeing the continuity of discipleship from the Gospels to the Epistles? Why?
2. How have you followed the example of Christ? Do you imitate him? Explain.
3. Could you tell the people to whom you minister, "Imitate me, as I imitate Christ"? Wouldn't it sound somewhat arrogant for us to say it? What did Paul mean by it? What would you mean by it? Give examples.

16

Apostolic Fathers:
Martyrs for the Name

Getting focused:

1. Have you ever experienced "persecution" for your faith? If so, how did you react? If not, how do you think that you would react?
2. Is there special spiritual value or blessing for those who have experienced persecution? Explain.

"The blood of the martyrs is indeed the seed of the Church. Dying we conquer. The moment we are crushed, that moment we go forth victorious."[1] This proud declaration of the church father Tertullian has been a rallying cry throughout church history. In it we have come to recognize that persecution brings growth and courage. Tradition emphasizes that most of the first disciples of Jesus, the Twelve, were martyrs for their faith in Jesus as the risen Christ. The word *martyr* comes from the Greek word *martus,* meaning witness. From its earliest days, the church has honored individuals who have witnessed to their faith in Christ by choosing to die rather than compromise their faith. As one student of the early martyrs says:

> The Christian martyrs demonstrated that serving and loving Jesus was more important than anything life could give them. By voluntarily accepting death when they could have saved their lives simply by repeating a seemingly innocuous formula, the martyrs testified not only to the centrality of Christ in their lives but also to their faith in the Resurrection and the life of the world to come.[2]

---

[1]Cited in the concluding sentence of the classic study by Herbert B. Workman, *Persecution in the Early Church,* reprint (Oxford: Oxford Univ. Press, 1980), 143.

[2]C. Bernard Ruffin, *The Days of the Martyrs: A History of the Persecution of Christians from Apostolic Times to the Time of Constantine* (Huntington, Ind.: Our Sunday Visitor, 1985), 1.

Even in my first days as a Christian, I understood the significance of this foundation of "witness in suffering" laid by the early church. I was challenged by their faith, yet I was chagrined by their sacrifice. I remember one occasion, standing in my kitchen talking with another new believer, saying, "I know this may seem foolish to say, but I really wish that we were experiencing some kind of persecution. Because then we would really be putting our faith on the line. It is so easy to be a Christian today in our circumstances. What would our faith be like if we were experiencing persecution?" Such may be the rash words of a new, zealous Christian, but that sentiment has always been a part of the church. Jesus gave a call to discipleship in his earthly ministry that set the tone for that sentiment:

> If anyone would come after me, he must deny himself and take up his cross daily and follow me. For whoever wants to save his life will lose it, but whoever loses his life for me will save it. What good is it for a man to gain the whole world, and yet lose or forfeit his very self? If anyone is ashamed of me and my words, the Son of Man will be ashamed of him when he comes in his glory and in the glory of the Father and of the holy angels. (Lk 9:23–26)

Since the days of the earliest church, men and women have responded to Jesus' radical summons, and many have received the strength and courage necessary to follow Jesus all the way into death. Readiness for martyrdom is a theme that runs consistently throughout Scripture. Sometimes rash (Thomas' statement in Jn 11:16),[3] sometimes boastful (Peter's statement in Lk 22:33),[4] sometimes prophetic (Jesus' words to Peter in Jn 21:18–19),[5] these statements of biblical characters reveal a deeply ingrained attitude of desiring to follow Jesus no matter what the cost. Persecution marked the fate of the church from its earliest days, yet it did not dim their passion for following Jesus. Luke captured the attitude of the apostles after they had experienced beatings from the Jewish Sanhedrin: "The apostles left the Sanhedrin, rejoicing because they had been counted worthy of suffering disgrace for the Name. Day after day, in the temple courts and from house to house, they never stopped teaching and proclaiming the good news that Jesus is the Christ" (Ac 5:41–42).

---

[3] "Let us also go, that we may die with Him."

[4] "Lord, I am ready to go with you to prison and to death."

[5] " 'I tell you the truth, when you were younger you dressed yourself and went where you wanted; but when you are old you will stretch out your hands, and someone else will dress you and lead you where you do not want to go.' Jesus said this to indicate the kind of death by which Peter would glorify God" (Jn 21:18–19).

By the time the apostles passed from the scene, martyrdom was a reality. And in the writings of the earliest church fathers, we find the same readiness to suffer for the name of the Master. The author of the *Martyrdom of Polycarp* wrote: "Blessed and noble, therefore, are all the martyrdoms that have taken place in accordance with the will of God (for we must reverently assign to God the power over all things). For who could fail to admire their nobility and patient endurance and loyalty to the Master" (*Mart. Pol.* 2.1–2).[6] Ignatius said: "I am not commanding you, as though I were somebody important. For even though I am in chains for the sake of the Name, I have not yet begun to be perfected in Jesus Christ" (*Eph.* 3.1).

These attitudes toward death for the sake of Jesus seem foreign to many of us who are not in situations where persecution is a reality. Yet we must appreciate that there is a direct link between them and the radical summons Jesus gave to take up the cross and follow him. When trying to understand discipleship, we must address the issue of martyrdom. We may not experience martyrdom ourselves, but suffering for Jesus' sake is a reality that every believer will in some way encounter. When we look at some of those who have gone before us who have given the ultimate sacrifice for Jesus—their lives—we can learn much from their example how to address whatever suffering and sacrifice we face in our day.

Our purpose in this chapter is to examine discipleship in the early church after the apostles passed from the earthly scene in order to learn what discipleship means while experiencing suffering. Suffering, persecution, and martyrdom were the stark realities of those in the early church. As we look to their experience, we actually look beyond them to Jesus, because their greatest desire was to follow Christ, regardless of the consequences. Polycarp, one of the early church fathers who experienced a martyr's death, when speaking of Christ's suffering on the cross for our sake, said: "Let us then be imitators of His endurance, and if we suffer for His Name's sake let us glorify Him. For this is the example which He gave us in Himself, and this is what we have believed" (*Phil.* 8.1–2).

THE IMPORTANCE OF THE APOSTOLIC FATHERS

Apostolic fathers has traditionally been used to designate the authors of the earliest extant Christian writings outside the New

---

[6]Unless otherwise noted, all translations of the apostolic fathers are from either Kirsopp Lake, *The Apostolic Fathers, with an English Translation*, 2 vols., *LCL*, reprint (Cambridge: Harvard, 1977), or from J. B. Lightfoot and J. R. Harmer, *The Apostolic Fathers,* ed. and rev. Michael W. Holmes, 2d ed. (Grand Rapids: Baker, 1989).

Testament.[7] These writings are important because they are a primary source for the study of early Christianity, especially the period after the majority of apostles passed from the scene (especially A.D. 70–150). They provide significant and often unparalleled glimpses of and insights into the lives of Christians and the Christian movement immediately following the apostles.[8] Such is the case for early conceptions of discipleship. At the time when the apostolic fathers wrote, the churches they addressed had been established for at least a half century. The early flush of conversion had passed for many of these churches, a mounting danger from heresy was exerting itself upon them, and increasing persecution from the Roman Empire was threatening their very existence. What was discipleship like under these conditions?

As we have done in our study of the biblical material, our study of the apostolic fathers will focus on specific terms, teaching, and concepts that reveal attitudes about discipleship. In addition, we will compare our findings with the biblical data to look for similarities and differences of discipleship life. Many of the same terms and concepts of discipleship that occur in the New Testament also occur in the apostolic fathers.[9] The writings that will anchor our study are those of Ignatius, bishop of the church at Antioch in Syria. Ignatius uses discipleship terminology more frequently than any apostolic father, revealing the most information about the development of discipleship in the days of the early church. Virginia Corwin observes, "The Ignatian letters have more references to imitation and discipleship

---

[7]The lists of writings vary, but the most commonly accepted collection includes *1 Clement, An Ancient Christian Sermon* (formerly known as 2 Clement), *The Letters of Ignatius, The Letter of Polycarp to the Philippians, The Martyrdom of Polycarp, The Didache, The Epistle of Barnabas, The Shepherd of Hermas, The Epistle to Diognetus,* and *The Fragments of Papias.* While we may assume that these documents were written by people who had some kind of influence from the apostles, explicit evidence for direct contact with the apostles is available primarily for Polycarp and Papias. The writings of three influential "bishops," Clement of Rome, Ignatius of Antioch, and Polycarp of Smyrna, have had the most profound influence on studies of the early church, but increasing attention is being given to all of the writings in the collection.

[8]For an excellent discussion of the significance, historical setting, and texts of the apostolic fathers, see Michael Holmes' revision of Lightfoot and Harmer, *The Apostolic Fathers.*

[9]Through the search capabilities of the computer data bank of *Thesaurus Linguae Graecae* (TLG) (housed at the University of California, Irvine), I examined all of the extant writings of the apostolic fathers, even the spurious writings, for the following terms: *disciple* (μαθητής) and *I make disciples* (μαθητεύω), *follower* and *I follow* (ἀκολουθ- stem), *believer* (πιστεύοντος; πιστοι), *brother/sister* (ἀδελφ- stem), *Christian* (Χριστιανός), *imitator* (μιμητής), *apostle* (ἀπόστολος), and *saints* (ἅγιοι).

than all the other Apostolic Fathers together."[10] Ignatius will anchor
our study, but we will briefly touch on the writings of the other
apostolic fathers as they contribute to a more complete understanding
of our subject.[11]

DISCIPLESHIP IN IGNATIUS

"Just as we become aware of a meteor only when, after travelling
silently through space for untold millions of miles, it blazes through
the atmosphere before dying in a shower of fire, so it is with Ignatius,
bishop of Antioch in Syria."[12] This description captures the brilliant
influence of the early church leader, Ignatius, bishop of the church at
Antioch. Ignatius is not a figure well-known to many modern-day
Christians, but his influence has been significant throughout church
history. We know virtually nothing of his early life. His apparently
long ministry in the region of Antioch in Syria went unrecorded in
church annals. We meet him for the first and only time for a few
weeks shortly before his death as a martyr in Rome early in the
second century. But in those few weeks Ignatius left a legacy that has
had a remarkable impact on the church. His legacy is in the form of
seven brief letters.

Ignatius was arrested during a time of persecution in Antioch and
was sent to Rome to be tried and executed. He traveled from Syria to
Rome in the company of ten Roman soldiers in approximately A.D.
110.[13] Along the route he wrote letters, five to churches located in
cities along the way (Ephesus, Magnesia, Tralles, Philadelphia, and
Smyrna); one to his friend Polycarp, bishop of the church at Smyrna;
and one to the church in Rome, alerting them to his impending arrival
there.[14] In these seven brief letters, Ignatius left a powerful mark

---

[10]Virginia Corwin, *St. Ignatius and Christianity in Antioch*, Yale Publications
in Religion 1 (New Haven: Yale Univ. Press, 1960), 228, n. 9.

[11]Later church fathers speak frequently of disciples and the life of discipleship
(e.g., Irenaeus and Eusebius), but the apostolic fathers reveal the earliest attitudes
about the concept of discipleship in the church following the passing of the
apostles.

[12]Lightfoot, Harmer, and Holmes, *Apostolic Fathers*, 79.

[13]There is a consensus regarding the general time of Ignatius's martyrdom,
during the reign of Trajan (A.D. 98–117), but there is debate concerning the exact
date. The date of A.D. 110 is an approximation. Cf. Lightfoot, Harmer, and Holmes,
Apostolic Fathers, 82.

[14]The middle recension of seven letters as the authentic corpus appears to be
the firmly held consensus of the majority of modern scholars. Cf. William R.
Schoedel, *Ignatius of Antioch: A Commentary on the Letters of Ignatius of
Antioch*, ed. Helmut Koester, Hermeneia (Philadelphia: Fortress, 1985), 3–7;
Lightfoot, Harmer, and Holmes, *Apostolic Fathers*, 82–83. For an extended, older
discussion, see J. B. Lightfoot, *The Apostolic Fathers: Revised Texts with*

upon church history. Ignatius is important because of the early date of his writings, reflecting unparalleled light upon conditions at a crucial time of church development. But, and this is the focus of our study, he is also important because of the impact of his attitude toward Christian life and ministry.

Ignatius was a complicated person. On the one hand, scholars suggest that he was full of self-doubt, attributable to the fact that he had lost control over warring factions in his church in Antioch. On the other hand, some scholars say that he had an inappropriately authoritarian attitude, which is displayed toward his own church and toward other churches and church leaders. Some point to his regular self-effacement and suggest that he had a low personal self-esteem. Others say that he had a naturally vigorous, impulsive, and energetic personality.[15] But all scholars point to Ignatius's remarkable attitude toward his impending martyrdom, even though they may point with differing interpretations of his attitude. Ignatius's attitude toward his martyrdom has unfailingly disturbed readers. What disturbs us the most is that he longs for his martyrdom, even begging his readers not to interfere with the Roman government's process. One observer notes, "The vivid, almost macabre eagerness with which Ignatius apparently anticipates his death has repelled many readers, and a good deal of unwarranted criticism (e.g., labeling him "neurotic") has been directed toward him."[16] It is in this very attitude toward martyrdom that we encounter a unique element of Ignatius's understanding of discipleship, an element that has had a profound impact upon the church's notion of discipleship ever since. I quote here a long, classic passage from Ignatius's letter to the Roman church. In its raw power and emotion this passage describes the utter horror of his impending martyrdom. But it also demonstrates Ignatius's incredible attitude toward that martyrdom and what it meant for him as a disciple of Jesus Christ.

> I am fighting wild beasts from Syria to Rome, through land and sea, by night and day, bound to ten leopards—which is a company of soldiers—who when well treated become worse. *By their mistreatment I become more of a disciple*, but "not for that reason I am justified." May I have the pleasure of wild beasts that have been prepared for me. I will even coax them to devour me promptly, not as they have done with some, whom they were too timid to touch. And if when I am willing and

---

Introductions, Notes, Dissertations, and Translations, two pts. in 5 vols., reprint (Grand Rapids: Baker, 1981), pt. 2, 1:233–430.

[15]For background to these views, see Schoedel, *Ignatius*, 10–15. See also Corwin, *St. Ignatius*, 21ff.; and Lightfoot, Harmer, and Holmes, *Apostolic Fathers*, 79–82.

[16]Lightfoot, Harmer, and Holmes, *Apostolic Fathers*, 81.

ready they are not, I will force them. Bear with me—I know what is best for me. *Now at last I am beginning to be a disciple.* May nothing visible or invisible envy me, so that I may reach Jesus Christ. Fire and cross and battles with wild beasts, mutilation, mangling, wrenching of bones, the hacking of limbs, the crushing of my whole body, cruel tortures of the devil—let these come upon me, only let me reach Jesus Christ! (*Rom.* 5.1.4–5.3.3; italics added for emphasis)

We stand amazed at such an attitude under such circumstances. What lies behind Ignatius's attitude? Is this attitude to be found in other apostolic fathers? What is Ignatius's understanding of discipleship, and how does it relate to the New Testament conception? What does this mean for our understanding of discipleship? To these perplexing questions we now turn.

Discipleship Terminology

Ignatius used many of the same discipleship terms that we find in the New Testament. The other apostolic fathers used some of this terminology but not to the extent of Ignatius. Intriguingly, Ignatius used the word *disciple* and related terms fourteen times, while in all the other apostolic fathers combined the word *disciple* occurs less than a dozen times. While Ignatius's abundant use of discipleship terminology has caused him to stand out prominently, he shares several common discipleship themes with the other apostolic fathers.

DISCIPLE

Ignatius used the word *disciple* more frequently than the other apostolic fathers. However, the term does occur in other writings of the Fathers, including the *Martyrdom of Polycarp* (17.3.2, 5; 22.2.1) and the anonymous letter to Diognetus (four times in 11.1–2).

Ignatius used the noun *disciple* (*mathētēs*),[17] the verb *I make/become a disciple* (*mathēteuō*),[18] and the rare noun *lesson* (*mathēteia*) once (*Trall.* 3.2.5). We will discuss categories of usage below more fully, but a few observations at this point will indicate the significance of "disciple" terms for Ignatius.

First, Ignatius used disciple terms in three seemingly contradictory ways. In some passages the word *disciple* simply designates a Christian. In other passages the word seems to designate the person who is a more committed Christian than other Christians. And in a number of other passages the word *disciple* seems to designate the

---

[17]μαθητής occurs nine times: Ignatius, *Eph.* 1.2.4; *Magn.* 9.1.6; 9.2.3; 10.1.3; *Trall.* 5.2.4; *Rom.* 4.2.4; 5.3.2; *Poly.* 2.1.1; 7.1.5.

[18]μαθητεύω occurs four times: Ignatius, *Eph.* 3.1.3; 10.1.4; *Rom.* 3.1.2; 5.1.4.

person who is a martyr. This surprising usage has caused much debate and confusion among students of discipleship over the years.

Second, when Ignatius used the verb *I make/become a disciple* (*mathēteuō*), the same verb used in the Great Commission of Matthew's gospel, he provided a unique link with the writings and activities of the early church.[19] A direct line was drawn from Matthew's record of the Great Commission of Jesus (Mt 28:19) to Luke's record of the activities of the apostolic church (Ac 14:21) to Ignatius's record of the life of the churches of the second century (*Eph.* 3.1.3; 10.1.4; *Rom.* 3.1.2; 5.1.4).

Third, in some contexts Ignatius seems to have drawn upon the "learner" aspect of the noun *mathētēs* (*Rom.* 3.1.2). We saw earlier that the semantical range of the noun certainly included the meaning "learner," but in common New Testament and Hellenistic secular usage the "adherent" factor was more in view. The "learner" aspect in Ignatius may be illustrated by his use of the rare noun *lesson* (*mathēteia*, *Trall.* 3.2.5), formed from the same stem as the noun *disciple* (*mathētēs*). This term does not occur in the New Testament and nowhere else in early Christian literature.

Fourth, although Ignatius referred to himself as a disciple, he did not consider himself to be an apostle (*Trall.* 7.1.4; *Rom.* 4.3.2). For Ignatius, "apostles" were the special and limited group of men that were the foundation of the church (cf. *Magn.* 6.1.5; 7.1.2; 13.2.3; *Phld.* 5.1.6; 9.1.5; *Smyrn.* 8.1.2). The "council of apostles" appears to be limited to the Twelve and to Paul (*Rom.* 4.3.2).

The use of disciple terms in the *Martyrdom of Polycarp* (written approximately A.D. 160, some fifty years after Ignatius) is also quite interesting. First, *mathētēs* is used to designate those persons who found martyrdom as "disciples and imitators of the Lord" (*Mart. Pol.* 17.3.2). This is similar to the martyr theme that we find in Ignatius.

Second, the term is also used to designate a mentor relationship between a Christian leader and a novice-trainee. For example, the author refers to Irenaeus as a "disciple of Polycarp" (*Mart. Pol.* 22.2.1).[20] Ignatius agrees with the concept of learning from and following the example of other Christians, but he does not use the term to designate a formal mentor relationship between two Christians.[21]

---

[19]A search of the apostolic fathers through the TLG data bank indicates that the verb does not occur elsewhere in these writings. Cf. also BAGD, *Greek-English Lexicon*, 486.

[20]The term also occurs in the longer conclusion found in the Moscow manuscript.

[21]One textually debated passage reads, "That I may be found to be your disciple at the resurrection (ἀναστάσει)" (Ignatius, *Poly.* 7.1.5). Lake (*Apostolic*

Third, "fellow-disciple" (*summathētēs*) occurs as a compound form in *Martyrdom of Polycarp*, but it does not occur in Ignatius. The author points to the martyrs, especially Polycarp, and prays that he too may join them as fellow disciples in martyrdom. "God grant that we too may be their companions and fellow-disciples" (*Mart. Pol.* 17.3.5). This is an interesting phenomenon, because "fellow-disciple" is quite rare in Hellenistic and early Christian usage. But it does occur once in the New Testament, when John records, "Thomas, who was called the Twin, said to his fellow disciples, 'Let us also go, that we may die with him'" (Jn 11:16 NRSV). Interestingly, this is also in a martyr context.

The word *disciple* also occurs in *The Epistle to Diognetus*, one of the latest in the collection of the apostolic fathers (c. A.D. 150–225) and called by J. B. Lightfoot "the noblest of early Christian writings."[22] In this anonymous apologetic tract to an unbeliever, the author uses the word *disciple* four times, all in one provocative passage.

> I am not talking about strange things, nor am I engaged in irrational speculation, but having been a *disciple* of Apostles, I am now becoming a teacher of the Gentiles. To those who are becoming *disciples* of the truth I try to minister in a worthy manner the teachings that have been handed down. Indeed, does anyone who has been rightly taught and has come to love the Word not seek to learn exactly the things openly made known by the Word to *disciples*? To them the Word appeared and revealed these things, speaking quite plainly as He did so; though not understood by unbelievers, He explained them to *disciples*, who, being regarded as faithful by Him, learned the mysteries of the Father. (*Diogn.* 11.1–2;[23] italics mine)

Several issues arise from this intriguing passage. First, since "disciples" are used opposite of "unbelievers," the phrase "becoming *disciples* of the truth" indicates conversion to Christianity. Second, as a "*disciple* of apostles" the writer was one who had been instructed by the apostles,[24] and who, in turn, was now a "teacher of the Gentiles." This expression indicates acquisition of the truth of the Gospel, as the phrase "those who are becoming *disciples* of the truth"

Fathers, 274, n. 3; and 275, n. 2) and Corwin (*St. Ignatius*, 228, n. 8) prefer this reading. Lightfoot (*Apostolic Fathers*, 304) and Schoedel (*Ignatius*, 278, n. 4) prefer the reading, "That I may be found to be a disciple by means of your prayer" (αἰτήσει). Schoedel argues convincingly against the former reading on the basis that a disciple in Ignatius is always a disciple of Jesus.

[22]Lightfoot, Harmer, and Holmes, *Apostolic Fathers*, 291.

[23]Lake concludes that this and the following chapters belong to a different document; cf. Lake, *Apostolic Fathers*, 2:349.

[24]Whether the writer was taught personally or through their writings is debated.

reveals. As we saw in Ignatius and the *Martyrdom of Polycarp*, this usage emphasizes the "learning" aspect. Third, this "learning" aspect is intimately linked with conversion. As one is taught the meaning of Christianity and receives it as one's own, that person becomes a "disciple of the truth," a Christian.

In the following pages we will see the importance of these observations for understanding discipleship in the apostolic fathers, but first I will make a few comments about related terminology.

FOLLOWER

We have seen that the Gospels regularly used *follow/follower* as an equivalent metaphorical expression for "discipleship" but that the term is found only rarely in the New Testament outside of the Gospels. Interestingly, the metaphorical discipleship sense of "follow" does not occur in Ignatius. Ignatius used the term to describe the physical act of going after someone or something (*Phld.* 11.1.3) or else to designate one who obeys or takes after the teachings or characteristics of another person or teaching (*Eph.* 14.1.5; *Phld.* 2.1.3; 3.3.2; *Smyrn.* 8.1.1). Clement likewise used "follow" in the sense of obeying or taking after the teachings or characteristics of another person or teaching (*1 Clem.* 14:1; 40:4).

Only rarely in the apostolic fathers does "follow" have a metaphorical sense that approximates "discipleship."[25] On one occasion Clement says that the proper duty of the Christian is to "follow the way of truth" (*1 Clem.* 35:5). However, a metaphorical sense similar to this is found in other terminology. For example, the author of *The Martyrdom of Polycarp* concludes his account with, "We bid you farewell, brothers, *as you walk by the word of Jesus Christ* which is in accord with the gospel; with whom be glory to God for the salvation of the holy elect; just as the blessed Polycarp was martyred, *in whose footsteps may we also be found* in the kingdom of Jesus Christ" (22.1; italics mine). Here the author speaks simultaneously of "walking by the word of Jesus" and being "in the footsteps" of Polycarp.

BROTHER/SISTER, CHRISTIAN, SAINT

In the same way that the New Testament writers referred to disciples by other names, so the apostolic fathers referred to disciples, believers in Jesus,[26] as "brothers/sisters," "Christians," and "saints."

---

[25]The substantive use of the verb ἀκολουθέω to designate a "follower" does not occur in the apostolic fathers.

[26]A fascinating phenomenon is that the word for "believer" (forms of πιστεύοντες and πίστις) occurs only rarely (e.g., Ignatius, *Magn.* 5.2.1).

The title *brothers/sisters* is used in the apostolic fathers in a manner reminiscent of biblical usage, implying that believers are members of the same family of God. The apostolic fathers regularly use the word *brothers* generically to designate local gatherings of believers.[27] Gender-specific reference is made to "sisters" and "brothers" who are individual members of the family of God (e.g., Ign. *Poly.* 5.1.2, 4; *Mart. Pol.* 20.1.3). This special relationship is not limited to the members of a local church, however, because those of other congregations in other locales are also referred to as their "brothers" (e.g., Ign. *Smyrn.* 12.1.1), and all believers everywhere are called "brothers" (e.g., *Mart. Pol.* 1.2.5), part of the same "brotherhood" (*1 Clem.* 2:4).[28] This is very similar to the way in which Jesus referred to his disciples and to the way in which the early church referred to one another.

The title *Christians* is also used in the apostolic fathers as a title for believers. It occurs regularly in Ignatius's letters and most frequently in the anonymous letter to Diognetus. Both in singular and plural forms the title *Christian(s)* designates those who are believers in Jesus Christ.[29] Referring to believers as "Christians" was probably becoming commonplace by this time as evidenced by Ignatius also using a related noun (*Christianity*)[30] and adjective (*christian, Trall.* 5.2.4) to designate the doctrine that is adopted, the ideology followed, and the lifestyle that results from sincere faith in Christ and his teaching. Significantly, the term *disciple* functions as a common referent for those called Christians, much as it did in the early days of Antioch, as Luke records (Ac 11:26). *Disciple* and *Christian* are near synonyms.

The expression *saints* also occurs in the apostolic fathers as a title for New Testament believers, i.e., disciples (Ign. *Smyrn.* 1.2.4; Pol. *Phil.* 1.1.4; 12.3; Lat. *sanctus*) or Old Testament prophets (Ign. *Phld.* 5.2.4), but it does not occur as frequently as *brothers/sisters* or *Christians*.

[27]E.g., Ignatius, *Eph.* 16.1.1; *Phld.* t.1.1; *1 Clem.* 13:1; 14:1; *Mart. Pol.* 1.1.1; 4.1.4; *Barn.* 5.5.1.

[28]Gerhard Lohfink, *Jesus and Community: The Social Dimension of Christian Faith* (Philadelphia: Fortress, 1984), 154–57.

[29]Singular = Ignatius, *Rom.* 3.2.3; *Poly.* 7.3.1; plural = Ignatius, *Eph.* 11.2.1; *Mag.* 4.1.1; *Diogn.* 1.1.2; 2.6.1; 3.2.2; 4.6.2; 6.1.2; et al.

[30]*Christianismos;* Ignatius, *Magn.* 10.1.3; 10.3.2, 3; *Rom.* 3.3.3; *Phld.* 6.1.3. The proper noun *Christianity* appears for the first time in Christian literature here in Ignatius. Its appearance is not surprising, because the proper noun *Christian* was already in use (cf. Ac 11:26; 26:28; 1Pe 4:16), and the term *Judaism* (cf. Ignatius *Magn.* 8:1) "provided a ready model for the creation of a noun to describe the distinctive identity of the Christian movement (Schoedel, *Ignatius*, 126, n. 1).

IMITATOR/IMITATE, EXAMPLE

We discovered in our study of the New Testament Epistles that the concept of "imitation" was closely related to Jesus' idea of discipleship. That same conceptual relationship is also found in the apostolic fathers. On four occasions Ignatius exhorted believers in various churches to be "imitators of the Lord." This meant to follow the example of Jesus in righteousness behavior (*Eph.* 1.1.3), in nonretaliation under persecution (*Eph.* 10.3.2), in disposition of character and endurance (*Trall.* 1.2.3), and in obedience to the will of the Father (*Phld.* 7.2.4). In turn, as pagans watched the good deeds of believers, they would follow their example and become disciples of Jesus (*Eph.* 10.1.4). Hence, imitation and discipleship are closely related.

Discipleship and imitation also converge when contemplating martyrdom. On one occasion Ignatius expressed his desire to be allowed to imitate the Lord to the point of being executed. "Allow me to be an imitator of the suffering of my God. If anyone has Him within himself, let him understand what I long for and sympathize with me, knowing what constrains me" (*Rom.* 6.3.1). Ignatius's desire to experience ultimate discipleship meant following Jesus to death. In like manner, Ignatius's desire to imitate Christ was so passionate that he saw his own imminent martyrdom in the light of imitating Jesus' suffering, and he assumed that all Christians would experience this same passion.

Although Clement did not use the word *imitate* (*mimeomai*) with reference to Christ, he did use related imitation terminology when he exhorted the church to follow the "example" (*hupogrammos*) Christ set in humility (*1 Clem.* 16:17) and good works (33:8). In addition, Clement emphasized another aspect of New Testament imitation: following the example of godly believers. He exhorted the church to be imitators (*mimētai*) of humility found in the the Old Testament prophets (17:1) and to follow the examples (*hupodeigma* and *hupogrammos*) set by other believers: e.g., the apostles, specifically Peter and Paul (5:4, 7; 6:1) and godly believers of his own day (63:1).

The "imitation" theme also occurs in Polycarp's *Epistle to the Philippians* and in the anonymous *Martyrdom of Polycarp.* In the *Martyrdom* the writer points either to Christ's death (17.3.3) or to martyrs like Polycarp (1.2.2; 19.1.5) as examples worthy of imitation. Polycarp himself, when speaking of Christ's suffering on the cross for our sake, said, "Let us then be imitators of His endurance, and if we suffer for His Name's sake let us glorify Him. For this is the example which He gave us in Himself, and this is what we have believed" (*Phil.* 8.1–2).

In those days of terrible persecution by the Roman Empire, the theme of following the example of Christ in suffering was a necessary stimulus to the faith of all those in the church.

Discipleship Characteristics

The apostolic fathers used many of the same discipleship terms as did the New Testament writers. When using the word *disciple,* the Fathers, especially Ignatius, used the term in a restricted manner. In the Gospels, and to a lesser degree in Acts, the word *disciple* was used as a title in narrative material simply to designate those who were believers. Many times the term could be used without special significance. On the other hand, a growing technicality surrounded the word *disciple* as Jesus developed his particular form of discipleship. That technicality implied a personal relationship with Jesus and an assumed progress of growth, especially in the goal of imitating and becoming like the Master. By the time of the early church, this technical understanding of what it meant to be a disciple of Jesus was firmly attached to the term. We can see that in the book of Acts the term is used somewhat unceremoniously as a title for a confessing Christian. However, the apostolic fathers did not use the term in this unceremonious manner. They tended to use *disciple* in a reverent sense that emphasized in context the technicality of the discipleship life of the Christian. This may have been influenced by a growing reverence for those disciples who walked with Jesus in his earthly ministry, but it almost certainly was influenced by the persecution the church was experiencing.

Overall, discipleship was understood as the development of the Christian life. However, the most perplexing feature of discipleship in Ignatius and some of the other apostolic fathers is the relationship to martyrdom. We noted above that Ignatius seemed to imply that the word *disciple* is a common referent for "believer" or "Christian." In several passages discipleship is simply the outworking of the Christian life. Yet we also noted that as he approached martyrdom Ignatius saw himself finally "becoming a disciple." In several passages discipleship seems to be a more advanced stage of the Christian life. What are we to make of these seemingly contradictory expressions of discipleship? In order to answer that question adequately we must take a closer look at both kinds of passages.

DISCIPLESHIP AS THE CHRISTIAN LIFE

Ignatius indicated that a person enters into and advances along the life of discipleship through conversion and Christian growth. When pagans "find God" they "become disciples" (*Eph.* 10.1.4). Once a person becomes a disciple, growth in discipleship transpires by living one's life in accordance with the characteristics of Christ and his teachings. Ignatius wrote to the church: "Having become His disciples, let us learn to live in accordance with Christianity. For whoever is called by any other name than this does not belong to God" (*Mag.* 10.1.3). Here he drew a contrast between the Judaizers, those who would lead the church back into legalism, and true disciples, those who "live in accordance with Christianity."

While Ignatius strongly emphasized that conversion results from faith, initiating the life of discipleship, he equally emphasized that endurance in the life of discipleship is the proof of belief. In his letter to the Magnesians he indicated that those who believe in the death and resurrection of Christ are disciples. He even pointed to the Old Testament prophets and called them "disciples in the Spirit" because they were awaiting Christ. The Christian life is centered on and flows from the mystery of the Cross.

> If, then, those who had lived in antiquated practices came to newness of hope, no longer keeping the Sabbath but living in accordance with the Lord's day, on which our life also arose through Him and His death (which some deny), the mystery through which we came to believe, and because of which we patiently endure, in order that we might be found to be disciples of Jesus Christ, our only teacher, how can we possibly live without Him? (Ign. *Magn.* 9.1.1–6)

The Cross and Resurrection determine the shape of Christian existence. Christ is the only Teacher of those who would call themselves disciples, because he provided the ultimate example of endurance in his obedience to the point of death. " 'Endurance' is a sign of discipleship precisely because, for Ignatius, Christ's teaching consists of his enactment of his Father's will in being obedient to the point of death."[31] Belief must be proven by endurance. Only those who are obedient prove to be disciples, and the conclusive proof is obedience to the point of death (cf. Ign. *Magn.* 9–10). As Ignatius saw the threat to the church from the Roman government and from the Judaizers, he declared that endurance and obedience are the proofs of true belief/discipleship. Conversion is the point at which one becomes a disciple, but true disciples will continue to grow in discipleship.

This is not to say that disciples will always obey perfectly. At times disciples will be wayward and will need to be brought back into line. Ignatius advised Polycarp on how to deal with wayward members of his church: "If you love good disciples, it is no credit to you; rather with gentleness bring the more troublesome ones into submission" (*Poly.* 2.1.1). Ignatius is as realistic as are the New Testament writers.

---

[31]Schoedel, *Ignatius of Antioch*, 124.

Obedience and endurance are the expected signs of discipleship, but perfection is not demanded as one traverses the path.

DEVELOPMENTAL DISCIPLESHIP

Discipleship in the apostolic fathers is clearly developmental. Although a Christian becomes a disciple through conversion, the life of a disciple (i.e., discipleship) is not a static phenomenon. Discipleship means growth and progress toward the goal of becoming more like Jesus. Simply by using the term *disciple* the authors conjure up an image of the Christian who is a committed follower of Jesus. To be a true disciple means that a person has made a definite conversion commitment to follow Jesus, and it is expected that the person who makes that commitment will carry it through to completion. This is especially significant for those who were experiencing persecution. During this time of persecution, if persons were charged with being a Christian, they could simply deny the name of Jesus and they would be set free. Those who continued to claim the name of Jesus demonstrated the reality of their faith. This was the ultimate demonstration that they were true followers, their vindication of faithfulness to the Name, to the reality of the Christian life, to Christian ministry.

Therefore, the time of conversion was a significant moment for considering the hardship that lay ahead. To claim the name of Jesus as Savior meant that one would surely experience persecution for the sake of the Name. This is an unmistakable illustration of Jesus' teaching on counting the cost of discipleship. Counting the cost not only meant the cost of what becoming a disciple meant, but also the cost of what the life of discipleship might entail. In the parables of counting the cost of discipleship, Jesus plainly pointed out the cost of what completing the process of discipleship would take (Lk 14:28–33). Jesus wanted people to recognize that discipleship was not simply the moment of conversion, but it included the life that would follow. It is this ongoing life that Ignatius, in particular, emphasized. The closer he came to the time of completing his life, the closer he was to being a completed disciple.[32]

Someone has said that "a disciple is always becoming more fully a disciple." That is similar to the developmental process that Ignatius emphasized. At the moment of conversion he became a disciple, but as he grew he became more like his Master, and the more like Jesus he became, the closer he came to the realization of the completed task of being made into the final likeness of Christ. This theme also

---

[32]Cf. Demetrios Trakatellis, "'Ακολούθει μου/Follow Me' (Mk 2:14): Discipleship and Priesthood," *GOThR* 30 (3, 1985): 283, 285.

continues the "already/not yet" tension the New Testament de-velops. An example of this is found especially in Paul, who emphasized that although he *already* counted the cost of knowing Christ for salvation, he did *not yet* know him fully. That knowledge was expanded through his life and would be perfected at the time of his death.

> But whatever was to my profit I now consider loss for the sake of Christ. What is more, I consider everything a loss compared to the surpassing greatness of knowing Christ Jesus my Lord, for whose sake I have lost all things. I consider them rubbish, that I may gain Christ and be found in him, not having a righteousness of my own that comes from the law, but that which is through faith in Christ—the righteousness that comes from God and is by faith. I want to know Christ and the power of his resurrection and the fellowship of sharing in his sufferings, becoming like him in his death, and so, somehow, to attain to the resurrection from the dead.
>
> Not that I have already obtained all this, or have already been made perfect, but I press on to take hold of that for which Christ Jesus took hold of me. Brothers, I do not consider myself yet to have taken hold of it. But one thing I do: Forgetting what is behind and straining toward what is ahead, I press on toward the goal to win the prize for which God has called me heavenward in Christ Jesus. (Php 3:7–14)

As with Paul, so with Ignatius. Ignatius wrote at a critical point in his life. For him, being a disciple was not a convenience. It would cost him his life. But this did not cause him to cringe from the challenge. In fact, facing martyrdom brought him into the stark realization that he was coming closer and closer to the fulfillment of his life of discipleship. He was closer to the end, closer to being with his Lord. And, in addition, as he faced martyrdom he realized that he was walking the same path of suffering and death that his Lord had walked and that most of the Twelve and Paul had walked.[33] He saw in his own martyrdom not a horror, but a privilege to walk as his Master had walked.

Later in church history this attitude would be taken to an extreme where men would seek out martyrdom in an ascetic fashion in order to gain meritorious salvation or a higher level of Christianity, such as sainthood. Such a conception is not biblical discipleship. In Ignatius, on the contrary, we find an example of discipleship that closely follows the model Jesus and the apostles developed.

---

[33]For a discussion of the view that readiness for martyrdom was a New Testament theme, see George Dragas, "Martyrdom and Orthodoxy in the New Testament Era—The Theme of Μαρτυπία As Witness to the Truth," *GOThR* 30 (3, 1985): 287–96.

IMITATION AND DISCIPLESHIP

We noted above that discipleship and imitation converge in Ignatius's thinking. The two notions are not precisely the same, but they have kindred meaning. Discipleship implies devotion to Christ and following his pattern. Imitation emphasizes the pattern but assumes the devotion. Corwin explains:

> The key to Ignatius' view of the Christian life is an understanding of the twin conceptions of imitation and discipleship, for they are central to his thinking. They give content to the choice that he urges, and in following the path that they indicate the Christian life is grounded securely, for it is provided both with an effective motive, in devotion to the Lord, and a pattern for life, in a general sense at least.[34]

Although some suggest that Ignatius adopted his imitation theme from Hellenistic philosophy,[35] close comparison of Ignatius's teaching with New Testament teaching indicates that Ignatius shaped his teaching after the model of Scripture, not Hellenism.[36] When Ignatius expressed his desire to be allowed to imitate the Lord to the point of being executed, his words reflected New Testament usage: "Allow me to be an imitator of the suffering of my God. If anyone has Him within himself, let him understand what I long for and sympathize with me, knowing what constrains me" (Ign. *Rom.* 6.3.1). Here Ignatius expressed what he believed every Christian should understand: the desire to be completely obedient, even if it means to suffer as did Christ. The context reveals clearly that Ignatius was very much in line with the New Testament authors for whom following Christ's example of submission implied suffering. The apostle Peter said, "To this you were called, because Christ suffered for you, leaving you an example, that you should follow in his steps" (1Pe 2:21).

We can also see discipleship and imitation merging in relationships between believers. Believers are to provide an example of godliness for pagans to follow (Ign. *Eph.* 10.1.4), and believers are to learn from one another (Ign. *Rom.* 3.1.2). The author of the *Martyrdom of Polycarp* suggests that in following the example of another believer one is said to be a disciple of that person (*Mart. Pol.* 22.2.1).

---

[34]Corwin, *St. Ignatius and Christianity in Antioch*, 227.

[35]E.g., Michael Atkinson, "Body and Discipleship," *Theology* 82 (1979): 279–87, who follows the highly influential article by Karl H. Rengstorf, "μαθητής," *TDNT* 4:415–61, esp. 460.

[36]Cf. Corwin, *St. Ignatius and Christianity in Antioch*, 227–37; H. H. Henrix, "Von der Nachahmung Gottes. Heiligkeit und Heiligsein im biblischen und jüdischen Denken," *Erbe und Auftrag* 65 (3, 1989): 177–87. While Henrix only briefly touches on Ignatius's attitude toward the Jewish heritage (pp. 186–87), the article is valuable for tracing the continuity of the imitation of God in the Jewish-Christian tradition.

Only one time does the New Testament speak of a believer having disciples (Ac 9:25: Saul's/Paul's disciples), but the theme of learning from and following the example of other believers is a thoroughly New Testament theme. The example often has to do with the way in which prior believers endured suffering. The writer to the Hebrews exhorts his readers to look back upon the Old Testament saints who suffered in faith and to follow Jesus' example of suffering (Heb 12:1–3), and Paul commends the Thessalonians, "For you, brothers, became imitators of God's churches in Judea, which are in Christ Jesus: You suffered from your own countrymen the same things those churches suffered from the Jews" (1Th 2:14).

Some have suggested that in his emphasis on imitation of Christ's suffering and martyrdom Ignatius is leaning toward a later church doctrine of "reenactment of Christ's passion." In later church doctrine a distinction was made between discipleship and imitation. Discipleship meant following after Christ, whereas imitation meant replicating Christlike qualities in order to attain sainthood. Following after Christ was seen as a category of faith and obedience that is stimulated by the grace of God, whereas imitation assumed the accomplishments of the dedicated person, the saint.[37] But the theme of imitation is not the same in Ignatius as is found in later church tradition. For Ignatius, imitation of Christ, even in suffering, was not a special saintliness. Rather, it was the calling of Christians in general.[38]

DISCIPLESHIP AS MARTYRDOM

While Ignatius's writings indicate that a person enters into and advances along the life of discipleship through conversion and Christian growth, he startles modern readers with language that seems to indicate that those approaching martyrdom experience discipleship in a unique manner. For example, Ignatius expresses an eagerness for "fighting with beasts at Rome, that by so doing I might be enabled to be a true disciple" (*Eph.* 1.2.4). As he considers

---

[37]See Schoedel, *Ignatius*, 30. Cf. Hans von Campenhousen, *Die Idee des Martyriums in der alten Kirche*, 2d ed. (Göttingen: Vandenhoeck & Ruprecht, 1964). This distinction is still seen in scholarly studies under the German technical terms *Nachfolge* (following after Christ) and *Nachahmung* (replicating Christlike qualities). E.g., cf. also Hans Dieter Betz, *Nachfolge und Nachahmung Jesu Christi im Neuen Testament*. BHT 37 (Tübingen: J. C. B. Mohr/Siebeck, 1967); Anselm Schulz, *Nachfolgen und Nachahmen: Studien über das Verhältnis der neutestamentlichen Jüngerschaft zur urchristlichen Vorbildethik*, SANT 6 (Munich: Kösel, 1962).

[38]Trakatellis, "'Ακολούθει μοι/Follow Me,'" 283, 285. For a discussion of "imitation" in the light of one of the most difficult passages of Ignatius's letters (*Rom.* 6.3.1), see Schoedel, *Ignatius*, 183–84.

imminent martyrdom by being devoured by wild beasts, he says, "Coax the wild beasts, that they may become my tomb and leave nothing of my body behind, lest I become a burden to someone once I have fallen asleep. Then I will truly be a disciple of Jesus Christ, when the world will no longer see my body" (*Rom.* 4.2.4). Ignatius exults in the spiritual benefit that martyrdom will finally bring: he will finally become a disciple.

> May I have the pleasure of wild beasts that have been prepared for me. I will even coax them to devour me promptly, not as they have done with some, whom they were too timid to touch. And if when I am willing and ready they are not, I will force them. Bear with me—I know what is best for me. Now at last I am beginning to be a disciple. (*Rom.* 5.3.2)

What are we to make of this kind of language related to discipleship? Some students of the early church have found here in Ignatius a two-level form of discipleship. That is, they suggest that, for Ignatius, it was only in experiencing martyrdom that he attained discipleship. If we take only one or two passages, this indeed might be the conclusion we reach. However, upon close examination of the seven passages in which Ignatius discusses discipleship and martyrdom, we can see that in each he gives vent to two thoroughly New Testament themes: (1) the Christian life is a developmental process that will be completed only at death and union with Christ, and (2) vindication of the reality of our Christian life and ministry is realized at death when we stand before the Lord. For example, as Ignatius contemplates the circumstances of his chains, which are producing great spiritual blessing, he gives us a unique perspective of his idea of discipleship: in facing imminent martyrdom he will finally "attain God" and in so doing finally become a disciple. "For I myself, though I am in chains and can comprehend heavenly things, the ranks of the angels and the hierarchy of principalities, things visible and invisible, for all this I am not yet a disciple. For we still lack many things, that we might not lack God" (*Trall.* 5.2.4). Schoedel comments, "Thus Augustine speaks of martyrs who 'endured so much to acquire God,' a future-oriented form of the theme of 'having' God (cf. Ign. *Magn.* 12).[39] A disciple in this sense is one who has attained spiritual fullness of God by being obedient to the point of death.

In a passage cited above, as Ignatius considers imminent martyrdom by being devoured by wild beasts, he says: "Coax the wild beasts, that they may become my tomb and leave nothing of my body behind, lest I become a burden to someone once I have fallen asleep. Then I will truly be a disciple of Jesus Christ, when the world will no

---

[39]Ibid., 145.

longer see my body" (Ign. *Rom.* 4.2.4). The disappearance of his body means that he will no longer be a burden to anyone (a remarkably Pauline theme), and it will also mark his complete transformation. He goes on: "If I suffer, I will be a freedman of Jesus Christ, and will rise up free in Him. In the meantime, as a prisoner I am learning to desire nothing" (*Rom.* 4.3.4). In passing from this world Ignatius realizes that he will finally attain true freedom, true perfection, which means true discipleship.[40]

A combination of the developmental and vindication aspect is clearly evident in a passage where Ignatius draws directly upon a Pauline statement: "I am fighting wild beasts from Syria to Rome, through land and sea, by night and day, bound to ten leopards— which is a company of soldiers—who when well treated become worse. By their mistreatment I become more of a disciple, but 'not for that reason I am justified'" (*Rom.* 5.1.4). Here Ignatius equates discipleship with justification and draws upon 1 Corinthians 4:4 to provide an illustrative principle. Ignatius sees his travel to Rome for martyrdom as a victory campaign against opposing forces. The Roman power is going down to defeat, but in a paradoxical way. Ignatius's victory will take the form of dying in the amphitheater and thus attaining God. His present sufferings are teaching him to become a disciple and are readying him for his justification. Citing Paul's words serves to emphasize the fact that Ignatius's justification is still future, the time when his perfection will be realized.[41] As Ignatius continues speaking of his imminent martyrdom, he exults in the spiritual benefit it will finally bring: he will finally become a disciple.

> May I have the pleasure of wild beasts that have been prepared for me. I will even coax them to devour me promptly, not as they have done with some, whom they were too timid to touch. And if when I am willing and ready they are not, I will force them. Bear with me—I know what is best for me. Now at last I am beginning to be a disciple. May nothing visible or invisible envy me, so that I may reach Jesus Christ. Fire and cross and battles with wild beasts, mutilation, mangling, wrenching of bones, the hacking of limbs, the crushing of my whole body, cruel tortures of the devil—let these come upon me, only let me reach Jesus Christ! (*Rom.* 5.3.1–3)

This is perhaps the most extreme statement in his letters, but it once again shows Ignatius's eagerness to undergo any suffering to attain

---

[40]Ibid., 176.
[41]Ibid., 179.

discipleship, which here means final attainment of being with Jesus Christ.

The same theme surfaces in Ignatius's letter to Polycarp. Since his church in Antioch is at peace as a result of the prayers of the Smyrnaeans and Polycarp, Ignatius is now free from anxiety. He can face his coming martyrdom with a heart that is free from the concerns of this world. Therefore, he covets their effective prayers for himself as well. For what does he want them to pray? ". . . that through suffering I reach God, that I may prove to be a disciple by means of your prayer" (*Pol.* 7.1.5). Schoedel comments, "The end of troubles in Antioch is evidently taken to indicate that Ignatius may expect his own troubles to be over; or more precisely, vindication of Ignatius in Antioch is taken to mean that the bishop may now have higher hopes of God's final approval."[42]

One other passage clarifies Ignatius's attitude toward discipleship in connection with martyrdom. When writing to the Ephesian believers, Ignatius gives strong admonitions based upon his authority as a bishop. However, he also points to the imperfection in his life, an imperfection that will be rectified only through growth as a disciple and through death. "I am not commanding you, as though I were somebody important. For even though I am in chains for the sake of the Name, I have not yet been perfected in Jesus Christ. For now I am only beginning to be a disciple, and I speak to you as my fellow-students. For I need to be trained by you in faith, instruction, endurance, and patience" (*Eph.* 3.1.1–3). Ignatius does not place himself above the Ephesian believers, even though he has the authority of a bishop. And he does not place himself above them because he is now "beginning to be a disciple." Discipleship does not place him in a higher category of sainthood. Rather, it simply shows that he is in process of actualizing his final goal of being with Christ after death. Indeed, these believers are his "fellow-learners."[43]

Therefore, martyrdom was seen by Ignatius as the time when he would attain final development of the discipleship process and when he would be fully vindicated as one who was a diligent and faithful servant of Jesus Christ. In that sense, true discipleship would be when he attained union with Christ through martyrdom. This desire did not deny the reality of present earthly discipleship, however. We saw above that Ignatius indicated elsewhere that a disciple is simply a Christian. What Ignatius shows us is that following Jesus into death

---

[42]Ibid., 278.

[43]Συνδιδασκαλίτης ("fellow-learners") is a *hapax legomenon* in Greek literature, most likely coined by Ignatius to indicate his unity with the church. See Schoedel, *Ignatius*, 48–49, n. 5.

brings the disciple into the final realization and proof of the reality of his or her relationship with Christ. In a powerful passage Ignatius contrasts those who are simply "Christian" in name with those who are "really Christians" and indicates that it is only in death that true Christians will prove the reality of their faith (*Magn.* 4.1.1).

> For just as there are two coinages, the one of God, the other of the world, and each has its own stamp impressed on it, so the unbelievers bear the stamp of this world, and the believers the stamp of God the Father in love through Jesus Christ, and unless we willingly choose to die through him in His passion, His life is not in us. (Ign. *Magn.* 5.1–2)

Willingness to be obedient, even unto death, was for Ignatius the proof that a person was a Christian, a true believer, a disciple.

IMPLICATIONS

The issue of martyrdom seems removed from our own cultural setting. How can we learn from these early believers who faced death so radically as a natural consequence of their true faith? In the past two millennia the church has taken both the biblical data and the teachings of the apostolic fathers to unwarranted extremes.

First, we can see that some later church fathers and even some modern Christian leaders misunderstood the radical commitment to discipleship displayed by Ignatius and others to be possible for only the spiritually elite within the church. Phillip Schaff notes that later church fathers referred to a special class of self-denying Christians (called *askētai*) who were held in high esteem by the church, who had special seats at worship and who "were considered the fairest ornaments of the church."[44] This later practice is often read back into earlier conceptions of discipleship. Origen "attached the notion of holiness to perfection and, therefore, to a certain group of Christians, a spiritual elite."[45] Throughout the Middle Ages this theme was echoed by monastic writers such as Bernard of Clairvaux (1091–1153), who looked on the monastic life as an imitation of the poverty, humility, and charity of the earthly Jesus.[46] But as we have noted, nowhere does Ignatius or the other apostolic fathers indicate that discipleship is an elitist conception. All Christians are disciples,

---

[44]Philip Schaff, *History of the Christian Church*, vol. 2 (Grand Rapids: Eerdmans, 1910), 388, 391. Some of the later Fathers who referred to the ἀσκηταί were Athenagoras, Tertullian, Origen, Eusebius, and Jerome, among others.

[45]John D. Zizioulas, "The Early Christian Community," in *Christian Spirituality—Origins to the Twelfth Century*, eds. Bernard McGinn and John Meyendorff (New York: Crossroad, 1985), 39.

[46]Avery Dulles, "Discipleship," *The Encyclopedia of Religion*, Mircea Eliade, ed. (New York: Macmillan, 1987), 4:363.

hence, the radical nature of discipleship displayed by Ignatius is a personal extension of his own Christian life. Schoedel says, "It is one-sided to find here [Ign. *Rom.* 6.3] decisive evidence that Ignatius has moved beyond the conception of following Christ in the New Testament and exalted the achievement of a special saintliness above the commitment to the Christian mission and its concern to illuminate the whole of human existence in light of the cross."[47] Although later Fathers would find in Ignatius a seedbed for elitist teaching, such was not the intention of Ignatius.

Second, we can see in a related way how some later church fathers misunderstood the apostolic fathers' attitude toward martyrdom to be an indication that the calling to suffering or martyrdom creates a special saintliness. Soon after Ignatius's and Polycarp's martyrdom, the influential church father Irenaeus suggested that martyrdom was the highest form of spirituality. Irenaeus spoke of "the true and perfect disciple of Christ as the one who is ready to go with him to the cross. True spirituality always involves some form of death. The ascetic and the martyr are for this reason the true spirituals of the church."[48] In the fourth century, Antony and the Desert Fathers saw the monastic and hermetical life as an "unbloody martyrdom" and thus as perfect discipleship.[49] Ignatius saw God's will for his life to include martyrdom, but this calling does not make him an elitist, and this calling is not for all others. As Cyril Richardson says, "Others may reach the divine through their own particular sufferings, which may not include martyrdom. The will of God may not be the same for all believers."[50] Ignatius appeared comfortable with a tension between discipleship as a present reality and as a future hope made perfect through martyrdom.

In our day we find many who go to these same extremes while misinterpreting the biblical data and the apostolic fathers. We can find in our own day those who speak in elitist terminology of disciples as a special category of committed Christians. We can also find those who speak of a special saintliness for those who suffer martyrdom.[51]

On the other hand, we can find many in our day who display a radical commitment to Christ in the most difficult circumstances, even those who suffer martyrdom on account of the Name, yet who

---

[47]Schoedel, *Ignatius*, 183.

[48]Zizioulas, "The Early Christian Community," 39.

[49]Dulles, "Discipleship," 363.

[50]Cyril Charles Richardson, *The Christianity of Ignatius of Antioch* (New York: Columbia, 1935), 24.

[51]Dulles, "Discipleship," 363. See our earlier discussion of various discipleship models in chap. 2.

see their actions as a natural extension of the Christian life. Many understand that their life of discipleship has included a challenge to count the cost of giving their comfort, their careers, their families, and their lives for the sake of the Name of Jesus. They have renounced all in counting the cost of becoming a disciple and of carrying out that life, and they see their calling as simply an extension of the Christian life. Recently I read a story that has driven home for me the fact that even in our day we must all count the cost of Jesus' call to follow him.

In Kabul, Afghanistan, during 1964, a fourteen-year-old boy, Zia Nodrat, enrolled in the NOOR Institute for the Blind. He already knew the whole Qur'an by heart. In Western terms that would be like a blind English speaker memorizing the complete New Testament in Greek, since Arabic was not Zia's mother tongue. While attending his classes in Braille in the Institute for the Blind, Zia also mastered English. He did this by listening and repeating what he heard on a transistor radio from Christian radio programs coming into his country. Finally, he shared with a few persons that he had received Jesus the Messiah as his personal Savior. They asked him if he realized that he could be killed for this, since the Islamic Law of Apostasy for anyone leaving Islam is death. Zia answered, "I have counted the cost and am willing to die for the Messiah, since he has already died on the cross for me." Zia went on to graduate from the Institute for the Blind. He then became the first blind student to attend and graduate from a sighted high school in Afghanistan. After that he graduated with a law degree from the University of Kabul and then graduated from Goethe Institute in Germany. Zia translated the New Testament from Iranian Persian into his own Afghan Dari dialect, which was published by the Pakistan Bible Society in Lahore. The third edition was published by Cambridge University Press in 1989.

Because of his faith in Christ, Zia faced regular persecution from the Muslim government of Afghanistan during the 1960s and 1970s and later by the communist government of the late 1970s. He was imprisoned by the communists in the early 1980s and was subjected to regular torture until his release in 1985. After his release from prison, Zia felt led by the Lord to travel with another blind man to Pakistan to minister among the refugee Afghans who had fled there. He started an Institute for the Blind in Pakistan.

On March 23, 1988, Zia was kidnapped by a fanatical Muslim group called Hisbe Islami ("the Party of Islam"). He was accused of being a CIA agent because he knew English, a KGB spy because he knew Russian, and an apostate from Islam because he was a Christian. Zia was beaten for hours with rods. A sighted person can brace and flinch when the blow comes. But a blind person cannot see the club coming and thus gets the full force, like the torture the Lord Jesus Christ experienced when he was blindfolded and then struck (Lk 22:64). Zia's wife and three daughters were with him when he was kidnapped. Soon after, his wife gave birth to a beautiful boy who looks much like his father. No one knows whether Zia ever heard that he had a son.

The latest word, though not absolutely certain, is that Hisbe Islami murdered Zia. Before he was kidnapped, he had told a friend that if this party ever captured him they would kill him. This same party caught two Pakistani Christians taking relief items to needy Afghans and tortured them. Before releasing them, one of the captors said, "We are not going to kill you the way we killed Zia Nodrat." In addition, an Afghan news reporter on the northwest frontier of Pakistan claims to have evidence that Hisbe Islami murdered Zia in a cruel way.[52]

In this dramatic story of Zia Nodrat we can see that the call to martyrdom Ignatius faced is a startling reality even in our day. In fact, some statisticians reckon that millions of people have been martyred for their faith in Christ in the twentieth century.[53]

I could easily feel guilty in the face of the story of Zia and the statistics of these martyrs around the world. Rather, I want to be challenged. I happen to have been called to be a disciple in completely different circumstances—circumstances that have not occasioned much physical suffering and certainly not martyrdom. Yet I know that I am not any less a disciple. Neither in biblical teaching nor in the apostolic fathers is discipleship earned through martyrdom. Discipleship is the Christian life, and each of us has been called to different forms of that life. As I read of such stories of sacrifice, suffering, and martyrdom in our own day, as I read of the early Fathers like Ignatius and Polycarp, as I read of the deaths of believers in Scripture, I am challenged to recognize that I am nonetheless a disciple of Jesus Christ and that I must daily count the cost and bear the cross that Christ has called me to carry. In so doing I seek first the kingdom of God and His righteousness. Such is the essence of discipleship for all believers.

In those days of terrible persecution by the Roman Empire, the theme of following the example of Christ in suffering was a necessary

---

[52]Excerpted from a pamphlet called *The Story of Zia Nodrat* (Toronto: Fellowship of Faith). I first became acquainted with the story of this remarkable person through a powerful chapel message by Prof. J. Christy Wilson at Talbot School of Theology in March 1991.

[53]David B. Barrett and Todd M. Johnson, *Our Globe and How to Reach It: Seeing the World Evangelized by* A.D. *2000 and Beyond*, Globe Evangelization Movement: The A.D. 2000 Series (Birmingham, Ala.: New Hope, 1990), 18, 44, 48.

stimulus to the faith of all those in that early, harried church. The *Martyrdom of Polycarp* concludes with an exhortation that is directed toward all the "brothers" and sounds a note that is reminiscent of the diverse expressions of discipleship found in the New Testament: "We bid you farewell, brothers, as you walk by the word of Jesus Christ which is in accord with the gospel; with whom be glory to God for the salvation of the holy elect; just as the blessed Polycarp was martyred, in whose footsteps may we also be found in the kingdom of Jesus Christ" (22).

I pray that Christ's example in suffering and the example of all the disciples through the years will be a stimulus to our faith as well.

Following up:

1. What suffering have you experienced in your life? How has it helped you to grow as a Christian? How would you advise others to handle similar kinds of suffering?
2. What should we do when various kinds of difficulties come our way? Should we avoid them, should we eagerly encounter them, or what? Explain how your answer relates to realistic Christian living.

PART VI

TOWARD THE THIRD
MILLENNIUM

Our journey through the world of discipleship is almost at an end. We first looked at various forms of discipleship that existed in the Old Testament world of ancient Israel, in the Greco-Roman world, and in first-century Judaism. We then followed Jesus through his ministry, seeing what he was doing in his unique form of discipleship. Then we looked through the eyes of each Evangelist, seeing from their own vantage point what discipleship meant to them. After that we saw how the concept of discipleship was carried out in the early church once the Master, Jesus Christ, had ascended to the Father. We saw this from the perspective of the narrative of the book of Acts as well as from the perspective of the teachings of the Epistles and Revelation. We also saw how the concept of discipleship was understood by the persecuted church after the apostles had passed from the earthly scene.

Only one more trail needs to be explored—the trail that leads to our own world. Jesus' call to men and women to follow him occurred nearly two thousand years ago. What does following the Master mean now as we face the third millennium of the Christian era? The intention of this study has been to attempt to cross the barrier of time, culture, and technology to hear Jesus' call as did those men and women so long ago. In this final section we will explore some of the expectations and implications of following the Master toward the third millennium of the Christian era. We will also see how some of the principles of this study have been carried out in a real life situation.

Now that the journey of this study is almost at an end, I pray that our journey of following the Master in this life has been enriched and will be fruitful until he returns!

17

Jesus' Discipleship Expectations

Getting focused:

1. What does Jesus expect of you as his disciple? What do others—your church, your family, your school—expect of you as a disciple of Jesus? What do you expect of yourself?
2. How does discipleship relate to the Christian life? What place does discipleship have in the local church?
3. Is it easier or harder to grow as Jesus' disciple in your family than in the church or in a parachurch organization? Explain.

Expectations held up by ourselves, by others, and by God of what we are to be, how we are to act, and what we are to look like can be incentives toward growth, can provide goals toward which to work, and can be guidelines for proper conduct. But expectations can also be a cloud of pressure forcing us to conform, a straitjacket of regulations stifling creativity and freedom, or a burden of guilt producing fear that we may step out of line. Jesus came calling men and women to a wonderful adventure called discipleship. It is an adventure because none of us has ever passed this way before. It is new to each of us every day of our lives. Each time we take another turn in the path of life, new vistas of opportunity and challenge await us. Jesus has high expectations for each of us, indeed, too high for any of us to attain. But at the same time as he holds up those expectations, he calls us to follow him where we have never been before, which requires creativity, freedom, and fearlessness.

Jesus' expectations are not designed to be burdens that would hinder our trek on the path of discipleship. But we make burdens of various kinds of expectations. We can settle into comfortable ways of walking which are safe and predictable because we have mastered them, and then we can place them on other people, expecting them to walk as we walk. We can adopt expectations that are not designed for us, or at least not for this place on the path, and they can hinder our movement. We can adopt expectations of other masters who cause us to think that Jesus wants them for us when in reality he may not.

In a recent premarital counseling session with a delightful young couple, I asked, "Are you the man or woman of God your future spouse needs?" I could see both of them struggling with that question because of their perceptions of what was expected in order to be called a man or woman of God. The young lady almost broke into tears because she had such high expectations that she could not bring herself to say that she had even partially arrived. She understood that perfection was not required, but she labored under the burden of expectations nonetheless.

Her situation reminds me of the young sailor I mentioned in an earlier chapter. You will remember that he was the sincere young man whose perceptions of discipleship were such that he wrung his hands and cried out, "When will I finally be a disciple of Jesus? What else do I have to do? I want to be one so badly, but I just don't know what else to do!"[1] The young sailor labored under a certain model of discipleship that suggested that it was only when he became fully committed and then performed certain Christian activities that he could say that he had truly followed Jesus' call to follow him.

Both of these young people were sincere about following Jesus. We sympathize with them because they were struggling with unrealistic perceptions of God's calling on their lives. They felt guilty about not performing on a higher level. On the other hand, we could look at other young people (and older as well) who are complacent about their Christian lives. They seem content with mediocrity or with compromise. They never seem to get fired up about the Christian life. They do not catch the excitement of what it means to walk with Jesus every day.

Interestingly enough, both kinds of people—those who struggle with perfectionism and those who are complacent—may be influenced by faulty perceptions of discipleship expectations. An issue here is "institutionalism." When expectations become solidified as legalistic requirements, or when they stifle individuality in our walk with God, or when they become simply a program we impose on people, or when they become agents of manipulation to get people to perform as we want them to perform, institutionalism begins and discipleship is repressed. We shall return to the issue of

---

[1]See chap. 2.

institutionalism in the next chapter, but its relationship to faulty expectations is crucial.

Faulty perceptions of Jesus' discipleship expectations for us may have, in part, led to some of the differences of the discipleship models we discussed earlier. Each of the models is partially correct, because each is built on select passages of Scripture and certain stages of the historical development of the discipleship concept. However, some of the models are actually incorrect at points. I have tried to point out those errors as we have looked at the overall development of biblical discipleship. I will not rehearse all of the issues again here. However, I do need to point out that the errors we perpetuate in our forms of discipleship can lead to the problems that the people of the church and parachurch groups experience. For example, discipleship can be seen as such a lofty ideal that it can be understood to be only for the elite. Or else it can be understood as only for those who are actively performing Christian duties or disciplines or only for those who are involved in professional ministry. We can even imply that discipleship is optional—that is, it is something to be entered into only when one is ready to be truly committed to Christ.

DEFINITIONS, AGAIN!

This is where clearer definitions of the terms *disciple* and *discipleship* are vitally important. Accurate definitions hold up appropriate expectations of what God desires for us. We can see signs that clearer definitions of what it means to be a disciple of Jesus are beginning to be sought in several diverse quarters.

Some parachurch organizations that used "discipleship" as a focal point for specialized training are reevaluating their definitions because they recognize that they may have used terminology imprecisely. Their methodologies are sound and fruitful, but incorrect use of terminology has resulted in inappropriate expectations of the Christian life.

Some churches that have used *disciple/discipleship* as a byword for advanced training or as a title for clergy are reevaluating their doctrines in the light of Scripture. For example, the Roman Catholic Church has sometimes drawn a false dichotomy between laity and clergy on the basis of discipleship terminology. However, the Second Vatican Council (1962–65) introduced the vocabulary of discipleship into official Roman Catholicism. In twenty-seven cases, council documents use the term *disciple* as a virtual synonym for *Christian*. "In his first encyclical, *Redemptor hominis* (1979), John Paul II described the church as the 'community of disciples' in which Christ says to each and every member, 'Follow me' (no. 21)."[2] If the Roman Catholic Church follows up on that encyclical, the implications may be profound for their church doctrine.

Some Christian academic institutions are recognizing that, in preparing young men and women for ministry, much more than just intellectual preparation is required. The disciple is the whole person, and unless the intellectual aspect of the person is integrated fully with the emotional, psychological, physical, and spiritual aspects, we create one-dimensional ministers. This is a central challenge for Christian academic institutions as we move into the third millennium of the Christian era.

Earlier I stated my definition of a disciple of Jesus Christ: one who has come to Jesus for eternal life, has claimed him as Savior and God, and has embarked upon the life of following him. Discipleship and discipling imply the process of becoming like Jesus Christ. To be a disciple of Jesus Christ means living a fully human life in this world in union with Jesus Christ and growing in conformity to his image. In our discussion of discipleship in the early church of Acts, we discovered two important components of biblical discipleship. On the one hand, discipleship consists of being molded by the apostolic teaching, being empowered by an experience with the living God, and being a participant in a community of disciples. On the other hand, it involves both a way to walk and a mission to fulfill.[3]

These definitions offer an approximation of what Jesus intended in his Great Commission. As such, this delineates Jesus' expectations for his disciples.

IMPLICATIONS

We have considered implications of our study in each chapter. In this chapter, I would like to suggest a few broad implications of our overall study.

Discipleship Is the Christian Life

We have seen that discipleship can be understood in a narrow sense to speak of specific master-disciple relationships. We examined those relationships as they appeared in the ancient world and particularly as they appeared in the world of the New Testament.

---

[2]Avery Dulles, "Discipleship," *The Encyclopedia of Religion*, ed. Mircea Eliade (New York: Macmillan, 1987), 4:363.

[3]Cf. Charles H. Talbert, "Discipleship in Luke-Acts," in *Discipleship in the New Testament*, ed. Fernando F. Segovia (Philadelphia: Fortress, 1985), 62.

However, New Testament discipleship is also understood in a broader sense to speak of Christian life in general—what such a way of life requires, implies, and entails.[4] Since discipleship implies a process of growth, scholars suggest that in its broadest sense discipleship is the metaphor most descriptive of the doctrine of "progressive sanctification."[5]

This is an important implication because it emphasizes that our entire life is to be brought into the discipleship process. If we do not bring our entire life into the discipleship process, we run the danger of compartmentalizing and/or dichotomizing our Christian lives. We can see many examples of the way in which the Christian life is compartmentalized and dichotomized. For example, our spiritual life is often treated separately from our careers or intellectual life. Many people have had successful careers in the business world and in their churches, but they are treated separately. Many older men and women I have spoken with have been active leaders in their churches, yet they have never learned how to intelligently and compassionately share their faith in their work places. Another example is young people who are dating. They often have difficulty knowing how to have a dating relationship that combines both the spiritual and romantic domains. I once heard a lady give a message in which she suggested that couples should not have intense times of prayer on dates because it could lead to inappropriate physical intimacy. Her intentions are good, and I think I understand what she means, but an underlying dichotomy between the spiritual on the one hand and the relational, physical, and emotional makeup of the dating relationship on the other hand, was created in the minds of several couples I spoke to afterward.

Earlier we discussed one difficult discipleship passage from Luke's gospel, in which an expert in the law stood up to test Jesus.

"Teacher," he asked, "what must I do to inherit eternal life?"

---

[4]Fernando F. Segovia, "Introduction: Call and Discipleship—Toward a Re-examination of the Shape and Character of Christian Existence in the New Testament," in *Discipleship in the New Testament*, ed. Segovia, 2.

[5]E.g., Everett Harrison draws a distinction between "spiritual life," "ethical life," and "social life," in his discussion of the "Christian life." However, his emphasis upon discipleship crosses over all those boundaries and may be seen as the unifying title of the Christian life. Cf. Everett F. Harrison, *The Apostolic Church* (Grand Rapids: Eerdmans, 1985), 140–49. Richard Calenberg concludes that "every believer at the point of exercising saving faith becomes a disciple of Jesus in a general sense." He then goes on to emphasize that not every believer is at every moment of the Christian life actively committed to the process of discipleship. He thereby makes discipleship equivalent to "progressive sanctification." Cf. Richard D. Calenberg, "The New Testament Doctrine of Discipleship" (unpublished Th.D. diss., Grace Theological Seminary, 1981), 245–46.

"What is written in the Law?" he replied. "How do you read it?"

He answered, " 'Love the Lord your God with all your heart and with all your soul and with all your strength and with all your mind'; and, 'Love your neighbor as yourself.' "

"You have answered correctly," Jesus replied. "Do this and you will live." (Lk 10:25–28)

Entrance to discipleship, eternal life, involves love for God and neighbor with all our heart, soul, strength, and mind. Growth in discipleship is no less all-encompassing.

John Calvin was one of the great intellectual giants of the church. But in his classic little treatise of the Christian life, Calvin assumed the whole Christian life to be the right subject of discipleship.

> The gospel is not a doctrine of the tongue, but of life. It cannot be grasped by reason and memory only, but it is fully understood when it possesses the whole soul, and penetrates to the inner recesses of the heart. Let nominal Christians cease from insulting God by boasting themselves to be what they are not, and let them show themselves disciples not unworthy of Christ, their Master. We must assign first place to the knowledge of our religion, for that is the beginning of salvation. But our religion will be unprofitable, if it does not change our heart, pervade our manners, and transform us into new creatures.[6]

When we point to discipleship as the Christian life, we address the whole person in relationship to Jesus Christ.

Discipleship Is a Process

We should also go one step further and suggest that discipleship is a process. If we view discipleship as the Christian life, we will naturally assume that it is a lifelong process. Too often we speak of a discipleship "program" that we have taken or initiated. While very few of the leaders of these programs suggest that once we have gone through their series we are now a finished product, they seldom show how the program fits with the ongoing process of one's life.

As Calvin suggested, we must not just develop our intellect or memory. We must develop as well-rounded people. And we must see this as a process that continues over the entire length of one's life. Discipleship is not simply a book or set of tapes that one goes through to reach maturity. The process certainly may include a curriculum; however, discipleship is much more process oriented.

---

[6]John Calvin, *Golden Booklet of the True Christian Life,* reprint (Grand Rapids: Baker, 1952), 17. The *Golden Booklet* was originally published as a part of the *Institutes,* under the title "On the Life of the True Christian Man," or in later editions under the title "On the Christian Life."

I am impressed increasingly by the central place the home plays in this process. Parenting, in particular, has taught me the most about discipleship being addressed to the whole person. One of the most natural places to develop disciples of Jesus is in the home. Paul repeatedly emphasizes the need for the leaders of the church to have their family relationships in order (e.g., 1Ti 3:4–5, 12; Tit 1:6–7). The training ground for leadership in the church is leadership at home. Hence, the beginning point of discipleship is what we are doing with our children. We are to lead them toward Jesus, introduce them to Jesus, and prepare them for life with Jesus after they leave home. While general principles of child rearing can be applied to every child, each child is unique and needs special attention in individualized growth. As children grow through the various stages of life, they have different needs and should be directed differently. As they approach maturity, they gain both independence and responsibility. The measure of their maturity is often found in how they balance both. As they continue on into adulthood, they pass on to their children the principles learned in their own process.

Those very same principles are at the heart of what discipling in the church is all about. This period of time can be the most productive for training future disciplers in the church.

We need to be very careful to balance the biological family discipleship process with the spiritual family discipleship process. Some of the most productive people in the church will be those individuals who have learned about the process of discipleship in the home. For those who have not learned the process through a Christian home setting (possibly through the lack of Christian parents), the family of God provides that which is lacking. Disciples are indeed the family of God (cf. Mt 12:46–50). Both of God's institutions, the family and the church, have been ordained for the role of providing guidance through the process of discipleship.

Discipleship Is the Ministry of the Church

Building upon the first two implications, I would like to suggest that discipleship is the ministry of the church. We often look at discipleship as one particular program of the church. It may well be that this is where some of the discipleship models we looked at earlier came into existence. They developed from looking at only limited aspects of biblical teaching on discipleship, and they ended up developing a program that accentuated that one segment of biblical teaching. It is not as though they are wrong; they are simply too narrowly focused, and, for some, even reductionistic. The danger here is that our churches and parachurch organizations can become one-dimensional, involved in training one-dimensional people.

Candidates for "discipleship training" in many churches are enrolled in a variety of programs, including spiritual disciplines, mentoring, intensive Bible study, small groups, leadership development, evangelism, commitment development, social activism, church growth, spiritual gifts, and missionary activity. The title *discipleship* is attached to the training, and the people in the church gain the impression that this one area is primarily what discipleship is all about.

These training programs are good. And I agree that they can all be referred to as "discipleship." However, I believe that we need to move toward a more integrative understanding. I suggest that we need to be even broader when conceiving of discipleship training. If discipleship is the Christian life, and if discipleship is a process, then the church needs to address itself to all areas in the process of the Christian's life.

Some of us are called to specific areas of ministry and service not intended for all disciples, which means that there should be different forms of discipleship training. In one sense, the goal of the church is to help all believers grow as disciples. This is the basic meaning of discipleship. In another sense, even as Jesus called aside certain people for specific responsibilities and gave them the necessary training, we should be doing the same. Any preparation, whether it is for Sunday school teachers, elders, or even pastors, should be considered as being precise forms of discipleship training.

However, in the broadest sense, if we are to raise healthy disciples in our churches, we must begin to understand and to develop men and women who are in the process of growth as disciples in every area of life: secular and sacred, family and church, spiritual and material, intellectual and emotional.

FOLLOWING THE MASTER INTO LIFE

I love the journey of life. And when all is finished, I would like to be remembered, not as a teacher or as a scholar or even as a husband or father, as important as all of those are to me, but rather as a disciple of the Master, Jesus Christ. To be remembered as a disciple of Jesus means that people remember me for living life to the full as I follow Jesus into every area of life into which he leads me. This in turn means that I am the best husband and father, teacher or scholar, when I have my eyes fixed on Jesus and am developing as his disciple.

Although some of us may have become weary of talk about discipleship in the past several years, we can never really talk about it too much, because it was through the discipleship relationship that Jesus designed to draw us into the most intimate fellowship with himself. We should, therefore, pursue even more vigorously a clear understanding of what it means to be a disciple.

But we should not in any way stop there. Discipleship was intended to be lived, not simply studied. One of my graduate students came into my office the other day and asked, "Dr. Wilkins, are you going to include a practical program of discipleship in your book?" What a leading question! I said, "Todd, I don't really have a program!" But then, intriguingly, he said, "Why don't you just try to tell them how you live it out?" In the next chapter, our final chapter, I will attempt to take Todd's advice. There are literally hundreds of books and tapes and seminars that teach discipleship programs. I have dozens of them sitting on the shelves around me as I write. Some of them are quite simple and straightforward. Others are so complex that they could keep you occupied until the Lord returns! Some are broadly based; others are quite narrowly focused. Although I have been involved in "discipleship" ministries for most of my Christian life, I do not have a program to give you. Instead, in the last chapter I will try to give you an idea of what I am doing in my own life and ministries right now to develop as a disciple.

My purpose in this book was to give you, fellow disciples of Jesus Christ, a more complete understanding of the historical and biblical data that surrounds the concept of discipleship. I continue to pray for you, as I promised I would in the first chapter, that this study will enrich your understanding of God's Word and his purposes in your life.

Following up:

1. What were your expectations of what it meant to be a disciple prior to reading this book? How have they changed? How have they remained the same?
2. Are there areas of your life that you have not considered to be in the realm of concern for discipleship? Explain. What areas of your life do you believe have been affected most by discipleship growth?
3. What would your church or ministry be like if all involved lived out the message that the expectations of discipleship found in the Gospels are expectations for all Christians, not just for a few committed ones? What can you do to help bring this about?

18

Walking with the Master in Your World

Getting focused:

1. What impressions come to mind when you think of a surfer? Is it possible for a surfer to be a disciple of Jesus? Explain.
2. After John the Baptist died, why did his disciples not all become disciples of Jesus?
3. Can there be a difference between the church as an "institution" and the church as a group of disciples of Jesus? What is that difference?
4. Why do people have difficulties fitting into churches?

Balancing expectations with the adventure of discipleship is tricky business. I have found that striving for that balance is absolutely essential in our daily lives and in our outreach to the world, because following Jesus into the world means that we will go places others have not gone and be with people who have no idea of the kinds of expectations we carry. Walking with Jesus in the world of surfing is an excellent example.[1]

Surfing is a compelling force in our family, not only because we live in a beach town and not only because it is such a wonderful sport, but also because my wife and I have found that it is a challenging avenue of ministry to our community.

This became especially evident when we entered into the teen years with our older daughter. We love these years with our children, but as parents we do not enter them alone. Since friends are one of the most important elements of the teenager's life, we knew that one

---

[1]This chapter first appeared in somewhat different form in an article for *Discipleship Journal.* Cf. Michael J. Wilkins, "Surfers and Other Disciples," *Discipleship Journal*, no. 62, vol. 11 (March/April 1991), 8–14.

way of staying in touch with our teenager was to become involved with her friends. Thus started some memorable times in our lives.

One summer I took between six and fifteen junior high and high school kids, both boys and girls, surfing every Tuesday morning. They began calling themselves the "Tuesday Tubes" group. I would pick them up at 6:30 in the morning and we would surf spots near towns called "T-Street," "Trestles," or "Churches." We often would walk for about a mile down a steep, winding trail to get to our own favorite isolated surf spot called "Trails." After that early morning surf session we would all go out for breakfast at Luv Burger and get the pancake and eggs special.

My wife was called "Mom" by most of the kids on the block. I could hardly ever come home from work without finding a half-dozen surfboards and wetsuits all over and that many kids in the kitchen getting a snack.

We had a wonderful time with those kids and also a wonderful ministry! Not one of them went to church. Nearly all of them came from broken homes, often single-parent homes, and some of them had never met either their mom or their dad. What incredible needs were to be found within this group of kids! We got most of them going to the youth group at church, and before long all of them, except maybe one or two, made commitments to Christ. My wife and I developed a discipleship relationship with these kids. What a wonderful opportunity to love them, to provide a touch of a home life that some of them had never known, to introduce them to the love of Jesus.

But the minute I mention that word—*discipleship*—is when the issue becomes complex. For the most part, each of us have heard the word *disciple* and have an image of what a disciple is to be like. We have an idea of what a true disciple should be, what he or she should act like, what his or her lifestyle should be. And that is exactly the issue with which my wife and I were presented. What do we want these young surfers to be like? Should they be like the brand of disciple that our church or organization or Christian school turns out? What kind of a disciple do we want them to look like? One of the most convicting passages of all with respect to this issue is Luke 6:40, where our Lord indicates that a disciple, when he is fully trained, will be *like his teacher*. Do we want these wonderfully moldable young surfers to look just like us? That's scary!

These are important questions, because each of us, if we are truly obedient to the Great Commission, will have our own little group of "surfers" whom the Lord is turning into disciples right before our eyes. It is that group within your church or parachurch organization or in your neighborhood whom God has given you. And our challenge is to ask ourselves, "What kind of disciples will we forge these young lives into?"

The Gospels are the primary place to find the answer to that question, but we are immediately struck with the intriguing phenomenon raised in our study of discipleship in the ancient world. Although we all have heard of Jesus' twelve disciples, we should be aware that when Jesus came to earth in the first century several other types of individuals were called "disciples." The term *disciple* was used generally to designate a follower who was committed to a recognized leader or teacher. Some of the greatest hindrances to following Jesus in the first century were the expectations people carried when they heard Jesus' message or which they brought into their relationship with him. Those expectations were a result of the other types of disciples they saw in existence or which they were themselves before they became Jesus' disciples. One of the commonly recognized points of conflict Jesus had with Judaism was institutionalism. Jesus rebuked the Pharisees for transgressing the commandments of God for the sake of their traditions (Mt 15:3). Hierarchical ambition and recognition of place within the scribal and pharisaical organizations was seen to suppress the working of the kingdom of God and was denounced as hypocritical (Mt 23).

In this chapter we will put to work what we have studied to this point. We will look at the four particular types of disciples found in the gospel record and view them from the standpoint of their expectations and the institution in which they found themselves when Jesus came on the scene. Most importantly, what was Jesus' evaluation of them as recorded in the Gospels? When we understand the dynamics of expectations and institutionalism, we can be that much clearer about our task of making disciples of those to whom God has called us to minister.

DISCIPLES OF MASTERS OTHER THAN JESUS

We saw in our earlier study of discipleship in first-century Judaism that there were a variety of types of disciples who were active in Israel when Jesus began his earthly ministry. How should they have responded to Jesus?

Disciples of Moses—*Devoted Traditionalists*

The Jews who questioned the parents of the man born blind (Jn 9:18ff.) attempted to scorn the man by saying that, although *he* was a disciple of Jesus, *they* were "disciples of Moses" (v. 28). I refer to this type of disciple as "devoted traditionalists." They focused on their privilege to have been born Jews who had a special relation to God through Moses (cf. v. 29). Any true Jew would have called himself a "disciple of Moses" in this sense, regardless of any secondary commitments to other groups in Israel, because God had specially chosen the Jews as his people to be a witness to the world. But we see in this passage that these Jews were so focused on their privileged position that they missed the witness that the Law of Moses was to have to Jesus.

This is the danger of those I call "church kids," those who have been privileged to grow up in a Christian home, who believe that somehow they are all right just because they grew up going to church and believing the right things. Church kids face a great danger because spiritual things can be so familiar to them that Jesus is never real to them. It is what some refer to as the difference between "environmental Christianity" and true discipleship.

But this can also be the danger of those who have been in the church so long that "their way" of doing things is the right way. At times we can be so focused on the way things have been done that we are not attuned to what God is doing right now. Both of these attitudes can contribute to what used to be called the "generation gap."

Disciples of the Pharisees—*Academic Religionists*

The "disciples of the Pharisees" (Mt 22:15–16; Mk 2:18) were adherents of the Pharisaic party, possibly belonging to one of the academic institutions. The Pharisees centered their activities on study and strict application of the Old Testament, developing a complex system of oral interpretations of the law.

These "disciples" were supremely dedicated people, but I refer to them as "academic religionists," the precursors of the later rabbinical school tradition. The Pharisees had a tendency to do the right things according to their interpretations without having their hearts rightly motivated (Mt 15:7–9). Jesus' denunciations of certain Pharisees are among the most scathing in Scripture (e.g., 5:20; 23:1–39). Recognizing the evil intentions of the "disciples of the Pharisees" who had been sent to trap him, Jesus called them "hypocrites" (22:15–18).

Such is the idea that many today have of what it means to be a disciple of Jesus. There are two dangers here. One danger is found in more liberally oriented churches. One can get the idea in some of these churches that if we know certain truths and live them out (e.g., the Ten Commandments, the Sermon on the Mount, the Golden Rule) religiously that we somehow "earn" salvation. Today there is a widespread belief that we become right with God by being good, by doing the right things. This is to fall into the trap of legalism, against which both Jesus and Paul preached.

The other danger is found in evangelical Bible churches, para-church groups, and schools. Here the emphasis is on study. The essence of discipleship is studying the Bible. It is an overintellectualizing of the Christian life, which often brings with it an attitude of arrogance and superiority. The "cloistered" academic life is the highest life. I once had a student tell me that his ideal of the Christian life was when he would be able to study and pray for eight to ten hours every day. That is not discipleship; that is ascetic monasticism. Jesus brought us to himself to walk with him in the world with the good news of salvation.

Disciples of John the Baptist—*Members of a Movement*

The disciples of John (Mk 2:18; Jn 1:35) were courageous men and women who had left the status quo of institutional Judaism to follow the prophet John the Baptist. I refer to this type of disciple as "members of a movement." They were attached more to the movement of God through the prophet than to ritual practices or traditions.

These disciples are a complex group. From them came the first followers of Jesus (Jn 1:35ff.). Some of John's disciples remained in contact with Jesus during his ministry in Galilee (Mt 14:12). Yet on at least one occasion they joined forces with the disciples of the Pharisees to question the practices of Jesus and his disciples (Mk 2:18–22).

I mentioned earlier that in the early 1970s my wife and I were a part of what was called then the Jesus Movement. It was a wonderful time, where God moved among the "hippies," and we were called to follow Jesus. We had our own songs and forms of worship and styles of relationships. But the tragedy was that for many it was just another high. I remember a song called "Take Another Hit of Jesus" that came out not long after I became a Christian. When the excitement wore off, many went looking for another high. Of the fifty-plus of our really close friends in the movement, my wife and I know of only a handful who are walking with Jesus today.

Apparently some of John the Baptist's disciples were so committed to him that they missed the true significance of Jesus' identity and missed becoming a disciple of Jesus. They were more committed to the movement than to God's revelation through Jesus.

Disciples of Jesus Who Left Him—*Dedicated Revolutionists*

In John 6:60–66 we find what may be the most tragic disciples of all. During the beginning stages of Jesus' ministry a large group of "disciples" attached themselves to him. Some, apparently thinking that Jesus was merely a revolutionary prophet, left him when he disappointed their expectations. I refer to this type of disciple as "dedicated revolutionists." They seemed to be looking for a leader to overthrow the Romans and to restore the rule to Israel. Many of them left homes and jobs to follow Jesus; some were even ready to die for their cause. This attitude is radical on the surface, but when we look deeper we see people who wanted God to conform to their way of thinking. They were willing to be disciples, but on their terms and according to their expectations. When Jesus did not do things their way, they left him.

THE DANGERS OF INSTITUTIONALISM

The tragedy is that each of these types of disciples were involved with various religious practices that *should* have prepared the way for them to become followers of Jesus. Remember that for the Jews in the Old Testament all discipleship relations were supposed to lead to discipleship to God alone. Now that God had come to earth in Jesus, the true disciple was to focus on him alone. The true disciple was to know Jesus so well, to follow him so closely, that the ultimate goal was to be conformed to his image (cf. Ro 8:28–29). But, instead, they missed the One for whom they were waiting, primarily because their religious practices had become so important that they overlooked the appearance of God among them. These groups continued to exist even after Jesus' ascension, and their rituals and traditions became their primary focus of practice.[2]

This points to one of the great dangers of any kind of discipleship program: focusing so much on the *practices* of discipleship that we lose sight of the *goal*. We see in these disciples what I refer to as the "dangers of institutionalism."

Institutions are designed to promote individuals, to minister to individuals so that the individuals are equipped to handle life on their own. Institutions are a means to an end, and the end is a person who is equipped to walk with God through life. But what often

---

[2]For a valuable study of the similarities and dissimilarities of the Jesus movement and these other groups within Israel, see Max Wilcox, "Jesus in the Light of His Jewish Environment," *Aufstieg und Niedergang der Römischen Welt*, 2, 25, 1, ed. H. Temporini and W. Haase (Berlin: Walter de Gruyter, 1982), 131–95.

happens is that our institutions become so important to that goal that sometimes we turn things around and our institutions become more important than the individual, and the individual is then made to serve the institution.[3] In this case the institution becomes the end, and the individual is the means to the end of serving the institution.

We suggested in the last chapter that when expectations become solidified as legalistic requirements, or when they stifle individuality in our walk with God, or when they become simply a program we impose on people, or when they become agents of manipulation to get people to perform as we want them to perform, institutionalism begins and discipleship is repressed.

Think of the institution you are in. Whether it is a church, a parachurch organization, a new movement, or a little discipleship group like my wife and I have had with teenagers, we need to ask ourselves some tough questions.

1. Are we making disciples *of our institutions,* or are our institutions making *disciples of Jesus?*
2. Are our disciples proficient at *programs* or at living a radical *relationship* with Jesus?
3. Does our attachment to our institutions isolate us from the world or equip us for changing the world?
4. Are people focusing on *us* because of the importance of our programs, or are we—and our programs—the "means to the end" so that people see *Jesus* more clearly?

It is important for modern disciples of Jesus to exam our practices to see how "institutional" we are becoming. The tendency toward institutionalism can stifle true discipleship. Institutions are not bad per se as long as we realize the end for which they are designed.

Jesus established the church as his functioning body on the earth in his absence. The church is designed to draw people into a loving fellowship with the Lord Jesus Christ and his people. The church can be seen as an institution created by God to promote his purposes on the earth. But it is possible for our churches or organizations to fall into the trap of cold, religious institutionalism, where the church is the end instead of the means, if we do not heed the dangers of institutionalism.

---

[3]Recently sociological theory applied to New Testament exegesis has explored the area of "institutionalism." It has much to offer us by way of simply helping us understand the dynamics of institutions. Once we understand common dynamics of institutions generally, we can compare those generalizations with Jesus' teaching to see what we are doing that differs from what he wants for discipleship in his church. We will not so much focus on the technical, sociological definition of institutionalism, but upon the entrenchment of expectations.

PREVENTING INSTITUTIONALISM
THROUGH BALANCED DISCIPLESHIP

What is the solution? How can we prevent institutionalism? I suggest two key ingredients: Jesus' example and balance. Jesus' example of making disciples in his earthly ministry is the model for us to follow as we fulfill his commission to "make disciples of all nations" (Mt 28:18–20). The early church made the change to the new day of the risen Christ but continued to follow Jesus as Master. In addition, we must be balanced as we follow Jesus' example. If we go too far in trying to avoid institutionalism, we can end up missing out on the profitable methods and practices that institutions have to offer. On the other hand, if we go too far in employing the methods of any particular institution, we may end up creating disciples of that institution instead of disciples of Jesus.

My wife and I have experienced times of both joy and discouragement with our wonderful young surfer friends. We have made mistakes, but the Lord continues to encourage us to follow his example. The following points come from what we have learned in our own growth in working with these young disciples.

Focus on Personalized Discipleship

When Jesus called men and women to follow him, he offered a personal relationship with himself, not simply an alternative lifestyle or different religious practices or a new social organization. While some of the sectarians within Judaism created man-made separations between the "righteous" and the "unrighteous" by their regulations and traditions, Jesus broke through those barriers by calling to himself those who, in the eyes of sectarians, did not seem to enjoy the necessary qualifications for fellowship with him (Mt 9:9–13; Mk 2:13–17). Discipleship means the beginning of a new life in intimate fellowship with a living Master and Savior.

We must challenge ourselves to take Jesus' position. Many young surfers come from backgrounds where attitudes, lifestyles, and standards are quite different from traditional Christian circles. It is easy to look at the surface and miss the great needs that lie within. We must be ready to extend our fellowship to those who differ from traditional Christian appearances.

We have tried to emphasize to these young surfers that, while discipleship to Jesus will inevitably bring about changes of lifestyle, their new life primarily means that they are entering into a personal relationship with him. Becoming a Christian does not mean that they have to act or talk or look like the members of any one particular church or organization. They need to know that Jesus takes them as they are and offers a personalized life of discipleship.

The first exposure to personalized Bible reading and prayer is crucial for determining the vitality of this new life. We took a group of these surfers on a six-hour trip so that they could compete in a statewide surf contest. We bought contemporary looking, paperback Bibles for each of them. Most of them had never had their own Bible, and they were "stoked"! Spontaneously, on their own, they gathered each evening to read together and to pray. The emphasis was on hearing God speak to them personally through his Word and on them speaking to God personally through prayer.

Here is where we try to encourage a balance of the traditional institutional approaches and personalized approaches. We encourage them to get involved in established churches and organizations where they can identify with and learn from the larger body of Christ. On the other hand, groups of surfers studying the Bible together and holding each other accountable often provide the individualized attention that is needed to help them start walking with Jesus right from where he calls them.

Challenge Them to Count the Cost

Jesus' gracious call to discipleship was accompanied by an intense command to count the cost of discipleship. The call to be a disciple in Jesus' lifetime meant to count the cost of full allegiance to him. Jesus recognized that various securities in this life can be a substitute for allegiance to him. The command to count the cost of discipleship meant exchanging the securities of this world for security in him. For some this meant riches (Mt 19:16–26), for others it meant attachment to family (Mt 8:21–22; Lk 14:25–27), for still others it meant nationalistic feelings of superiority (Lk 10:25–37).

Surfers tend to be somewhat "free spirited." They like to think of themselves as unhindered by normal restraints. Jesus' command to count the cost sounds harsh in their ears. Yet we have found that their own commitment to surfing helps them understand Jesus' demand. Counting the cost marks their everyday life. Surfing is one of the most difficult of all sports, requiring utmost commitment, training, and conditioning. Many people say that they would like to surf; many even try it for a while; but the difficulty of the sport soon discourages most. To continue surfing requires that they count the cost of the commitment, the physical difficulty, and the danger. While free-spirited surfers delight in the gracious offer of discipleship, they readily understand the cost that is required for single-mindedly following Jesus. Nothing is more despised by a true surfer than a "poser," a person who plays the role of surfer but does not really surf. The challenge to count the cost of discipleship means the difference between posing as a disciple and living as one.

Help Them to Become Like Jesus

Jesus declared that to be a disciple is to become like the Master (Mt 10:24–25; Lk 6:40). Becoming like Jesus includes going out with the same message, ministry, and compassion (Mt 10:5ff.); practicing the same religious and social traditions (Mt 12:1–8; Mk 2:18–22); belonging to the same family of obedience (Mt 12:46–50); exercising the same servanthood (Mk 10:42–45; Mt 20:26–28; Jn 13:12–17); and experiencing the same suffering (Mt 10:16–25; Mk 10:38–39). The true disciple was to know Jesus so well, was to have followed him so closely, that he or she would become like him. The ultimate goal was to be conformed to his image (cf. Lk 6:40; Ro 8:28–29).

A practical way of helping our young surfer friends to become like Jesus was to focus on the three marks of a disciple of Jesus, which, in fact, were the central marks of Jesus' own life: abiding in the Word (Jn 8:31–32), loving one another (13:34–35), and bearing fruit (15:8).[4] I see these three marks as ways in which we can focus our efforts in personal discipleship as well as in discipleship that occurs within the church. In fact, I suggest that when we look at the viability of various "programs" in the church or of individual relationships, we ask whether or not they contribute toward these three marks of Jesus' disciples. If so, press on! If not, they may be extraneous.

THROUGH ABIDING IN JESUS' WORD

True discipleship means abiding in Jesus' words as the truth for every area of life (cf. Jn 8:31–32). Abiding in Jesus' words does not mean perpetual Bible study. Rather, it means to know and to live in what Jesus says about life. Instead of listening to the world's values, disciples must listen to what Jesus says. This begins with salvation (cf. Peter's example in Jn 6:66–69) but involves every other area of life as well.

For example, self-image is extremely important to these young surfers. The world will tell them that they will find personal fulfillment only when they are the best surfer, when they have the right surfboard or wetsuit sponsors, when they win the world championship. But to abide in Jesus' words means to live with what he says about them: that God loves them and that they are his special

---

[4]See chap. 12 for a full treatment of these marks of discipleship.

creatures who will be fulfilled only when they are in right relationship with him.

We must spend time comparing the words of the world with the words of Jesus and then support young people as they attempt to abide in Jesus' words.

THROUGH LOVING ONE ANOTHER

True discipleship also means loving one another as Jesus loved his disciples (Jn 13:34–35). Love is not something for a special category of committed Christians. Love is a distinguishing mark of all disciples of Jesus, made possible because of regeneration—where a change has been made in the heart of the believer by God's love—and because of an endless supply of love from God, who is love (cf. 1Jn 4:12–21).

Surfers have a natural bond between them because of their shared devotion to the sport. But jealousy, envy, and rivalry easily arise as a result of the competition and the huge egos that often develop from being in the spotlight. When commitment to each other is of a higher priority than coming out on top in the surf world, the love of Jesus stands out starkly.

I remember one occasion vividly. Two of our young girls were getting ready to go out and surf in the California state high school surfing championships. Although they would soon be competing with each other, they stood near the shoreline and prayed together. With that kind of commitment, personal ambition is placed in proper perspective.

THROUGH BEARING FRUIT

Jesus also said that the true disciple will bear fruit. What is this fruit? The fruit of the Spirit (Gal 5:22–26), new converts (Jn 4:3–38; 15:16), righteousness, and good works (Php 1:11; Col 1:10). This is the chance for us show these young people how to allow the Spirit of God to guide every area of their lives and to become like Jesus in their characteristics, their witness, and their outreach.

Just recently one of the young boys, now a senior in high school, was baptized in a local church. As he gave his testimony before the church, he emphasized that his baptism was his declaration to the world that he was walking with Jesus. The church has played a vital role in providing the necessary support, encouragement, and training so that he can demonstrate to the world that Jesus is real in his life.

Lead the Way into the World

Here is where a crucial characteristic of a disciple of Jesus comes into focus. It is one thing to declare to be a Christian within the church or among other Christian friends. It is another thing to live that commitment out in the world. Living a Christ-centered life in the world often marks the distinction between institutionalism and discipleship.

But since these young surfers have very few models of how to do this, it is imperative that we go out there with them. That means surfing with them (there is not much difficulty persuading me to do that!); going to contests with them; getting involved in the surfing organizations; and providing guidance, support, and comfort in times of temptation and trial. It means providing a model of how to live in the same world as they live in. As we are salt and light, as we walk the narrow path, as we love and provide hope to the world, we become the living example for them to follow. This is close to Paul's admonition, "Follow my example, as I follow the example of Christ" (1Co 11:1).

FOLLOWING JESUS' PATH

Institutions come and go. Whether we are entrenched conservatives who cling to traditions that have worked so wonderfully or whether we are flaming revolutionaries who are contending for a new way of experiencing discipleship, we must be intent upon following Jesus' way. The work of any church or parachurch organization must be directed toward this goal of discipleship: to get people to be committed to Jesus first, with only secondary commitment to a particular church or group. We must develop followers of the Master, not adherents of a particular method.

Many of these young surfers have rough edges and do not look or act like those who have been raised in Christian circles. We have tried to get them involved in churches and groups ranging anywhere from Bible churches to mainline churches to charismatic churches to contemporary parachurch organizations, and we have watched many of them slowly drop out. This has broken our hearts, but I think it has happened because the Christian institutions have lost interest in these kids primarily because these kids are "different." They don't fit; they don't have much to offer.

One afternoon I had a long conversation with one young boy who had been virtually abandoned by his own family. His mother was in jail at the time on cocaine charges. His father had abandoned the family at birth. This fifteen-year-old boy and his sister were drifting around from family to family trying to find a place to live. But on top of all of this, this young boy was finding it difficult fitting into traditional Christian circles. At the end of our talk he looked over at me with great big tears in his eyes and said, "Doc, my whole life was changed when I met your family. And no matter how little I look like I have, I've got Jesus now. And He's never going to leave me."

Throughout our lives we all will be presented with opportunities to be involved in great ministries in which we will be helping others to grow spiritually and in which we ourselves will be challenged as to the "right" way to grow. We must never let any great ministry take the place of this simple truth: *Our ministries are intended to make disciples of Jesus in his way.*

While walking down the long, winding path to go surfing, some of the kids would run ahead and beat the rest of us into the water. Some would stand at the top of the trail and watch the surf for quite a while, wondering if the waves were going to be good enough that day to make the long walk worthwhile. Others would fool around and get off the path, climbing up and down the cliffs where they were not supposed to go. They were old enough to be responsible for themselves, but I would be concerned until I had them all down at the beach with me. I couldn't walk for them. I could only show them the way down the path.

Some of the kids have gotten off the path of discipleship since those days. Some are still standing at the top of the trail, not fully committed to walking with Jesus. Others have run on ahead and are experiencing fullness in their life with Jesus. We continue to be concerned about them all, praying for them all, waiting for them all to join us in the fellowship of Jesus. We cannot live their lives for them. But we can keep on walking with Jesus down the path and try to show them the way.

Following up:

1. How could each of these discipleship groups that existed in Palestine when Jesus came on the scene have retained the strengths of their background while becoming disciples of Jesus?
2. What signs of institutionalism can be found in your church or group? In your own life? What can be done to create discipleship to Jesus, instead?
3. Are you more comfortable among Christians or non-Christians? Why?
4. In what ways are you currently helping your own group of "surfers" to walk with Jesus in the world?

Selected Bibliography
by Categories

The following bibliography is intended as a resource tool for those who would like to do further research and read about the biblical and historical phenomenon of disciples and discipleship. Each category is designed for specialized reading. Hundreds of books and articles have been written within each category. Those listed here have been among the most influential in various circles. Some entries have been listed more than once if they have special value for more than one category. Standard reference tools such as commentaries have not been included here. The reader should consult the footnotes for such citations.

A. GENERAL STUDIES OF DISCIPLESHIP

1. Scholarly

Arensen, Allen G. "Making Disciples According to Christ's Plan." *Evangelical Missions Quarterly* 16, no. 2 (1980): 103–6.

Atkinson, Michael. "Body and Discipleship." *Theology* 82 (Issue 688, 1979): 279–87.

Badke, William B. "Was Jesus a Disciple of John?" *Evangelical Quarterly* 62, no. 3 (1990): 195–204.

Bammel, Ernst. *Jesu Nachfolger, Nachfolgeüberlieferungen in der Zeit des frühen Christentums.* Studia Delitzschiana, Dritte Folge 1. Heidelberg: Lambert Schneider, 1988.

_____. "What Is Thy Name?" *NovT* 12 (1970): 223–28.

Beernaert, P. Mourlon. "Converting to the Gospel." *LumVit* 42, no. 4 (1987): 369–79.

Betz, Hans Dieter. *Nachfolge und Nachahmung Jesu Christi im Neuen Testament.* BHT 37. Tübingen: Mohr/Siebeck, 1967.

Blauvelt, Livingston, Jr. "Does the Bible Teach Lordship Salvation?" *BS* 143 (569, 1986): 37–45.

Bock, Darrell L. "A Review of *The Gospel According to Jesus.*" *BS* 146 (581, 1989): 21–40.

Calenberg, Richard D. "The New Testament Doctrine of Discipleship." Unpublished doctoral dissertation, Grace Theological Seminary, 1981.

Crouzel, H. "L'imitation et la 'suite' de Dieu et du Christ dans les premiers siècles chrétiens, ainsi que leurs sources gréco—romaines et hébraïques." *Jahrbuch für Antike und Christentum* (*JAC*) 21 (1978): 7–41.

Culver, Robert Duncan. "Apostles and the Apostolate in the New Testament." *BS* 134 (534, 1977): 131–43.

DeRidder, Richard R. *Discipling the Nations.* 1971, reprint. Grand Rapids: Baker, 1975.

Dragas, George. "Martyrdom and Orthodoxy in the New Testament Era—The Theme of Μαρτυρία As Witness to the Truth." *GOThR* 30, no. 3 (1985): 287–96.

Drushal, M. E. "Implementing Theory Z in the Church: Managing People as Jesus Did." *Ashland Theological Bulletin* 20 (1988): 47–62.

Dunn, James D. G. *Jesus and Discipleship: Understanding Jesus Today.* Edited by Howard Clark Kee. Cambridge: Cambridge University Press, 1991.

Freyne, Seán. *The Twelve: Disciples and Apostles. A Study in the Theology of the First Three Gospels.* London: Sheed & Ward, 1968.

Green, Michael P. "The Meaning of Cross-Bearing." *BS* 140 (558, 1983): 117–33.

Happel, Stephen, and James J. Walter. *Conversion and Discipleship: A Christian Foundation for Ethics and Doctrine.* Philadelphia: Fortress, 1986.

Henrix, H. H. "Von der Nachahmung Gottes. Heiligkeit und Heiligsein im biblischen und jüdischen Denken." *Erbe und Auftrag* 65, no. 3 (1989): 177–87.

Kingsbury, Jack Dean. "On Following Jesus: The 'Eager' Scribe and the 'Reluctant' Disciple (Matthew 8.18–22)." *NTS* 34 (1988): 45–59.

Kruse, Colin G. *New Testament Models for Ministry: Jesus and Paul.* 1983. Reprint. Nashville, Tenn.: Thomas Nelson, 1985.

Kvalbein, Hans. "'Go Therefore and Make Disciples. . .': The Concept of Discipleship in the New Testament." *Themelios* 13 (1988): 48–53.

Luter, A. Boyd. "Discipleship and the Church." *BS* 137 (57, 1980): 267–73.

———. "A New Testament Theology of Discipling." Unpublished Th.D. dissertation, Dallas Theological Seminary, 1985.

Marcus, Joel. "Entering into the Kingly Power of God." *JBL* 107, no. 4 (1988): 663–75.

Melbourne, Bertram L. *Slow To Understand: The Disciples in Synoptic Perspective.* Lanham, Md.: University Press of America, 1988.

Müller, Dietrich. "Disciple/μαθητής." *NIDNTT* 1:483–90.

Rengstorf, Karl H. "Διδάσκω, διδάσκαλος." *TDNT* 2:135–65.

_____. "μαθητής." *TDNT* 4:415–61.

Sawicki, Marianne. "How to Teach Christ's Disciples: John 1:19–37 and Matthew 11:2–15." *LexThQ* 21, no. 1 (1986): 14–26.

Schulz, Anselm. *Nachfolgen und Nachahmen: Studien über das Verhältnis der neutestamentlichen Jüngerschaft zur urchristlichen Vorbildethik.* SANT 6. Munich: Kösel-Verlag, 1962.

Schweizer, Eduard. *Lordship and Discipleship.* Translated and revised by the author. *SBT* 28. 1955. London: SCM, 1960.

Seccombe, David P. "Take Up Your Cross." In *God Who is Rich in Mercy: Essays Presented to D. B. Knox.* Edited by Peter T. O'Brien and David G. Peterson. Homebush, Australia: Anzea, 1986.

Segovia, Fernando F., ed. *Discipleship in the New Testament.* Philadelphia: Fortress, 1985.

Trakatellis, Demetrios. "'Ακολούθει μοι/Follow Me' (Mk 2:14): Discipleship and Priesthood." *GOThR* 30, no. 3 (1985): 271–85.

Vincent, John James. *Disciple and Lord: The Historical and Theological Significance of Discipleship in the Synoptic Gospels.* Dissertation zur Erlangung der Doktorwuerde der Theologischen Fakultaet der Universitaet Basel, 1960. Sheffield: Sheffield Academic Press, 1976.

_____. "Discipleship and Synoptic Studies." *Theologische Zeitschrift* 16 (1960): 456–569.

Wagner, C. Peter. "What Is 'Making Disciples'?" *Evangelical Missions Quarterly* 9 (1973): 285–93.

Wilkins, Michael J. "Barabbas." "Bartholomew." "Belief/Believers." "Brother/Brotherhood." "Christian." "Imitate/Imitators." *The Anchor Bible Dictionary.* Edited by David Noel Freedman. Five vols. Garden City, N.Y.: Doubleday, forthcoming.

_____. *The Concept of Disciple in Matthew's Gospel: As Reflected in the Use of the Term Μαθητής.* NovTSup 59. Leiden: E. J. Brill, 1988.

_____. "Disciple." "Discipleship." *Dictionary of Jesus and the Gospels.* Edited by Joel Green and Scot McKnight. Consulting editor I. Howard Marshall. Downers Grove, Ill.: InterVarsity Press, 1992.

_____. "Named and Unnamed Disciples in Matthew: A Literary/Theological Study." *SBLSP* 30. Atlanta: Scholars, 1991.

2. Popular

Arn, Win, and Charles Arn. *The Master's Plan for Making Disciples.* Pasadena: Church Growth Press, 1982.

Augsburger, Myron S. *Invitation to Discipleship.* Scottdale, Pa.: Herald Press, 1969.

Boice, James Montgomery. *Christ's Call to Discipleship*. Chicago: Moody, 1986.

Bonhoeffer, Dietrich. *The Cost of Discipleship*. Translated by R. H. Fuller. 2d rev. ed. New York: Macmillan, 1963.

Bruce, Alexander Balmain. *The Training of the Twelve*. 1871, reprint. Grand Rapids: Kregel, 1971.

Chandapilla, P. T. *The Master Trainer*. Bombay: Gospel Literature Service, 1974.

Coleman, Robert E. *The Master Plan of Discipleship*. Old Tappan, N.J.: Fleming H. Revell, 1987.

————. *The Master Plan of Evangelism*. 2d ed. Old Tappan, N.J.: Fleming H. Revell, 1964.

Coppedge, Allan. *The Biblical Principles of Discipleship*. Grand Rapids: Zondervan, 1989.

Cosgrove, Francis M. *Essentials of Discipleship*. Colorado Springs: NavPress, 1980.

Eims, Leroy. *The Lost Art of Disciple Making*. Grand Rapids/Colorado Springs: Zondervan/NavPress, 1978, pp. 61ff., 83ff., 181–88.

Fryling, Alice, ed. *Disciplemakers' Handbook: Helping People Grow in Christ*. Downers Grove, Ill.: InterVarsity Press, 1989.

Griffiths, Michael. *The Example of Jesus*. The Jesus Library, ed. Michael Green. Downers Grove, Ill.: InterVarsity Press, 1985.

Hadidian, Allen. *Successful Discipling*. Chicago: Moody, 1979.

Hanks, Billie Jr., and William A. Shell, eds. *Discipleship: The Best Writings from the Most Experienced Disciple Makers*. Grand Rapids: Zondervan, 1981.

Hartman, Doug, and Doug Sutherland. *Guidebook to Discipleship*. Irvine, Calif.: Harvest House, 1976.

Hendrix, John, and Loyd Householder, eds. *The Equipping of Disciples*. Nashville: Broadman, 1977.

Henrichsen, Walter A. *Disciples Are Made—Not Born*. Wheaton, Ill.: Victor Books, 1974.

Hodges, Zane C. *Absolutely Free: A Biblical Reply to Lordship Salvation*. Grand Rapids/Dallas: Zondervan/Redención Viva, 1989.

————. *The Gospel Under Siege: A Study on Faith and Works*. Dallas: Redención Viva, 1981.

Howard, David M. *The Great Commisstion for Today*. Downers Grove, Ill.: InterVarsity Press, 1976.

Hull, Bill. *Disciple Making Church*. Old Tappan, N.J.: Fleming H. Revell, 1990.

————. *Jesus Christ Disciplemaker: Rediscovering Jesus' Strategy for Building His Church*. Colorado Springs: NavPress, 1984.

Kuhne, Gary W. *The Dynamics of Discipleship Training: Being and Producing Spiritual Leaders.* Grand Rapids: Zondervan, 1978.

Liddell, Eric H. *The Disciplines of the Christian Life.* Nashville: Abingdon, 1985. (Formerly known as *A Manual of Christian Discipleship.*)

————. "The Muscular Christianity of Eric Liddell: The Olympic Runner and Missionary on Discipleship." *Christianity Today,* June 14, 1985, 23–25.

MacArthur, John F. *The Gospel According to Jesus: What Does Jesus Mean When He Says "Follow Me"?* Grand Rapids: Zondervan, 1988.

MacDonald, William. *True Discipleship.* Kansas City, Kans.: Walterick, 1975.

Martin, John R. *Ventures in Discipleship: A Handbook for Groups or Individuals.* Scottdale, Pa.: Herald Press, 1984.

Mayhall, Jack. *Discipleship: The Cost and the Price.* Wheaton: Victor, 1984.

McGavran, Donald A., and Win Arn. *How to Grow a Church.* Glendale, Calif.: Gospel Light, 1973.

Neighbour, Ralph W. *The Journey into Discipleship.* Lay Renewal, 1974.

Ortiz, Juan Carlos. *Disciple.* Carol Stream, Ill.: Creation House, 1975.

Phillips, Keith. *The Making of a Disciple.* Old Tappan, N.J.: Fleming H. Revell, 1981.

Powell, Paul W. *The Complete Disciple.* Wheaton, Ill: Victor Books, 1982.

Richards, Lawrence O. *A Practical Theology of Spirituality.* Grand Rapids: Zondervan, 1987.

Ryrie, Charles C. *So Great Salvation: What It Means to Believe in Jesus Christ.* Wheaton, Ill.: Victor Books, 1989.

Sanders, J. Oswald. *Spiritual Maturity.* Chicago: Moody, 1962.

Sine, Tom, *Taking Discipleship Seriously: A Radical Biblical Approach.* Valley Forge: Judson Press, 1985.

Sugden, Christopher. *Radical Discipleship.* London: Marshall, Morgan & Scott, 1981.

Wagner, C. Peter. *Stop the World I Want to Get On.* Glendale, Calif.: Regal Books, 1974.

————. "What Is 'Making Disciples'?" *Evangelical Missions Quarterly* 9 (1973): 285–93.

Wallis, Jim. *Agenda for Biblical People.* New York: Harper & Row, 1976.

Warr, Gene. *You Can Make Disciples.* Waco: Word, 1978.

Warren, Max. *I Believe in the Great Commission.* Grand Rapids: Eerdmans, 1976.

Watson, David. *Called and Committed: World Changing Discipleship*. London/Wheaton: Hodder & Stoughton/Harold Shaw, 1981/1982.

Wilkins, Michael J. "Radical Discipleship." *Sundoulos*. Alumni publication of Talbot School of Theology (Fall 1988), 1–2.

————. "Surfers and Other Disciples." *Discipleship Journal*. Vol. 112, no 62 (March/April 1991): 8–14.

Willard, Dallas. *The Spirit of the Disciplines: Understanding How God Changes Lives*. San Francisco: Harper & Row, 1988.

Wilson, Carl. *With Christ in the School of Disciple Building: A Study of Christ's Method of Building Disciples*. Grand Rapids: Zondervan, 1976.

Yohn, Rick. *Now That I'm a Disciple*. Irvine, Calif.: Harvest House, 1976.

3. Dictionary Articles

Albin, T. R. "Disciple, Discipleship." *Dictionary of Christianity in America*. Daniel G. Reid, coordinating editor. Downers Grove, Ill.: InterVarsity Press, 1990.

Barron, B. "Shepherding Movement (Discipleship Movement)." *Dictionary of Christianity in America*. Daniel G. Reid, coordinating editor. Downers Grove, Ill.: InterVarsity Press, 1990.

Dulles, Avery. "Discipleship." *The Encyclopedia of Religion*. Mircea Eliade, editor-in-chief. New York: Macmillan, 1987. 4:361–64.

Eller, V. M. "Discipleship." *The Brethren Encyplopedia*. Donald F. Durnbaugh, ed. Philadelphia: The Brethren Encyclopedia, 1983. 1:386.

Fabry, H. J. *"chbhl."* TDOT. Vol. 4. Edited by G. J. Botterweck and H. Ringgren. Translated by D. E. Green. Grand Rapids: Eerdmans, 1980.

Gould, George P. "Disciple." *Dictionary of Christ and the Gospels*. New York: Scribners, 1905. 1:457–59.

Held, M. L. "Disciples." *New Catholic Encyclopedia*. Prepared by the editorial staff at the Catholic University of America, Washington, D.C. New York: McGraw–Hill, 1967. 4:895.

Hawthorne, Gerald F. "Disciple." *The Zondervan Pictorial Encyclopedia of the Bible*. Merrill C. Tenney, general editor. Five vols. Grand Rapids: Zondervan, 1975. 2:129–31.

Helm, Paul. "Disciple." *Baker Encyclopedia of the Bible*. Walter A. Elwell, general editor. Grand Rapids: Baker, 1988.

Hillyer, Norman. *"sopher."* NIDNTT. Vol. 3. Grand Rapids: Zondervan, 1978.

Jastrow, Marcus, ed. *A Dictionary of the Targumim, the Talmud Babli and Yerushalmi, and the Midrashic Literature.* New York: Pardes, 1950.

Jenni, Ernst. *"lmdh." THAT.* Edited by Ernst Jenni and Claus Westermann. Vol. 2. München: Chr. Kaiser, 1971.

Kaiser, Walter C. *"lamadh." TWOT.* Edited by R. Laird Harris, Gleason L. Archer, Jr., and Bruce K. Waltke. Chicago: Moody, 1980.

Léon-Dufour, Xavier, ed. *Dictionary of Biblical Theology.* 2d. ed. New York: Seabury, 1973.

Meye, Robert P. "Disciple." *The International Standard Bible Encyclopedia.* Four vols. Geoffrey W. Bromiley, general editor. Rev. ed. Grand Rapids: Eerdmans, 1979. 1:947–48.

Müller, Dietrich. "Disciple/μαθητής." Colin Brown, translator and editor. *New International Dictionary of New Testament Theology.* Grand Rapids: Zondervan, 1975. 1:483–90.

Müller, Dietrich, and Colin Brown. "Apostle/ἀποστέλλω." Translated and edited by Colin Brown. *New International Dictionary of New Testament Theology.* Grand Rapids: Zondervan, 1975. 1:126–37.

Müller, H.-P. *"Chakham." TDOT.* Vol. 4. Translated by David E. Green. Grand Rapids: Eerdmans, 1980.

Nepper-Christensen, Poul. "μαθητής." *Exegetisches Wörterbuch zum Neuen Testament.* Vol. 2. Edited by Horst Balz and Gerhard Schneider. Stuttgart: W. Kohlhammer, 1982.

Parker, Pierson. "Disciple." *The Interpreter's Dictionary of the Bible.* George Arthur Buttrick, editor. Nashville: Abingdon, 1962. 1:845.

Plummer, Alfred. "Disciple." *Dictionary of the Apostolic Church.* Edited by James Hastings. New York: Scribner, 1915. 1:301–3.

Rabinowitz, Louis Isaac. "Talmid Hakham." *Encyclopedia Judaica.* Sixteen vols. Jerusalem: Macmillan, 1971.

Rainey, Anson. F. "Scribe, Scribes." *The Zondervan Pictorial Encyclopedia of the Bible.* Merrill C. Tenney, general editor. Five vols. Grand Rapids: Zondervan, 1975. 5:298–302.

Rengstorf, Karl H. "ἀπόστολος." *TDNT* 1:69–75.

_____. "διδάσκω, διδάσκαλος." *TDNT* 2: 135–65.

_____. "δώδεκα." *TDNT* 2:321–28.

_____. "μαθητής." *TDNT* 4:415–61.

Souvay, Charles L. "Disciple." *The Catholic Encyclopedia.* Edited by Charles G. Herbermann et al. New York: The Encyclopedia Press, 1913. 4:29.

Wilkins, Michael J. "Barabbas." "Bartholomew." "Belief/Believers." "Brother/Brotherhood." "Christian." "Imitate/Imitators." *The An-*

chor Bible Dictionary. Edited by David Noel Freedman. Five vols. Garden City, N.Y.: Doubleday, 1992.

―――. "Disciple." "Discipleship." *Dictionary of Jesus and the Gospels.* Edited by Joel Green and Scot McKnight. Consulting editor I. Howard Marshall. Downers Grove, Ill.: InterVarsity Press, 1992.

B. FOUNDATIONS OF DISCIPLESHIP
IN THE OLD TESTAMENT

Albright, William F. Samuel. *The Beginnings of the Prophetic Movement: The Goldenson Lecture of 1961. In Interpreting the Prophetic Tradition: The Goldenson Lectures 1955–1966.* The Library of Biblical Studies. Edited by H. O. Orlinsky. New York: Hebrew Union College, 1969.

Bryce, G. E. A *Legacy of Wisdom: The Egyptian Contribution to the Wisdom of Israel.* Lewisburg: Bucknell University Press, 1979.

Clarke, M. L. *Higher Education in the Ancient World.* Albuquerque: University of New Mexico Press, 1971.

Clements, R. E. *Prophecy and Tradition.* Atlanta: John Knox,1975.

Crenshaw, James L. *Old Testament Wisdom: An Introduction.* Atlanta: John Knox, 1981.

―――. ed. *Studies in Ancient Israelite Wisdom.* New York: KTAV 1976.

de Vaux, Roland. *Ancient Israel: Its Life and Institutions.* Translated by John McHugh. New York: McGraw-Hill, 1961.

Demsky, A. "Education (Jewish) In the Biblical Period." *Encyclopedia Judaica.* Jerusalem, 1971, VI.

Drazin, Nathan. *History of Jewish Education from 515 B.C.E. to 220 C.E. (During the Periods of the Second Commonwealth and the Tannaim).* Baltimore: Johns Hopkins, 1940.

Ellison, H. L. *The Prophets of Israel: From Ahijah to Hosea.* Grand Rapids: Eerdmans, 1969.

Eppstein, V. "Was Saul Also Among the Prophets?" ZAW 81 (1969) 287–304.

Freeman, Hobart E. *An Introduction to the Old Testament Prophets.* Chicago: Moody, 1968.

Gerhardsson, Birger. *Memory and Manuscript: Oral Tradition and Written Transmission in Rabbinic Judaism and Early Christianity.* Translated by Eric Sharpe. Lund: C. W. K. Gleerup, 1961.

Gerstenberger, Erhard. "Covenant and Commandment." *JBL* 84 (1965) 51–65.

―――. "The Woe-Oracles of the Prophets." *JBL* 81 (1962) 249–263.

_____. *Wesen und Herkunft des 'apodiktischen' Rechts. WMANT* 20. Neukirchen-Vluyn: Neukirchener, 1965.

Goldin, J. "Several Sidelights of a Torah Education in Tannaite and Early Amorical Times." In *Ex Orbe Religionum: Studia Geo Widengren. Pars Prior. Studies in the History of Religions.* Supplements to *Numen.* XXI. Leiden: E. J. Brill, 1972.

Hanson, Paul D. *The People Called: The Growth of Community in the Bible.* San Francisco: Harper & Row, 1986.

Hengel, Martin. *Judaism and Hellenism: Studies in Their Encounter in Palestine During the Early Hellenistic Period.* 2 vols. Translated by John Bowden. *WUNT* 10. 2d. ed. Philadelphia: Fortress, 1974.

_____. *The Charismatic Leader and His Followers.* Translated by J. Greig. 1968. New York: Crossroad, 1981.

Hermisson, Hans-Jürgen. *Studien zur israelitischen Spruchweisheit. WMANT* 28. Neukirchen-Vluyn: Neukirchener Verlag, 1968.

Humphreys, W. Lee. "The Motif of the Wise Courtier in the Book of Proverbs." *Israelite Wisdom: Theological and Literary Essays in Honor of Samuel Terrien.* Edited by J. Gammie, W. Brueggemann, W. L. Humphreys, J. Ward. Missoula, Montana: Scholars Press, 1978.

Koch, Klaus. *The Prophets: Volume I, The Assyrian Period.* Translated by M. Kohl. Philadelphia: Fortress, 1983.

Lang, Bernhard. *Die weisheitliche Lehrrede: Eine Untersuchung von Sprache 1–7. SBS* 54. Stuttgart: Kath. Bibelwerk; 1972.

_____. *Monotheism and the Prophetic Minority: An Essay in Biblical History and Sociology.* The Social World of Biblical Antiquity Series 1. Sheffield: Almond, 1983.

Légasse, S. "Scribes et disciples de Jésus." *RB* 68 (1961) 321–45; 481–506.

Lemaire, André. *Les écoles et la formation de la Bible dans l'ancien Israël.* Fribourg/Göttingen: Universitaires/Vandenhoeck & Ruprecht, 1981.

_____. "Sagesse et ecoles." *VT* XXXIV (1984) 270–81. Lénhardt, Pierre. "Voies de la continuité juive: Aspects de la relation maître-disciple d'aprés la littérature rabbinique ancienne," *RSR* 66 (1978) 489–516.

Lindblom, Johannes. *Prophecy in Ancient Israel.* Oxford: Blackwell, 1962.

_____. "Wisdom in the Old Testament Prophets." *Wisdom in Israel and in the Ancient Near East: Presented to Professor Harold Henry Rowley.* Edited by M. Noth and D. Winton Thomas. *VTSup* III. Leiden: E. J. Brill, 1955.

Marrou, Henri I. *A History of Education in Antiquity.* Translated by George Lamb. 3d. ed. New York: Sheed and Ward, 1956.

McKane, William. *Prophets and Wise Men, SBT* 44. Naperville, Ill.: Alec R. Allenson,1965.

Mettinger, Tryggve D. *Solomonic State Officials: A Study of the Civil Government Officials of the Israelite Monarchy. ConB OTS* 5. Lund: Gleerup, 1971.

Mirsky, S. K. "The Schools of Hillel, R. Ishmael, and R. Akiba in Pentateuchal Interpretation." *Essays Presented to Chief Rabbi Israel Brodie on the Occasion of His Seventieth Birthday.* Edited by Zimmels, Rabbinowitz, Finestein. London: Soncino, 1967.

Murphy, Roland E. "Assumptions and Problems in Old Testament Wisdom Research." *CBQ* 29 (1967) 101–12.

————. "Wisdom—Theses and Hypotheses." *Israelite Wisdom: Theological and Literary Essays in Honor of Samuel Terrien.* Edited by J. Gammie, W. Brueggemann, W. L. Humphreys, J. Ward. Missoula, Montana: Scholars Press, 1978.

Neusner, Jacob. *The Rabbinic Traditions about the Pharisees Before 70.* 3 vols. Leiden: E. J. Brill, 1971.

Olivier, J. P. J. "Schools and Wisdom Literature." *JNSL* IV (1975) 49–60.

Perdue, Leo G. *Wisdom and Cult: A Critical Analysis of the Views of Cult in the Wisdom Literatures of Israel and the Ancient Near East. SBLDS* 30. Missoula, Montana: Scholars, 1977.

Porter, J. R. "The Origins of Prophecy in Israel." In *Israel's Prophetic Tradition: Essays in Honour of Peter R. Ackroyd.* Edited by R. Coggins, A. Phillips, and M. Knibb. Cambridge: Cambridge University Press, 1982.

Schilling, Othmar. "Amt und Nachfolge im Alten Testament und in Qumran." *Volk Gottes: zum Kirchenverständnis der Katholischen, Evangelischen, und Anglikanischen Theologie. Festgabe für Josef Höfer.* Edited by Remigius Bäumer und Heimo Dolch. Freiberg: Herder, 1967.

Schulz, Anselm. *Nachfolgen und Nachahmen: Studien über das Verhältnis der neutestamentlichen Jüngerschaft zur urchristlichen Vorbildethik. SANT* 6. Munich: Kösel-Verlag, 1962.

Scott, R. B. Y. *The Way of Wisdom.* New York: Macmillan, 1971.

Sigal, Philip. *Judaism: The Evolution of a Faith.* Revised and edited by Lillian Sigal. Grand Rapids: Eerdmans, 1988.

Terrien, Samuel. "Amos and Wisdom." *Studies in Ancient Israelite Wisdom.* Edited by James L. Crenshaw. 1962, reprint New York: KTAV 1976.

Urbach, Ephraim E. *The Sages: Their Concepts and Beliefs.* Translated by Israel Abrahams, 2 vols. 2d ed. Jerusalem: Magnes Press, 1979.

Vincent, John James. "Disciple and Lord: The Historical and Theological Significance of Discipleship in the Synoptic Gospels." Dissertation zur Erlangung der Doktorwuerde der Theologischen Fakultaet der Universitaet Basel, 1960. Sheffield: Academy, 1976.

von Rad, Gerhard. "The Joseph Narrative and Ancient Wisdom." *Studies in Ancient Israelite Wisdom*. Edited by James L. Crenshaw. New York: *KTAV* 1976.

————. *The Message of the Prophets*. Translated by D. M. G. Stalker. New York: Harper and Row, 1962.

————. *Wisdom in Israel*. N.d.; *ET* 1972. Nashville: Abingdon, 1984.

Whybray, R. N. *The Intellectual Tradition in the Old Testament*. BZAW 135. Berlin: Walter de Gruyter,1974.

Wilson, Robert R. *Prophecy and Society in Ancient Israel*. Philadelphia: Fortress, 1980.

————. *Sociological Approaches to the Old Testament*. GBS: OT Series. Philadelphia: Fortress, 1984. Wolff, Hans Walter. *Amos the Prophet: The Man and His Background*. Translated by F. McCurley, 1964. Philadelphia: Fortress, 1973.

————. "Micah the Moreshite—The Prophet and His Background." *Israelite Wisdom: Theological and Literary Essays in Honor of Samuel Terrien*. Edited by J. Gammie, W. Brueggemann, W. L. Humphreys, J. Ward. Missoula, Montana: Scholars Press, 1978.

Wood, Leon. *The Prophets of Israel*. Grand Rapids: Baker, 1979.

Young, Edward J. *My Servants the Prophets*. Grand Rapids: Eerdmans, 1955.

C. DISCIPLESHIP IN THE NEW TESTAMENT SOCIAL MILIEU

Badke, William B. "Was Jesus a Disciple of John?" *Evangelical Quarterly* 62, no. 3 (1990): 195–204.

Bammel, Ernst. *Jesu Nachfolger, Nachfolgeüberlieferungen in der Zeit des frühen Christentums*. Studia Delitzschiana, Dritte Folge 1. Heidelberg: Lambert Schneider, 1988.

Barnett, Paul. *Behind the Scenes of the New Testament*. Downers Grove, Ill.: InterVarsity Press, 1990.

Dunn, James D. G. *Jesus and Discipleship. Understanding Jesus Today*. Edited by Howard Clark Kee. Cambridge: Cambridge University Press, 1992.

————. "Pharisees, Sinners, and Jesus." *The Social World of Formative Christianity and Judaism*. Essays in tribute to Howard Clark Kee. Philadelphia: Fortress, 1988.

————. *Unity and Diversity in the New Testament: An Inquiry into the Character of Earliest Christianity.* 2d ed. London/Philadelphia: SCM/Trinity, 1990.

Gager, John G. *Kingdom and Community: The Social World of Early Christianity.* Englewood Cliffs, N.J.: Prentice-Hall, 1975.

Gray, Vivienne. "*MIMESIS* in Greek Historical Theory." *American Journal of Philology* 108, no. 3 (1987): 467–86.

Hanson, Paul D. *The People Called: The Growth of Community in the Bible.* San Francisco: Harper & Row, 1986. See esp. 430–38.

Hengel, Martin. *The Charismatic Leader and His Followers.* Translated by J. Greig. New York: Crossroad, 1981.

Hollingsworth, Mark. "Rabbi Jesus and Rabbi John: Opponents and Brothers." *BT* 28, no. 5 (1990): 284–90.

Horsley, Richard A. *Jesus and the Spiral of Violence: Popular Jewish Resistance in Roman Palestine.* San Francisco: Harper & Row, 1987.

————. *Sociology and the Jesus Movement.* New York: Crossroad, 1989.

Horsley, Richard A., and John S. Hanson. *Bandits, Prophets, and Messiahs: Popular Movements at the Time of Jesus.* Minneapolis: Winston, 1985.

Lohfink, Gerhard. *Jesus and Community: The Social Dimension of Christian Faith.* Philadelphia: Fortress, 1984.

Malina, Bruce J. *Christian Origins and Cultural Anthropology: Practical Models for Biblical Interpretation.* Atlanta: John Knox, 1986.

————. *The New Testament World: Insights from Cultural Anthropology.* Atlanta: John Knox, 1981.

Murphy-O'Connor, Jerome. "John the Baptist and Jesus: History and Hypotheses." *NTS* 36 (1990): 359–74.

Neusner, Jacob; William S. Green; and Ernest Frerichs, eds. *Judaisms and Their Messiahs at the Turn of the Christian Era.* Cambridge: Cambridge University Press, 1987.

Neyrey, Jerome H. "Social Science Modeling and the New Testament: A Biblical Scholar's View of *Christian Origins and Cultural Anthropology.*" *BThB* 16, no. 3 (1986): 107–10.

Perkins, Pheme. *Jesus As Teacher. Understanding Jesus Today.* Edited by Howard Clark Kee. Cambridge: Cambridge University Press, 1990.

Saldarini, Anthony J. *Pharisees, Scribes and Sadducees in Palestinian Society: A Sociological Approach.* Wilmington, Del.: Michael Glazier, 1988.

Sanders, E. P. *Jesus and Judaism.* Philadelphia: Fortress, 1985.

Segal, Alan F. *Rebecca's Children: Judaism and Christianity in the Roman World*. Cambridge: Harvard University Press, 1986.

Sigal, Philip. *Judaism: The Evolution of a Faith*. Revised and edited by Lillian Sigal. Grand Rapids: Eerdmans, 1988.

Theissen, Gerd. *Sociology of Early Palestinian Christianity*. Translated by John Bowden. Philadelphia: Fortress, 1978.

Tidball, Derek. *The Social Context of the New Testament: A Sociological Analysis*. Grand Rapids: Zondervan, 1984.

White, L. Michael. "Shifting Sectarian Boundaries in Early Christianity." *BJRLMan* 70, no. 3 (1988): 7–24.

White, Leland J. "The Bible, Theology and Cultural Pluralism: A Theologian's View of Christian Origins and Cultural Anthropology." *BThB* 16, no. 3 (1986): 111–15.

Wilcox, Max. "Jesus in the Light of His Jewish Environment." *Aufstieg und Niedergang der Römischen Welt*. Edited by H. Temporini and W. Haase. Berlin: Walter de Gruyter, 1982. 2, 25, 1:131–95.

Wilkins, Michael J. *The Concept of Disciple in Matthew's Gospel: as Reflected in the Use of the Term Μαθητής*, NovTSup 59. Leiden: E. J. Brill, 1988.

————. "Named and Unnamed Disciples in Matthew: A Literary/Theological Study." *SBLSP* 30. Atlanta: Scholars, 1991.

Witherington, Ben III. *The Christology of Jesus*. Minneapolis: Fortress, 1990.

D. THE APOSTLES

For extensive studies of the apostles, see:

Brownrigg, Ronald. *The Twelve Apostles*. New York: Macmillan, 1974.

Budge, Ernest A. Wallis. *The Contendings of the Apostles*. Two vols. London: H. Frowde, 1901.

Bruce, F. F. *Paul: Apostle of the Heart Set Free*. Grand Rapids: Eerdmans, 1977.

————. *Peter, Stephen, James and John: Studies in Non-Pauline Christianity*. Grand Rapids: Eerdmans, 1979.

For surveys of the apostles, see standard Bible dictionary/encyclopedia articles; e.g.:

Anchor Bible Dictionary. Edited by David Noel Freedman. Garden City, N.Y.: Doubleday, forthcoming.

Baker Encyclopedia of the Bible. General editor, Walter A. Elwell. Two vols. Grand Rapids: Baker, 1988.

The Illustrated Bible Dictionary. Edited by J. D. Douglas and N. Hillyer. Three vols. Leicester/Wheaton: InterVarsity Press/Tyndale House, 1980.

The International Standard Bible Encyclopedia. Revised edition. Edited by Geoffrey W. Bromiley. Grand Rapids: Eerdmans, 1979–86.

The Interpreter's Dictionary of the Bible and Supplement. Edited by G. A. Buttrick. New York: Abingdon, 1962–77.

The Zondervan Pictorial Encyclopedia of the Bible. Edited by Merrill C. Tenney. Five vols. Grand Rapids: Zondervan, 1975.

For devotional studies of the apostles, see, e.g.:

Barclay, William. *The Master's Men*. Nashville: Abingdon, 1959.

Flynn, Leslie B. *The Twelve*. Wheaton, Ill.: Victor Books, 1982.

Griffith, Leonard. *Gospel Characters: The Personalities Around Jesus*. Grand Rapids: Eerdmans, 1976.

Lockyer, Herbert. *All the Apostles of the Bible*. Grand Rapids: Zondervan, 1972.

For discussions of the apocryphal traditions about the apostles, see, e.g.:

Hennecke, Edgar. *New Testament Apocrypha*. Two vols. Edited by Wilhelm Schneemelcher. Philadelphia: Westminster, 1963–65.

E. WOMEN DISCIPLES IN THE BIBLICAL ACCOUNT

Beare, Patrick. "Mary, the Perfect Disciple: A Paradigm for Mariology." *Theological Studies* 41 (1981): 461–504.

Carmody, Desise Lardner. *Biblical Woman: Contemporary Reflections on Scriptural Texts*. New York: Crossroad, 1989.

D'Angelo, Mary Rose. "Women in Luke-Acts: A Redactional View." *JBL* 109, no. 3 (1990): 441–61.

Fischer, Kathleen. *Women at the Well: Feminist Perspectives on Spiritual Direction*. New York/Mahwah: Paulist, 1988.

Heine, Susanne. *Women and Early Christianity: A Reappraisal*. Translated by John Bowden. Minneapolis: Augsburg, 1988.

Hengel, Martin. "Maria Magdalena und die Frauen als Zeugen." In *Abraham unser Vater*, Festschrift for O. Michel. Edited by O. Betz et. al. Arbeiten zur Geschichte des Spätjudentums und Urchristentums 5 (1963): 243–56.

Love, Stuart L. "The 'Place' of Women in Certain Public Teaching Settings in Matthew's Gospel: A Sociological Inquiry." Unpublished paper presented to the Social Science Study Group, SBL annual meeting, Anaheim, California, November 20, 1989. Special thanks to Professor Love for supplying me with a personal copy of his paper.

Maly, Eugene. "Women and the Gospel of Luke." *BThB* 10 (1980): 99–104.

Martini, Carlo M. *Women in the Gospels*. New York: Crossroad, 1990.

Minear, Paul. "Jesus' Audiences According to Luke." *NovT* 16 (1974): 81–109.

Munro, Winsome. "Women Disciples in Mark?" *CBQ* 44 (1982): 225–41.

Neal, Hazel G. *Bible Women of Faith*. Anderson, Ind.: Warner, 1955.

Osborne, Grant R. "Women in Jesus' Ministry." *Westminster Theological Journal* 51 (1989): 259–91.

Quesnell, Quentin. "The Women at Luke's Supper." In *Political Issues in Luke-Acts*. Edited by Richard Cassidy and Philip Scharper. Maryknoll, N.Y.: Orbis, 1983, pp. 59–79.

Ryan, Rosalie. "The Women from Galilee and Discipleship in Luke." *BThB* 15, no. 2 (1985): 56–59.

Schüssler-Fiorenza, Elizabeth. *In Memory of Her: A Feminist Theological Reconstruction of Christian Origins*. New York: Crossroad, 1983.

Sigal, Lillian. "Images of Women in Judaism." In an appendix to *Judaism: The Evolution of a Faith*. By Philip Sigal. Revised and edited by Lillian Sigal. Grand Rapids: Eerdmans, 1988.

Stagg, Evelyn, and Frank Stagg. *Woman in the World of Jesus*. Philadelphia: Westminster, 1978.

Tetlow, Elizabeth. *Women and Ministry in the New Testament*. New York: Paulist, 1980.

Witherington, Ben III. *The Christology of Jesus*. Minneapolis: Fortress, 1990.

_____. "On the Road with Mary Magdalene, Joanna, Susanna and Other Disciples: Luke 8:1–3." *ZNW* 70 (1979): 243–48.

_____. *Women in the Earliest Churches*. SNTSMS 59. Cambridge, Eng.: Cambridge University Press, 1988.

_____. *Women in the Ministry of Jesus: A Study of Jesus' Attitude Toward Women and Their Roles as Reflected in His Earthly Ministry*. SNTSMS 51. Cambridge: Cambridge University Press, 1984.

Wold, Margaret. "'Women of Faith and Spirit': Profiles of Fifteen Biblical Witnesses." Minneapolis: Augsburg, 1987.

F. DISCIPLESHIP STUDIES ACCORDING TO NEW TESTAMENT LITERARY GROUPINGS

1. Matthew

Bauer, David R. *The Structure of Matthew's Gospel*. Sheffield: Almond Press, 1988.

Bornkamm, Günther; Gerhard Barth; and Heinz Joachim Held. *Tradition and Interpretation in Matthew*. Translated by Percy Scott. Reprint. Philadelphia: Westminster, 1963.

Doyle, B. Rod. "Matthew's Intention As Discerned by His Structure." *Revue Biblique* 95, no. 1 (1988): 34–54.

Edwards, Richard A. *Matthew's Story of Jesus*. Philadelphia: Fortress, 1985.

⸺. "Uncertain Faith: Matthew's Portrait of the Disciples." In *Discipleship in the New Testament*. Edited by Fernando F. Segovia. Philadelphia: Fortress, 1985.

Freyne, Seán. *The Twelve: Disciples and Apostles. A Study in the Theology of the First Three Gospels*. London: Sheed & Ward, 1968.

Howard, David M. *The Great Commisstion for Today*. Downers Grove, Ill.: InterVarsity Press, 1976.

Howell, David B. *Matthew's Inclusive Story: A Study in the Narrative Rhetoric of the First Gospel*. JSNTSup 42. Sheffield: Sheffield Academic Press, 1990.

Kingsbury, Jack Dean. "The Developing Conflict Between Jesus and the Jewish Leaders in Matthew's Gospel: A Literary-Critical Study." *CBQ* 49 (1987): 57–73.

⸺. "The Figure of Peter in Matthew's Gospel as a Theological Problem." *JBL* 98 (1979): 78.

⸺. *Matthew as Story*. 2d ed. Minneapolis: Fortress, 1988.

⸺. "On Following Jesus: The 'Eager' Scribe and the 'Reluctant' Disciple (Matthew 8.18–22)." *NTS* 34 (1988): 45–59.

⸺. "The Verb AKOLOUTHEIN ('To Follow') as an Index of Matthew's View of His Community." *JBL* 97 (1978): 56–73.

Lincoln, Andrew T. "Matthew—A Story for Teachers?" *The Bible in Three Dimensions: Essays in Celebration of Forty Years of Biblical Studies in the University of Sheffield*. Edited by David J. A. Clines, Stephen E. Fowl, and Stanley E. Porter. JSOTSup 87. Sheffield: Sheffield Academic Press, 1990.

Love, Stuart L. "The 'Place' of Women in Certain Public Teaching Settings in Matthew's Gospel: A Sociological Inquiry." Unpublished paper presented to the Social Science Study Group, SBL annual meeting, Anaheim, California, November 20, 1989. Special thanks to Professor Love for supplying me with a personal copy of his paper.

Luz, Ulrich. "Die Jünger im Matthäusevangelium." *ZNW* 62 (1971): 141–71. Reprinted as "The Disciples in the Gospel According to Matthew." Translated and edited by Graham Stanton. In *The Interpretation of Matthew*. IRT 3, 1971. London/Philadelphia: SPCK/Fortress, 1983.

Minear, Paul S. *Matthew: The Teacher's Gospel.* New York: Pilgrim, 1982.

Orton, David E. *The Understanding Scribe: Matthew and the Apocalyptic Ideal.* JSNTSup 25. Sheffield: Sheffield Academic Press, 1989.

Sawicki, Marianne. "How to Teach Christ's Disciples: John 1:19–37 and Matthew 11:2–15." *LexThQ* 21, no. 1 (1986): 14–26.

Sheridan, Mark. "Disciples and Discipleship in Matthew and Luke." *BThB* 3 (1973): 235–55.

Thysman, R. *Communauté et directives éthiques: la catéchèse de Matthieu.* Recherches et Synthèses: Section d'exégèse, no. 1. Gembloux: Duculot, 1974.

Trotter, Andrew H. "Understanding and Stumbling: A Study of the Disciples' Understanding of Jesus and His Teaching in the Gospel of Matthew." Ph.D. dissertation, Cambridge University, 1987.

Warren, Max. *I Believe in the Great Commission.* Grand Rapids: Eerdmans, 1976.

Wilkins, Michael J. *The Concept of Disciple in Matthew's Gospel: As Reflected in the Use of the Term Μαθητής. NovTSup* 59. Leiden: E. J. Brill, 1988.

―――. "Named and Unnamed Disciples in Matthew: A Literary/Theological Study." *SBLSP* 30. Atlanta: Scholars, 1991.

―――. "The Use of ΜΑΘΗΤΣ in the New Testament." Unpublished M.Div. thesis, Talbot Theological Seminary, 1977.

Zumstein, Jean. *La Condition du Croyant dans L'Evangile Selon Matthieu.* Orbis Biblicus et Orientalis 16. Göttingen: Vandenhoeck & Ruprecht, 1977.

2. Mark

Best, Ernest. *Following Jesus: Discipleship in the Gospel of Mark.* JSNTSup 4. Sheffield: Sheffield Academic Press, 1981.

―――. *Disciples and Discipleship: Studies in the Gospel According to Mark.* Edingburgh: T. & T. Clark, 1986.

Black, C. Clifton. *The Disciples According to Mark: Markan Redaction in Current Debate.* JSNTSup 27. Sheffield: Sheffield Academic Press, 1989.

Budesheim, Thomas L. "Jesus and the Disciples in Conflict with Jerusalem." *Zeitschrift für die neutestamentliche Wissenschaft* 62 (1971): 190–209.

Crossan, John Dominic. "Empty Tomb and Absent Lord (Mark 16:1–8)." In *The Passion in Mark: Studies on Mark 14–16.* Edited by Werner Heinz Kelber. Philadelphia: Fortress, 1976, 135–52.

Daris, Sergio. "6. Marco, Vangelo 2:1–26. Papiri letterari dell' Universita; Cattolica di Milano." *Aegyptus* 52 (1972): 80–88.

Donahue, John R. *The Theology and Setting of Discipleship of Mark.* The 1983 Pere Marquette Theology Lecture. Milwaukee: Marquette University Press, 1983.

Donaldson, James. "Called to Follow—A Twofold Experience of Discipleship in Mark." *BThB* 5 (1975): 67–77.

Focant, Camille. "L'Incompréhension des Disciples dans le deuxième Evangile." *Revue Biblique* 82 (1985): 161–85.

Freyne, Seán. *The Twelve: Disciples and Apostles. A Study in the Theology of the First Three Gospels.* London: Sheed & Ward, 1968.

Guelich, Robert A. *Mark 1–8:26.* WBC 34A. Dallas: Word, 1989.

Kelber, Werner Heinz. "Apostolic Tradition and the Form of the Gospel." *In Discipleship in the New Testament.* Edited by Fernando F. Segovia. Philadelphia: Fortress, 1985.

_____. *The Kingdom in Mark: A New Place and a New Time.* Philadelphia: Fortress, 1974.

_____. "Mark 14:32–42: Gethsemane. Passion Christology and Discipleship Failure." *Zeitschrift für die neutestamentliche Wissenschaft* 63 (1972): 166–87.

_____. *Mark's Story of Jesus.* Philadelphia: Fortress, 1979.

_____. *The Passion in Mark: Studies on Mark 14–16.* Edited by Werner Heinz Kelber. Philadelphia: Fortress, 1976.

Kingsbury, Jack Dean. *Conflict in Mark: Jesus, Authorities, and Disciples.* Minneapolis: Fortress, 1989.

Klein, Günther. "Die Verleugnung des Petrus. Eine traditionsgeschichtliche Untersuchung." *Zeitschrift für Theologie und Kirche* 58 (1961): 285–328.

Kuby, Alfred. "Zur Konzeption des Markus-Evangeliums." *Zeitschrift für die neutestamentliche Wissenschaft* 49 (1958): 52–64.

Lincoln, A. T. "The Promise and the Failure: Mark 16:7, 8." *JBL* 108, no. 2 (1989): 283–300.

Malbon, Elizabeth Struthers. "Disciples/Crowds/Whoever: Markan Characters and Readers." *NovT* 28, no. 2 (1986): 104–30.

_____. "The Jewish Leaders in the Gospel of Mark: A Literary Study of Marcan Characterization." *JBL* 108, no. 2 (1989): 259–81.

Marshall, Christopher D. *Faith As a Theme in Mark's Narrative.* SNTMS 64. Cambridge: Cambridge University Press, 1989.

Matera, Frank J. "The Incomprehension of the Disciples and Peter's Confession (Mark 6,14–8,30)." *Biblica* 70, no. 2 (1989): 153–72.

_____. *What Are They Saying About Mark?* New York: Paulist, 1987.

Meye, Robert P. *Jesus and the Twelve: Discipleship and Revelation in Mark's Gospel.* Grand Rapids: Eerdmans, 1968.

Munro, Winsome. "Women Disciples in Mark?" *CBQ* 44 (1982): 225–41.

Myers, Ched. *Binding the Strong Man. A Political Reading of Mark's Story of Jesus.* Maryknoll, N.Y.: Orbis, 1988.

Reploh, Karl-Georg. *Markus—Lehrer der Gemeinde: Eine redaktionsgeschichtliche Studie zu den Jüngerperikopen des Markus-Evangeliums.* Stuttgarter biblische Monographien 9. Stuttgart: Katholisches Bibelwerk, 1969.

Stock, Augustine. *Call to Discipleship: A Literay Study of Mark's Gospel.* Good News Studies 1. Wilmington, Del.: Michael Glazier, 1982.

Sweetland, Dennis M. *Our Journey with Jesus. Discipleship According to Mark.* Good News Studies 22. Wilmington, Del.: Michael Glazier, 1987.

Tannehill, Robert C. "The Disciples in Mark: The Function of a Narrative Role." *JR* 57 (1977): 386–405. Reprinted in *The Interpretation of Mark.* Edited by William Telford. Issues in Religion and Theology 7. Philadelphia/London: Fortress/SPCK, 1985.

Thomas, John Christopher. "Discipleship in Mark's Gospel." In *Faces of Renewal: Studies in Honor of Stanley M. Horton.* Edited by Paul Elbert. Peabody, Mass.: Hendrickson, 1988.

Trakatellis, Demetrios. "'Ἀκολούθει μοι/Follow Me' (Mk 2:14): Discipleship and Priesthood." *GOThR* 30, no. 3 (1985): 271–85.

Trocmé, Etienne. *The Formation of the Gospel According to Mark.* Translated by Pamela Gaughan. Philadelphia: Westminster, 1975.

Tyson, Joseph. "The Blindness of the Disciples in Mark." *JBL* 80 (1961): 261–68. (Reprinted in Christopher Tuckett, editor, *The Messianic Secret. IRT* 1. Philadelphia/London: Fortress/SPCK, 1983, pp. 35–43).

Weeden, Theodore John, Sr. "The Conflict Between Mark and His Opponents Over Kingdom Theology." *SBLSP* 1973 (Cambridge, Mass.: SBL, 1973), 115–34.

————. The Heresy That Necessitated Mark's Gospel. *Zeitschrift für die neutestamentliche Wissenschaft* 59 (1968): 145–58 (reprinted in *The Interpretation of Mark.* Edited by William Telford. *IRT* 7. Philadelphia/London: Fortress/SPCK, 1985, pp. 64–77).

————. *Mark—Traditions in Conflict.* Philadelphia: Fortress, 1971.

Wink, Walter. "The Education of the Apostles: Mark's View of Human Transformation." *Religious Education* 83, no. 2 (1988): 277–90.

Wrede, William. *The Messianic Secret.* Translated by J. C. G. Greig. Cambridge: James Clarke, 1971.

3. Luke

Degenhardt, H.-J. *Lukas—Evangelist der Armen. Besitz und Besitz-verzicht nach den lukanischen Schriften: Eine traditions- und redaktionsgeschichtliche Untersuchung.* Stuttgart: Katholisches Bibelwerk, 1965.

Dollar, Harold E. "A Biblical-Missiological Exploration of the Cross-Cultural Dimensions in Luke-Acts." Unpublished Ph.D. dissertation, Fuller Theological Seminary, 1990.

Ellis, E. Earle. *The Gospel of Luke.* NCB. Rev. ed. Grand Rapids/London: Eerdmans/Marshall, Morgan & Scott, 1974.

Fitzmyer, Joseph A. *The Gospel According to Luke (I–IX): Introduction, Translation, and Notes.* AB 28. Garden City, N.Y.: Doubleday, 1981, pp. 235–57.

————. *Luke the Theologian: Aspects of His Teaching.* New York: Paulist, 1989.

Freyne, Seán. *The Twelve: Disciples and Apostles. A Study in the Theology of the First Three Gospels.* London: Sheed & Ward, 1968.

Giles, Kevin N. "The Church in the Gospel of Luke." *Scottish Journal of Theology* 34 (1981): 121–46.

Kingsbury, Jack Dean. *Conflict in Luke: Jesus, Authorities, and Disciples.* Minneapolis: Fortress, 1991.

Martin, Ralph P. "Salvation and Discipleship in Luke's Gospel." *Interpretation* 30 (1976): 366–80.

McCasland, S. V. " 'The Way.' " *JBL* 77 (1958): 222–30.

O'Toole, Robert F. "Luke's Message in Luke 9:1–50." *CBQ* 49 (1987): 74–89.

————. "Parallels Between Jesus and His Disciples in Luke-Acts: A Further Study." *Biblische Zeitschrift* 27 (1983): 195–212.

Repo, Eero. *Der "Weg" als Selbstbezeichnung des Urchristentums: Eine traditionsgeschichtliche und semasiologische Untersuchung.* Annales Academiae scientarum fennicae B132/2. Helsinki: Soumalainen Tiedeakatemia, 1964.

Rhee, Sung-Yul (Victor). "The Concept of Discipleship in Luke-Acts." Unpublished Th.M. thesis, Talbot School of Theology, 1989.

Rice, George E. "Luke's Thematic Use of the Call to Discipleship." *Andrews University Seminary Studies* 19 (1981): 51–58.

Richard, Earl. "Luke—Writer, Theologian, Historian: Research and Orientation of the 1970's." *BThB* 12 (1983): 3–15.

Ryan, Rosalie. "The Women from Galilee and Discipleship in Luke." *BThB* 15 (2, 1985): 56–59.

Sheridan, Mark. "Disciples and Discipleship in Matthew and Luke." *BThB* 3 (1973): 235–55.

Sweetland, Dennis M. *Our Journey with Jesus. Discipleship According to Luke-Acts.* Good News Studies 23. Wilmington, Del.: Michael Glazier, 1990.

Talbert, Charles H. "Discipleship in Luke-Acts." In *Discipleship in the New Testament.* Edited by Fernando F. Segovia. Philadelphia: Fortress, 1985.

_____. *Reading Luke: A Literary and Theological Commentary on the Third Gospel.* New York: Crossroad, 1984.

4. John

Black, C. Clifton. "Christian Ministry in Johannine Perspective." *Interpretation* 44 (1990): 29–41.

Brown, R. E. *The Community of the Beloved Disciple: The Life, Loves, and Hates of an Individual Church in New Testament Times.* New York: Paulist, 1979, pp. 25–28.

de Jonge, M. "The Fourth Gospel: The Book of the Disciples." In *Jesus: Stranger from Heaven and Son of God. Jesus Christ and the Christians in Johannine Perspective.* SBLSBS 11. Missoula: Scholars, 1977, pp. 1–27.

Jiménez, R. Moreno. "El discípulo de Jesucristo, según el evangelio de S. Juan." *EstBib* 30 (1971): 269–311.

Koester, Craig. "Hearing, Seeing, and Believing in the Gospel of John." *Biblica* 70 (1989): 327–48.

Laney, J. Carl. "Abiding Is Believing: The Analogy of the Vine in John 15:1–6." *BS* 146 (581, 1989): 55–66.

Sawicki, Marianne. "How to Teach Christ's Disciples: John 1:19–37 and Matthew 11:2–15." *LexThQ* 21 (1, 1986): 14–26.

Schnackenburg, R. "Exkurs 17: Jünger, Gemeinde, Kirche im Johannesevangelium." In *Das Johannesevangelium.* Three vols. *HTKNT* 4. Freiburg: Herder, 1967–1975. 3:231–45.

Schulz, Anselm. *Nachfolgen und Nachahmen: Studien über das Verhältnis der neutestamentlichen Jüngerschaft zur urchristlichen Vorbildethik.* SANT 6. Munich: Kösel-Verlag, 1962, pp. 137–44, 161–76.

Segovia, Fernando F. " 'Peace I Leave with You; My Peace I Give to You': Discipleship in the Fourth Gospel." In *Discipleship in the New Testament.* Edited by Fernando F. Segovia. Philadelphia: Fortress, 1985.

Smith, Dwight Moody. *Johannine Christianity: Essays on Its Setting, Sources, and Theology.* Columbia, S.C.: University of South Carolina, 1984.

Winbery, C. L. "Abiding in Christ: The Concept of Discipleship in John." *ThE* 38 (1988): 104–20.

5. Acts

Dollar, Harold E. "A Biblical-Missiological Exploration of the Cross-Cultural Dimensions in Luke-Acts." Ph.D. dissertation, Fuller Theological Seminary, 1990.

Dulles, Avery. *A Church to Believe In: Discipleship and the Dynamics of Freedom*. New York, 1982.

Dunn, James D. G. *Unity and Diversity in the New Testament: An Inquiry into the Character of Earliest Christianity*. 2d ed. London/Philadelphia: SCM/Trinity, 1990.

Gager, John G. *Kingdom and Community: The Social World of Early Christianity*. Englewood Cliffs, N.J.: Prentice-Hall, 1975.

Harrison, Everett F. *The Apostolic Church*. Grand Rapids: Eerdmans, 1985.

Kyrtatas, Dimitris J. *The Social Structure of the Early Christian Communities*. London: Verso, 1987.

Lohfink, Gerhard. *Jesus and Community: The Social Dimension of Christian Faith*. Philadelphia: Fortress, 1984.

Luter, A. Boyd. "Discipleship and the Church." *BS* 137 (547, 1980): 267–73.

O'Toole, Robert F. "Parallels Between Jesus and His Disciples in Luke-Acts: A Further Study." *Biblische Zeitschrift* 27 (1983): 195–212.

Rhee, Sung-Yul (Victor). "The Concept of Discipleship in Luke-Acts." Th.M. thesis, Talbot School of Theology, 1989.

Talbert, Charles H. "Discipleship in Luke-Acts." In *Discipleship in the New Testament*. Edited by Fernando F. Segovia. Philadelphia: Fortress, 1985.

6. Epistles

Dragas, George. "Martyrdom and Orthodoxy in the New Testament Era—The Theme of Μαρτυρία As Witness to the Truth." *GOThR* 30, no. 3 (1985): 287–96.

Dulles, Avery. *A Church to Believe In: Discipleship and the Dynamics of Freedom*. New York, 1982.

Dunn, James D. G. *Unity and Diversity in the New Testament: An Inquiry into the Character of Earliest Christianity*. 2d ed. London/Philadelphia: SCM/Trinity, 1990.

Gray, Vivienne. "*MIMESIS* in Greek Historical Theory." *American Journal of Philology* 108, no. 3 (1987): 467–86.

Harrison, Everett F. *The Apostolic Church*. Grand Rapids: Eerdmans, 1985.

Henrix, H. H. "Von der Nachahmung Gottes. Heiligkeit und Heiligsein im biblischen und jüdischen Denken." *Erbe und Auftrag* 65,
no. 3 (1989): 177–87.

Kruse, Colin G. *New Testament Models for Ministry: Jesus and Paul.*
1983, reprint. Nashville: Thomas Nelson, 1985.

Luter, A. Boyd. "Discipleship and the Church." *BS* 137 (547, 1980):
267–73.

Malinowski, Francis X. "The Brave Women of Philippi." *BThB* 15,
no. 2 (1985): 60–63.

Morrison, Karl F. *The Mimetic Tradition of Reform in the West.*
Princeton: Princeton, 1982.

Tinsley, E. J. *The Imitation of God in Christ: An Essay on the
Biblical Basis of Christian Spirituality.* London: SCM, 1960.

7. Postapostolic Church

Baus, Karl. *From the Apostolic Community to Constantine.* With a
"General Introduction to Church History" by Hubert Jedin.
London: Burns & Oates, 1980.

Berry, Grinton. *Foxe's Book of Martyrs.* Reprint. Grand Rapids:
Baker, 1990.

Betz, Hans Dieter. *Nachfolge und Nachahmung Jesu Christi im
Neuen Testament.* BHT 37. Tübingen: Mohr/Siebeck, 1967.

Brown, Raymond E., and John P. Meier. *Antioch and Rome: New
Testament Cradles of Catholic Christianity.* Ramsey, N.J.: Paulist,
1983.

Campenhausen, Hans von. *Die Idee des Martyriums in der alten
Kirche.* 2d ed. Göttingen: Vandenhoeck & Ruprecht, 1964.

————. *Ecclesiastical Authority and Spiritual Power in the Church
of the First Three Centuries.* Translated by J. A. Baker. Stanford,
Calif.: Stanford University Press, 1969.

————. *Tradition and Life in the Church: Essays and Lectures in
Church History.* Philadelphia: Fortress, 1968.

Corwin, Virginia. *St. Ignatius and Christianity in Antioch.* New
Haven: Yale, 1960.

Davies, John Gordon. *The Early Christian Church.* New York: Holt,
Rinehart & Winston, 1965.

Dragas, George. "Martyrdom and Orthodoxy in the New Testament
Era—The Theme of Μαρτυρία As Witness to the Truth." *GOThR*
30, no. 3 (1985): 287–96.

Fox, Robin Lane. *Pagans and Christians.* San Francisco: Harper &
Row, 1986.

Frend, W. H. C. *Martyrdom and Persecution in the Early Church: A
Study of a Conflict from the Maccabees to Donatus.* 1965, reprint.
Grand Rapids: Baker, 1981.

————. *The Rise of Christianity*. Philadelphia: Fortress, 1984.

Horbury, William. *Suffering and Martrydom in the New Testament*. Cambridge: Cambridge University Press, 1981.

Kyrtatas, Dimitris J. *The Social Structure of the Early Christian Communities*. London: Verso, 1987.

Lightfoot, J. B. *The Apostolic Fathers: Revised Texts with Introductions, Notes, Dissertations, and Translations*. Two parts in 5 volumes. 1889–1890, reprint. Grand Rapids: Baker, 1981.

Lightfoot, J. B., and J. R. Harmer. *The Apostolic Fathers*. Edited and revised by Michael W. Holmes. 1891, 2d ed. Grand Rapids: Baker, 1989.

Richardson, Cyril Charles. *The Christianity of Ignatius of Antioch*. New York: Columbia University Press, 1935.

Ruffin, C. Bernard. *The Days of the Martyrs: A History of the Persecution of Christians from Apostolic Times to the Time of Constantine*. Huntington, Ind.: Our Sunday Visitor, 1985.

Schoedel, William R. *Ignatius of Antioch: A Commentary on the Letters of Ignatius of Antioch*. Edited by Helmut Koester. Hermeneia Commentary Series. Philadelphia: Fortress, 1985.

Schulz, Anselm. *Nachfolgen und Nachahmen: Studien über das Verhältnis der neutestamentlichen Jüngerschaft zur urchristlichen Vorbildethik*. SANT 6. Munich: Kösel-Verlag, 1962.

Staniforth, Maxwell. *Early Christian Writings—The Apostolic Fathers*. New York: Dorset, 1968.

Tinsley, E. J. "The imitatio Christi in the Mysticism of St. Ignatius of Antioch." *Studia Patristica*. Vol. 2. Eds. Kurt Aland and F. L. Cross. Berlin: Akademie, 1957.

————. *The Imitation of God in Christ: An Essay on the Biblical Basis of Christian Spirituality*. London: SCM, 1960.

Torrance, Thomas F. *The Doctrine of Grace in the Apostolic Fathers*. Grand Rapids: Eerdmans, 1948.

Trakatellis, Demetrios. "'Ακολούθει μοι/Follow Me' (Mk 2:14): Discipleship and Priesthood." *GOThR* 30, no. 3 (1985): 271–85.

Walsh, Michael. *The Triumph of the Meek: Why Early Christianity Succeeded*. San Francisco: Harper & Row, 1986.

Workman, Herbert B. *Persecution in the Early Church*. 1906, reprint. Oxford: Oxford University Press, 1980.

Zizioulas, John D. "The Early Christian Community." In *Christian Spirituality—Origins to the Twelfth Century*. Edited by Bernard McGinn and John Meyendorff. New York: Crossroad, 1985.

Person Index

Aberbach, M. 55n, 296n
Agnew, Francis 258n
Albright, William F. 126n, 161n, 177, 180n, 185n, 253n
Alford, Henry 254n
Allen, W. C. 181n
Allison, Dale C., Jr. 209n
Atkinson, Michael 327n
Aune, David 97n
Baab, O. J. 140n, 213n
Bacon, Benjamin W. 182n, 183n
Badke, William B. 104n, 190n
Barker, Kenneth 54n
Barnett, Paul 101n
Barr, James 284n
Barrett, C. K. 83n, 91n, 101n, 102n, 157n, 227n, 230n, 231n, 233n, 234n, 235n
Barrett, David B. 335n
Bauer, David R. 186n
Bernard, John H. 230n, 234n
Best, Ernest 105n, 199n, 210n
Betz, Hans Dieter 78n, 96n, 305, 306–8n, 328n
Black, C. Clifton 195n
Blair, E. P. 176n
Blauvelt, Livingston 26
Boice, James M. 32
Bonhoeffer, Dietrich 25, 31–32
Borgen, Peder 83n
Bornkamm, Günther 87, 109n, 180n
Brandon, G. F. 96n
Brown, Colin 259n
Brown, Raymond E. 91n, 156n, 157n, 226n, 228, 229n, 230n, 231n, 234, 235n
Bruce, A. B. 33n, 36–37, 147n, 150n, 152n, 278n
Bruce, F. F. 248–49n, 252–53n, 255, 257n, 259n, 264n, 266, 268n, 276n, 277n
Bultmann, Rudolf 96n, 178n, 295n
Caird, G. B. 284n
Calenberg, Richard D. 268n, 343n
Calvin, John 344
Campenhousen, Hans von, 308n, 328n
Caragounis, Chrys 153n, 185n, 264n
Carmignac, Jean 88n
Carson, Donald A. 136n, 152n, 156n, 161n, 163n, 187n, 188n, 209n, 262n, 263n
Chandapilla, P. T. 30n
Charlesworth, James H. 96n, 233n
Coenen, L. 105n

Coleman, Robert E. 33n
Conzelmann, Hans 181n, 185
Coppedge, Allan 27n
Corwin, Virginia 314, 315n, 316n, 327
Cotterell, Peter 248n, 284n
Craigie, Peter C. 58n
Crenshaw, James L. 65n
Cullman, Oscar 91n, 97n, 153n, 185n, 264n
Culpepper, Alan R. 89n
Davies, W. D. 209n
Degenhardt, H. J. 29n
de Jonge, M. 226n
DeRidder, Richard 33n, 190n
Dodd, Charles A. 233n
Dollar, Harold E. 261n, 267n
Doyle, B. Rod 186n
Dragas, George 326n
Drushal, M. E. 30n
Dulles, Avery 271n, 273, 288n, 306n, 332n, 333n, 342n
Dunn, James D. G. 97n, 100n, 101n, 139n, 244n, 260n, 264n, 278n
Eims, Leroy 27n, 30n
Elliot, J. Keith 178n
Ellis, E. Earle 127n, 207n, 213–14n, 220n
Feuillet, Andre 60n
Fisher, Fred L. 27n
Fitzmyer, Joseph A. 136n, 153n, 173n, 189n, 207n, 210n, 256n
Focant, Camille 199n
Foster, Richard J. 135n
France, R. T. 161n, 162n
Freyne, Seán 150n, 259n, 272n
Fryling, Alice 32n
Gager, John G. 99n, 260n
Geldenhuys, Norval 216n
Gerhardsson, Birger 97n
Getz, Gene A. 276n
Gill, David W. 244
Godet, F. 230n, 234n
Golka, Friedemann W. 65n
Goppelt, Leonhard 178n
Gould, George P. 251n
Green, Michael P. 131n, 214n, 302n
Griffiths, Michael 32n
Gruenewald, Max 132n
Grundmann, Walter 300n
Guelich, Robert A. 152n, 163n, 197n
Guthrie, Donald 139n, 154n, 213n, 217–18n, 227n, 259n, 272, 295n
Habermann, A. M. 88n
Hadidian, Allen 32n

Subject Index

Abiding, 226, 236, 303; in Jesus' word, 357. *See also* Discipleship, marks of.
Abraham, 53, 149, 188, 220
Accountability, 143
AIDS, 246
Alexander the Great, 72, 76
Ambition, 201
Andrew, 102, 152, 155
Antioch, disciples first called Christians, 250
Apollo, 75
Apollos, 251
Apologists, 301
Apostle(ship). *See* Call.
Apostles, definition, 149, 150, 260
Apostolic fathers, definition of, 313; importance, 313-36; martyrs for the name, 311–13
Ascension, 147, 286
Ascetic Monastecism, 352
Augustine, 239

Baptizing, 189
Bartholomew, 159–60
Bear(ing) the cross, 25, 135, 136, 213, 215, 217, 302
Bearing fruit, 358–59; definition, 303. *See also* Discipleship, marks of, fruit.
Believers, 102, 294, 295; are disciples, 221–89; equality of, 192; in Jesus Christ, 26–28, 31, 32, 37; marked by Jesus, 224–39; post-Easter, 256; referent for disciple, 208; transition to term from "disciple" 282. *See also* Disciple.
Boot camp, 67
Branch analogy, 238
Branch(es), 306
Breaking of bread. *See* Communion of believers.
Brother/Sister(s), 38, 39, 141, 287, 320, 321; definition, 296
Brotherhood, 297, 321
Brothers, Jesus called two sets of, 104, 140, 213. *See also* James and John. *See also* Peter and Andrew.
Bubble(s), Biola, 145, 167; Christian, 145, 147; forms of, 168

Caleb, 59
Call, called, calling, at the heart of discipleship, 54; distinctions between, 148; enabling, 107, 113; growth, 133; his people to represent him, 53, 54; Jesus', 99, 104–8; Jesus initiates, 107; kingdom of God, 111; Master's, 54; pattern, 107; responses to, 106, 107, 108; to account, 139; to become fellow-workers, 187; to believe, 111; to discipleship/apostleship, 111, 112, 187; to leave post attachments, 286; to salvation, 111, 133, 186; to service, 133,186; unrealistic perceptions of God's, 340; various calls, 106, 107
Cana of Galilee, 103
Capernaum, 102
Christ, as Lord, 27; fulfillment of the law, 304; 'in' 132; incarnate example of God, 308; mind of, 302; pattern for obedience, 304
Christian(s), 38, 39, 119, 208, 287, 299–302, 321; as lights, 304; cultural, 204; disciple a referent for, 45; first time occurring in Scripture, 250; Gentiles, 297; indicated contempt and hostility, 250; life, 17; modern, 289; new, 17; origin of the term, 300; true, 25
Church, 298, 299; a new creation, 247; age, dawning of, 248; body of Christ, 257; disciples, 256–58; early fathers, 233; experienced persecution, 237; faithfulness to the mission, 268; future, 239; God's new creation, 257; post-apostolic, 18; practice of the, 274
Clement, 320, 322
Commitment, Jesus' call to, 28; faith vs. works, 183; personal, 108; radical, 70
Communion of believers, 276
Community, as family, 140; balance, 139; body of Christ, 270; Christian discipleship, 32; definition, 139; disciples became, 270; eschatological, 29; ingrediants, 270; life, 139–41; messianic, 149; metaphor for, 305; necessity of, 245–47; object of Jesus' ministry, 183; of disciples, 207; of faith, 141, 243–80, 271; one in the spirit, 266
Complacency, 340
Conversion, 31, 191, 324; author's, 204; confused with commitment, 33
Converts, assembly of, 257; new, 238, 358; prospective, 221

Scripture Index